Date: 12/13/17

GRA 741.5 ADV V.2
DeMatteis, J. M.,
The adventures of Augusta
Wind. The last story /

D1462428

**PALM BEACH COUNTY
LIBRARY SYSTEM**
3650 Summit Boulevard
West Palm Beach, FL 33406-4198

The Adventures of AUGUSTA WIND

THE LAST STORY

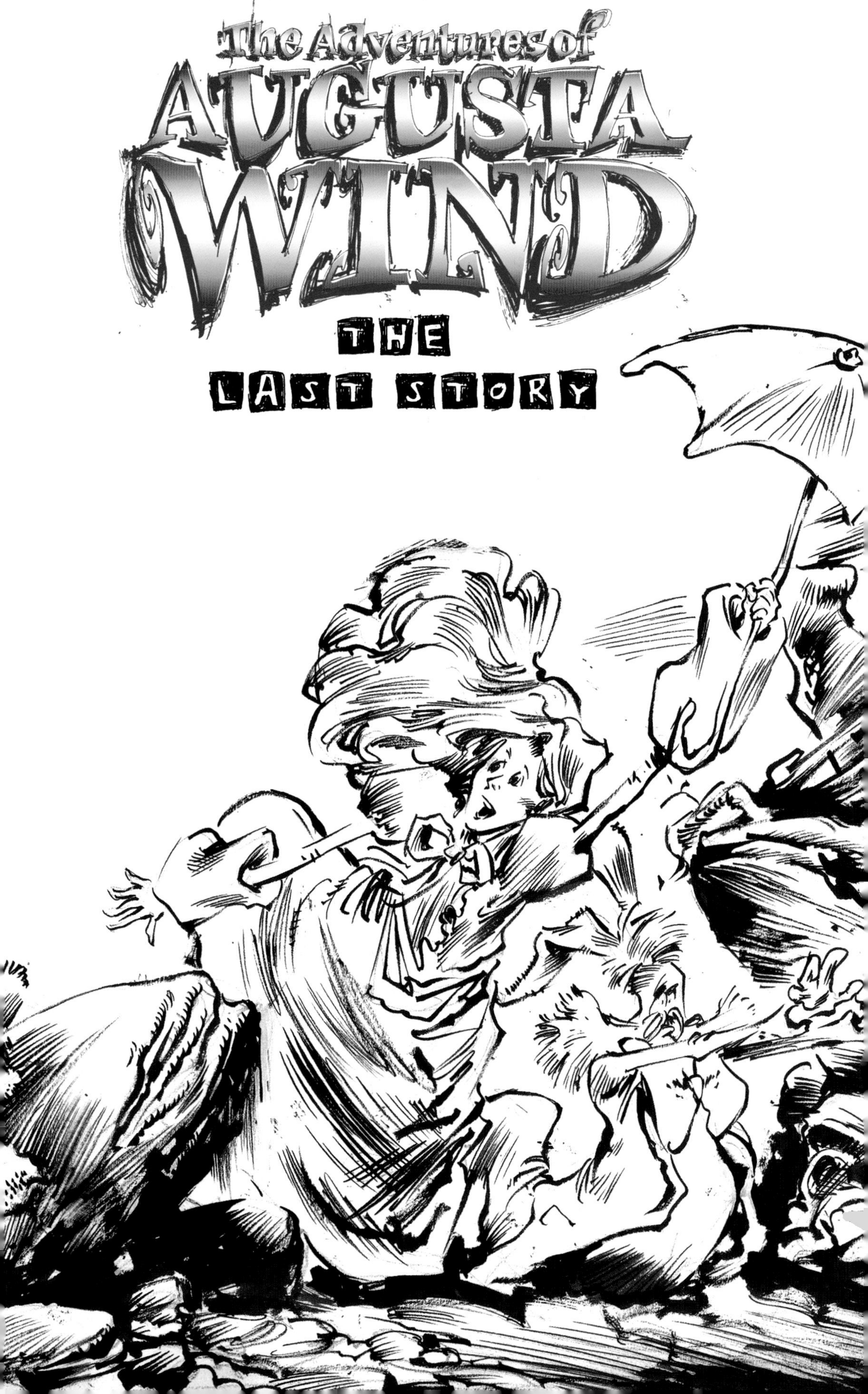

Become our fan on Facebook **facebook.com/idwpublishing**
Follow us on Twitter **@idwpublishing**
Subscribe to us on YouTube **youtube.com/idwpublishing**
See what's new on Tumblr **tumblr.idwpublishing.com**
Check us out on Instagram **instagram.com/idwpublishing**

www.IDWPUBLISHING.com

Ted Adams, CEO & Publisher
Greg Goldstein, President & COO
Robbie Robbins, EVP/Sr. Graphic Artist
Chris Ryall, Chief Creative Officer
David Hedgecock, Editor-in-Chief
Laurie Windrow, Sr. VP of Sales & Marketing
Matthew Ruzicka, CPA, Chief Financial Officer
Dirk Wood, VP of Marketing
Lorelei Bunjes, VP of Digital Services
Jeff Webber, VP of Digital Publishing & Business Development
Jerry Bennington, VP of New Product Development

ISBN: 978-1-63140-249-4   20 19 18 17   1 2 3 4

THE ADVENTURES OF AUGUSTA WIND, VOLUME 2: THE LAST STORY. APRIL 2017. FIRST PRINTING. © 2017 J.M. DeMatteis and Vassilis Gogtzilas. All Rights Reserved. The IDW logo is registered in the U.S. Patent and Trademark Office. IDW Publishing, a division of Idea and Design Works, LLC. Editorial offices: 2765 Truxtun Road, San Diego, CA 92106. Any similarities to persons living or dead are purely coincidental. With the exception of artwork used for review purposes, none of the contents of this publication may be reprinted without the permission of Idea and Design Works, LLC. Printed in Korea.
IDW Publishing does not read or accept unsolicited submissions of ideas, stories, or artwork.

Originally published as THE ADVENTURES OF AUGUSTA WIND, VOL. 2: THE LAST STORY issues #1–5.

For international rights, contact licensing@idwpublishing.com

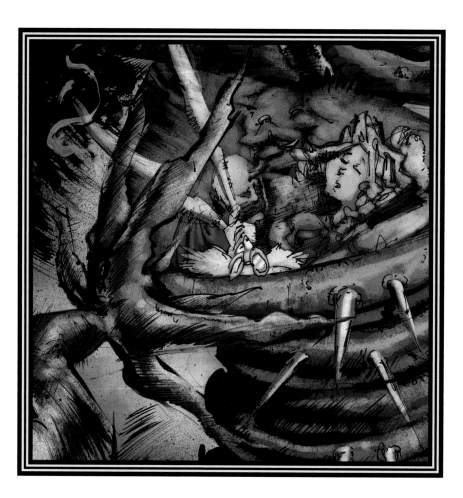

CREATED BY
J.M. DeMATTEIS WRITER + VASSILIS GOGTZILAS ARTIST

COLORS BY CARLOS BADILLA
LETTERS BY TOM B. LONG
SERIES EDITS BY SARAH GAYDOS
ASSISTANT EDITS BY CHRIS CERASI

COVER BY VASSILIS GOGTZILAS
COVER COLORS BY CARLOS BADILLA
COLLECTION EDITS BY
JUSTIN EISINGER & ALONZO SIMON
COLLECTION DESIGN BY CLAUDIA CHONG
PUBLISHER TED ADAMS

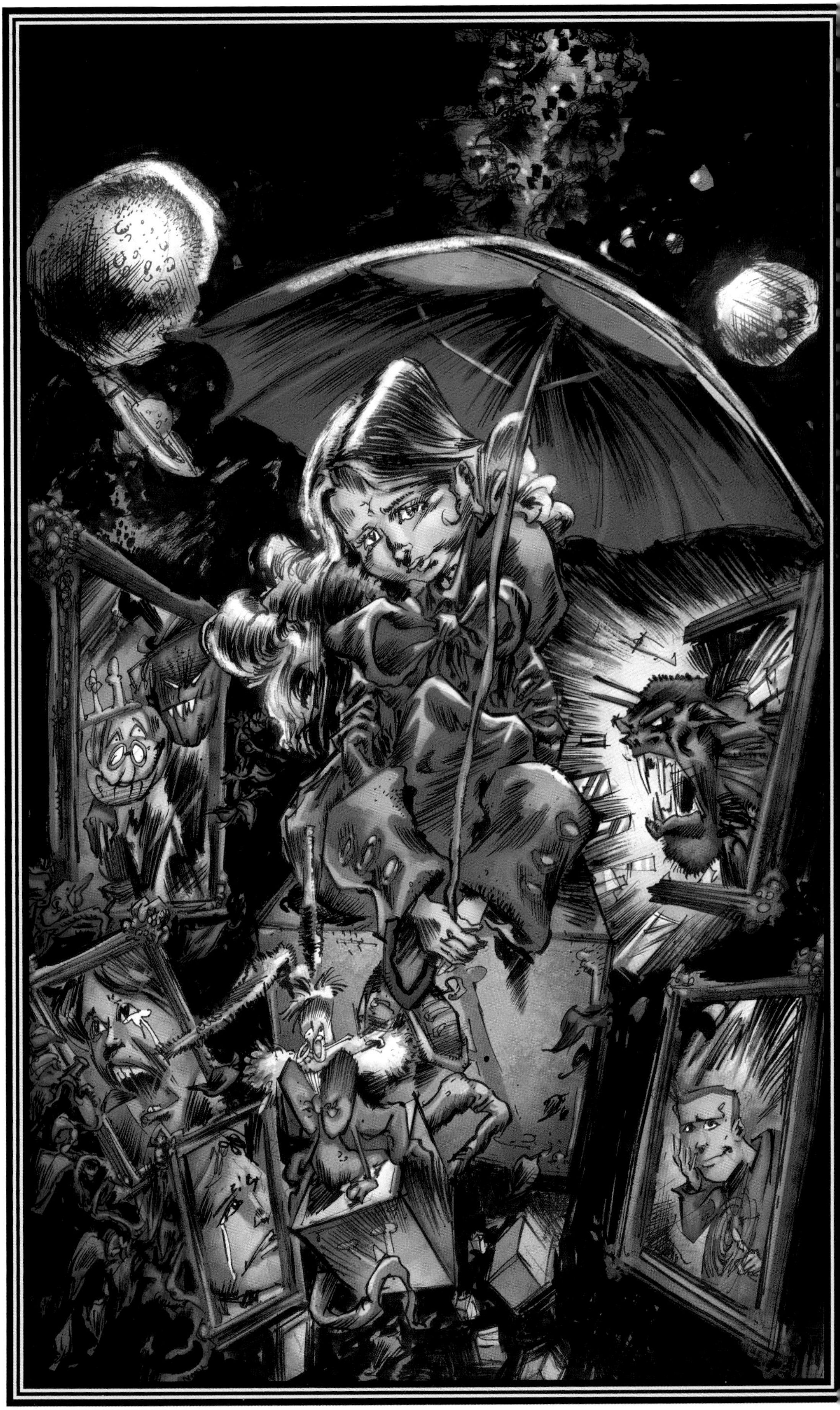

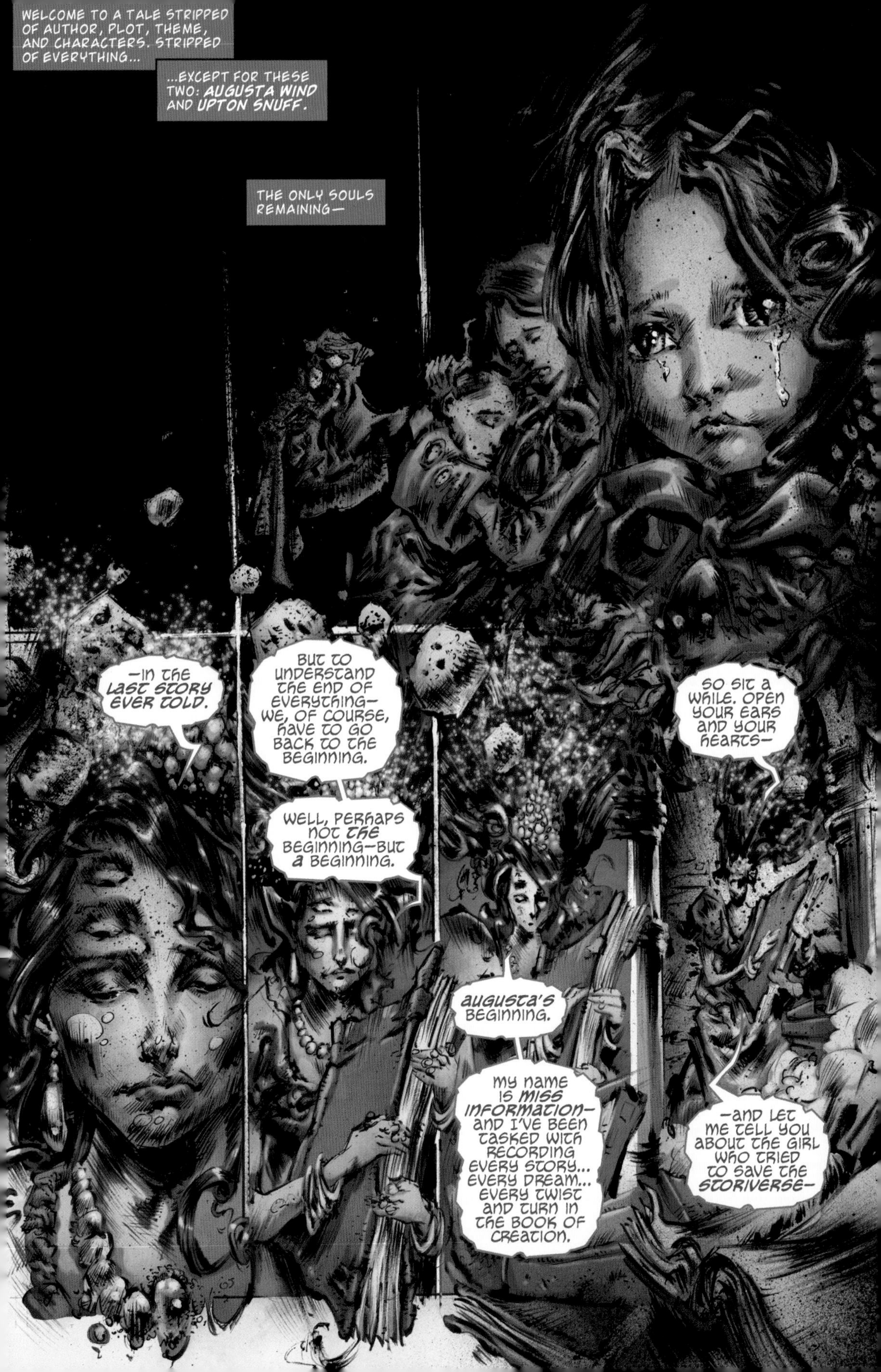
WELCOME TO A TALE STRIPPED OF AUTHOR, PLOT, THEME, AND CHARACTERS. STRIPPED OF EVERYTHING...
...EXCEPT FOR THESE TWO: AUGUSTA WIND AND UPTON SNUFF.
THE ONLY SOULS REMAINING—
—IN THE LAST STORY EVER TOLD.
BUT TO UNDERSTAND THE END OF EVERYTHING—WE, OF COURSE, HAVE TO GO BACK TO THE BEGINNING.
WELL, PERHAPS NOT THE BEGINNING—BUT A BEGINNING.
AUGUSTA'S BEGINNING.
MY NAME IS MISS INFORMATION—AND I'VE BEEN TASKED WITH RECORDING EVERY STORY... EVERY DREAM... EVERY TWIST AND TURN IN THE BOOK OF CREATION.
SO SIT A WHILE. OPEN YOUR EARS AND YOUR HEARTS—
—AND LET ME TELL YOU ABOUT THE GIRL WHO TRIED TO SAVE THE STORIVERSE—

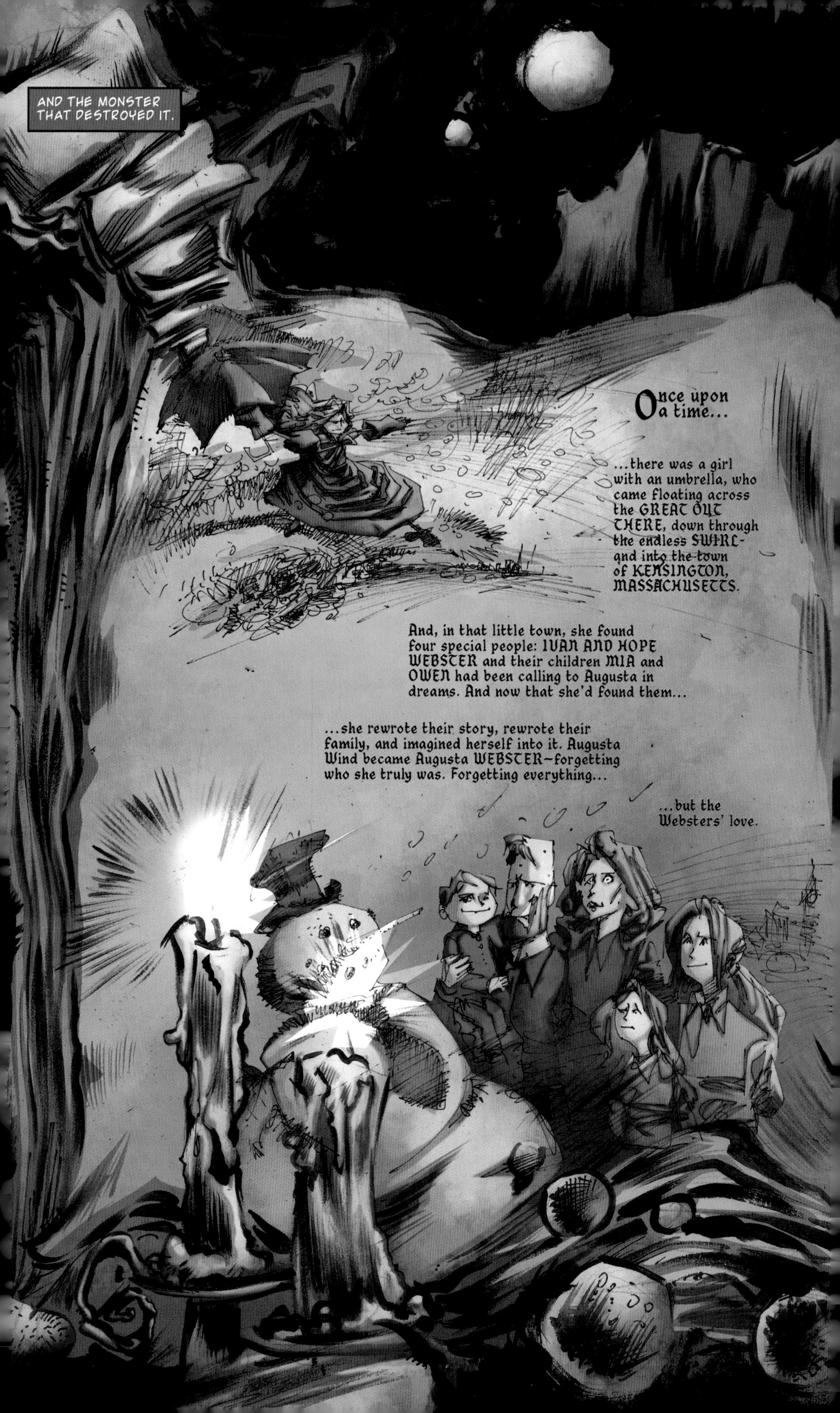
AND THE MONSTER THAT DESTROYED IT.
Once upon a time...
...there was a girl with an umbrella, who came floating across the GREAT OUT THERE, down through the endless SWIRL– and into the town of KENSINGTON, MASSACHUSETTS.
And, in that little town, she found four special people: IVAN AND HOPE WEBSTER and their children MIA and OWEN had been calling to Augusta in dreams. And now that she'd found them...
...she rewrote their story, rewrote their family, and imagined herself into it. Augusta Wind became Augusta WEBSTER—forgetting who she truly was. Forgetting everything...
...but the Websters' love.

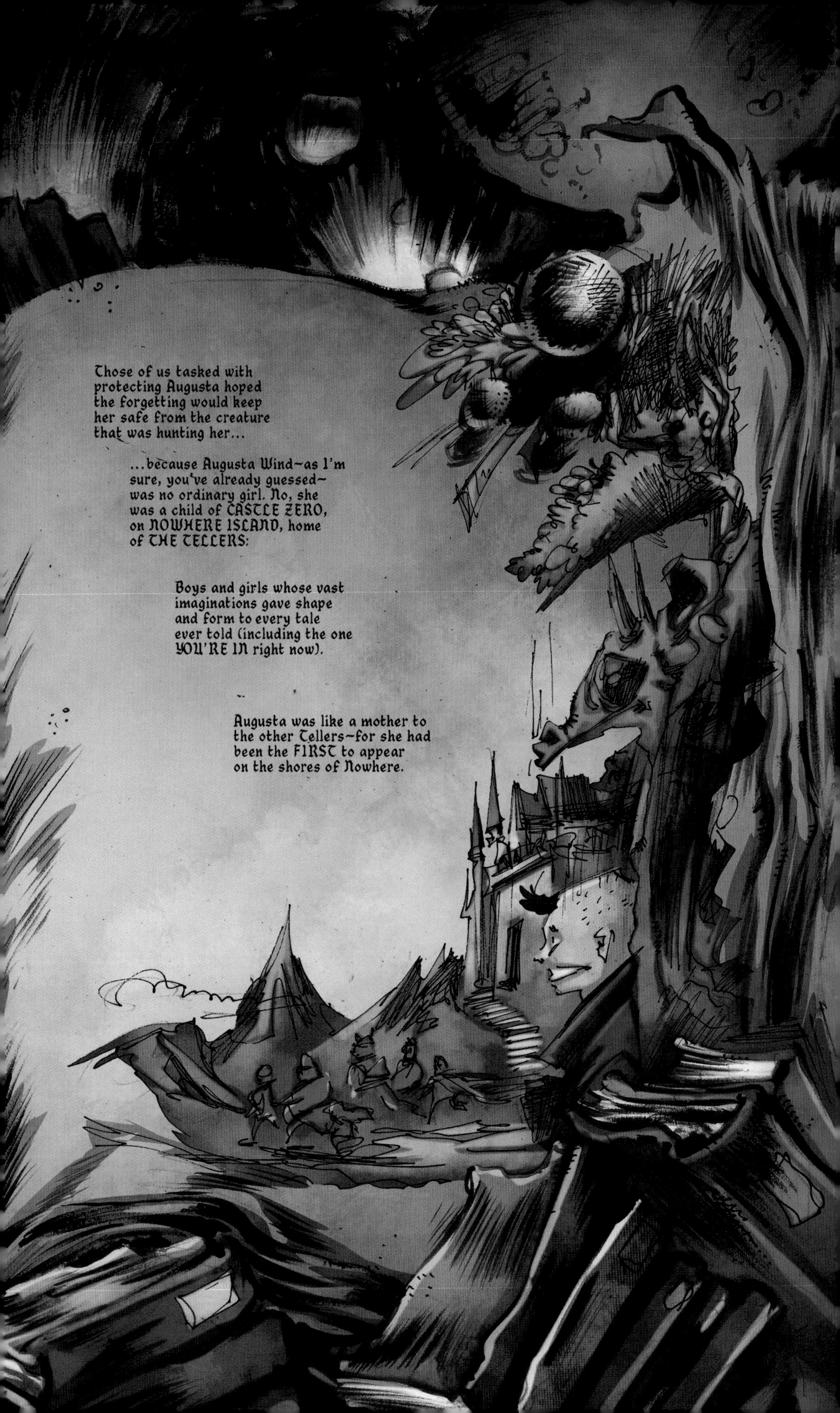
Those of us tasked with protecting Augusta hoped the forgetting would keep her safe from the creature that was hunting her...
...because Augusta Wind~as I'm sure, you've already guessed~ was no ordinary girl. No, she was a child of CASTLE ZERO, on NOWHERE ISLAND, home of THE TELLERS:
Boys and girls whose vast imaginations gave shape and form to every tale ever told (including the one YOU'RE IN right now).
Augusta was like a mother to the other Tellers~for she had been the FIRST to appear on the shores of Nowhere.

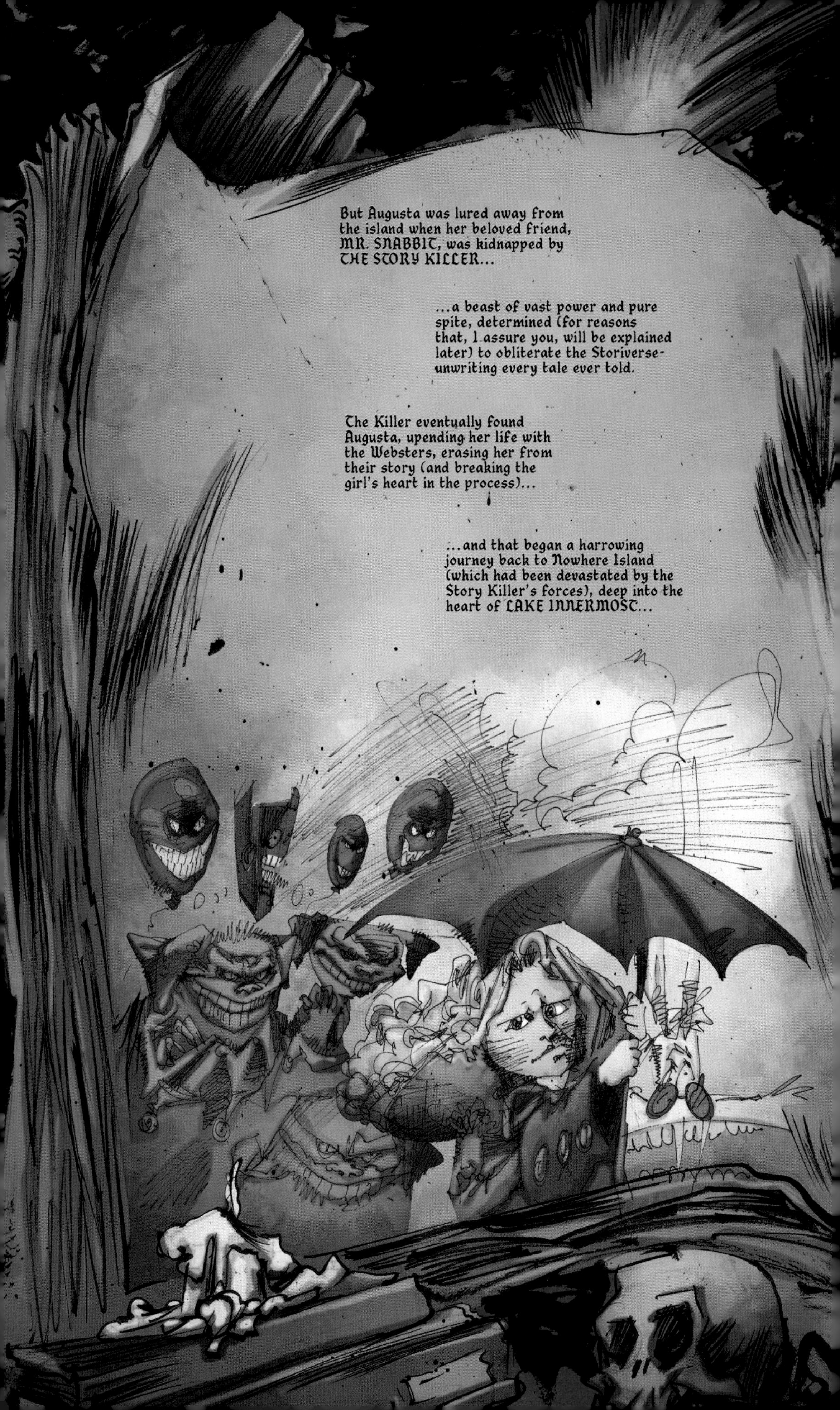
But Augusta was lured away from the island when her beloved friend, MR. SNABBIT, was kidnapped by THE STORY KILLER...
...a beast of vast power and pure spite, determined (for reasons that, I assure you, will be explained later) to obliterate the Storiverse-unwriting every tale ever told.
The Killer eventually found Augusta, upending her life with the Websters, erasing her from their story (and breaking the girl's heart in the process)...
...and that began a harrowing journey back to Nowhere Island (which had been devastated by the Story Killer's forces), deep into the heart of LAKE INNERMOST...

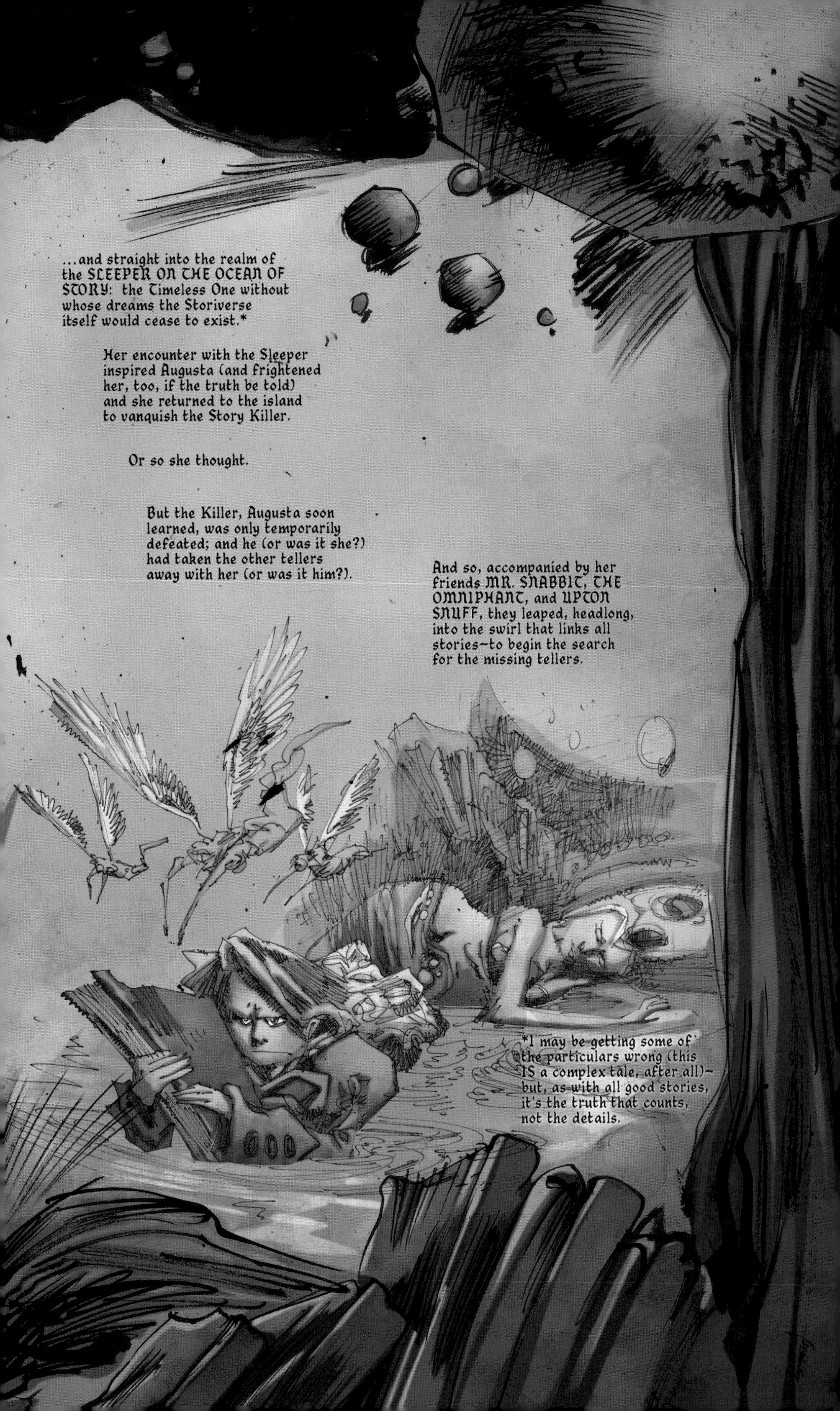
...and straight into the realm of the SLEEPER ON THE OCEAN OF STORY: the Timeless One without whose dreams the Storiverse itself would cease to exist.*
Her encounter with the Sleeper inspired Augusta (and frightened her, too, if the truth be told) and she returned to the island to vanquish the Story Killer.
Or so she thought.
But the Killer, Augusta soon learned, was only temporarily defeated; and he (or was it she?) had taken the other tellers away with her (or was it him?).
And so, accompanied by her friends MR. SNABBIT, THE OMNIPHANT, and UPTON SNUFF, they leaped, headlong, into the swirl that links all stories–to begin the search for the missing tellers.
*I may be getting some of the particulars wrong (this IS a complex tale, after all)– but, as with all good stories, it's the truth that counts, not the details.

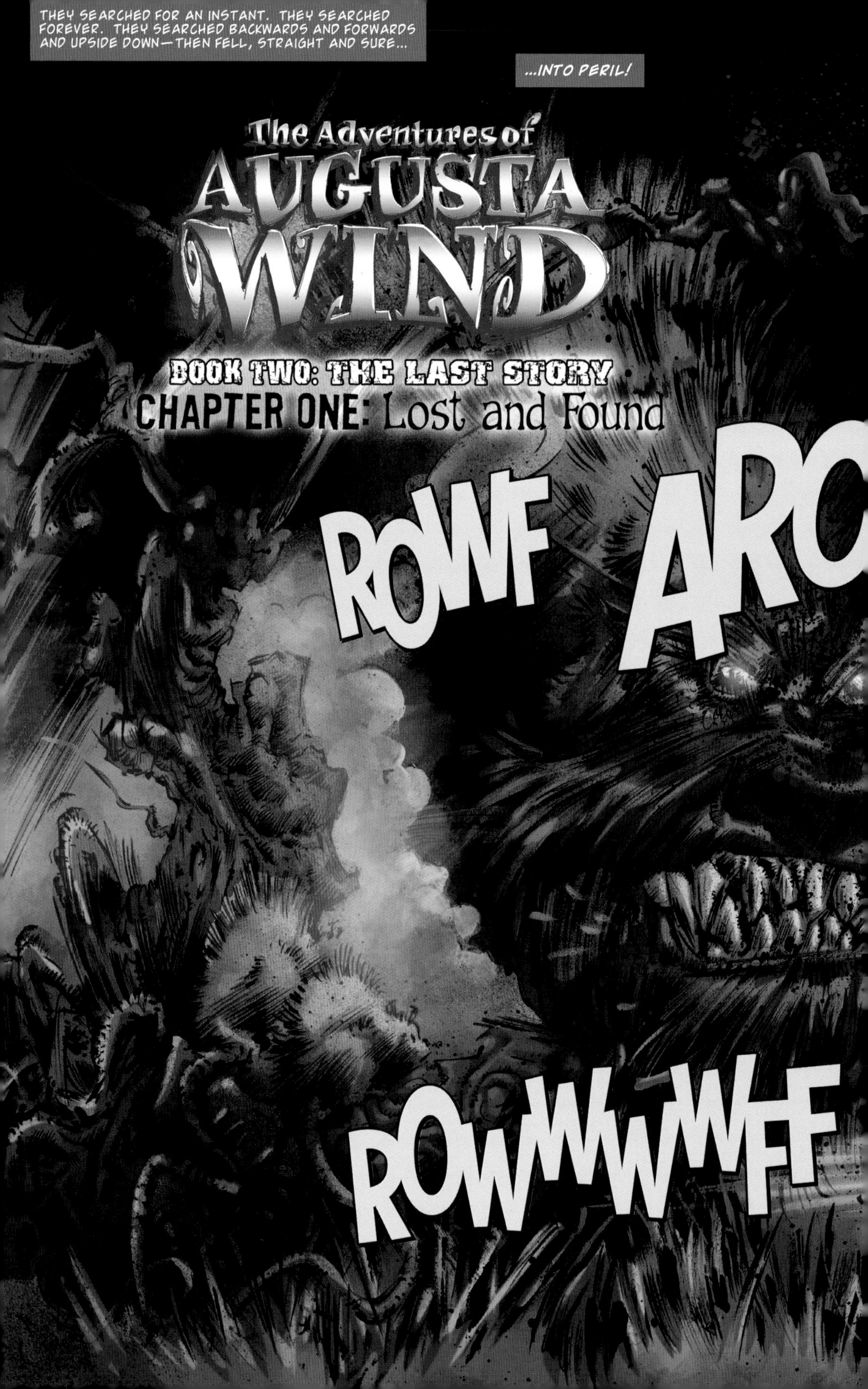
THEY SEARCHED FOR AN INSTANT. THEY SEARCHED FOREVER. THEY SEARCHED BACKWARDS AND FORWARDS AND UPSIDE DOWN—THEN FELL, STRAIGHT AND SURE...
...INTO PERIL!
The Adventures of AUGUSTA WIND
BOOK TWO: THE LAST STORY
CHAPTER ONE: Lost and Found
ROWF
ARO
ROWWWWFF

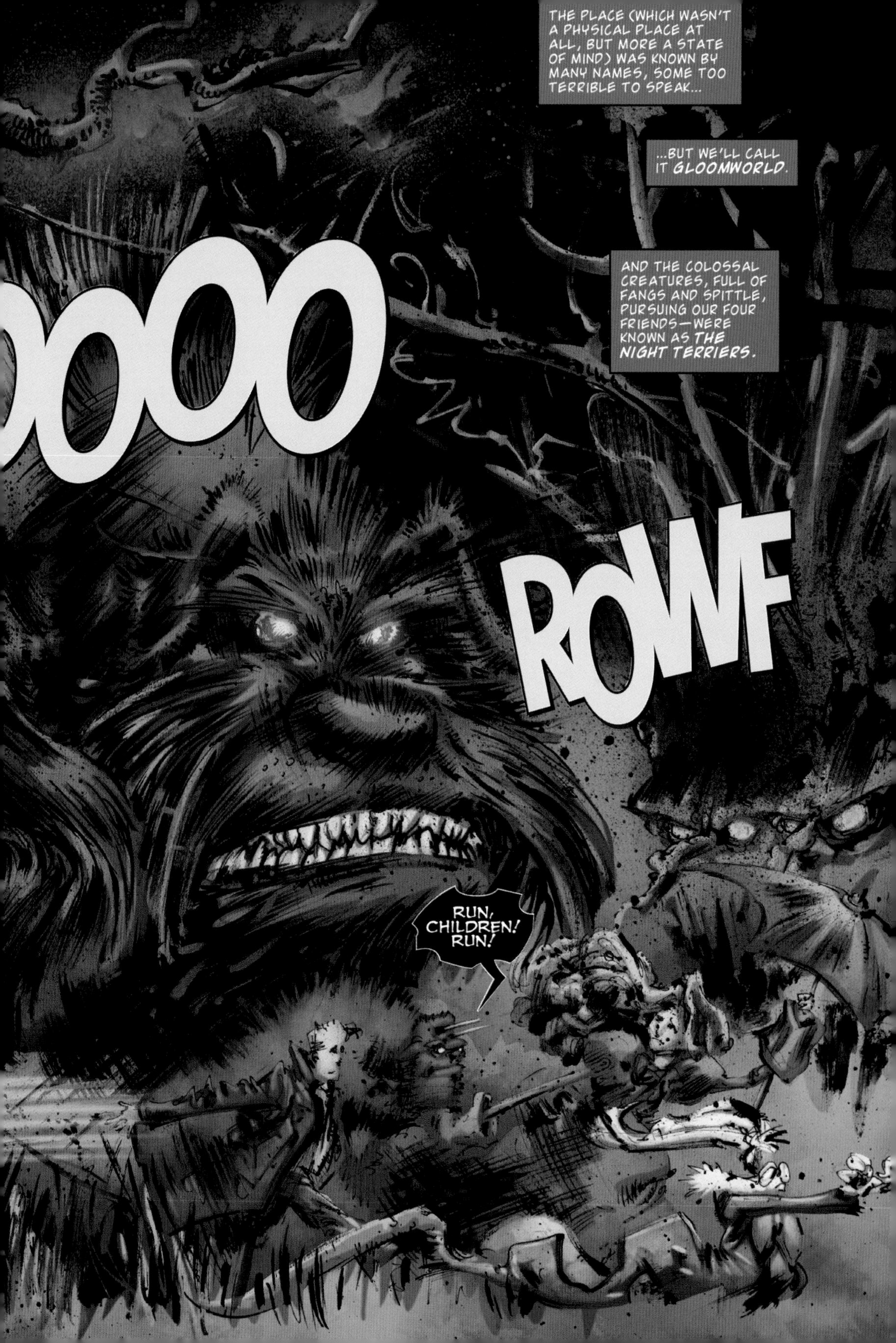
THE PLACE (WHICH WASN'T A PHYSICAL PLACE AT ALL, BUT MORE A STATE OF MIND) WAS KNOWN BY MANY NAMES, SOME TOO TERRIBLE TO SPEAK...
...BUT WE'LL CALL IT GLOOMWORLD.
AND THE COLOSSAL CREATURES, FULL OF FANGS AND SPITTLE, PURSUING OUR FOUR FRIENDS—WERE KNOWN AS THE NIGHT TERRIERS.
OOOO
ROWF
RUN, CHILDREN! RUN!

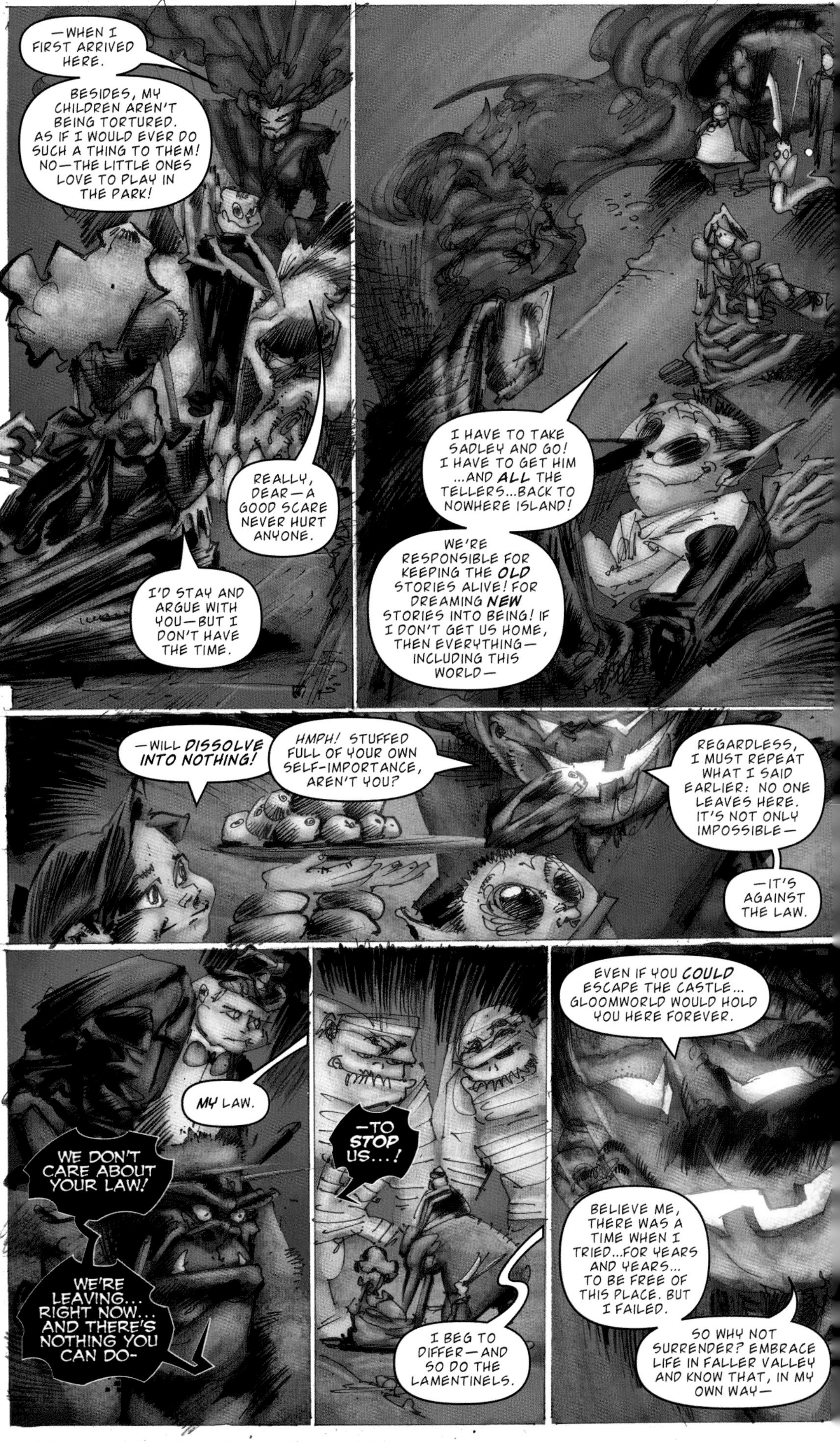
—WHEN I FIRST ARRIVED HERE.
BESIDES, MY CHILDREN AREN'T BEING TORTURED. AS IF I WOULD EVER DO SUCH A THING TO THEM! NO—THE LITTLE ONES LOVE TO PLAY IN THE PARK!
REALLY, DEAR—A GOOD SCARE NEVER HURT ANYONE.
I'D STAY AND ARGUE WITH YOU—BUT I DON'T HAVE THE TIME.
I HAVE TO TAKE SADLEY AND GO! I HAVE TO GET HIM ...AND ALL THE TELLERS...BACK TO NOWHERE ISLAND!
WE'RE RESPONSIBLE FOR KEEPING THE OLD STORIES ALIVE! FOR DREAMING NEW STORIES INTO BEING! IF I DON'T GET US HOME, THEN EVERYTHING—INCLUDING THIS WORLD—
—WILL DISSOLVE INTO NOTHING!
HMPH! STUFFED FULL OF YOUR OWN SELF-IMPORTANCE, AREN'T YOU?
REGARDLESS, I MUST REPEAT WHAT I SAID EARLIER: NO ONE LEAVES HERE. IT'S NOT ONLY IMPOSSIBLE—
—IT'S AGAINST THE LAW.
MY LAW.
WE DON'T CARE ABOUT YOUR LAW!
WE'RE LEAVING... RIGHT NOW... AND THERE'S NOTHING YOU CAN DO-
—TO STOP US...!
I BEG TO DIFFER—AND SO DO THE LAMENTINELS.
EVEN IF YOU COULD ESCAPE THE CASTLE... GLOOMWORLD WOULD HOLD YOU HERE FOREVER.
BELIEVE ME, THERE WAS A TIME WHEN I TRIED...FOR YEARS AND YEARS... TO BE FREE OF THIS PLACE. BUT I FAILED.
SO WHY NOT SURRENDER? EMBRACE LIFE IN FALLER VALLEY AND KNOW THAT, IN MY OWN WAY—

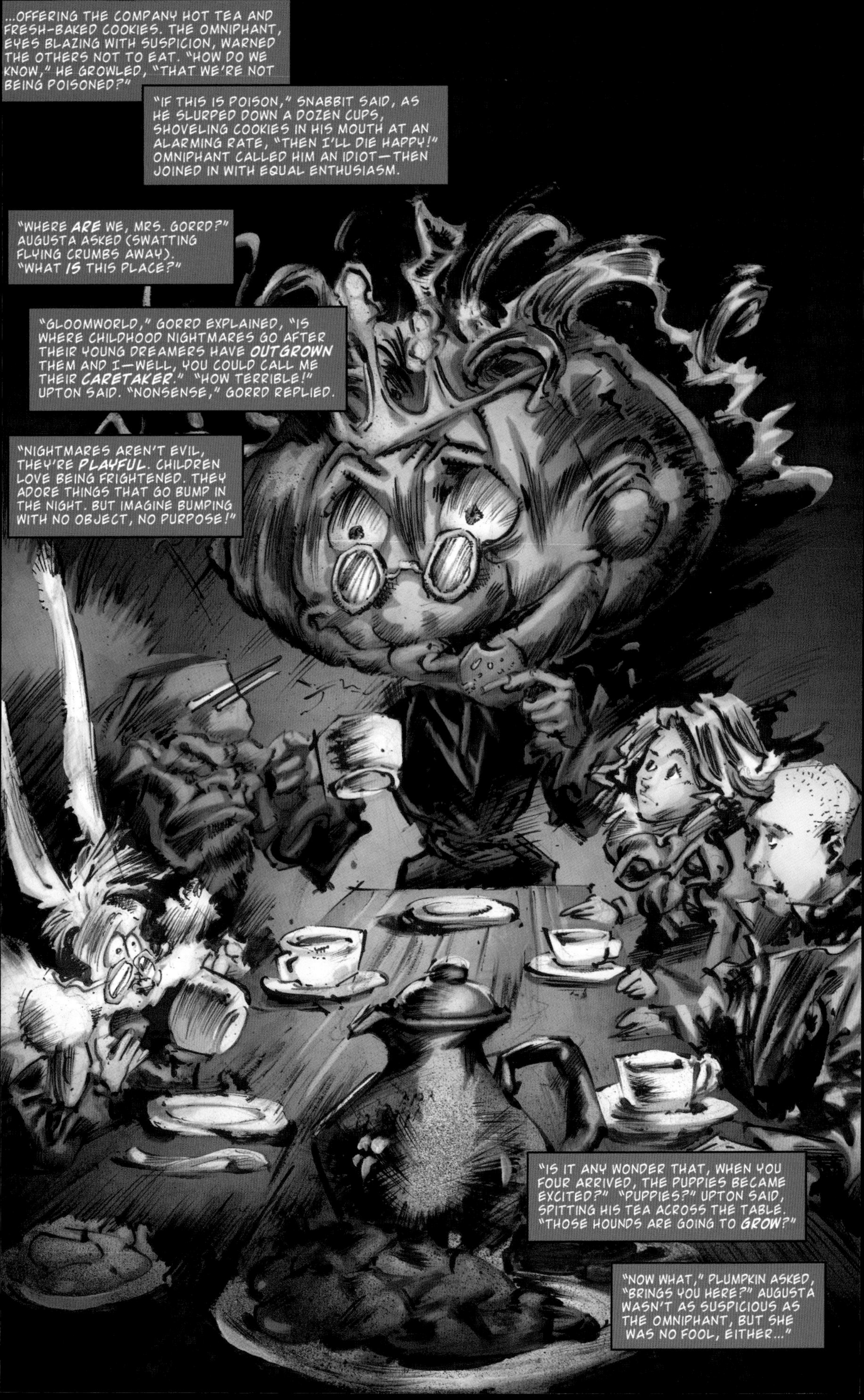
...OFFERING THE COMPANY HOT TEA AND FRESH-BAKED COOKIES. THE OMNIPHANT, EYES BLAZING WITH SUSPICION, WARNED THE OTHERS NOT TO EAT. "HOW DO WE KNOW," HE GROWLED, "THAT WE'RE NOT BEING POISONED?"
"IF THIS IS POISON," SNABBIT SAID, AS HE SLURPED DOWN A DOZEN CUPS, SHOVELING COOKIES IN HIS MOUTH AT AN ALARMING RATE, "THEN I'LL DIE HAPPY!" OMNIPHANT CALLED HIM AN IDIOT—THEN JOINED IN WITH EQUAL ENTHUSIASM.
"WHERE *ARE* WE, MRS. GORRD?" AUGUSTA ASKED (SWATTING FLYING CRUMBS AWAY). "WHAT *IS* THIS PLACE?"
"GLOOMWORLD," GORRD EXPLAINED, "IS WHERE CHILDHOOD NIGHTMARES GO AFTER THEIR YOUNG DREAMERS HAVE *OUTGROWN* THEM AND I—WELL, YOU COULD CALL ME THEIR *CARETAKER*." "HOW TERRIBLE!" UPTON SAID. "NONSENSE," GORRD REPLIED.
"NIGHTMARES AREN'T EVIL, THEY'RE *PLAYFUL*. CHILDREN LOVE BEING FRIGHTENED. THEY ADORE THINGS THAT GO BUMP IN THE NIGHT. BUT IMAGINE BUMPING WITH NO OBJECT, NO PURPOSE!"
"IS IT ANY WONDER THAT, WHEN YOU FOUR ARRIVED, THE PUPPIES BECAME EXCITED?" "PUPPIES?" UPTON SAID, SPITTING HIS TEA ACROSS THE TABLE. "THOSE HOUNDS ARE GOING TO *GROW*?"
"NOW WHAT," PLUMPKIN ASKED, "BRINGS YOU HERE?" AUGUSTA WASN'T AS SUSPICIOUS AS THE OMNIPHANT, BUT SHE WAS NO FOOL, EITHER..."

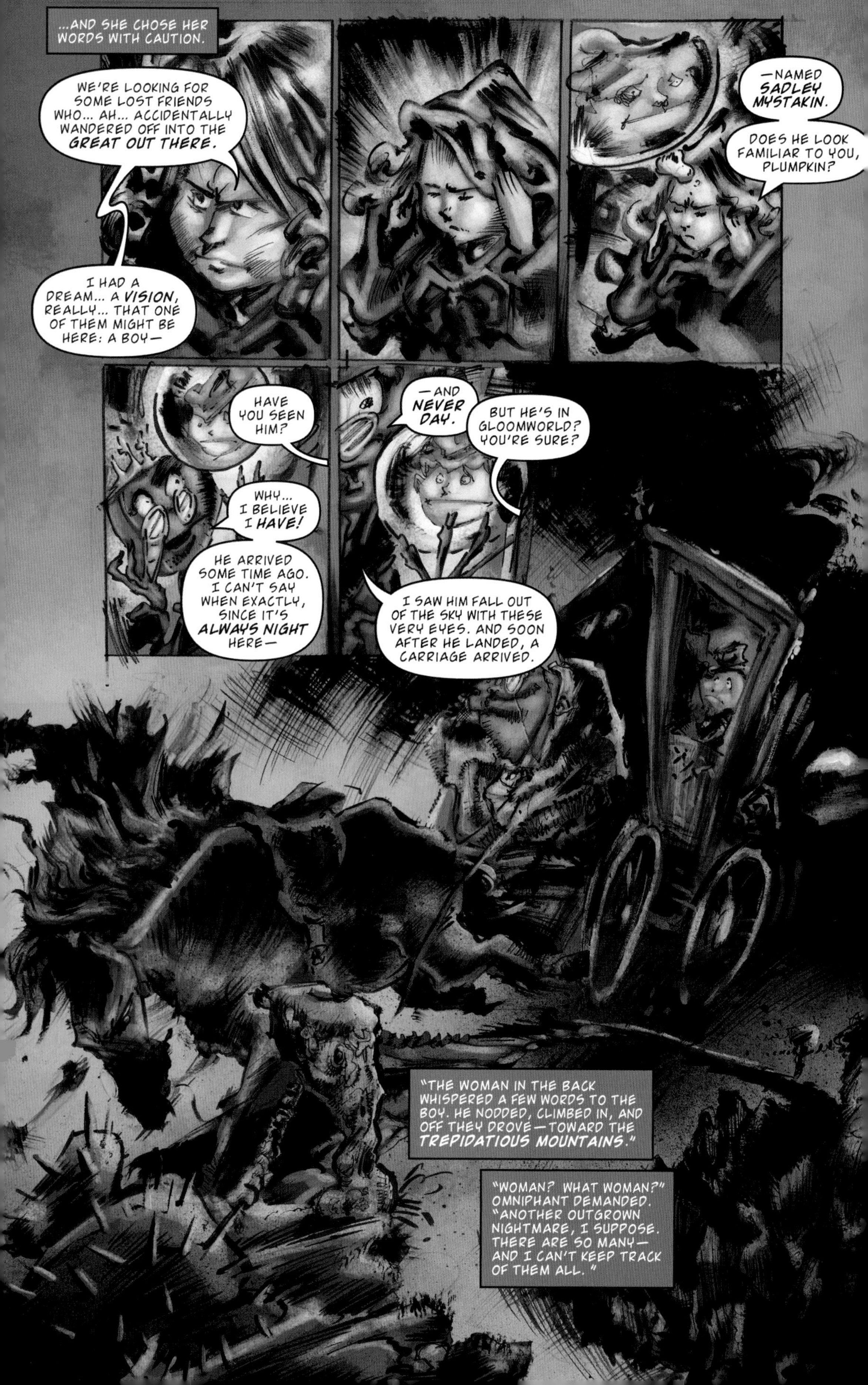

...AND SHE CHOSE HER WORDS WITH CAUTION.
WE'RE LOOKING FOR SOME LOST FRIENDS WHO... AH... ACCIDENTALLY WANDERED OFF INTO THE GREAT OUT THERE.
I HAD A DREAM... A VISION, REALLY... THAT ONE OF THEM MIGHT BE HERE: A BOY—
—NAMED SADLEY MYSTAKIN.
DOES HE LOOK FAMILIAR TO YOU, PLUMPKIN?
HAVE YOU SEEN HIM?
WHY... I BELIEVE I HAVE!
HE ARRIVED SOME TIME AGO. I CAN'T SAY WHEN EXACTLY, SINCE IT'S ALWAYS NIGHT HERE—
—AND NEVER DAY.
BUT HE'S IN GLOOMWORLD? YOU'RE SURE?
I SAW HIM FALL OUT OF THE SKY WITH THESE VERY EYES. AND SOON AFTER HE LANDED, A CARRIAGE ARRIVED.
"THE WOMAN IN THE BACK WHISPERED A FEW WORDS TO THE BOY. HE NODDED, CLIMBED IN, AND OFF THEY DROVE—TOWARD THE TREPIDATIOUS MOUNTAINS."
"WOMAN? WHAT WOMAN?" OMNIPHANT DEMANDED. "ANOTHER OUTGROWN NIGHTMARE, I SUPPOSE. THERE ARE SO MANY—AND I CAN'T KEEP TRACK OF THEM ALL."

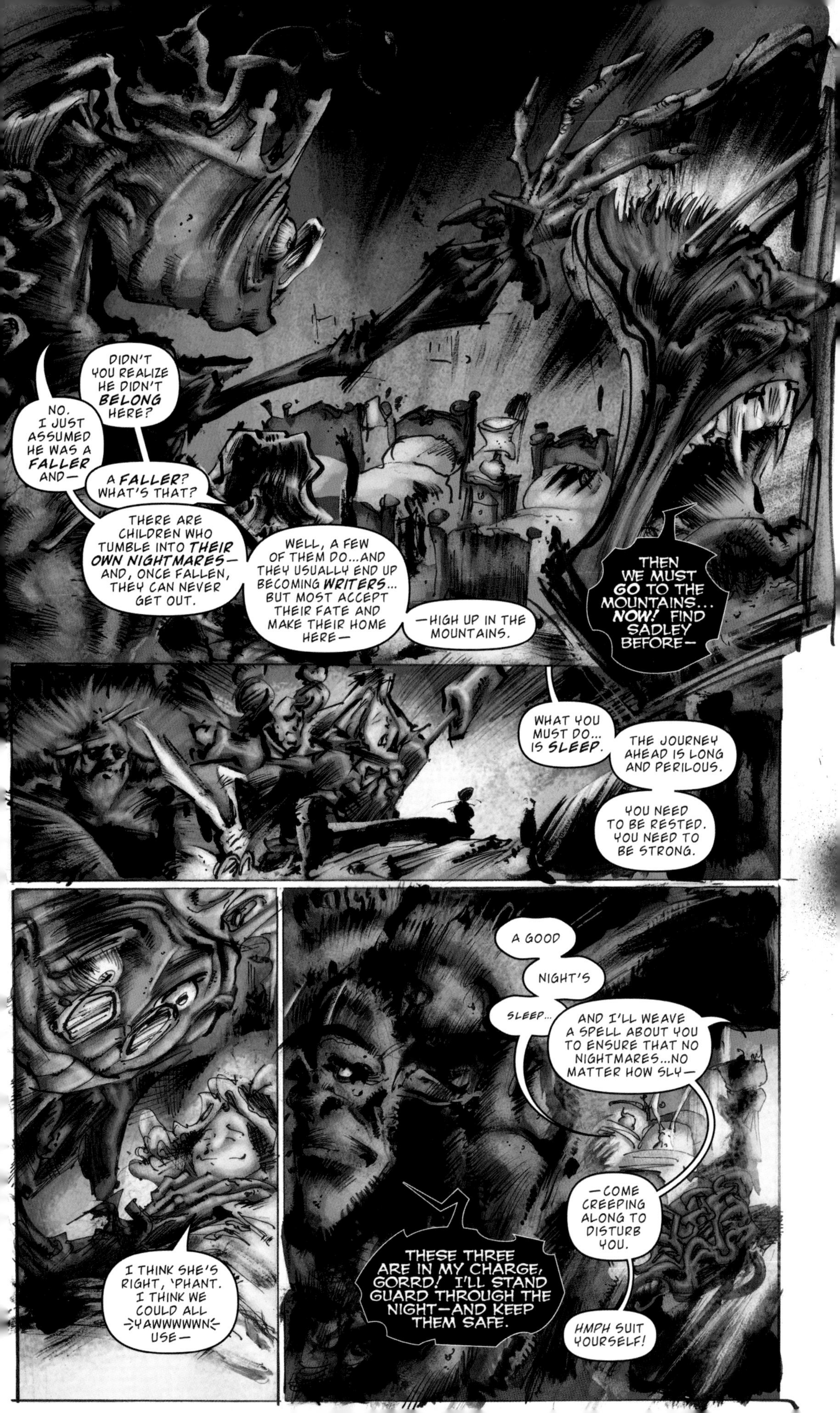

DIDN'T YOU REALIZE HE DIDN'T BELONG HERE?
NO. I JUST ASSUMED HE WAS A FALLER AND—
A FALLER? WHAT'S THAT?
THERE ARE CHILDREN WHO TUMBLE INTO THEIR OWN NIGHTMARES—AND, ONCE FALLEN, THEY CAN NEVER GET OUT.
WELL, A FEW OF THEM DO...AND THEY USUALLY END UP BECOMING WRITERS... BUT MOST ACCEPT THEIR FATE AND MAKE THEIR HOME HERE—
—HIGH UP IN THE MOUNTAINS.
THEN WE MUST GO TO THE MOUNTAINS... NOW! FIND SADLEY BEFORE—
WHAT YOU MUST DO... IS SLEEP.
THE JOURNEY AHEAD IS LONG AND PERILOUS.
YOU NEED TO BE RESTED. YOU NEED TO BE STRONG.
I THINK SHE'S RIGHT, 'PHANT. I THINK WE COULD ALL YAWWWWWN USE—
A GOOD
NIGHT'S
SLEEP...
AND I'LL WEAVE A SPELL ABOUT YOU TO ENSURE THAT NO NIGHTMARES...NO MATTER HOW SLY—
—COME CREEPING ALONG TO DISTURB YOU.
THESE THREE ARE IN MY CHARGE, GORRD! I'LL STAND GUARD THROUGH THE NIGHT—AND KEEP THEM SAFE.
HMPH SUIT YOURSELF!

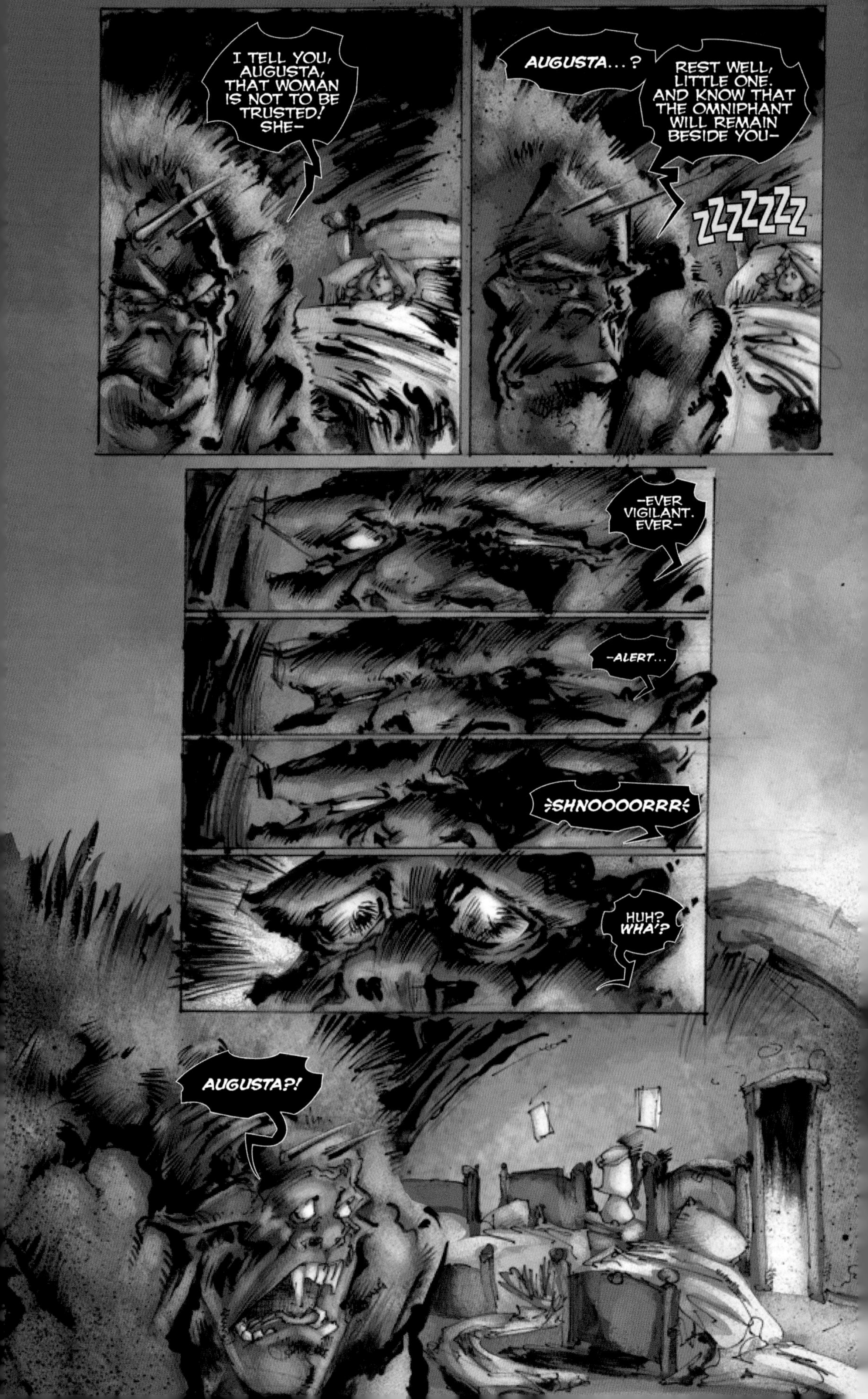
I TELL YOU, AUGUSTA, THAT WOMAN IS NOT TO BE TRUSTED! SHE-
AUGUSTA...?
REST WELL, LITTLE ONE. AND KNOW THAT THE OMNIPHANT WILL REMAIN BESIDE YOU-
ZZZZZZ
-EVER VIGILANT. EVER-
-ALERT...
SHNOOOORRR
HUH? WHA'?
AUGUSTA?!

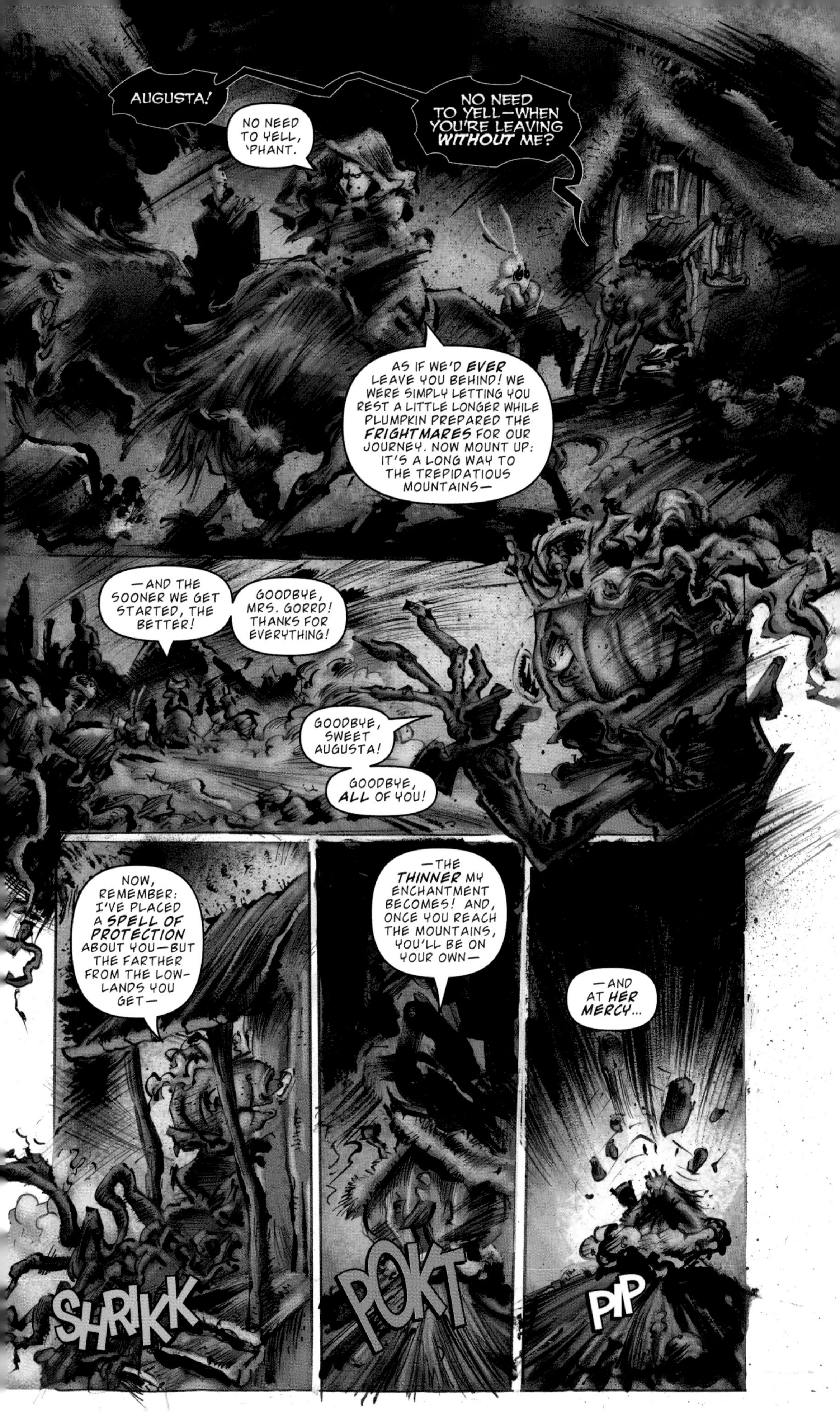
AUGUSTA!
NO NEED TO YELL, 'PHANT.
NO NEED TO YELL—WHEN YOU'RE LEAVING WITHOUT ME?
AS IF WE'D EVER LEAVE YOU BEHIND! WE WERE SIMPLY LETTING YOU REST A LITTLE LONGER WHILE PLUMPKIN PREPARED THE FRIGHTMARES FOR OUR JOURNEY. NOW MOUNT UP: IT'S A LONG WAY TO THE TREPIDATIOUS MOUNTAINS—
—AND THE SOONER WE GET STARTED, THE BETTER!
GOODBYE, MRS. GORRD! THANKS FOR EVERYTHING!
GOODBYE, SWEET AUGUSTA!
GOODBYE, ALL OF YOU!
NOW, REMEMBER: I'VE PLACED A SPELL OF PROTECTION ABOUT YOU—BUT THE FARTHER FROM THE LOW-LANDS YOU GET—
SHRIKK
—THE THINNER MY ENCHANTMENT BECOMES! AND, ONCE YOU REACH THE MOUNTAINS, YOU'LL BE ON YOUR OWN—
POKT
—AND AT HER MERCY...
PIP

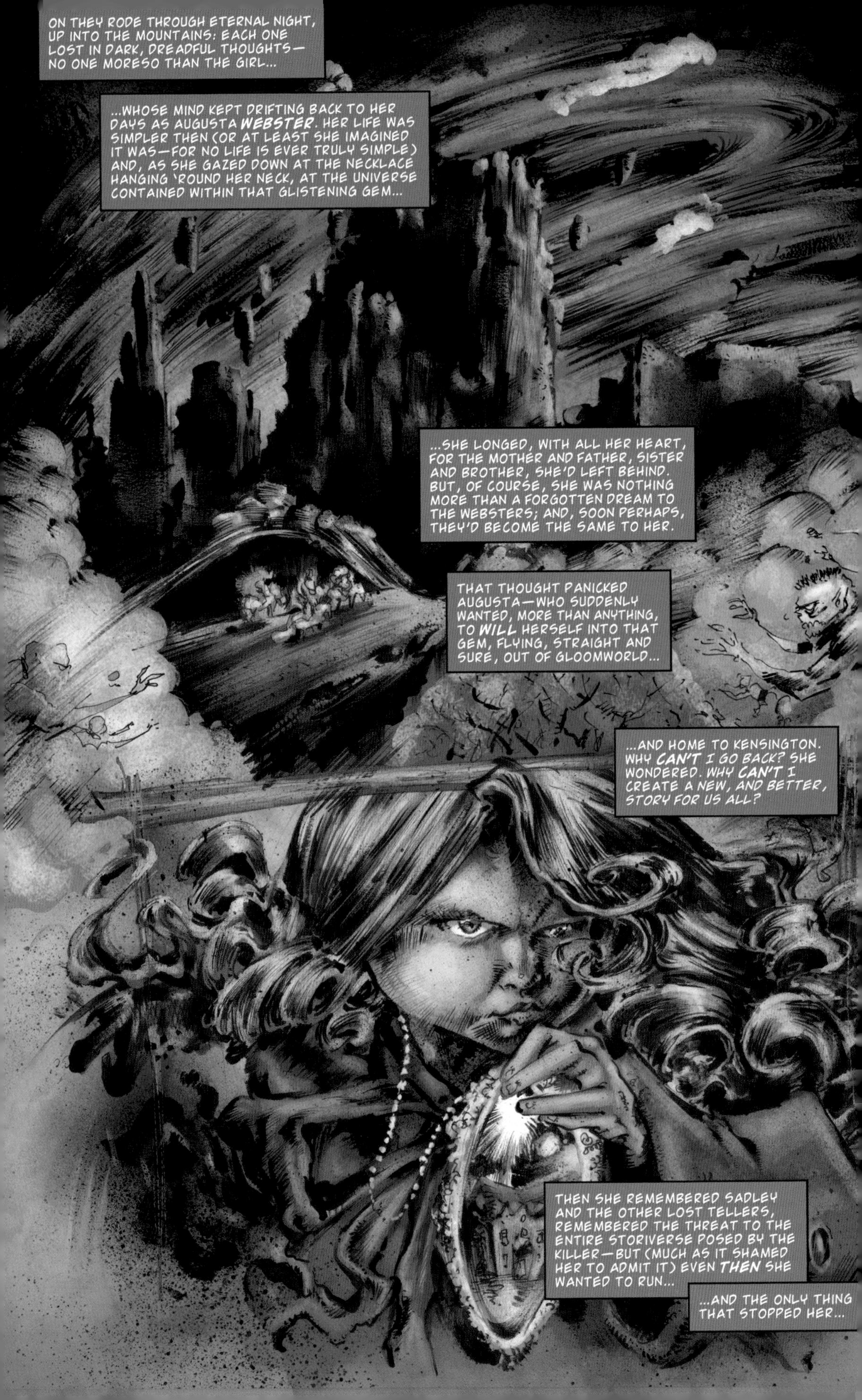
ON THEY RODE THROUGH ETERNAL NIGHT, UP INTO THE MOUNTAINS: EACH ONE LOST IN DARK, DREADFUL THOUGHTS— NO ONE MORESO THAN THE GIRL...
...WHOSE MIND KEPT DRIFTING BACK TO HER DAYS AS AUGUSTA WEBSTER. HER LIFE WAS SIMPLER THEN (OR AT LEAST SHE IMAGINED IT WAS—FOR NO LIFE IS EVER TRULY SIMPLE) AND, AS SHE GAZED DOWN AT THE NECKLACE HANGING 'ROUND HER NECK, AT THE UNIVERSE CONTAINED WITHIN THAT GLISTENING GEM...
...SHE LONGED, WITH ALL HER HEART, FOR THE MOTHER AND FATHER, SISTER AND BROTHER, SHE'D LEFT BEHIND. BUT, OF COURSE, SHE WAS NOTHING MORE THAN A FORGOTTEN DREAM TO THE WEBSTERS; AND, SOON PERHAPS, THEY'D BECOME THE SAME TO HER.
THAT THOUGHT PANICKED AUGUSTA—WHO SUDDENLY WANTED, MORE THAN ANYTHING, TO WILL HERSELF INTO THAT GEM, FLYING, STRAIGHT AND SURE, OUT OF GLOOMWORLD...
...AND HOME TO KENSINGTON. WHY CAN'T I GO BACK? SHE WONDERED. WHY CAN'T I CREATE A NEW, AND BETTER, STORY FOR US ALL?
THEN SHE REMEMBERED SADLEY AND THE OTHER LOST TELLERS, REMEMBERED THE THREAT TO THE ENTIRE STORIVERSE POSED BY THE KILLER—BUT (MUCH AS IT SHAMED HER TO ADMIT IT) EVEN THEN SHE WANTED TO RUN...
...AND THE ONLY THING THAT STOPPED HER...

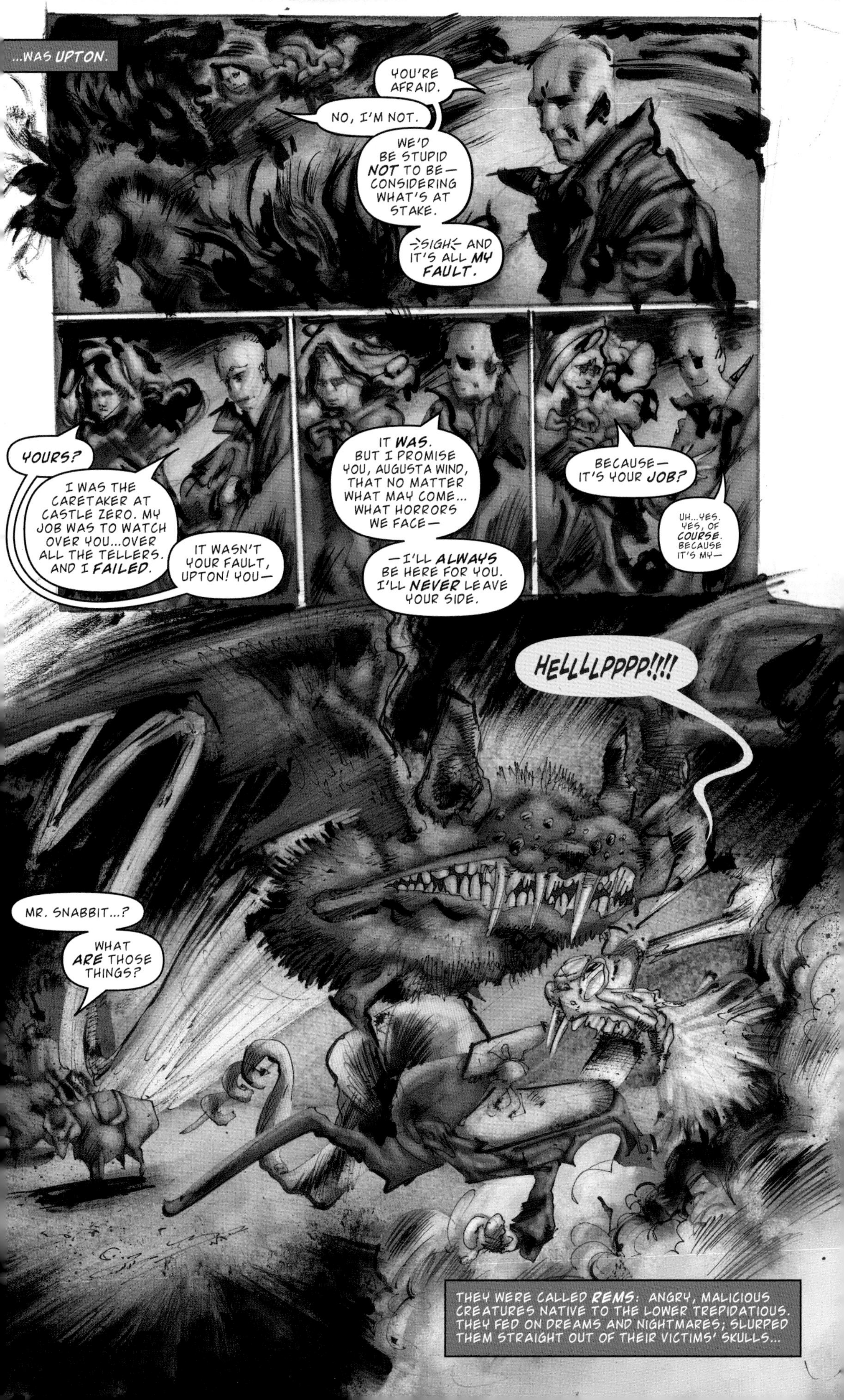
...WAS UPTON.
YOU'RE AFRAID.
NO, I'M NOT.
WE'D BE STUPID NOT TO BE— CONSIDERING WHAT'S AT STAKE.
⇒SIGH⇐ AND IT'S ALL MY FAULT.
YOURS?
I WAS THE CARETAKER AT CASTLE ZERO. MY JOB WAS TO WATCH OVER YOU...OVER ALL THE TELLERS. AND I FAILED.
IT WASN'T YOUR FAULT, UPTON! YOU—
IT WAS. BUT I PROMISE YOU, AUGUSTA WIND, THAT NO MATTER WHAT MAY COME... WHAT HORRORS WE FACE—
—I'LL ALWAYS BE HERE FOR YOU. I'LL NEVER LEAVE YOUR SIDE.
BECAUSE— IT'S YOUR JOB?
UH...YES. YES, OF COURSE. BECAUSE IT'S MY—
HELLLLPPPP!!!!
MR. SNABBIT...?
WHAT ARE THOSE THINGS?
THEY WERE CALLED REMS: ANGRY, MALICIOUS CREATURES NATIVE TO THE LOWER TREPIDATIOUS. THEY FED ON DREAMS AND NIGHTMARES; SLURPED THEM STRAIGHT OUT OF THEIR VICTIMS' SKULLS...

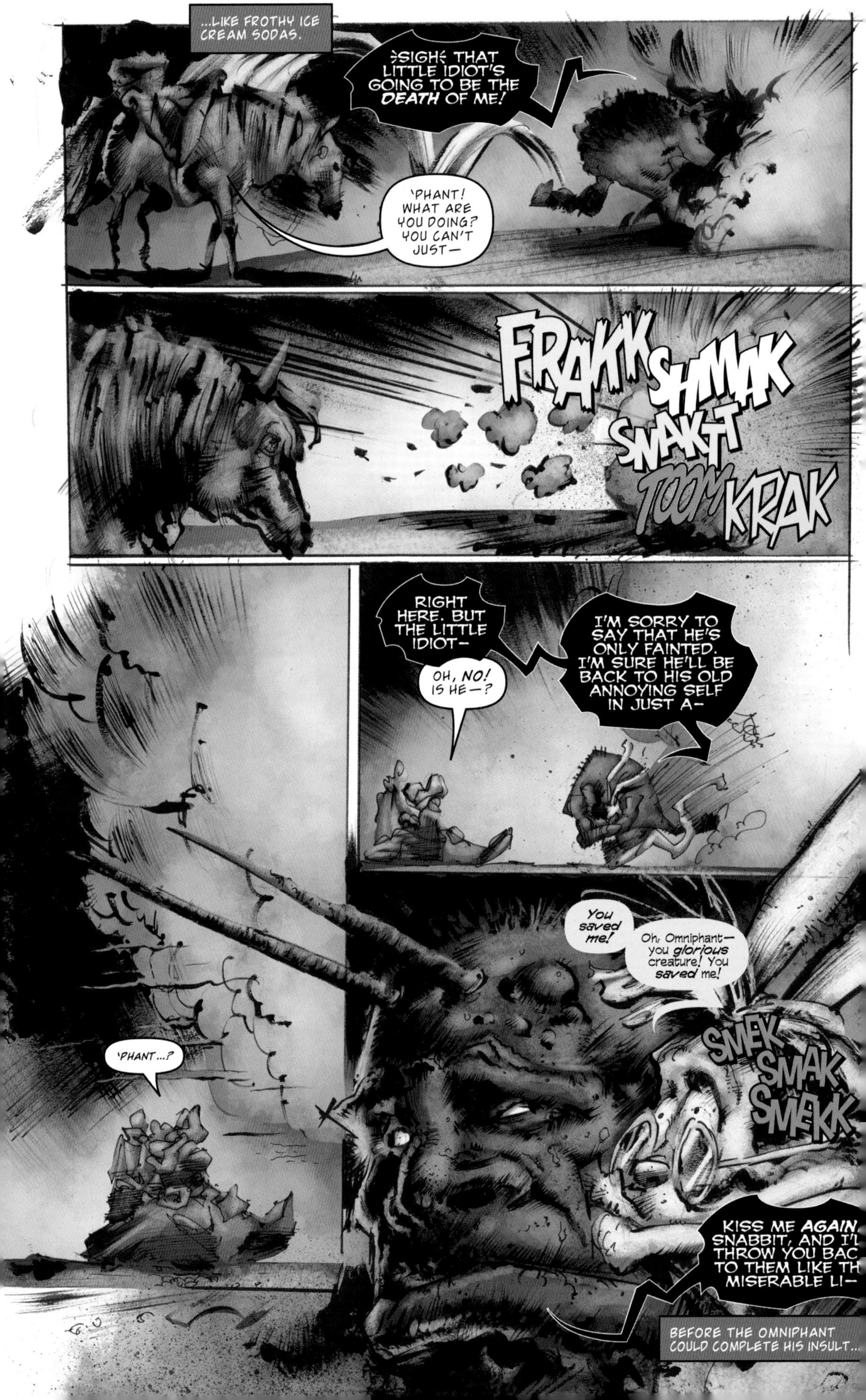
...LIKE FROTHY ICE CREAM SODAS.
>SIGH< THAT LITTLE IDIOT'S GOING TO BE THE *DEATH* OF ME!
'PHANT! WHAT ARE YOU DOING? YOU CAN'T JUST—
FRAKK SHMAK SNAKT TOOM KRAK
RIGHT HERE. BUT THE LITTLE IDIOT—
OH, *NO!* IS HE—?
I'M SORRY TO SAY THAT HE'S ONLY FAINTED. I'M SURE HE'LL BE BACK TO HIS OLD ANNOYING SELF IN JUST A—
'PHANT...?
You saved me!
Oh, Omniphant—you *glorious* creature! You *saved* me!
SMEK SMAK SMEKK
KISS ME *AGAIN*, SNABBIT, AND I'L THROW YOU BAC TO THEM LIKE TH MISERABLE LI—
BEFORE THE OMNIPHANT COULD COMPLETE HIS INSULT...

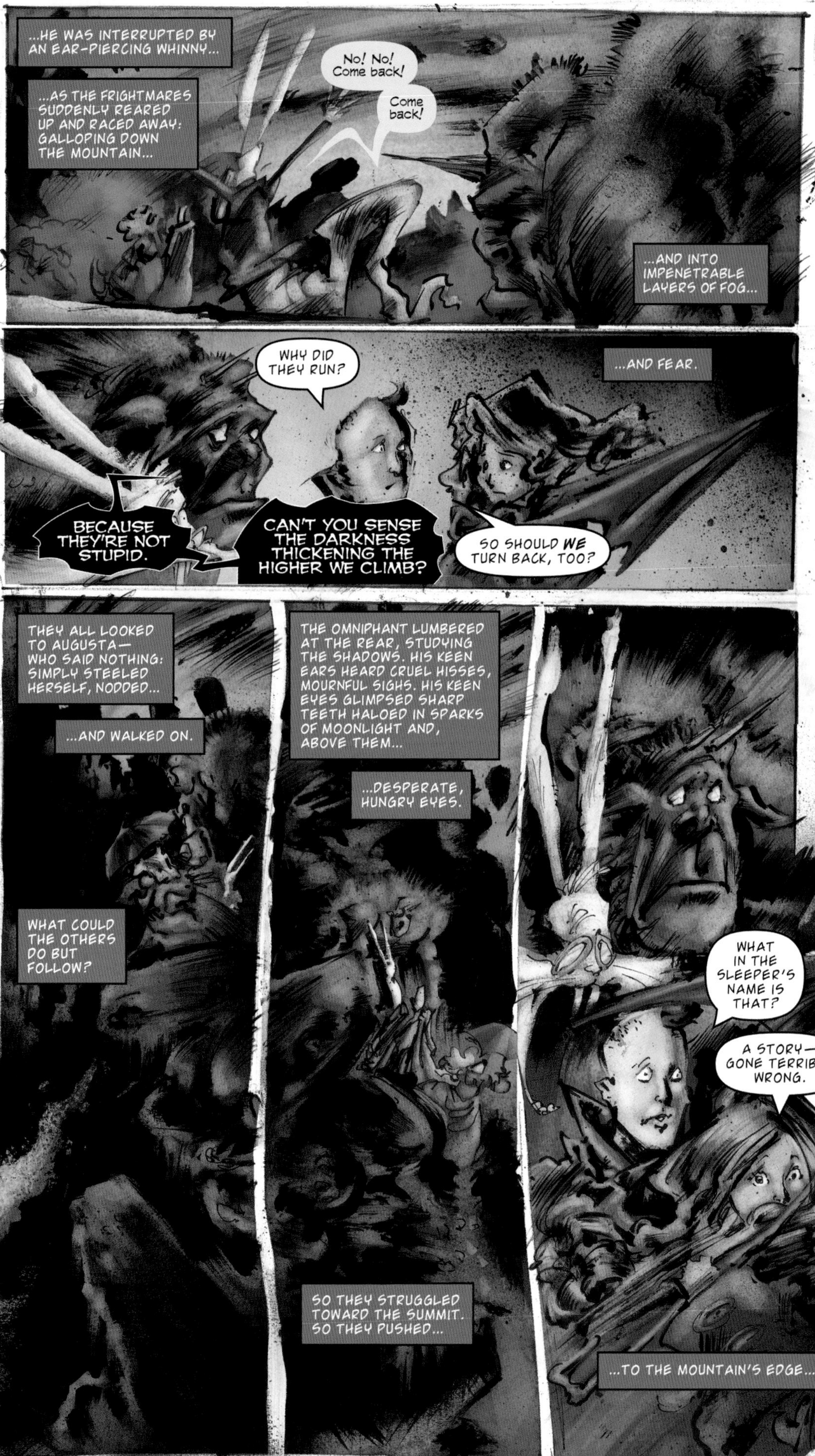
...HE WAS INTERRUPTED BY AN EAR-PIERCING WHINNY...
...AS THE FRIGHTMARES SUDDENLY REARED UP AND RACED AWAY: GALLOPING DOWN THE MOUNTAIN...
No! No! Come back!
Come back!
...AND INTO IMPENETRABLE LAYERS OF FOG...
WHY DID THEY RUN?
...AND FEAR.
BECAUSE THEY'RE NOT STUPID.
CAN'T YOU SENSE THE DARKNESS THICKENING THE HIGHER WE CLIMB?
SO SHOULD WE TURN BACK, TOO?
THEY ALL LOOKED TO AUGUSTA— WHO SAID NOTHING: SIMPLY STEELED HERSELF, NODDED...
...AND WALKED ON.
WHAT COULD THE OTHERS DO BUT FOLLOW?
THE OMNIPHANT LUMBERED AT THE REAR, STUDYING THE SHADOWS. HIS KEEN EARS HEARD CRUEL HISSES, MOURNFUL SIGHS. HIS KEEN EYES GLIMPSED SHARP TEETH HALOED IN SPARKS OF MOONLIGHT AND, ABOVE THEM...
...DESPERATE, HUNGRY EYES.
SO THEY STRUGGLED TOWARD THE SUMMIT. SO THEY PUSHED...
WHAT IN THE SLEEPER'S NAME IS THAT?
A STORY— GONE TERRIBLY WRONG.
...TO THE MOUNTAIN'S EDGE...

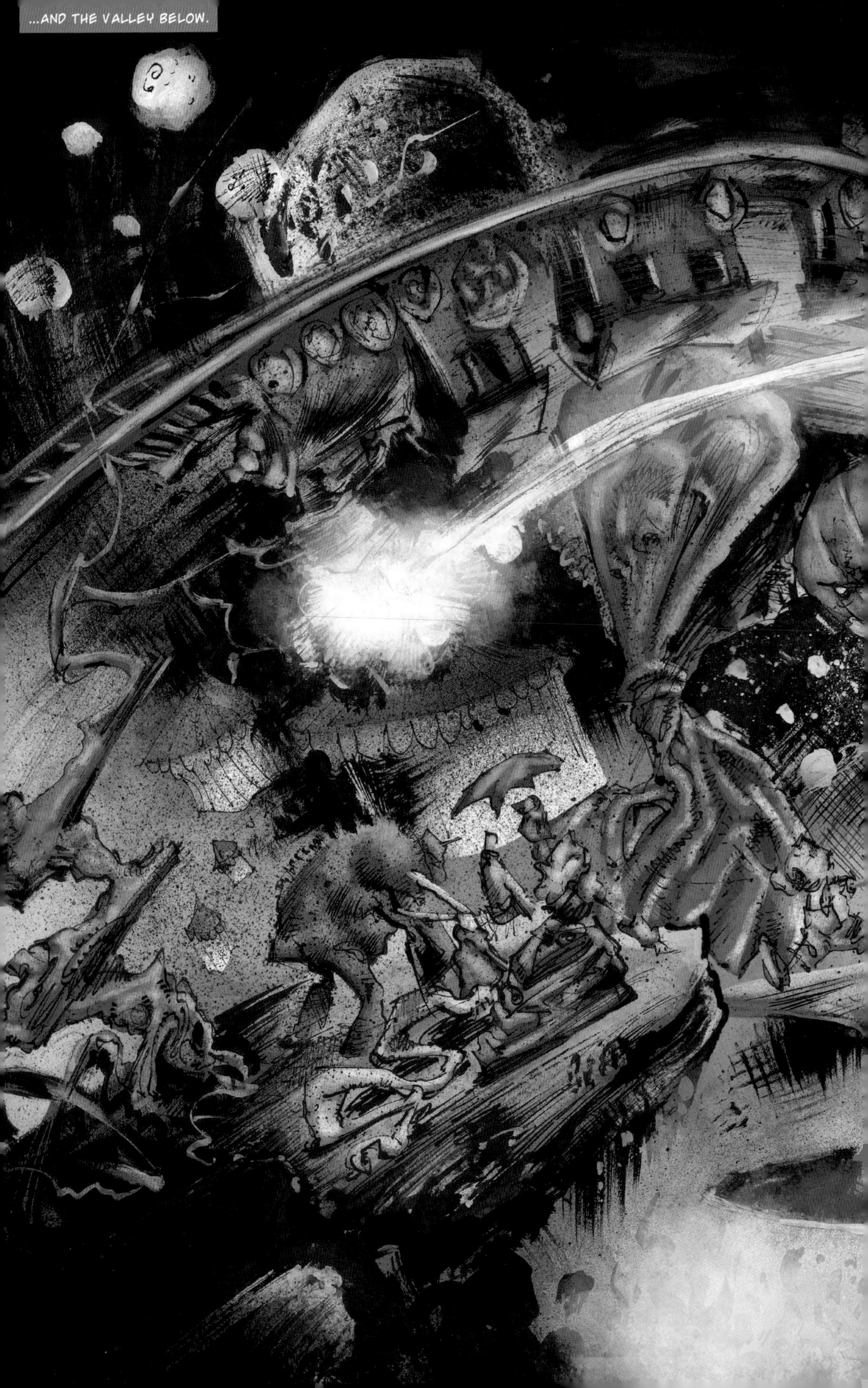
...AND THE VALLEY BELOW.

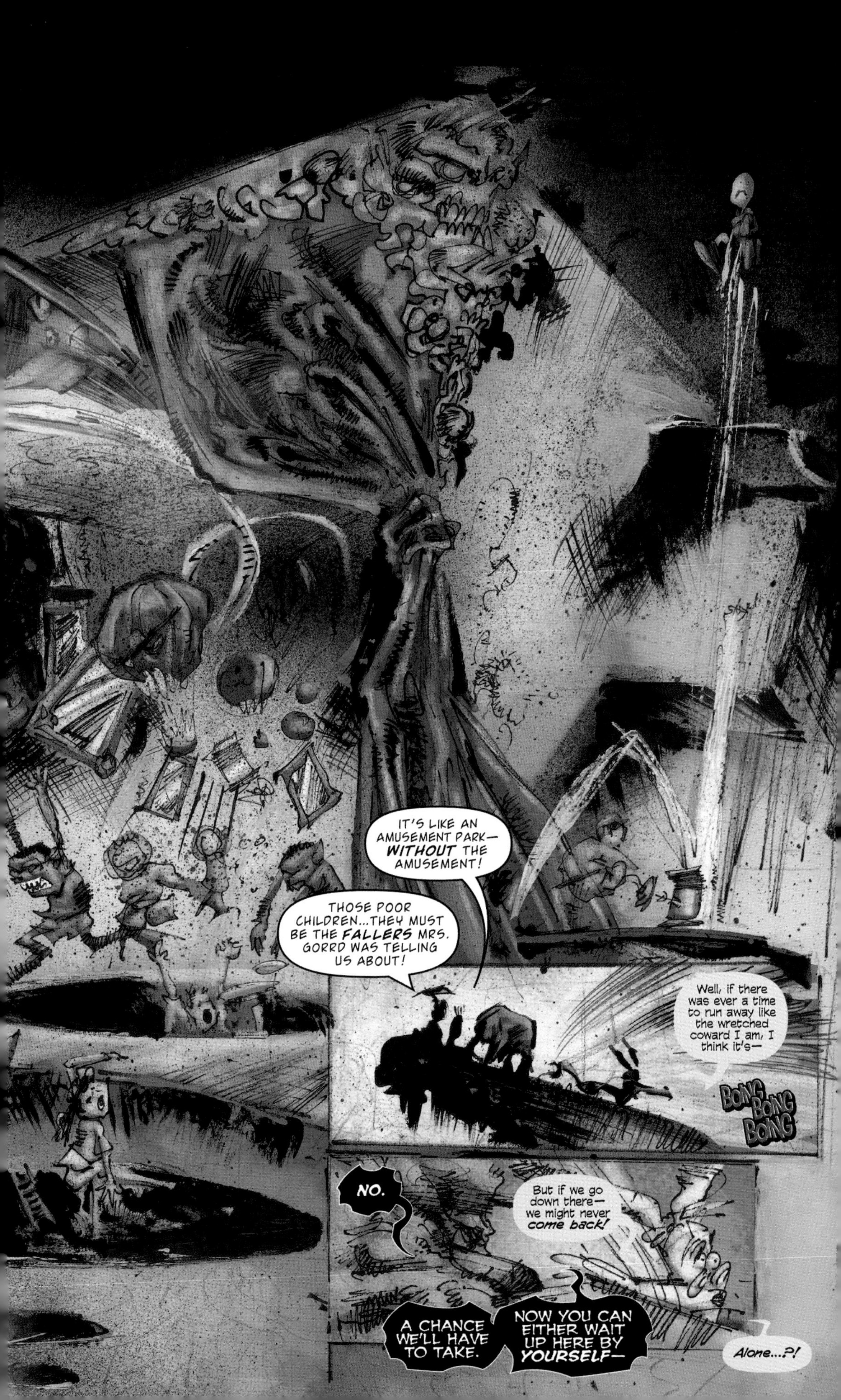

IT'S LIKE AN AMUSEMENT PARK— WITHOUT THE AMUSEMENT!
THOSE POOR CHILDREN...THEY MUST BE THE FALLERS MRS. GORRD WAS TELLING US ABOUT!
Well, if there was ever a time to run away like the wretched coward I am, I think it's—
BOING BOING BOING
NO.
But if we go down there— we might never come back!
A CHANCE WE'LL HAVE TO TAKE.
NOW YOU CAN EITHER WAIT UP HERE BY YOURSELF—
Alone...?!

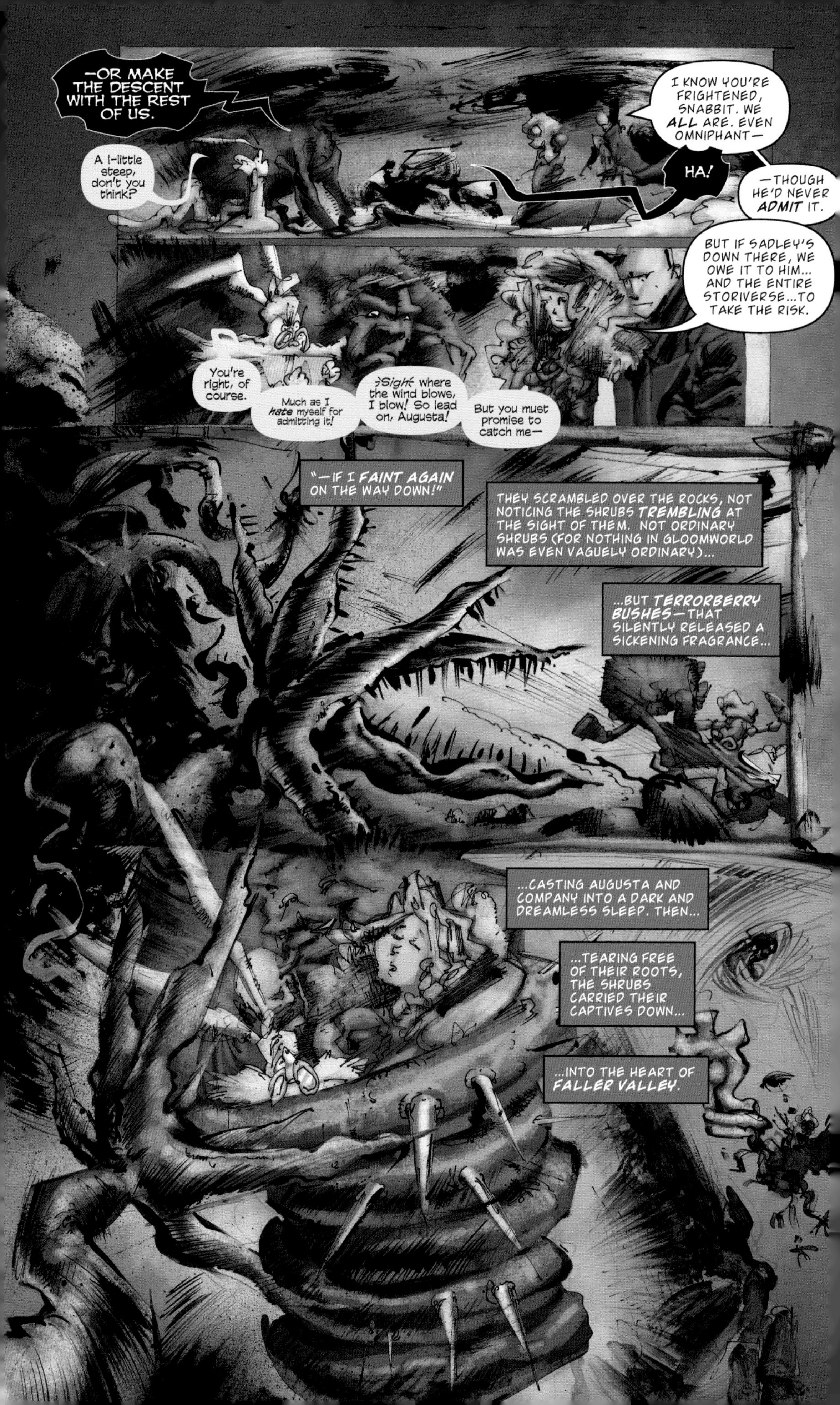

—OR MAKE THE DESCENT WITH THE REST OF US.
I KNOW YOU'RE FRIGHTENED, SNABBIT. WE ALL ARE. EVEN OMNIPHANT—
A l-little steep, don't you think?
HA!
—THOUGH HE'D NEVER ADMIT IT.
BUT IF SADLEY'S DOWN THERE, WE OWE IT TO HIM... AND THE ENTIRE STORIVERSE...TO TAKE THE RISK.
You're right, of course.
Much as I hate myself for admitting it!
Sigh where the wind blows, I blow! So lead on, Augusta!
But you must promise to catch me—
"—IF I FAINT AGAIN ON THE WAY DOWN!"
THEY SCRAMBLED OVER THE ROCKS, NOT NOTICING THE SHRUBS TREMBLING AT THE SIGHT OF THEM. NOT ORDINARY SHRUBS (FOR NOTHING IN GLOOMWORLD WAS EVEN VAGUELY ORDINARY)...
...BUT TERRORBERRY BUSHES—THAT SILENTLY RELEASED A SICKENING FRAGRANCE...
...CASTING AUGUSTA AND COMPANY INTO A DARK AND DREAMLESS SLEEP. THEN...
...TEARING FREE OF THEIR ROOTS, THE SHRUBS CARRIED THEIR CAPTIVES DOWN...
...INTO THE HEART OF FALLER VALLEY.

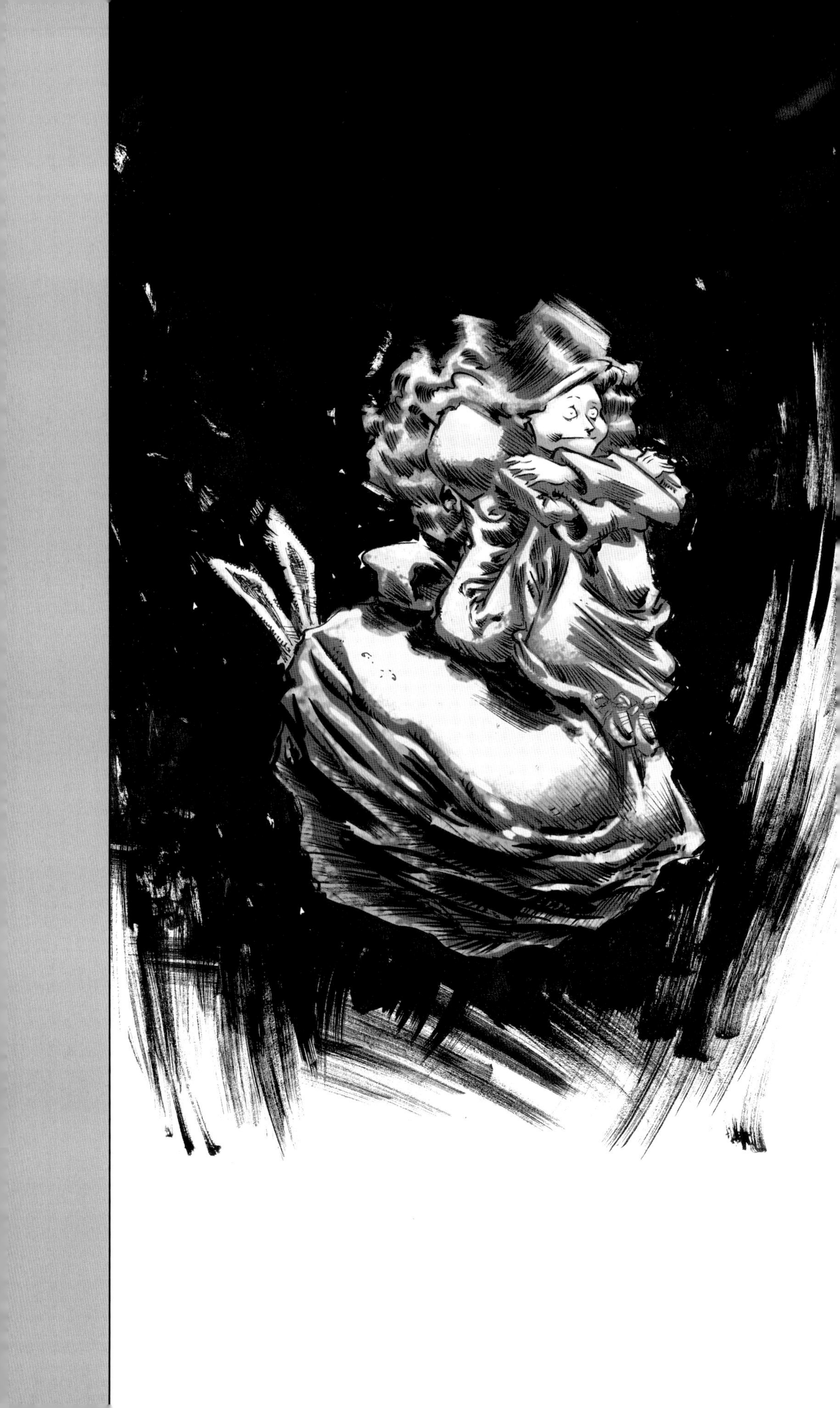

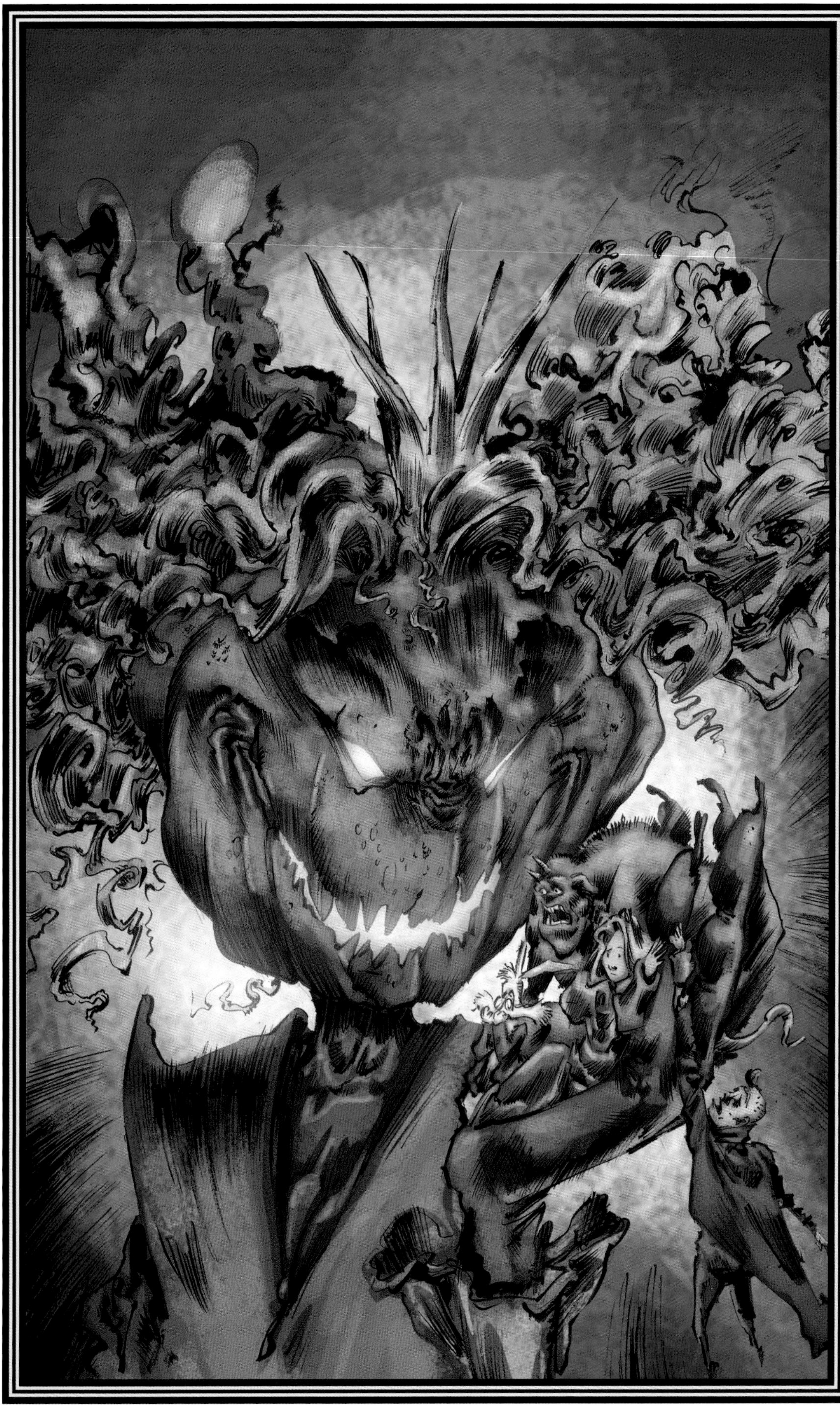

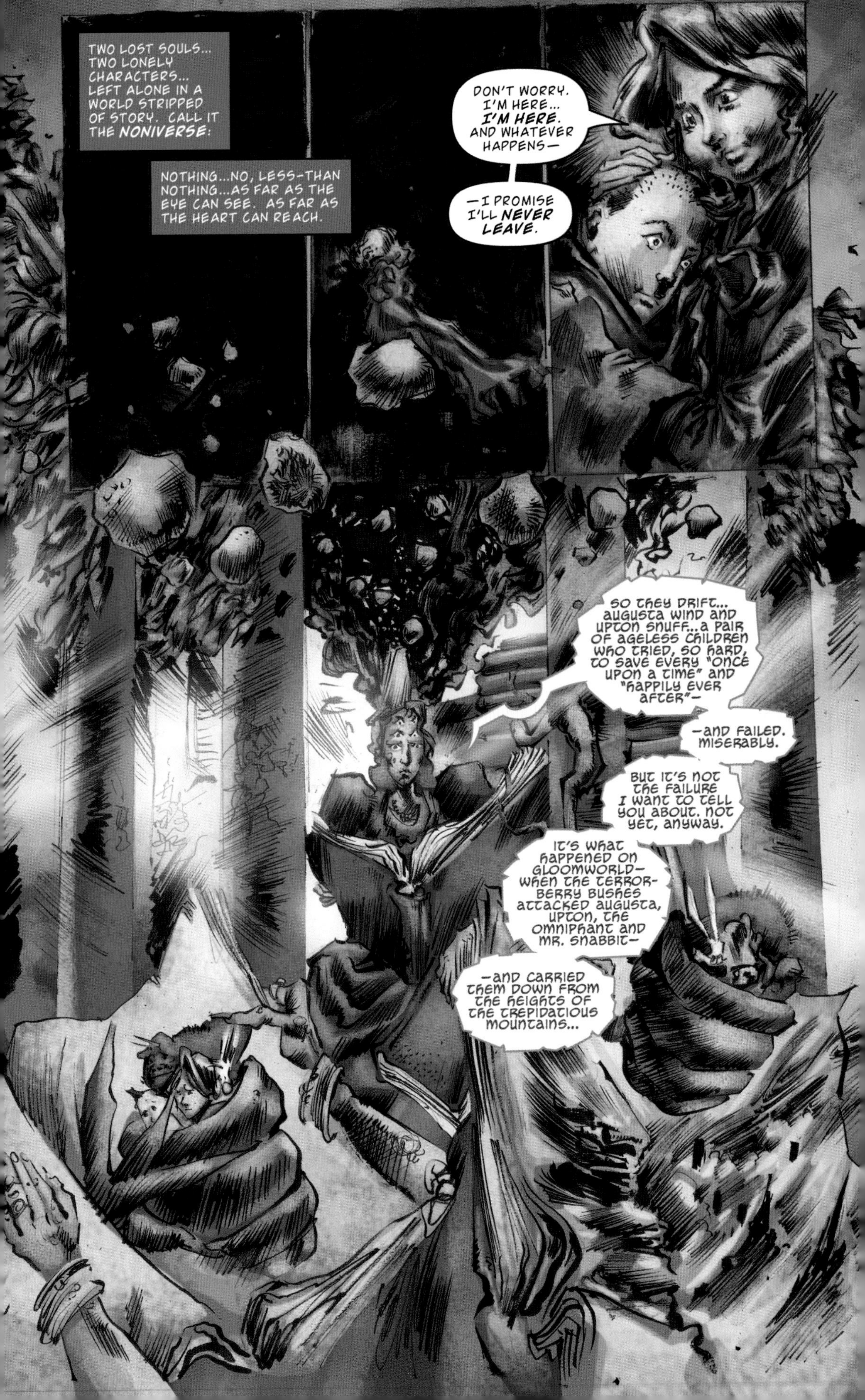
TWO LOST SOULS... TWO LONELY CHARACTERS... LEFT ALONE IN A WORLD STRIPPED OF STORY. CALL IT THE *NONIVERSE*:
NOTHING...NO, LESS-THAN NOTHING...AS FAR AS THE EYE CAN SEE. AS FAR AS THE HEART CAN REACH.
DON'T WORRY. I'M HERE... ***I'M HERE***. AND WHATEVER HAPPENS—
—I PROMISE I'LL ***NEVER LEAVE***.
SO THEY DRIFT... AUGUSTA WIND AND UPTON SNUFF...A PAIR OF AGELESS CHILDREN WHO TRIED, SO HARD, TO SAVE EVERY "ONCE UPON A TIME" AND "HAPPILY EVER AFTER"—
—AND FAILED. MISERABLY.
BUT IT'S NOT THE FAILURE I WANT TO TELL YOU ABOUT. NOT YET, ANYWAY.
IT'S WHAT HAPPENED ON GLOOMWORLD— WHEN THE TERROR-BERRY BUSHES ATTACKED AUGUSTA, UPTON, THE OMNIPHANT AND MR. SNABBIT—
—AND CARRIED THEM DOWN FROM THE HEIGHTS OF THE TREPIDATIOUS MOUNTAINS...

CHAPTER TWO: A Rude Awakening

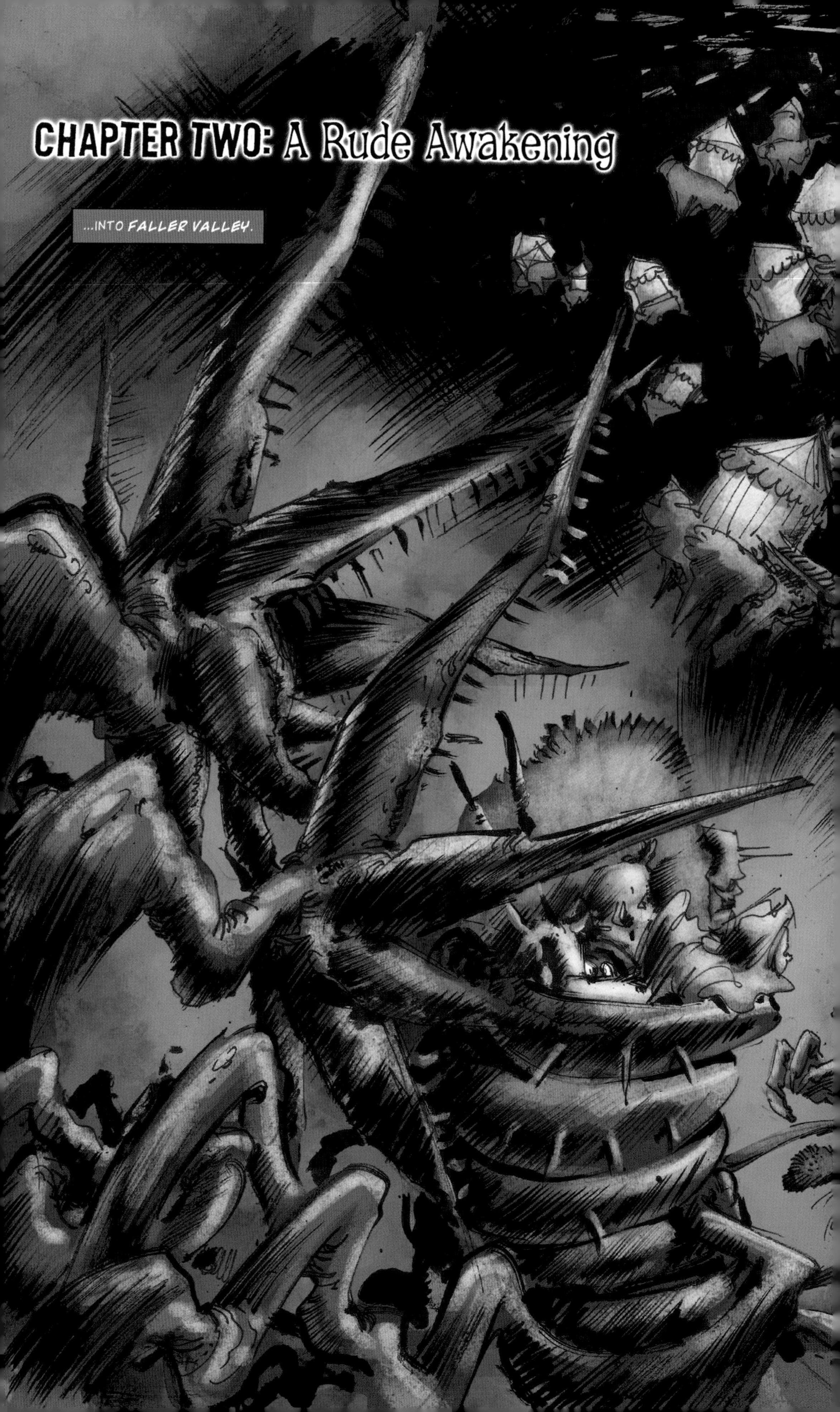
...INTO FALLER VALLEY.

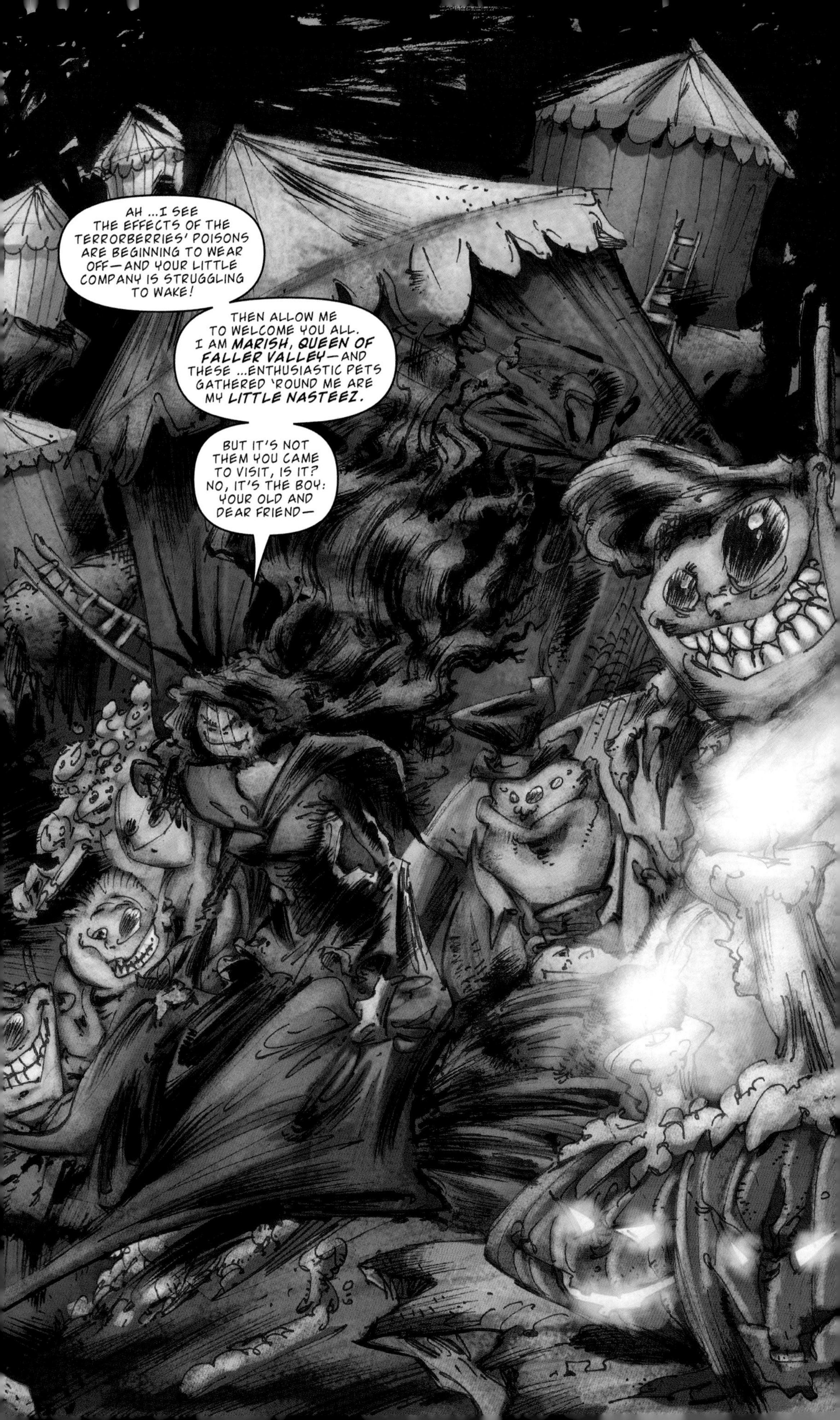
AH ...I SEE THE EFFECTS OF THE TERRORBERRIES' POISONS ARE BEGINNING TO WEAR OFF—AND YOUR LITTLE COMPANY IS STRUGGLING TO WAKE!
THEN ALLOW ME TO WELCOME YOU ALL. I AM MARISH, QUEEN OF FALLER VALLEY—AND THESE ...ENTHUSIASTIC PETS GATHERED 'ROUND ME ARE MY LITTLE NASTEEZ.
BUT IT'S NOT THEM YOU CAME TO VISIT, IS IT? NO, IT'S THE BOY: YOUR OLD AND DEAR FRIEND—

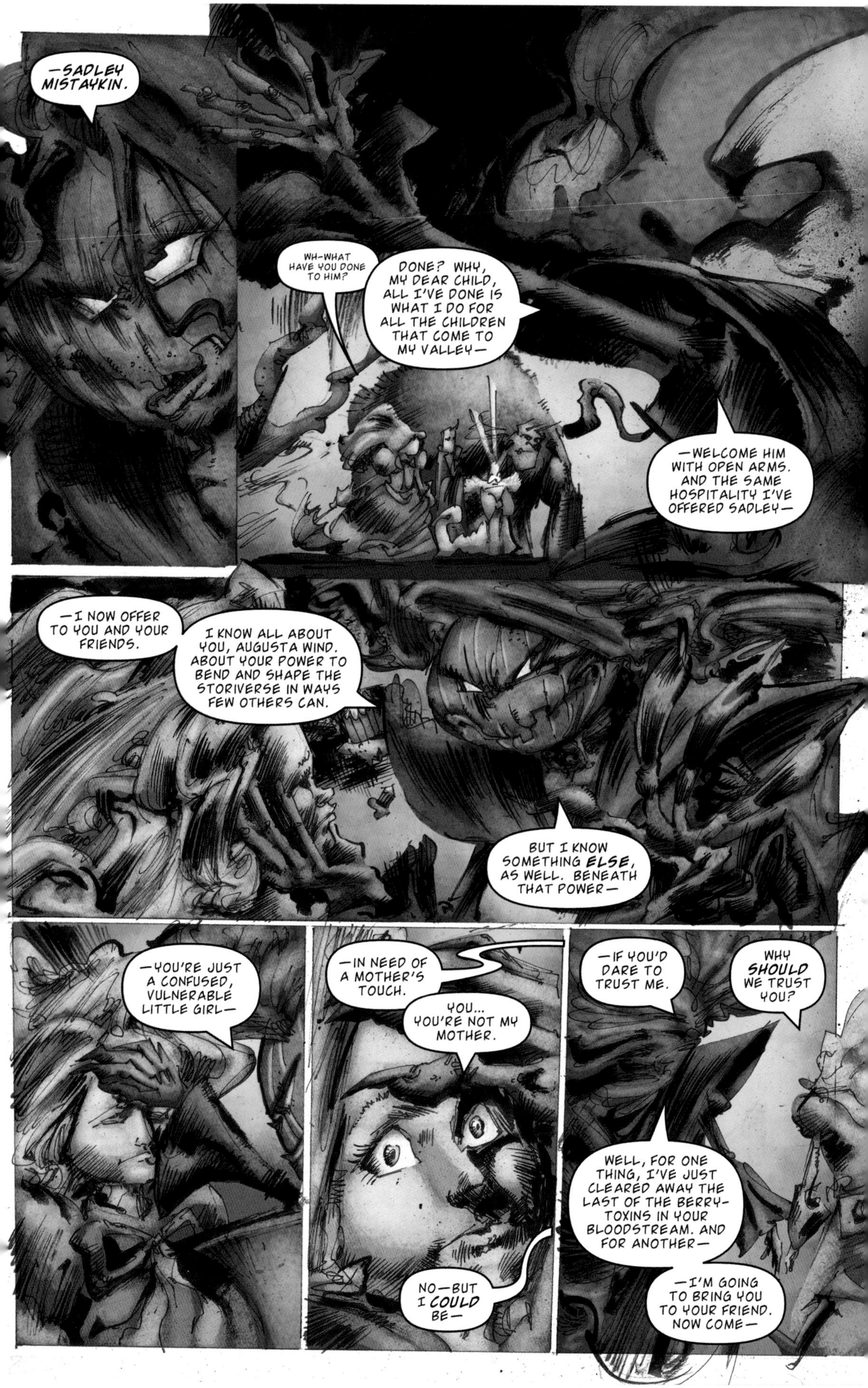
—SADLEY MISTAYKIN.
WH-WHAT HAVE YOU DONE TO HIM?
DONE? WHY, MY DEAR CHILD, ALL I'VE DONE IS WHAT I DO FOR ALL THE CHILDREN THAT COME TO MY VALLEY—
—WELCOME HIM WITH OPEN ARMS. AND THE SAME HOSPITALITY I'VE OFFERED SADLEY—
—I NOW OFFER TO YOU AND YOUR FRIENDS.
I KNOW ALL ABOUT YOU, AUGUSTA WIND. ABOUT YOUR POWER TO BEND AND SHAPE THE STORIVERSE IN WAYS FEW OTHERS CAN.
BUT I KNOW SOMETHING ELSE, AS WELL. BENEATH THAT POWER—
—YOU'RE JUST A CONFUSED, VULNERABLE LITTLE GIRL—
—IN NEED OF A MOTHER'S TOUCH.
YOU... YOU'RE NOT MY MOTHER.
NO—BUT I COULD BE—
—IF YOU'D DARE TO TRUST ME.
WHY SHOULD WE TRUST YOU?
WELL, FOR ONE THING, I'VE JUST CLEARED AWAY THE LAST OF THE BERRY-TOXINS IN YOUR BLOODSTREAM. AND FOR ANOTHER—
—I'M GOING TO BRING YOU TO YOUR FRIEND. NOW COME—

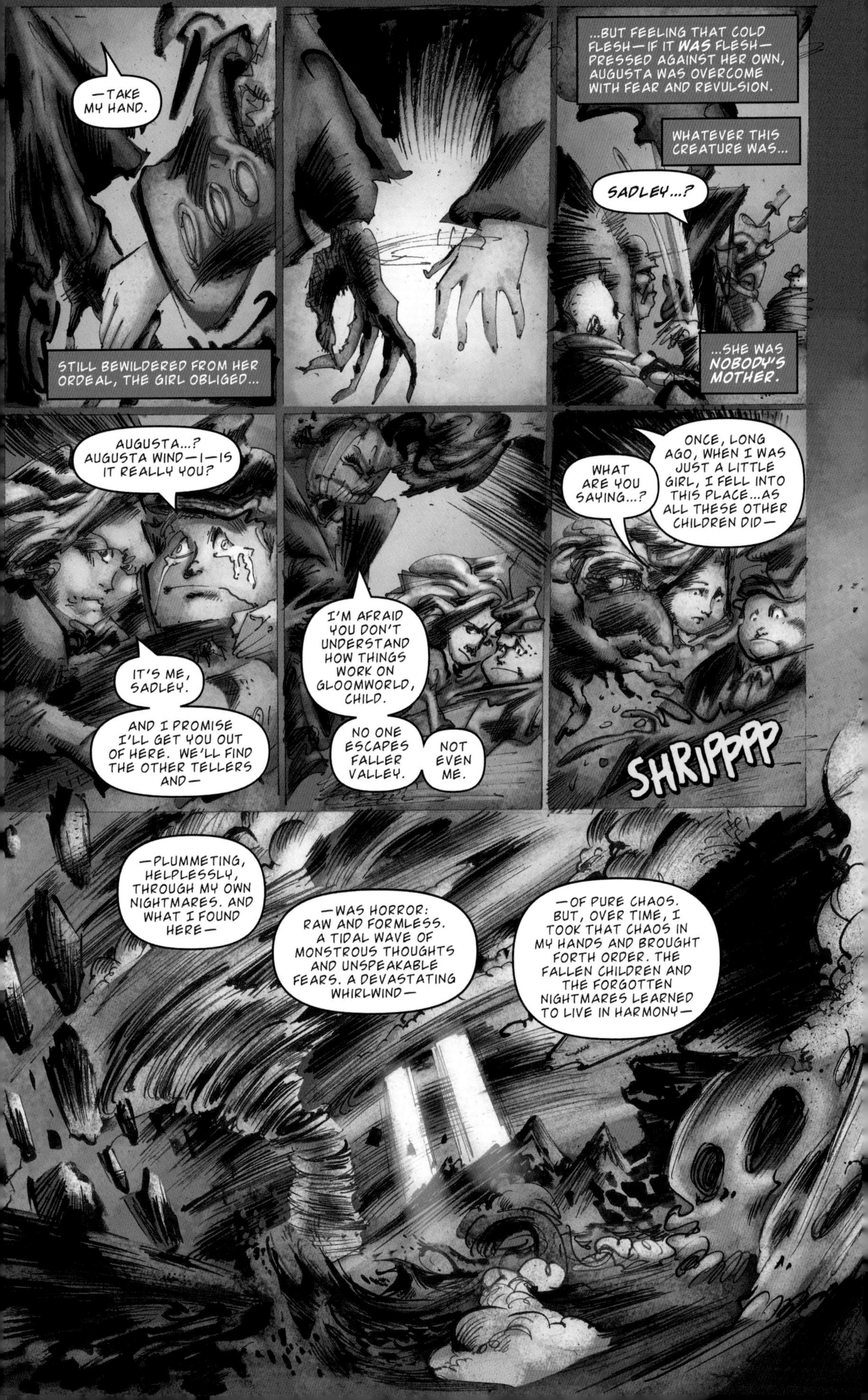
—TAKE MY HAND.
STILL BEWILDERED FROM HER ORDEAL, THE GIRL OBLIGED...
...BUT FEELING THAT COLD FLESH—IF IT WAS FLESH—PRESSED AGAINST HER OWN, AUGUSTA WAS OVERCOME WITH FEAR AND REVULSION.
WHATEVER THIS CREATURE WAS...
SADLEY...?
...SHE WAS NOBODY'S MOTHER.
AUGUSTA...? AUGUSTA WIND—I—IS IT REALLY YOU?
IT'S ME, SADLEY.
AND I PROMISE I'LL GET YOU OUT OF HERE. WE'LL FIND THE OTHER TELLERS AND—
I'M AFRAID YOU DON'T UNDERSTAND HOW THINGS WORK ON GLOOMWORLD, CHILD.
NO ONE ESCAPES FALLER VALLEY.
NOT EVEN ME.
WHAT ARE YOU SAYING...?
ONCE, LONG AGO, WHEN I WAS JUST A LITTLE GIRL, I FELL INTO THIS PLACE...AS ALL THESE OTHER CHILDREN DID—
SHRIPPPP
—PLUMMETING, HELPLESSLY, THROUGH MY OWN NIGHTMARES. AND WHAT I FOUND HERE—
—WAS HORROR: RAW AND FORMLESS. A TIDAL WAVE OF MONSTROUS THOUGHTS AND UNSPEAKABLE FEARS. A DEVASTATING WHIRLWIND—
—OF PURE CHAOS. BUT, OVER TIME, I TOOK THAT CHAOS IN MY HANDS AND BROUGHT FORTH ORDER. THE FALLEN CHILDREN AND THE FORGOTTEN NIGHTMARES LEARNED TO LIVE IN HARMONY—

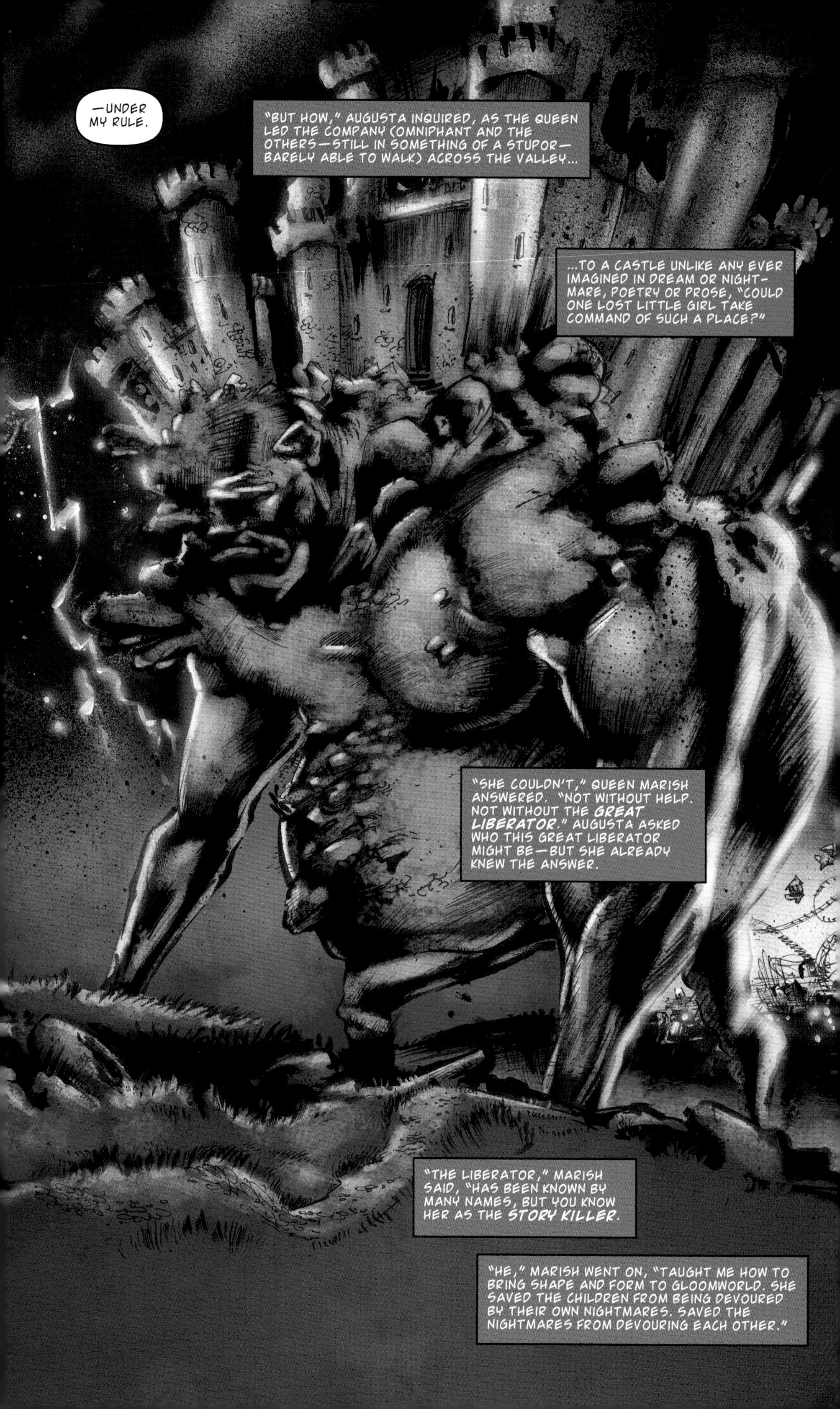
—UNDER MY RULE.
"BUT HOW," AUGUSTA INQUIRED, AS THE QUEEN LED THE COMPANY (OMNIPHANT AND THE OTHERS—STILL IN SOMETHING OF A STUPOR—BARELY ABLE TO WALK) ACROSS THE VALLEY...
...TO A CASTLE UNLIKE ANY EVER IMAGINED IN DREAM OR NIGHTMARE, POETRY OR PROSE, "COULD ONE LOST LITTLE GIRL TAKE COMMAND OF SUCH A PLACE?"
"SHE COULDN'T," QUEEN MARISH ANSWERED. "NOT WITHOUT HELP. NOT WITHOUT THE GREAT LIBERATOR." AUGUSTA ASKED WHO THIS GREAT LIBERATOR MIGHT BE—BUT SHE ALREADY KNEW THE ANSWER.
"THE LIBERATOR," MARISH SAID, "HAS BEEN KNOWN BY MANY NAMES, BUT YOU KNOW HER AS THE STORY KILLER.
"HE," MARISH WENT ON, "TAUGHT ME HOW TO BRING SHAPE AND FORM TO GLOOMWORLD. SHE SAVED THE CHILDREN FROM BEING DEVOURED BY THEIR OWN NIGHTMARES. SAVED THE NIGHTMARES FROM DEVOURING EACH OTHER."

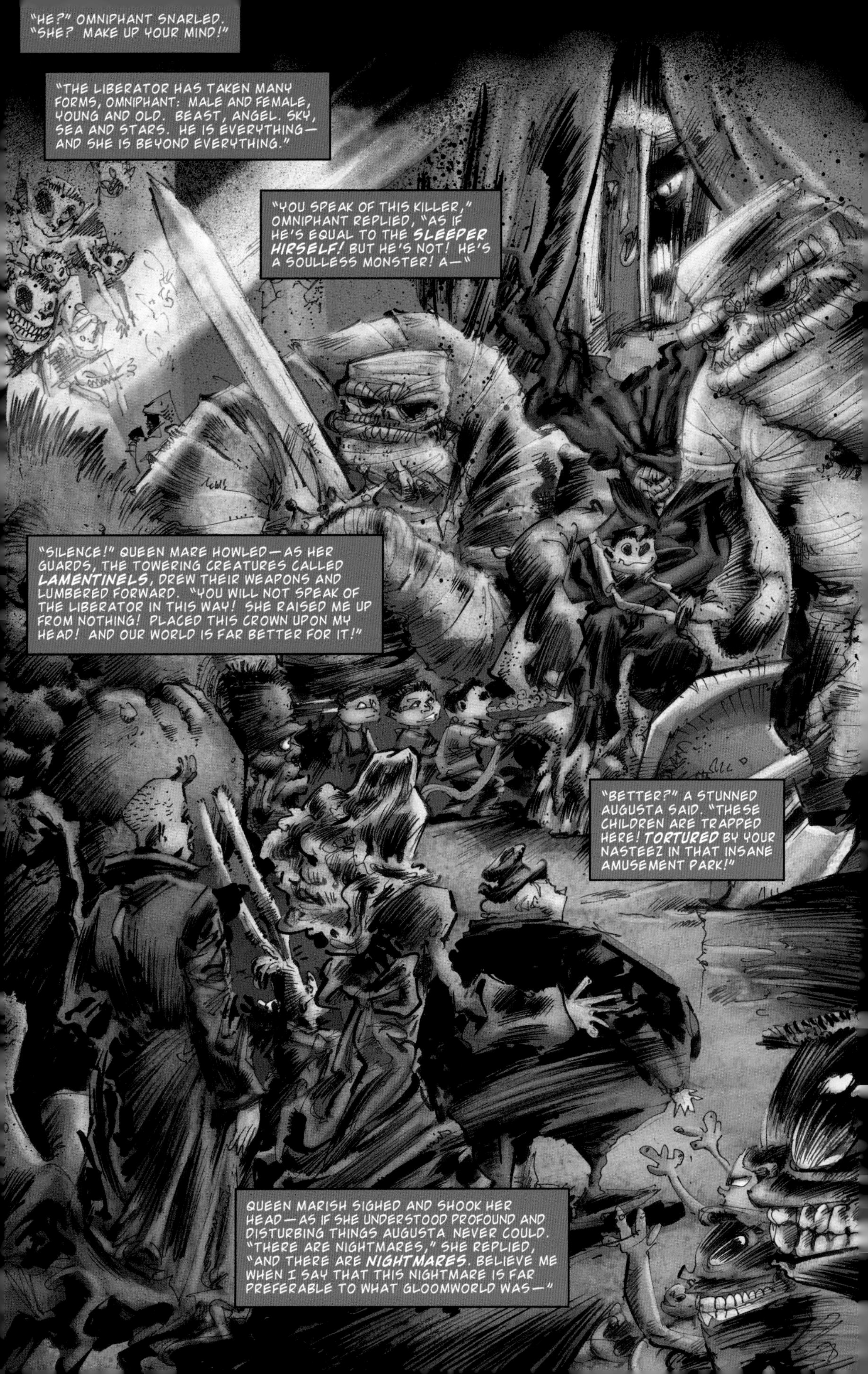
"HE?" OMNIPHANT SNARLED. "SHE? MAKE UP YOUR MIND!"
"THE LIBERATOR HAS TAKEN MANY FORMS, OMNIPHANT: MALE AND FEMALE, YOUNG AND OLD. BEAST, ANGEL. SKY, SEA AND STARS. HE IS EVERYTHING—AND SHE IS BEYOND EVERYTHING."
"YOU SPEAK OF THIS KILLER," OMNIPHANT REPLIED, "AS IF HE'S EQUAL TO THE SLEEPER HIRSELF! BUT HE'S NOT! HE'S A SOULLESS MONSTER! A—"
"SILENCE!" QUEEN MARE HOWLED—AS HER GUARDS, THE TOWERING CREATURES CALLED LAMENTINELS, DREW THEIR WEAPONS AND LUMBERED FORWARD. "YOU WILL NOT SPEAK OF THE LIBERATOR IN THIS WAY! SHE RAISED ME UP FROM NOTHING! PLACED THIS CROWN UPON MY HEAD! AND OUR WORLD IS FAR BETTER FOR IT!"
"BETTER?" A STUNNED AUGUSTA SAID. "THESE CHILDREN ARE TRAPPED HERE! TORTURED BY YOUR NASTEEZ IN THAT INSANE AMUSEMENT PARK!"
QUEEN MARISH SIGHED AND SHOOK HER HEAD—AS IF SHE UNDERSTOOD PROFOUND AND DISTURBING THINGS AUGUSTA NEVER COULD. "THERE ARE NIGHTMARES," SHE REPLIED, "AND THERE ARE NIGHTMARES. BELIEVE ME WHEN I SAY THAT THIS NIGHTMARE IS FAR PREFERABLE TO WHAT GLOOMWORLD WAS—"

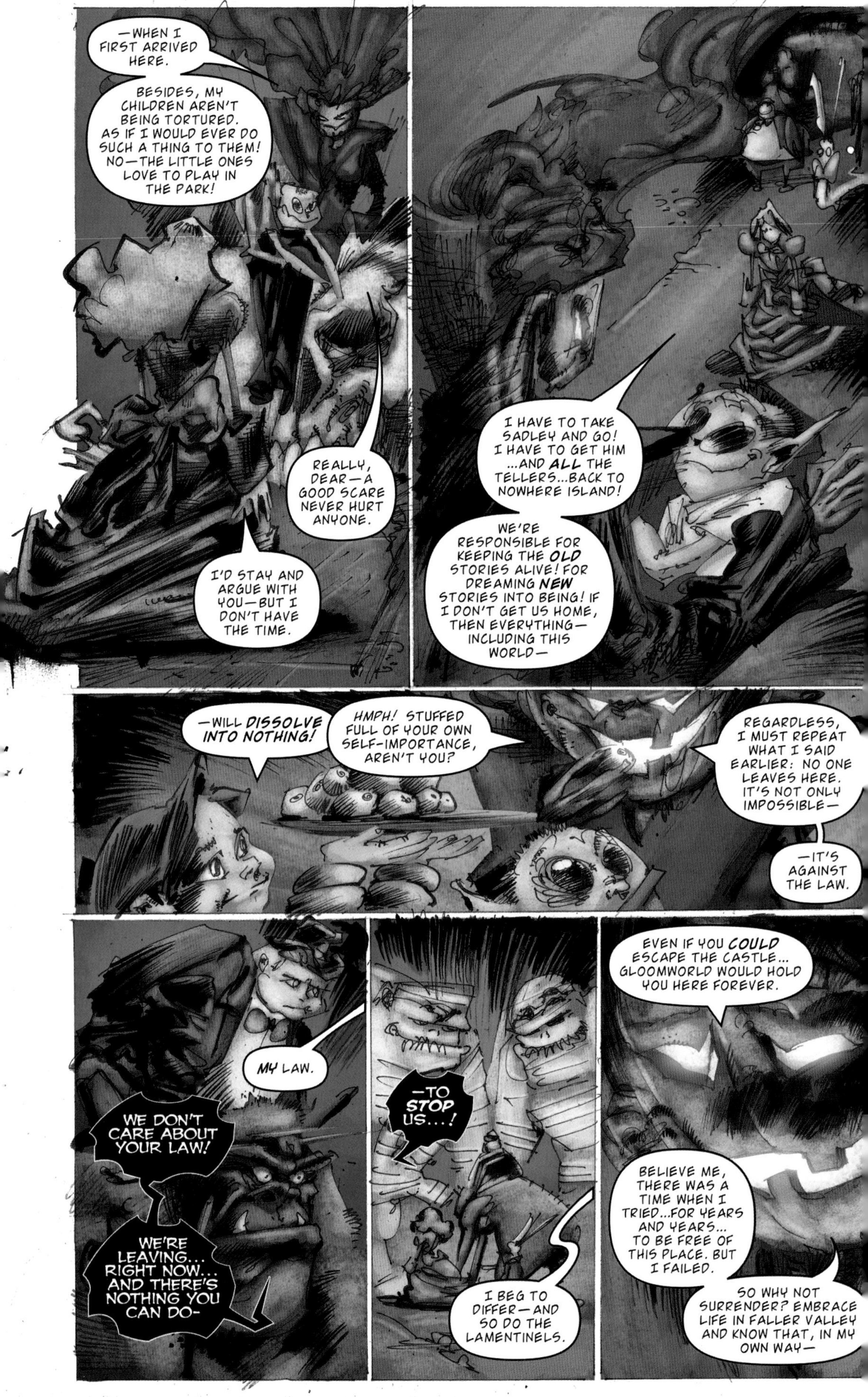
—WHEN I FIRST ARRIVED HERE.
BESIDES, MY CHILDREN AREN'T BEING TORTURED. AS IF I WOULD EVER DO SUCH A THING TO THEM! NO—THE LITTLE ONES LOVE TO PLAY IN THE PARK!
REALLY, DEAR—A GOOD SCARE NEVER HURT ANYONE.
I'D STAY AND ARGUE WITH YOU—BUT I DON'T HAVE THE TIME.
I HAVE TO TAKE SADLEY AND GO! I HAVE TO GET HIM ...AND ALL THE TELLERS...BACK TO NOWHERE ISLAND!
WE'RE RESPONSIBLE FOR KEEPING THE OLD STORIES ALIVE! FOR DREAMING NEW STORIES INTO BEING! IF I DON'T GET US HOME, THEN EVERYTHING—INCLUDING THIS WORLD—
—WILL DISSOLVE INTO NOTHING!
HMPH! STUFFED FULL OF YOUR OWN SELF-IMPORTANCE, AREN'T YOU?
REGARDLESS, I MUST REPEAT WHAT I SAID EARLIER: NO ONE LEAVES HERE. IT'S NOT ONLY IMPOSSIBLE—
—IT'S AGAINST THE LAW.
MY LAW.
WE DON'T CARE ABOUT YOUR LAW!
WE'RE LEAVING... RIGHT NOW... AND THERE'S NOTHING YOU CAN DO-
—TO STOP US...!
I BEG TO DIFFER—AND SO DO THE LAMENTINELS.
EVEN IF YOU COULD ESCAPE THE CASTLE... GLOOMWORLD WOULD HOLD YOU HERE FOREVER.
BELIEVE ME, THERE WAS A TIME WHEN I TRIED...FOR YEARS AND YEARS... TO BE FREE OF THIS PLACE. BUT I FAILED.
SO WHY NOT SURRENDER? EMBRACE LIFE IN FALLER VALLEY AND KNOW THAT, IN MY OWN WAY—

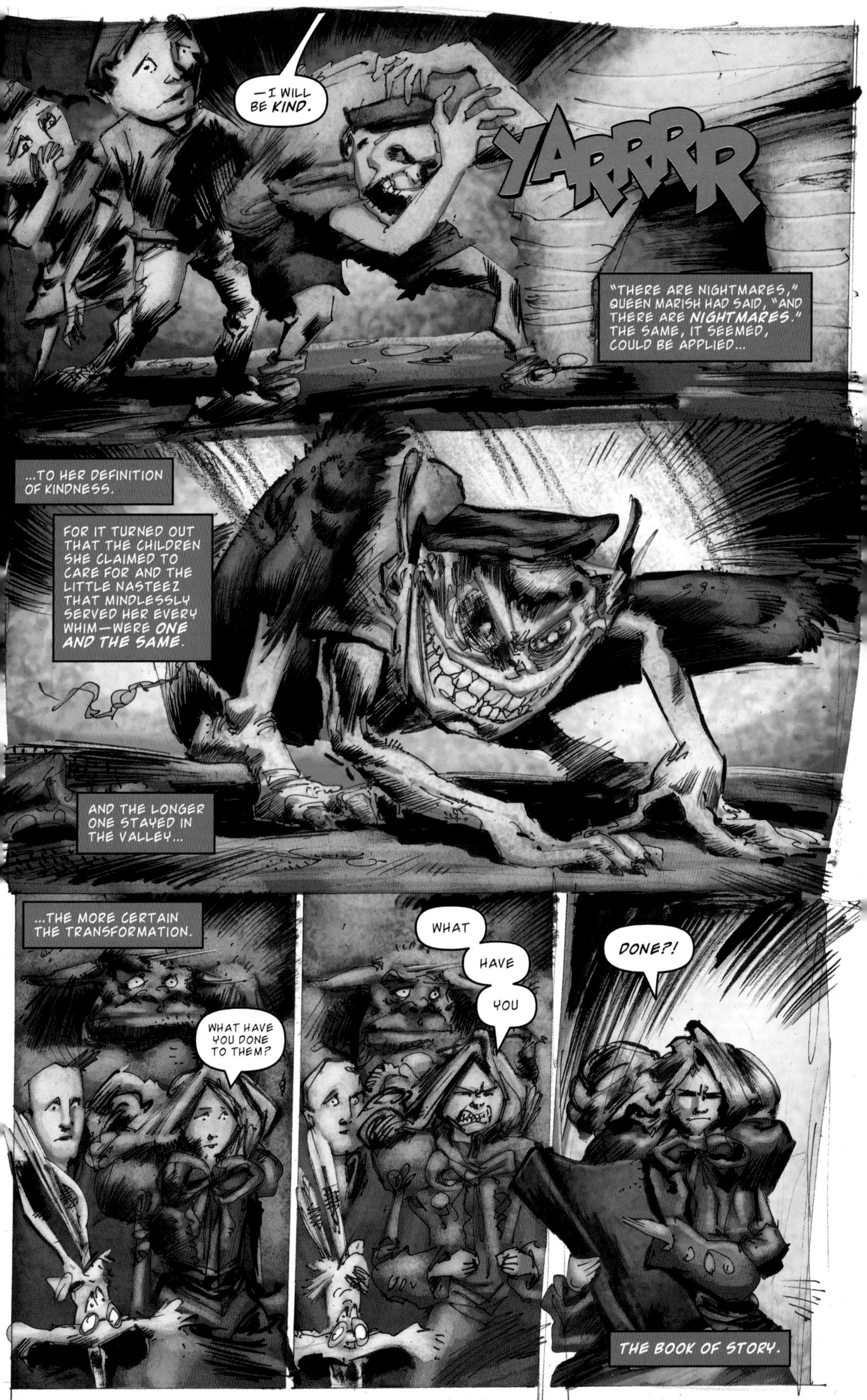
—I WILL BE KIND.
YARRRR
"THERE ARE NIGHTMARES," QUEEN MARISH HAD SAID, "AND THERE ARE NIGHTMARES." THE SAME, IT SEEMED, COULD BE APPLIED...
...TO HER DEFINITION OF KINDNESS.
FOR IT TURNED OUT THAT THE CHILDREN SHE CLAIMED TO CARE FOR AND THE LITTLE NASTEEZ THAT MINDLESSLY SERVED HER EVERY WHIM—WERE ONE AND THE SAME.
AND THE LONGER ONE STAYED IN THE VALLEY...
...THE MORE CERTAIN THE TRANSFORMATION.
WHAT HAVE YOU DONE TO THEM?
WHAT
HAVE
YOU
DONE?!
THE BOOK OF STORY.

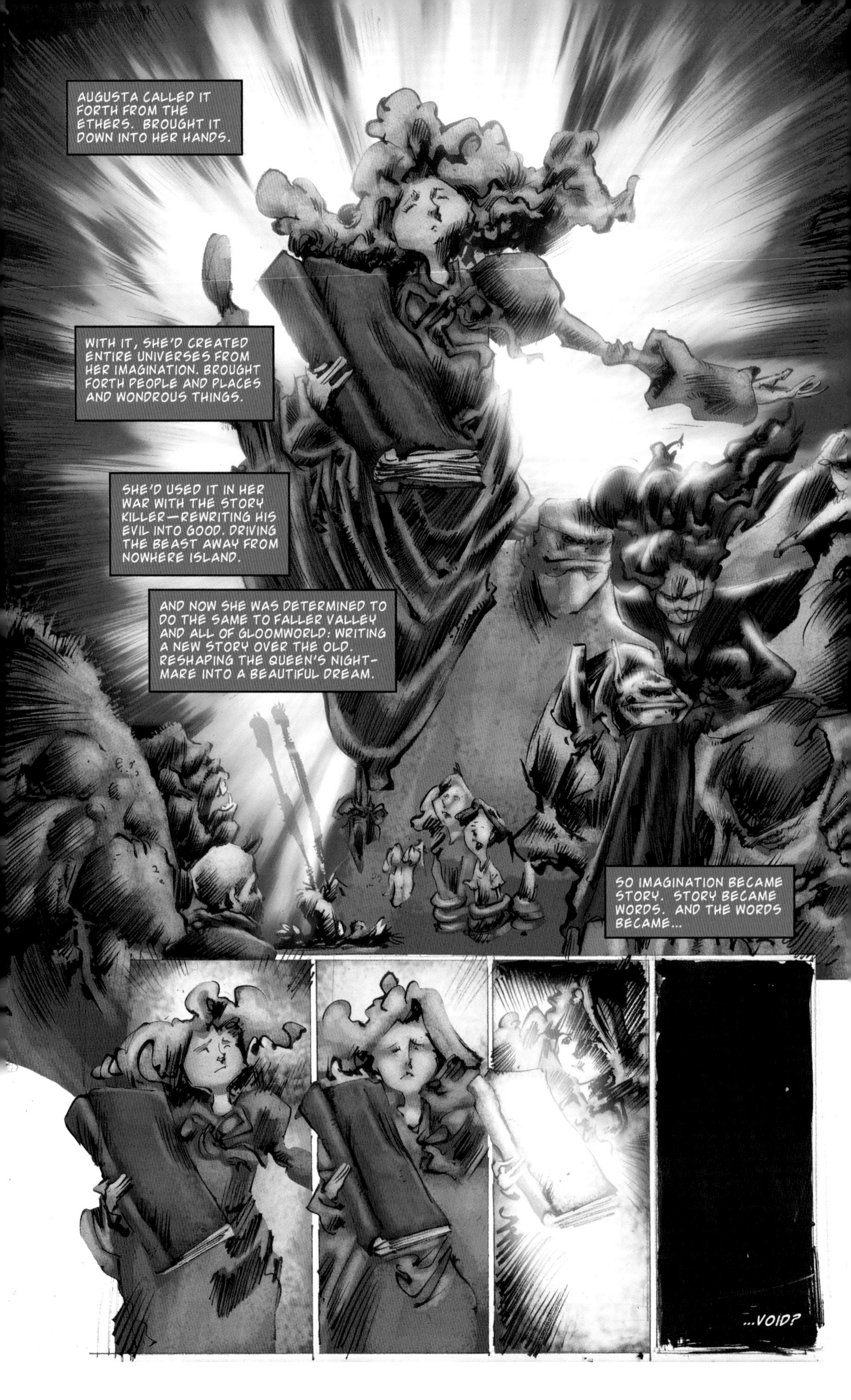
AUGUSTA CALLED IT FORTH FROM THE ETHERS. BROUGHT IT DOWN INTO HER HANDS.
WITH IT, SHE'D CREATED ENTIRE UNIVERSES FROM HER IMAGINATION. BROUGHT FORTH PEOPLE AND PLACES AND WONDROUS THINGS.
SHE'D USED IT IN HER WAR WITH THE STORY KILLER—REWRITING HIS EVIL INTO GOOD. DRIVING THE BEAST AWAY FROM NOWHERE ISLAND.
AND NOW SHE WAS DETERMINED TO DO THE SAME TO FALLER VALLEY AND ALL OF GLOOMWORLD: WRITING A NEW STORY OVER THE OLD. RESHAPING THE QUEEN'S NIGHT-MARE INTO A BEAUTIFUL DREAM.
SO IMAGINATION BECAME STORY. STORY BECAME WORDS. AND THE WORDS BECAME...
...VOID?

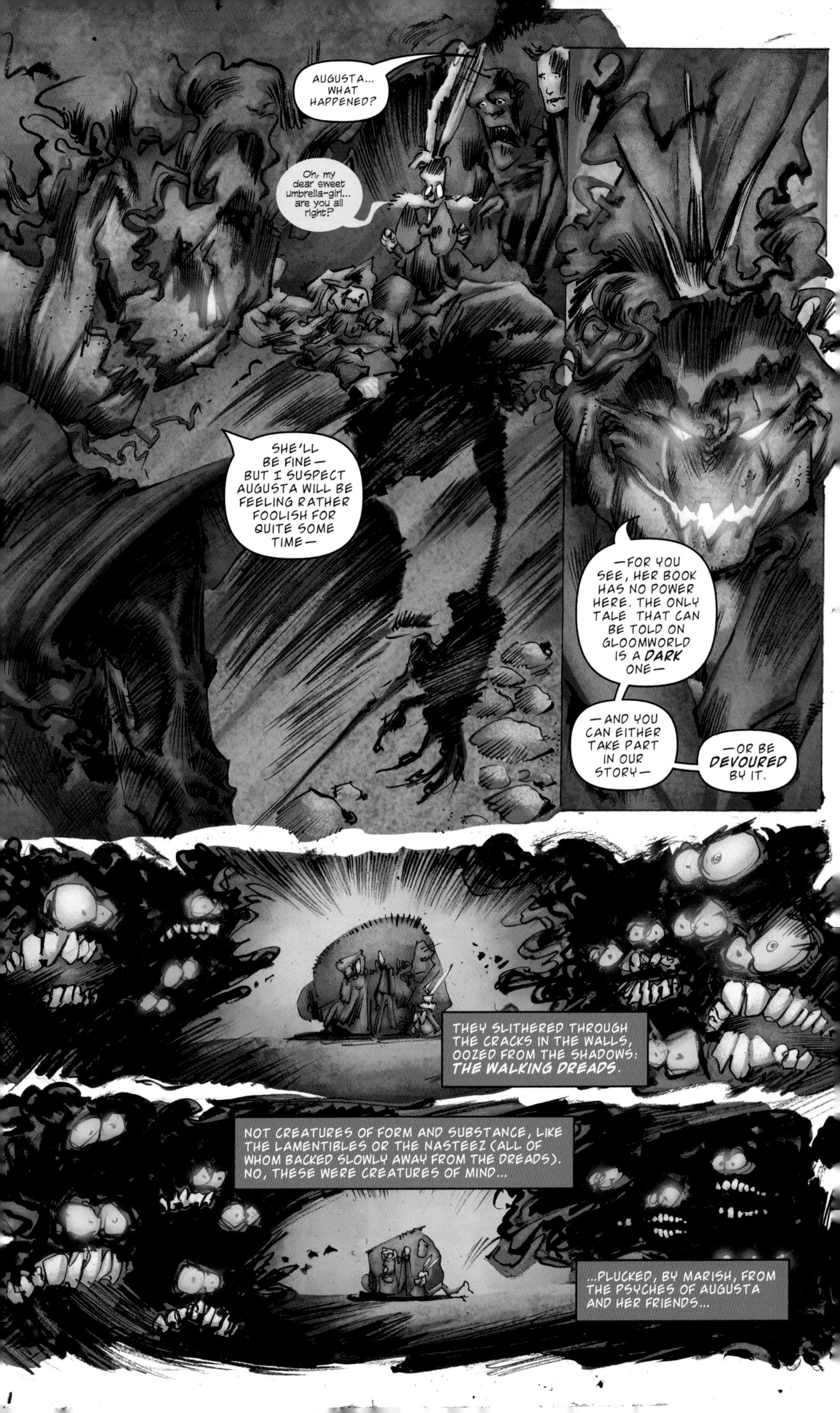
AUGUSTA... WHAT HAPPENED?
Oh, my dear sweet umbrella-girl... are you all right?
SHE'LL BE FINE— BUT I SUSPECT AUGUSTA WILL BE FEELING RATHER FOOLISH FOR QUITE SOME TIME—
—FOR YOU SEE, HER BOOK HAS NO POWER HERE. THE ONLY TALE THAT CAN BE TOLD ON GLOOMWORLD IS A DARK ONE—
—AND YOU CAN EITHER TAKE PART IN OUR STORY—
—OR BE DEVOURED BY IT.
THEY SLITHERED THROUGH THE CRACKS IN THE WALLS, OOZED FROM THE SHADOWS: THE WALKING DREADS.
NOT CREATURES OF FORM AND SUBSTANCE, LIKE THE LAMENTIBLES OR THE NASTEEZ (ALL OF WHOM BACKED SLOWLY AWAY FROM THE DREADS). NO, THESE WERE CREATURES OF MIND...
...PLUCKED, BY MARISH, FROM THE PSYCHES OF AUGUSTA AND HER FRIENDS...

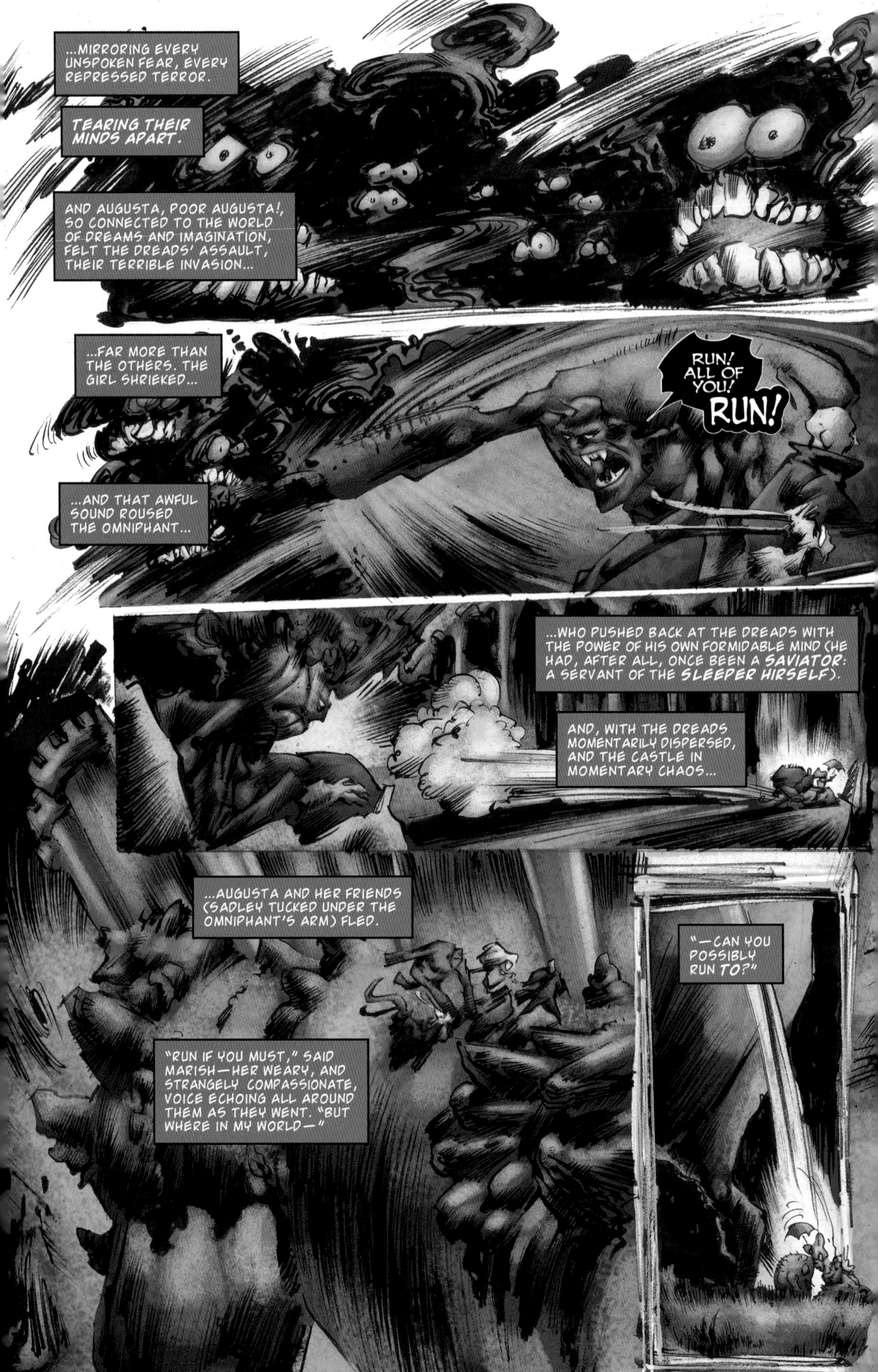

...MIRRORING EVERY UNSPOKEN FEAR, EVERY REPRESSED TERROR.
TEARING THEIR MINDS APART.
AND AUGUSTA, POOR AUGUSTA!, SO CONNECTED TO THE WORLD OF DREAMS AND IMAGINATION, FELT THE DREADS' ASSAULT, THEIR TERRIBLE INVASION...
...FAR MORE THAN THE OTHERS. THE GIRL SHRIEKED...
RUN! ALL OF YOU! RUN!
...AND THAT AWFUL SOUND ROUSED THE OMNIPHANT...
...WHO PUSHED BACK AT THE DREADS WITH THE POWER OF HIS OWN FORMIDABLE MIND (HE HAD, AFTER ALL, ONCE BEEN A SAVIATOR: A SERVANT OF THE SLEEPER HIRSELF).
AND, WITH THE DREADS MOMENTARILY DISPERSED, AND THE CASTLE IN MOMENTARY CHAOS...
...AUGUSTA AND HER FRIENDS (SADLEY TUCKED UNDER THE OMNIPHANT'S ARM) FLED.
"RUN IF YOU MUST," SAID MARISH—HER WEARY, AND STRANGELY COMPASSIONATE, VOICE ECHOING ALL AROUND THEM AS THEY WENT. "BUT WHERE IN MY WORLD—"
"—CAN YOU POSSIBLY RUN TO?"

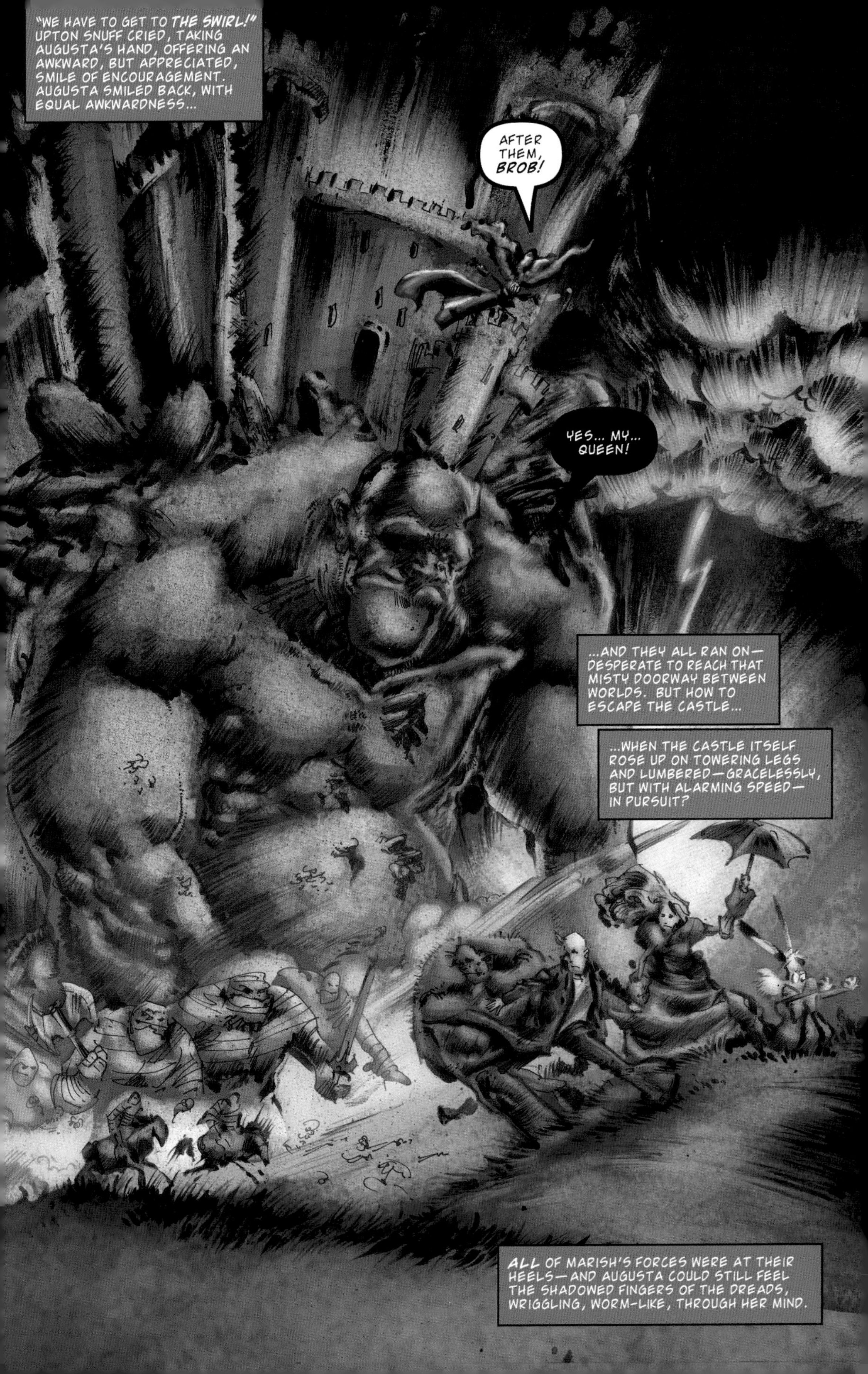
"WE HAVE TO GET TO ***THE SWIRL!***" UPTON SNUFF CRIED, TAKING AUGUSTA'S HAND, OFFERING AN AWKWARD, BUT APPRECIATED, SMILE OF ENCOURAGEMENT. AUGUSTA SMILED BACK, WITH EQUAL AWKWARDNESS...
AFTER THEM, ***BROB!***
YES... MY... QUEEN!
...AND THEY ALL RAN ON—DESPERATE TO REACH THAT MISTY DOORWAY BETWEEN WORLDS. BUT HOW TO ESCAPE THE CASTLE...
...WHEN THE CASTLE ITSELF ROSE UP ON TOWERING LEGS AND LUMBERED—GRACELESSLY, BUT WITH ALARMING SPEED—IN PURSUIT?
ALL OF MARISH'S FORCES WERE AT THEIR HEELS—AND AUGUSTA COULD STILL FEEL THE SHADOWED FINGERS OF THE DREADS, WRIGGLING, WORM-LIKE, THROUGH HER MIND.

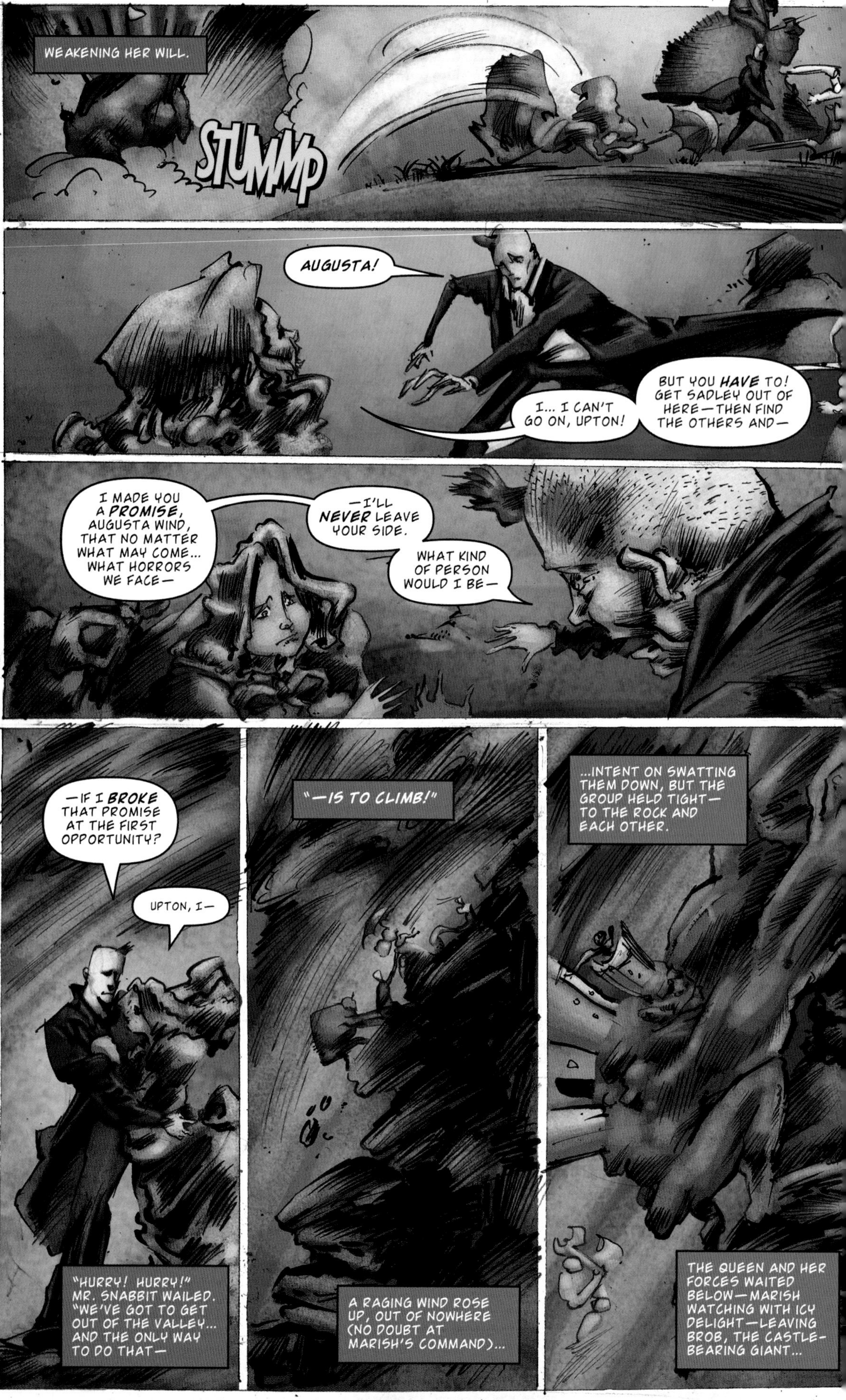
WEAKENING HER WILL.
STUMMP
AUGUSTA!
I... I CAN'T GO ON, UPTON!
BUT YOU HAVE TO! GET SADLEY OUT OF HERE—THEN FIND THE OTHERS AND—
I MADE YOU A PROMISE, AUGUSTA WIND, THAT NO MATTER WHAT MAY COME... WHAT HORRORS WE FACE—
—I'LL NEVER LEAVE YOUR SIDE.
WHAT KIND OF PERSON WOULD I BE—
—IF I BROKE THAT PROMISE AT THE FIRST OPPORTUNITY?
UPTON, I—
"HURRY! HURRY!" MR. SNABBIT WAILED. "WE'VE GOT TO GET OUT OF THE VALLEY... AND THE ONLY WAY TO DO THAT—
"—IS TO CLIMB!"
A RAGING WIND ROSE UP, OUT OF NOWHERE (NO DOUBT AT MARISH'S COMMAND)...
...INTENT ON SWATTING THEM DOWN, BUT THE GROUP HELD TIGHT—TO THE ROCK AND EACH OTHER.
THE QUEEN AND HER FORCES WAITED BELOW—MARISH WATCHING WITH ICY DELIGHT—LEAVING BROB, THE CASTLE-BEARING GIANT...

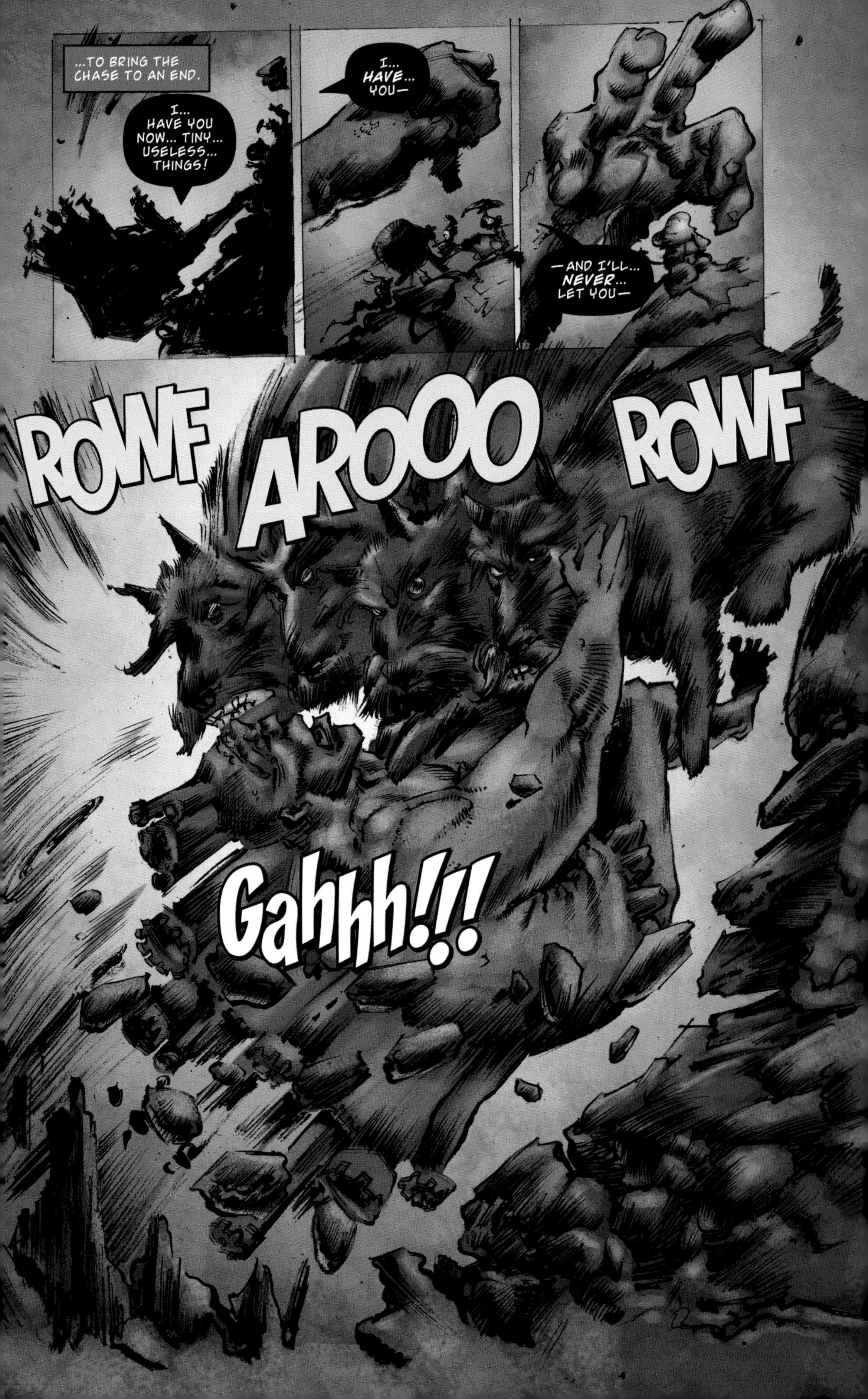
...TO BRING THE CHASE TO AN END.
I... HAVE YOU NOW... TINY... USELESS... THINGS!
I... HAVE... YOU—
—AND I'LL... NEVER... LET YOU—
ROWF
AROOO
ROWF
Gahhh!!!

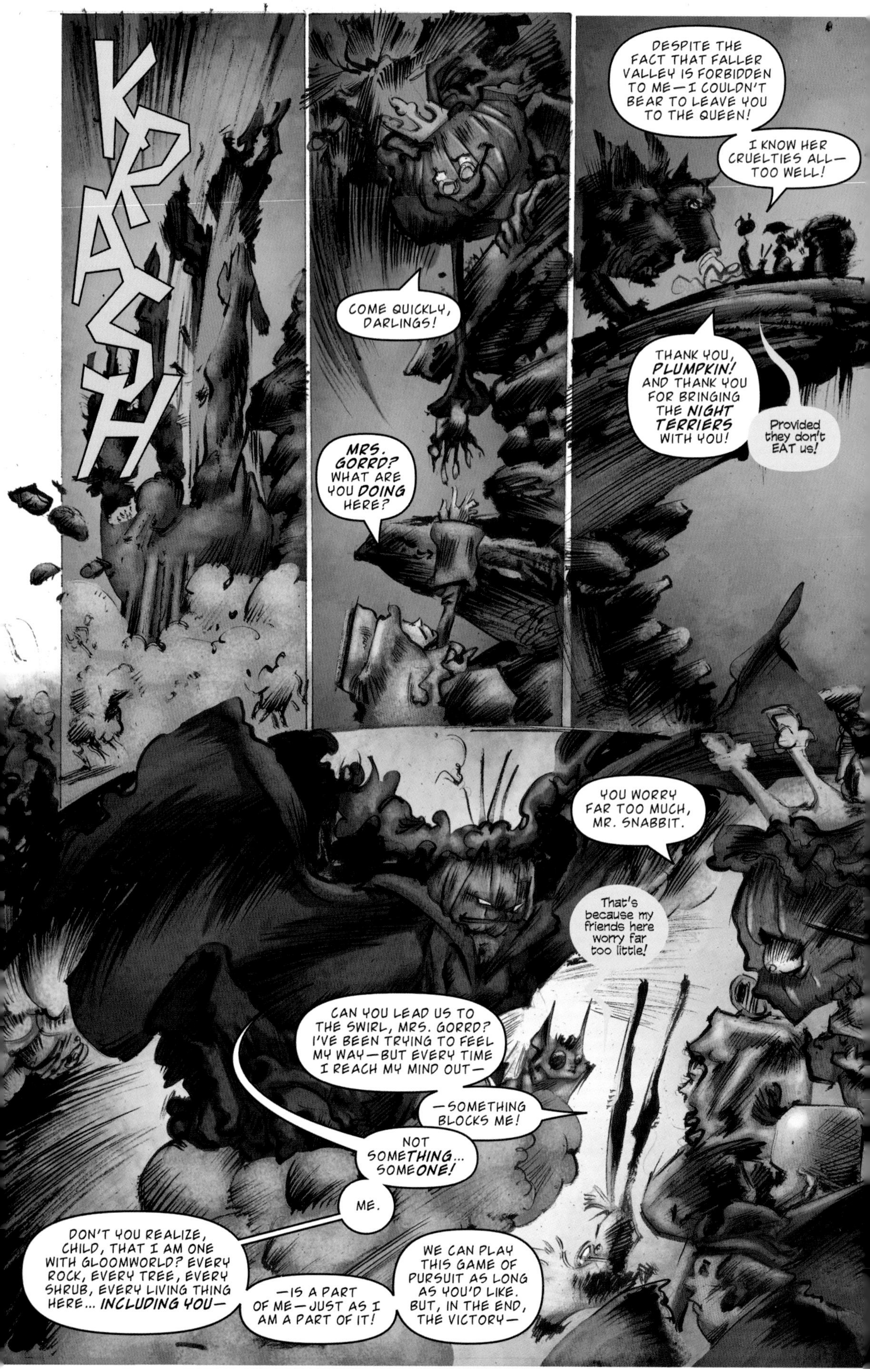
KRASH!
COME QUICKLY, DARLINGS!
MRS. GORRD? WHAT ARE YOU DOING HERE?
DESPITE THE FACT THAT FALLER VALLEY IS FORBIDDEN TO ME—I COULDN'T BEAR TO LEAVE YOU TO THE QUEEN!
I KNOW HER CRUELTIES ALL-TOO WELL!
THANK YOU, PLUMPKIN! AND THANK YOU FOR BRINGING THE NIGHT TERRIERS WITH YOU!
Provided they don't EAT us!
YOU WORRY FAR TOO MUCH, MR. SNABBIT.
That's because my friends here worry far too little!
CAN YOU LEAD US TO THE SWIRL, MRS. GORRD? I'VE BEEN TRYING TO FEEL MY WAY—BUT EVERY TIME I REACH MY MIND OUT—
—SOMETHING BLOCKS ME!
NOT SOMETHING... SOMEONE!
ME.
DON'T YOU REALIZE, CHILD, THAT I AM ONE WITH GLOOMWORLD? EVERY ROCK, EVERY TREE, EVERY SHRUB, EVERY LIVING THING HERE... INCLUDING YOU—
—IS A PART OF ME—JUST AS I AM A PART OF IT!
WE CAN PLAY THIS GAME OF PURSUIT AS LONG AS YOU'D LIKE. BUT, IN THE END, THE VICTORY—

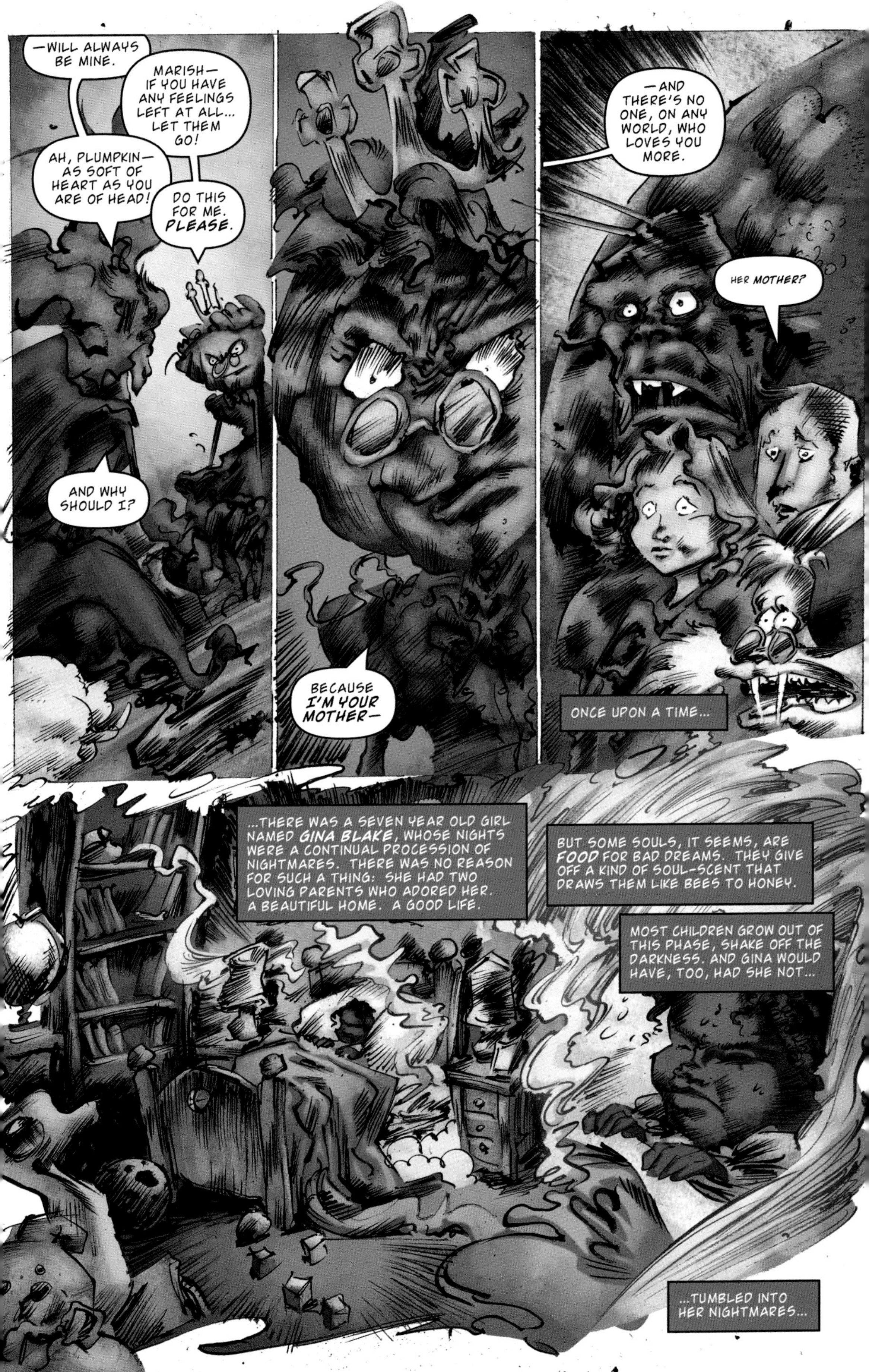
—WILL ALWAYS BE MINE.
MARISH— IF YOU HAVE ANY FEELINGS LEFT AT ALL... LET THEM GO!
AH, PLUMPKIN— AS SOFT OF HEART AS YOU ARE OF HEAD!
DO THIS FOR ME. PLEASE.
AND WHY SHOULD I?
BECAUSE I'M YOUR MOTHER—
—AND THERE'S NO ONE, ON ANY WORLD, WHO LOVES YOU MORE.
HER MOTHER?
ONCE UPON A TIME...
...THERE WAS A SEVEN YEAR OLD GIRL NAMED GINA BLAKE, WHOSE NIGHTS WERE A CONTINUAL PROCESSION OF NIGHTMARES. THERE WAS NO REASON FOR SUCH A THING: SHE HAD TWO LOVING PARENTS WHO ADORED HER. A BEAUTIFUL HOME. A GOOD LIFE.
BUT SOME SOULS, IT SEEMS, ARE FOOD FOR BAD DREAMS. THEY GIVE OFF A KIND OF SOUL-SCENT THAT DRAWS THEM LIKE BEES TO HONEY.
MOST CHILDREN GROW OUT OF THIS PHASE, SHAKE OFF THE DARKNESS. AND GINA WOULD HAVE, TOO, HAD SHE NOT...
...TUMBLED INTO HER NIGHTMARES...

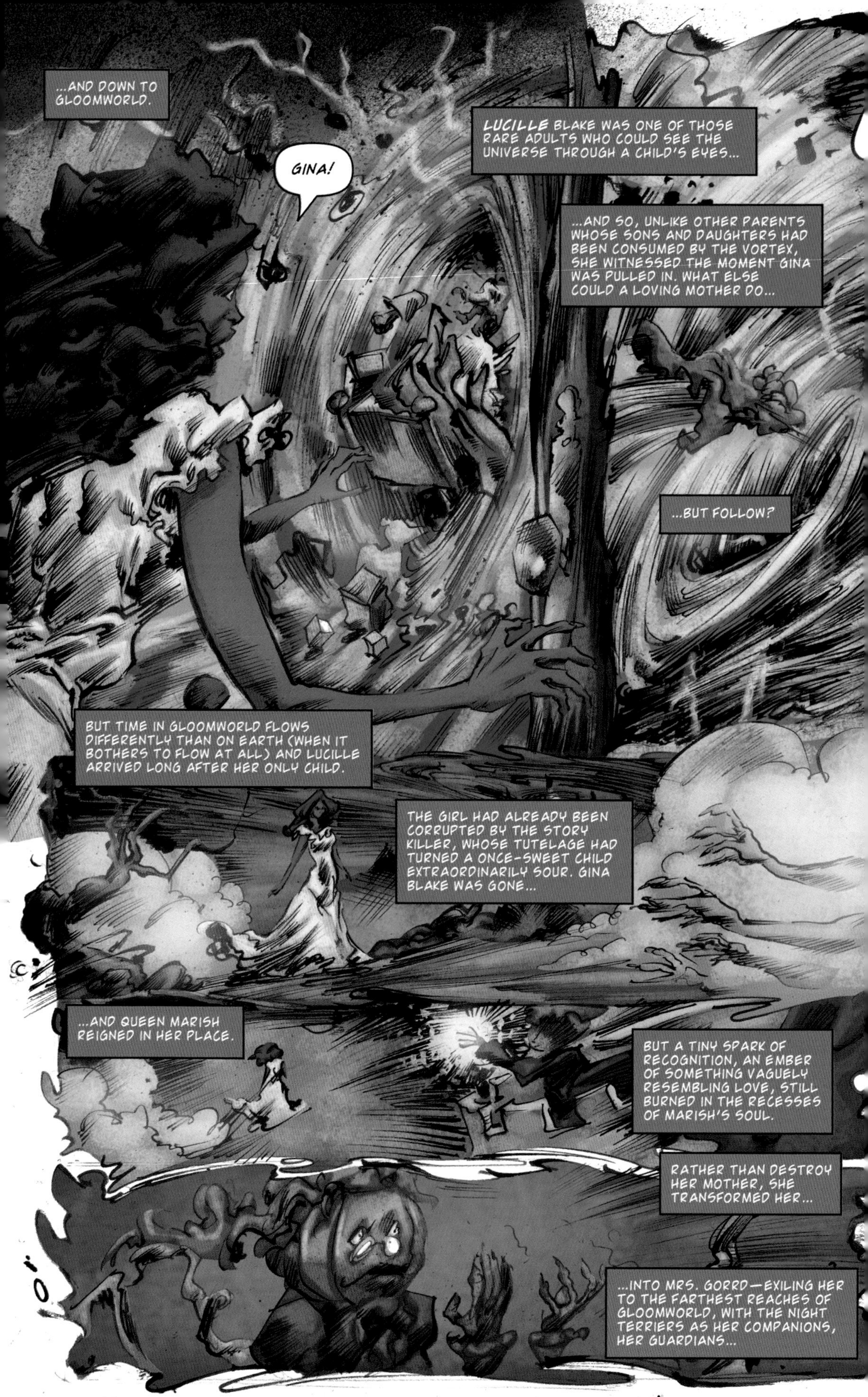

...AND DOWN TO GLOOMWORLD.
LUCILLE BLAKE WAS ONE OF THOSE RARE ADULTS WHO COULD SEE THE UNIVERSE THROUGH A CHILD'S EYES...
GINA!
...AND SO, UNLIKE OTHER PARENTS WHOSE SONS AND DAUGHTERS HAD BEEN CONSUMED BY THE VORTEX, SHE WITNESSED THE MOMENT GINA WAS PULLED IN. WHAT ELSE COULD A LOVING MOTHER DO...
...BUT FOLLOW?
BUT TIME IN GLOOMWORLD FLOWS DIFFERENTLY THAN ON EARTH (WHEN IT BOTHERS TO FLOW AT ALL) AND LUCILLE ARRIVED LONG AFTER HER ONLY CHILD.
THE GIRL HAD ALREADY BEEN CORRUPTED BY THE STORY KILLER, WHOSE TUTELAGE HAD TURNED A ONCE-SWEET CHILD EXTRAORDINARILY SOUR. GINA BLAKE WAS GONE...
...AND QUEEN MARISH REIGNED IN HER PLACE.
BUT A TINY SPARK OF RECOGNITION, AN EMBER OF SOMETHING VAGUELY RESEMBLING LOVE, STILL BURNED IN THE RECESSES OF MARISH'S SOUL.
RATHER THAN DESTROY HER MOTHER, SHE TRANSFORMED HER...
...INTO MRS. GORRD—EXILING HER TO THE FARTHEST REACHES OF GLOOMWORLD, WITH THE NIGHT TERRIERS AS HER COMPANIONS, HER GUARDIANS...

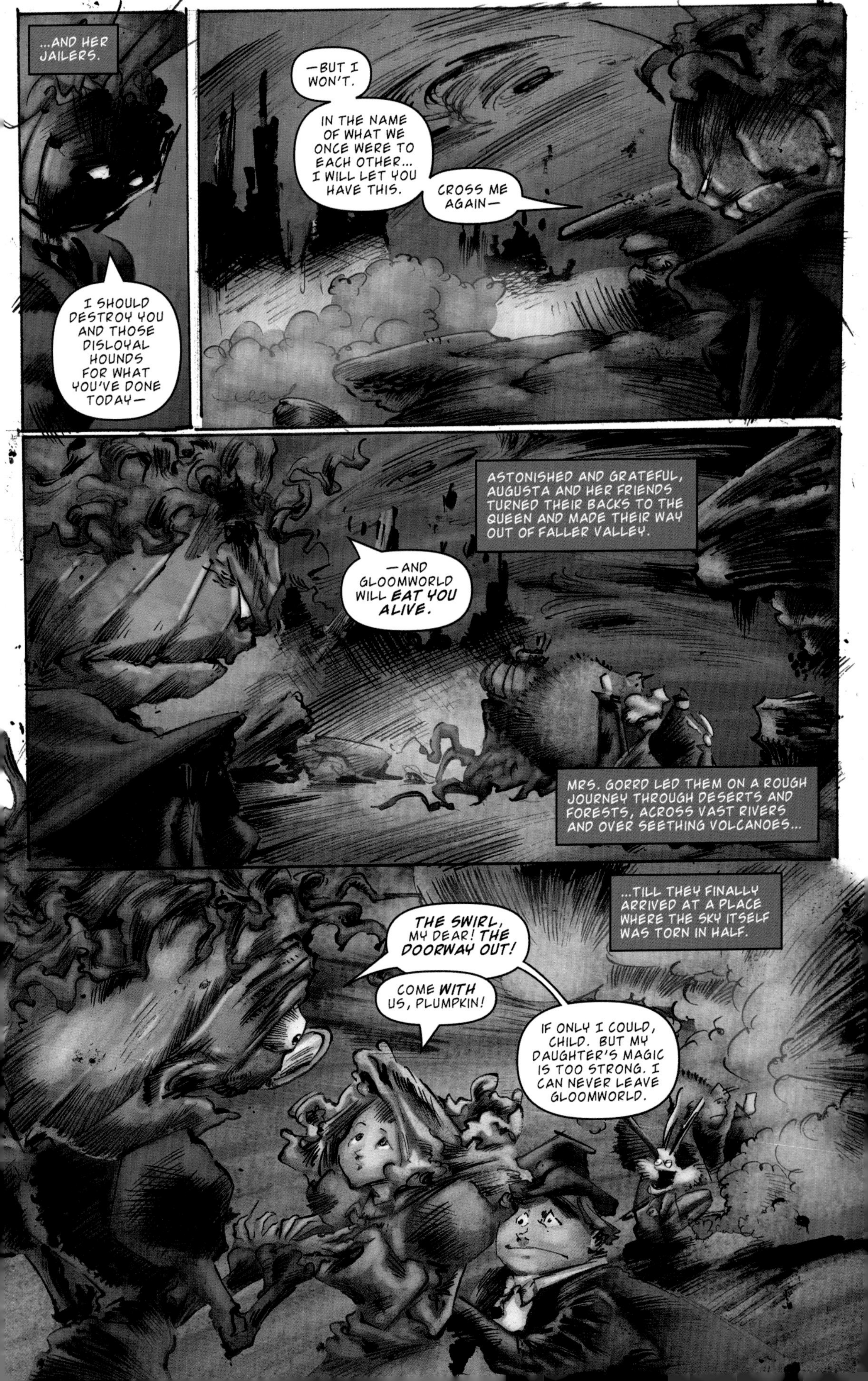
...AND HER JAILERS.
I SHOULD DESTROY YOU AND THOSE DISLOYAL HOUNDS FOR WHAT YOU'VE DONE TODAY—
—BUT I WON'T.
IN THE NAME OF WHAT WE ONCE WERE TO EACH OTHER... I WILL LET YOU HAVE THIS.
CROSS ME AGAIN—
ASTONISHED AND GRATEFUL, AUGUSTA AND HER FRIENDS TURNED THEIR BACKS TO THE QUEEN AND MADE THEIR WAY OUT OF FALLER VALLEY.
—AND GLOOMWORLD WILL EAT YOU ALIVE.
MRS. GORRD LED THEM ON A ROUGH JOURNEY THROUGH DESERTS AND FORESTS, ACROSS VAST RIVERS AND OVER SEETHING VOLCANOES...
...TILL THEY FINALLY ARRIVED AT A PLACE WHERE THE SKY ITSELF WAS TORN IN HALF.
THE SWIRL, MY DEAR! THE DOORWAY OUT!
COME WITH US, PLUMPKIN!
IF ONLY I COULD, CHILD. BUT MY DAUGHTER'S MAGIC IS TOO STRONG. I CAN NEVER LEAVE GLOOMWORLD.

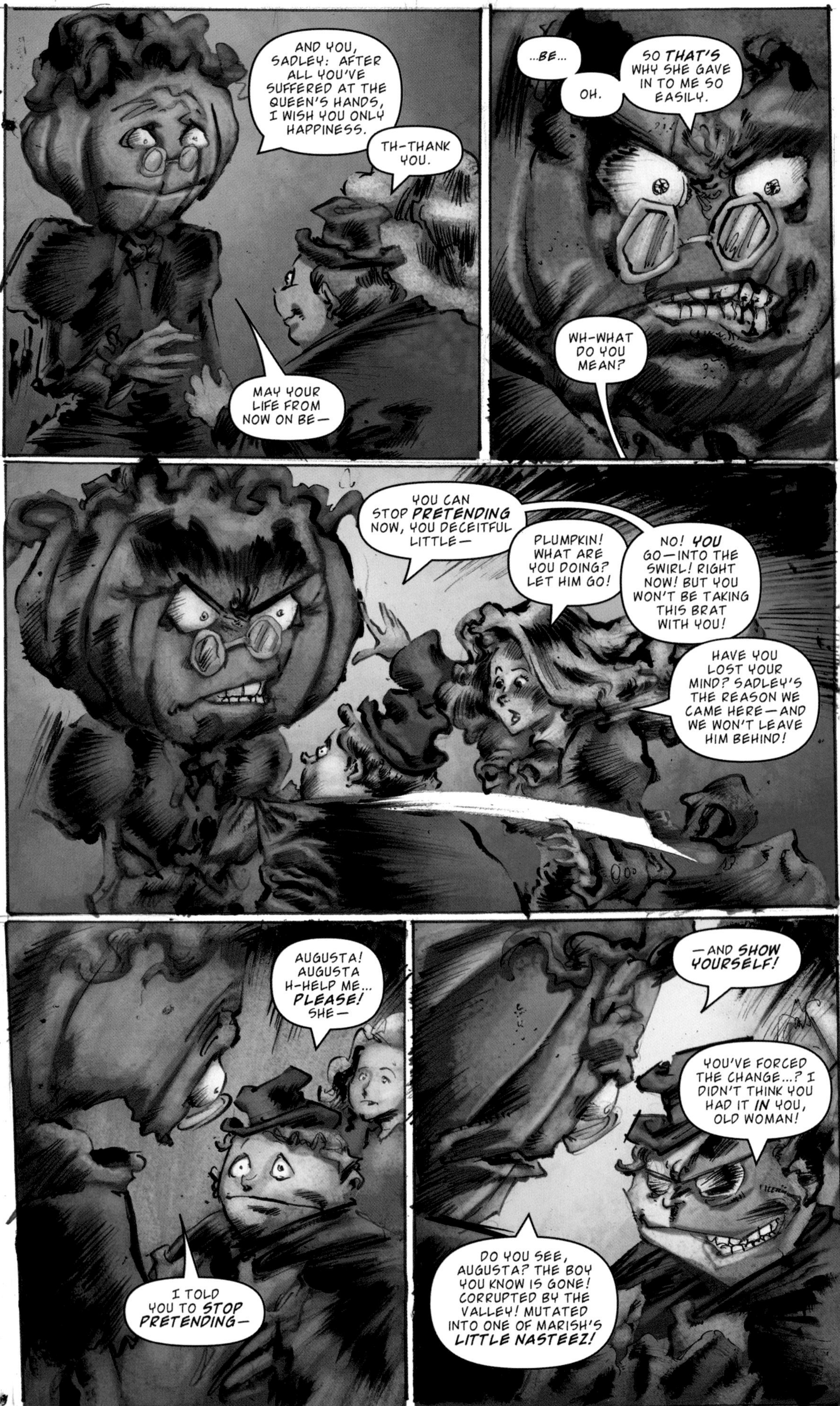
AND YOU, SADLEY: AFTER ALL YOU'VE SUFFERED AT THE QUEEN'S HANDS, I WISH YOU ONLY HAPPINESS.
TH-THANK YOU.
MAY YOUR LIFE FROM NOW ON BE—
...BE...
OH.
SO THAT'S WHY SHE GAVE IN TO ME SO EASILY.
WH-WHAT DO YOU MEAN?
YOU CAN STOP PRETENDING NOW, YOU DECEITFUL LITTLE—
PLUMPKIN! WHAT ARE YOU DOING? LET HIM GO!
NO! YOU GO—INTO THE SWIRL! RIGHT NOW! BUT YOU WON'T BE TAKING THIS BRAT WITH YOU!
HAVE YOU LOST YOUR MIND? SADLEY'S THE REASON WE CAME HERE—AND WE WON'T LEAVE HIM BEHIND!
AUGUSTA! AUGUSTA H-HELP ME... PLEASE! SHE—
I TOLD YOU TO STOP PRETENDING—
—AND SHOW YOURSELF!
YOU'VE FORCED THE CHANGE...? I DIDN'T THINK YOU HAD IT IN YOU, OLD WOMAN!
DO YOU SEE, AUGUSTA? THE BOY YOU KNOW IS GONE! CORRUPTED BY THE VALLEY! MUTATED INTO ONE OF MARISH'S LITTLE NASTEEZ!

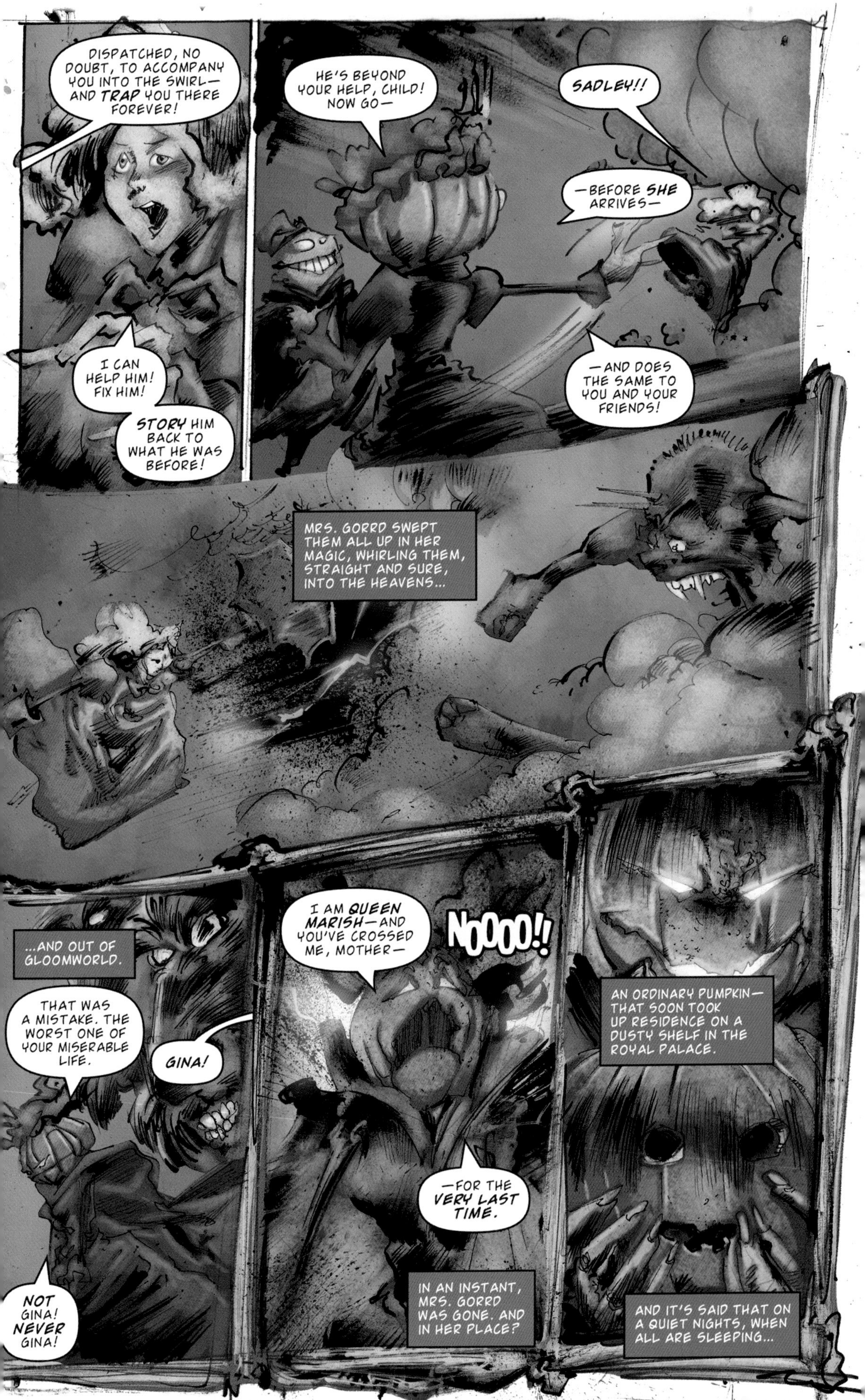
DISPATCHED, NO DOUBT, TO ACCOMPANY YOU INTO THE SWIRL— AND TRAP YOU THERE FOREVER!
I CAN HELP HIM! FIX HIM!
STORY HIM BACK TO WHAT HE WAS BEFORE!
HE'S BEYOND YOUR HELP, CHILD! NOW GO—
SADLEY!!
—BEFORE SHE ARRIVES—
—AND DOES THE SAME TO YOU AND YOUR FRIENDS!
MRS. GORRD SWEPT THEM ALL UP IN HER MAGIC, WHIRLING THEM, STRAIGHT AND SURE, INTO THE HEAVENS...
...AND OUT OF GLOOMWORLD.
THAT WAS A MISTAKE. THE WORST ONE OF YOUR MISERABLE LIFE.
GINA!
NOT GINA! NEVER GINA!
I AM QUEEN MARISH—AND YOU'VE CROSSED ME, MOTHER—
NOOOO!!
—FOR THE VERY LAST TIME.
IN AN INSTANT, MRS. GORRD WAS GONE. AND IN HER PLACE?
AN ORDINARY PUMPKIN— THAT SOON TOOK UP RESIDENCE ON A DUSTY SHELF IN THE ROYAL PALACE.
AND IT'S SAID THAT ON A QUIET NIGHTS, WHEN ALL ARE SLEEPING...

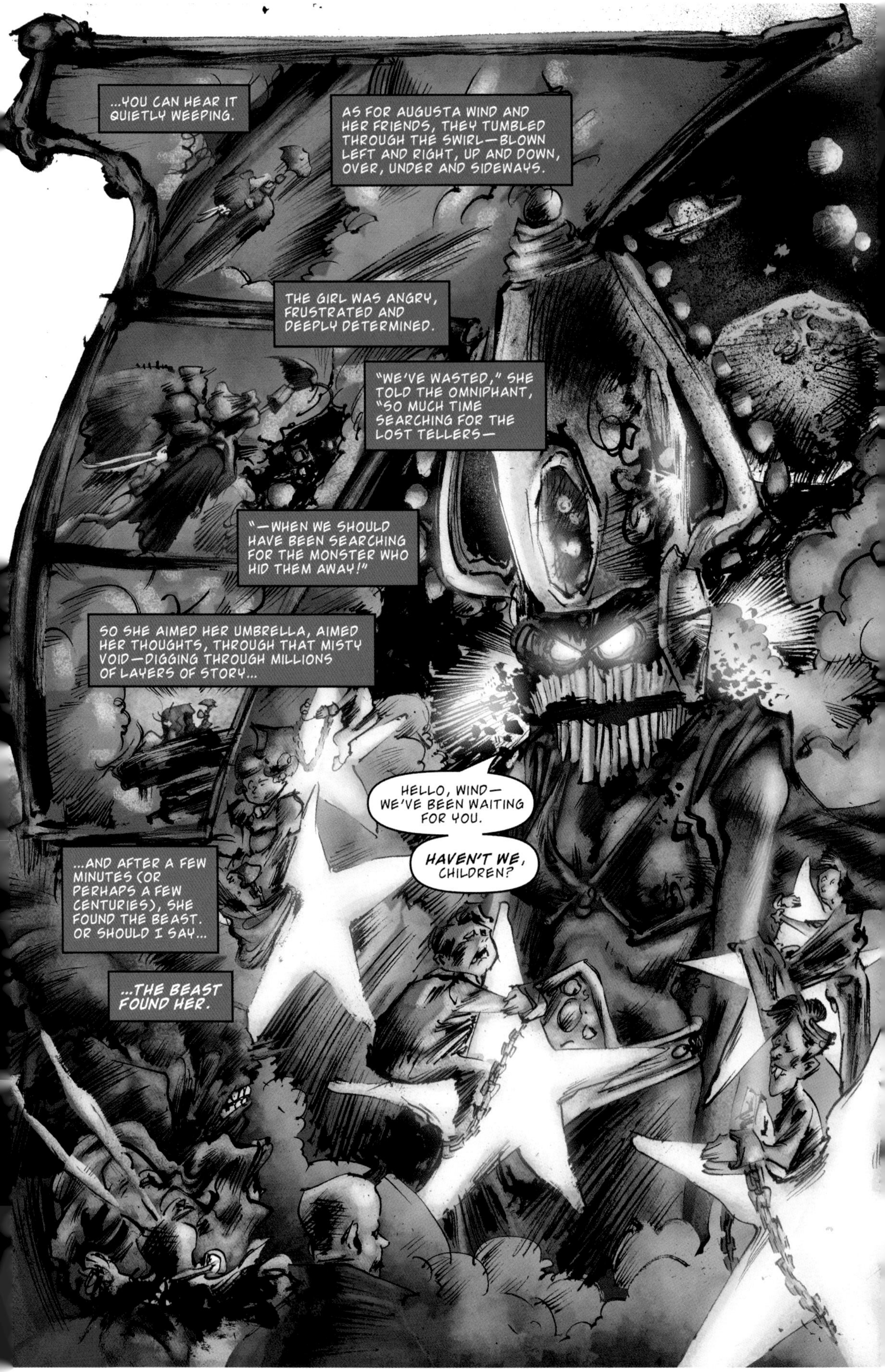

...YOU CAN HEAR IT QUIETLY WEEPING.
AS FOR AUGUSTA WIND AND HER FRIENDS, THEY TUMBLED THROUGH THE SWIRL—BLOWN LEFT AND RIGHT, UP AND DOWN, OVER, UNDER AND SIDEWAYS.
THE GIRL WAS ANGRY, FRUSTRATED AND DEEPLY DETERMINED.
"WE'VE WASTED," SHE TOLD THE OMNIPHANT, "SO MUCH TIME SEARCHING FOR THE LOST TELLERS—
"—WHEN WE SHOULD HAVE BEEN SEARCHING FOR THE MONSTER WHO HID THEM AWAY!"
SO SHE AIMED HER UMBRELLA, AIMED HER THOUGHTS, THROUGH THAT MISTY VOID—DIGGING THROUGH MILLIONS OF LAYERS OF STORY...
HELLO, WIND— WE'VE BEEN WAITING FOR YOU.
HAVEN'T WE, CHILDREN?
...AND AFTER A FEW MINUTES (OR PERHAPS A FEW CENTURIES), SHE FOUND THE BEAST. OR SHOULD I SAY...
...THE BEAST FOUND HER.

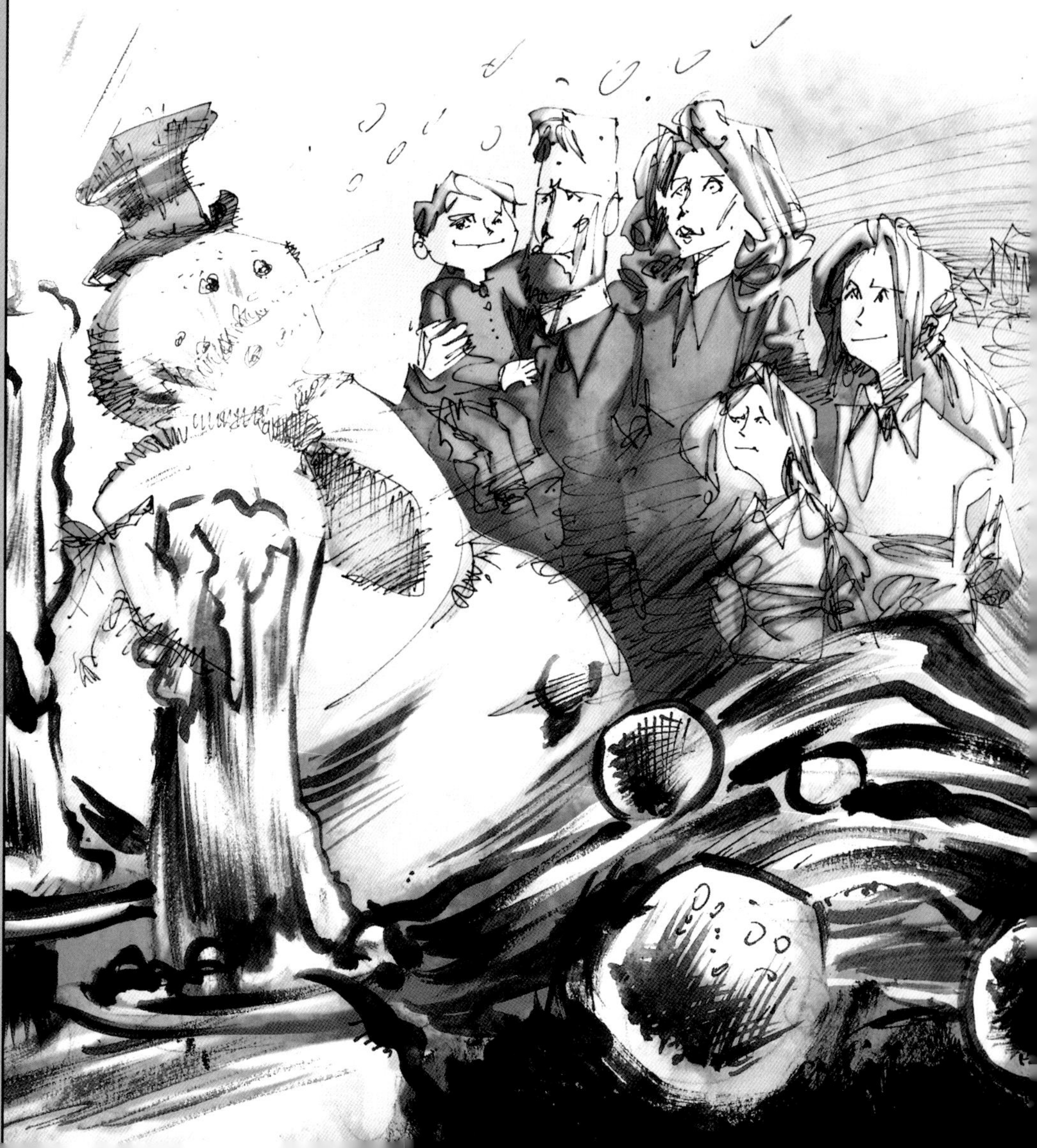

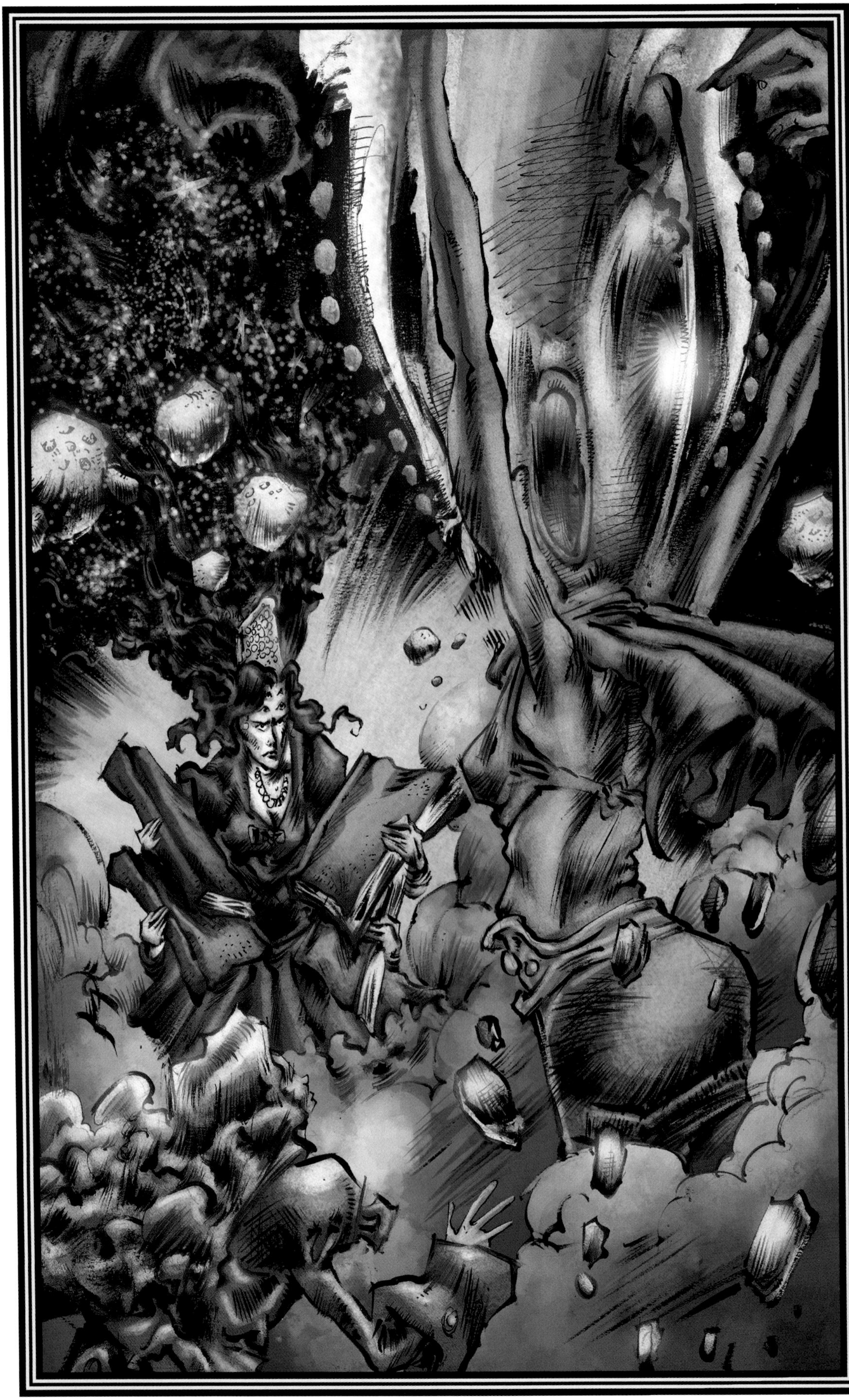

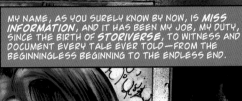

MY NAME, AS YOU SURELY KNOW BY NOW, IS *MISS INFORMATION*, AND IT HAS BEEN MY JOB, MY DUTY, SINCE THE BIRTH OF *STORIVERSE*, TO WITNESS AND DOCUMENT EVERY TALE EVER TOLD—FROM THE BEGINNINGLESS BEGINNING TO THE ENDLESS END.

I'VE LEARNED TO BE SOMEWHAT DISPASSIONATE ABOUT THE TELLING. TO REMAIN ALOOF FROM—ALTHOUGH NOT UNCARING ABOUT—EVENTS I RECORD. THIS *PARTICULAR* TALE, THOUGH, PRESENTS ME WITH SOMETHING OF A CHALLENGE, SINCE IT INCLUDES THE RATHER DISTURBING DETAILS...

...OF MY OWN DEATH.

CHAPTER THREE: OMEGUS

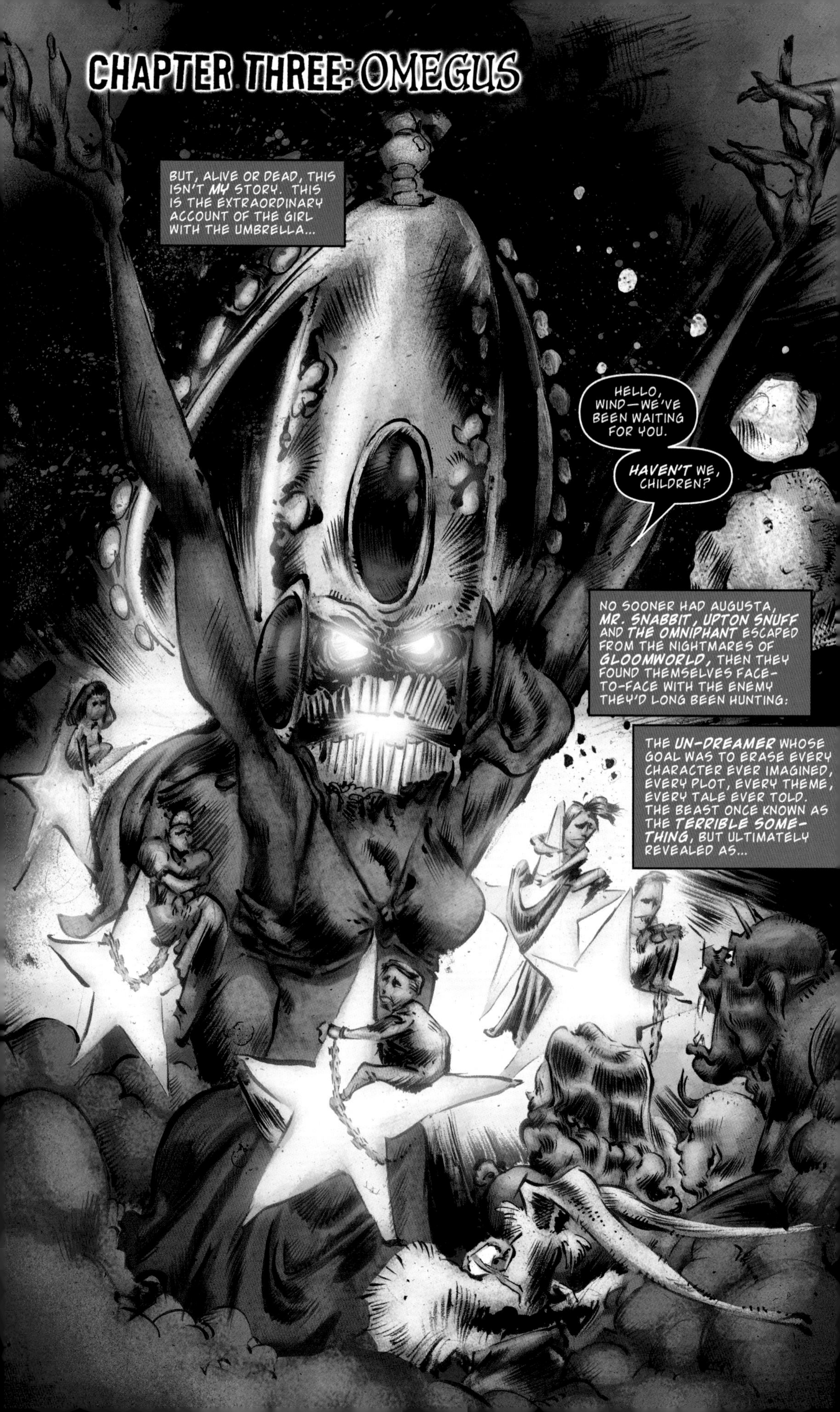
BUT, ALIVE OR DEAD, THIS ISN'T MY STORY. THIS IS THE EXTRAORDINARY ACCOUNT OF THE GIRL WITH THE UMBRELLA...
HELLO, WIND—WE'VE BEEN WAITING FOR YOU.
HAVEN'T WE, CHILDREN?
NO SOONER HAD AUGUSTA, MR. SNABBIT, UPTON SNUFF AND THE OMNIPHANT ESCAPED FROM THE NIGHTMARES OF GLOOMWORLD, THEN THEY FOUND THEMSELVES FACE-TO-FACE WITH THE ENEMY THEY'D LONG BEEN HUNTING:
THE UN-DREAMER WHOSE GOAL WAS TO ERASE EVERY CHARACTER EVER IMAGINED, EVERY PLOT, EVERY THEME, EVERY TALE EVER TOLD. THE BEAST ONCE KNOWN AS THE TERRIBLE SOME-THING, BUT ULTIMATELY REVEALED AS...

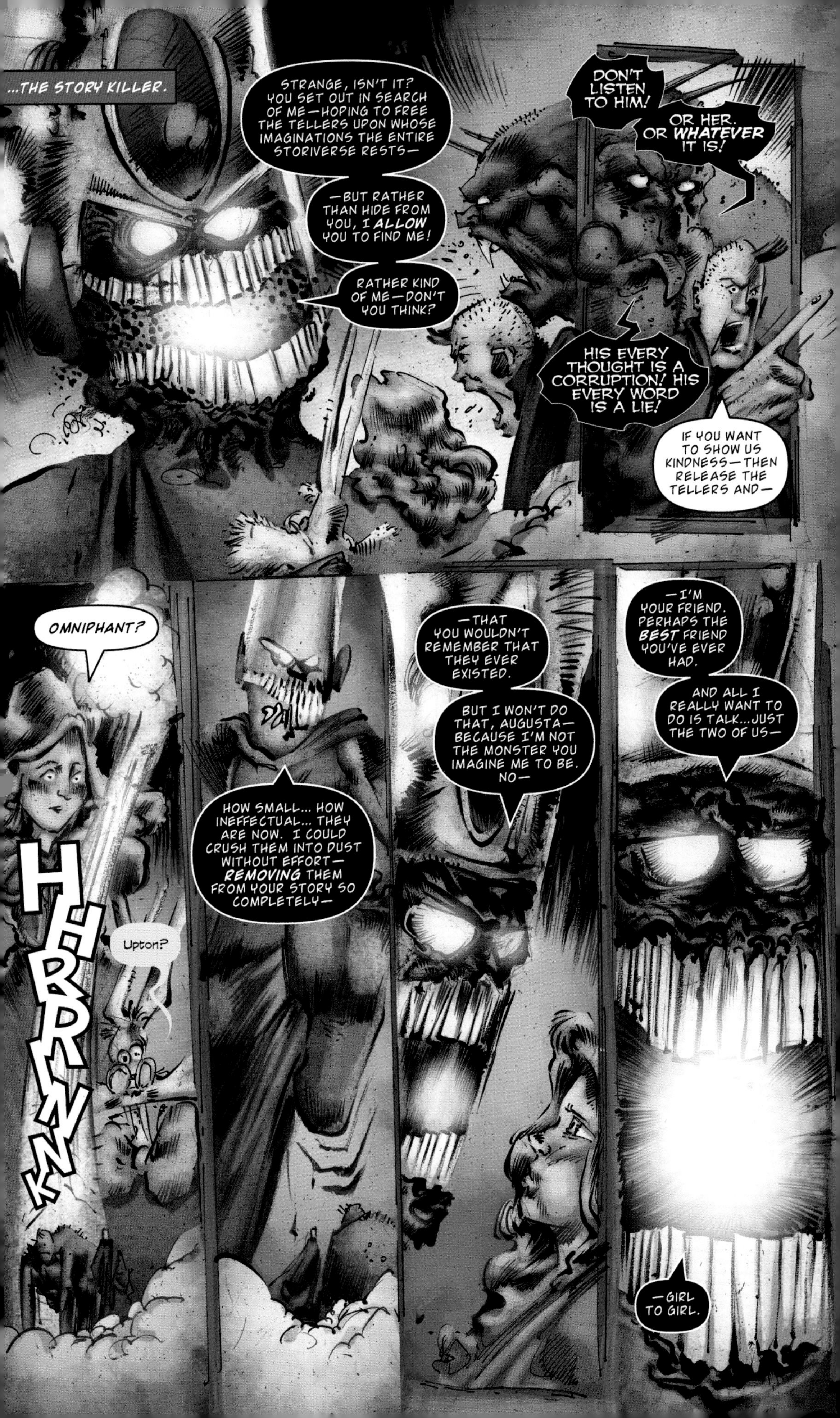
...THE STORY KILLER.
STRANGE, ISN'T IT? YOU SET OUT IN SEARCH OF ME—HOPING TO FREE THE TELLERS UPON WHOSE IMAGINATIONS THE ENTIRE STORIVERSE RESTS—
—BUT RATHER THAN HIDE FROM YOU, I ALLOW YOU TO FIND ME!
RATHER KIND OF ME—DON'T YOU THINK?
DON'T LISTEN TO HIM!
OR HER. OR WHATEVER IT IS!
HIS EVERY THOUGHT IS A CORRUPTION! HIS EVERY WORD IS A LIE!
IF YOU WANT TO SHOW US KINDNESS—THEN RELEASE THE TELLERS AND—
OMNIPHANT?
HHRRNNK
Upton?
HOW SMALL... HOW INEFFECTUAL... THEY ARE NOW. I COULD CRUSH THEM INTO DUST WITHOUT EFFORT—REMOVING THEM FROM YOUR STORY SO COMPLETELY—
—THAT YOU WOULDN'T REMEMBER THAT THEY EVER EXISTED.
BUT I WON'T DO THAT, AUGUSTA—BECAUSE I'M NOT THE MONSTER YOU IMAGINE ME TO BE. NO—
—I'M YOUR FRIEND. PERHAPS THE BEST FRIEND YOU'VE EVER HAD.
AND ALL I REALLY WANT TO DO IS TALK...JUST THE TWO OF US—
—GIRL TO GIRL.

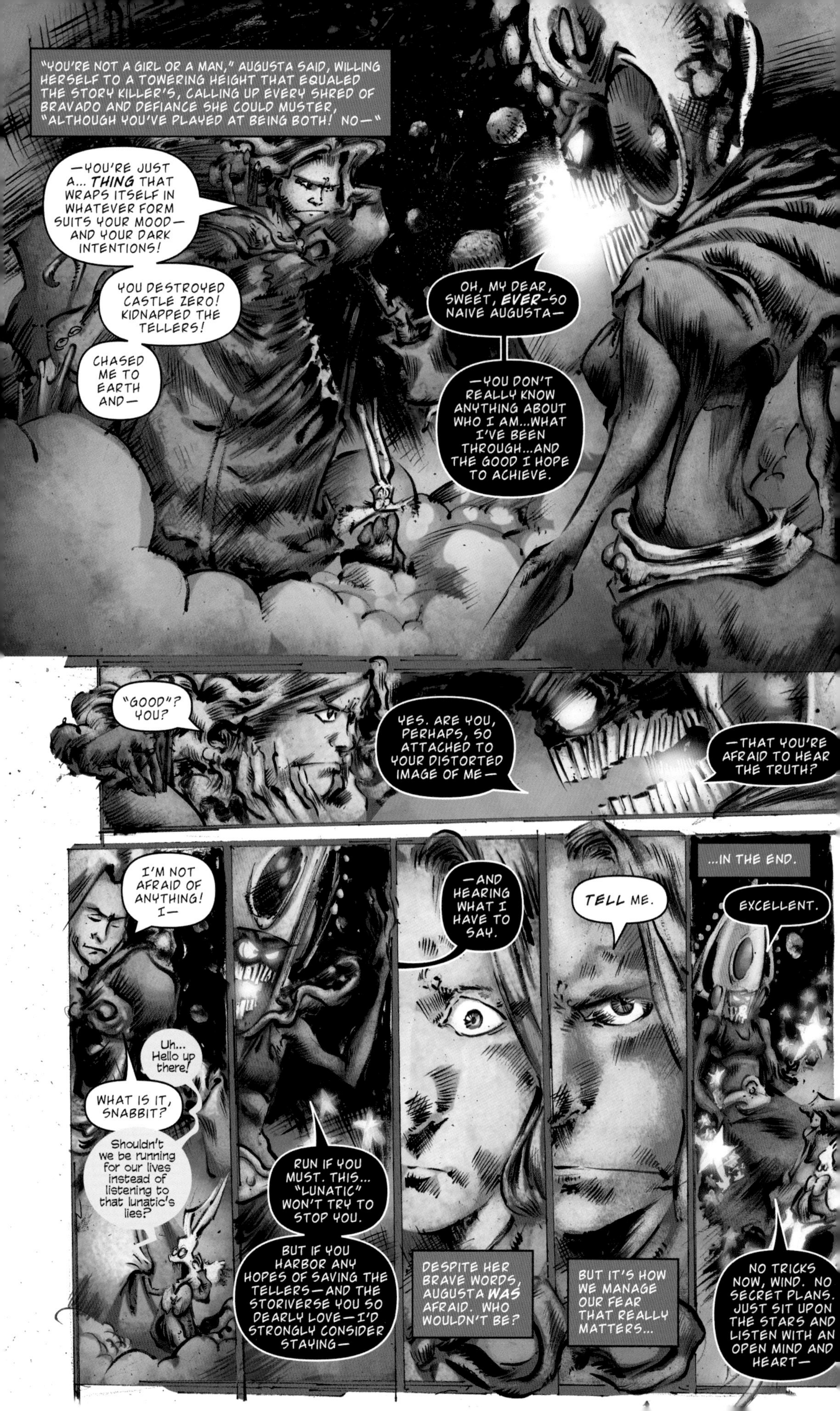
"YOU'RE NOT A GIRL OR A MAN," AUGUSTA SAID, WILLING HERSELF TO A TOWERING HEIGHT THAT EQUALED THE STORY KILLER'S, CALLING UP EVERY SHRED OF BRAVADO AND DEFIANCE SHE COULD MUSTER, "ALTHOUGH YOU'VE PLAYED AT BEING BOTH! NO—"
—YOU'RE JUST A... THING THAT WRAPS ITSELF IN WHATEVER FORM SUITS YOUR MOOD— AND YOUR DARK INTENTIONS!
YOU DESTROYED CASTLE ZERO! KIDNAPPED THE TELLERS!
CHASED ME TO EARTH AND—
OH, MY DEAR, SWEET, EVER-SO NAIVE AUGUSTA—
—YOU DON'T REALLY KNOW ANYTHING ABOUT WHO I AM...WHAT I'VE BEEN THROUGH...AND THE GOOD I HOPE TO ACHIEVE.
"GOOD"? YOU?
YES. ARE YOU, PERHAPS, SO ATTACHED TO YOUR DISTORTED IMAGE OF ME—
—THAT YOU'RE AFRAID TO HEAR THE TRUTH?
I'M NOT AFRAID OF ANYTHING! I—
Uh... Hello up there!
WHAT IS IT, SNABBIT?
Shouldn't we be running for our lives instead of listening to that lunatic's lies?
RUN IF YOU MUST. THIS... "LUNATIC" WON'T TRY TO STOP YOU.
BUT IF YOU HARBOR ANY HOPES OF SAVING THE TELLERS—AND THE STORIVERSE YOU SO DEARLY LOVE—I'D STRONGLY CONSIDER STAYING—
—AND HEARING WHAT I HAVE TO SAY.
DESPITE HER BRAVE WORDS, AUGUSTA WAS AFRAID. WHO WOULDN'T BE?
TELL ME.
BUT IT'S HOW WE MANAGE OUR FEAR THAT REALLY MATTERS...
...IN THE END.
EXCELLENT.
NO TRICKS NOW, WIND. NO SECRET PLANS. JUST SIT UPON THE STARS AND LISTEN WITH AN OPEN MIND AND HEART—

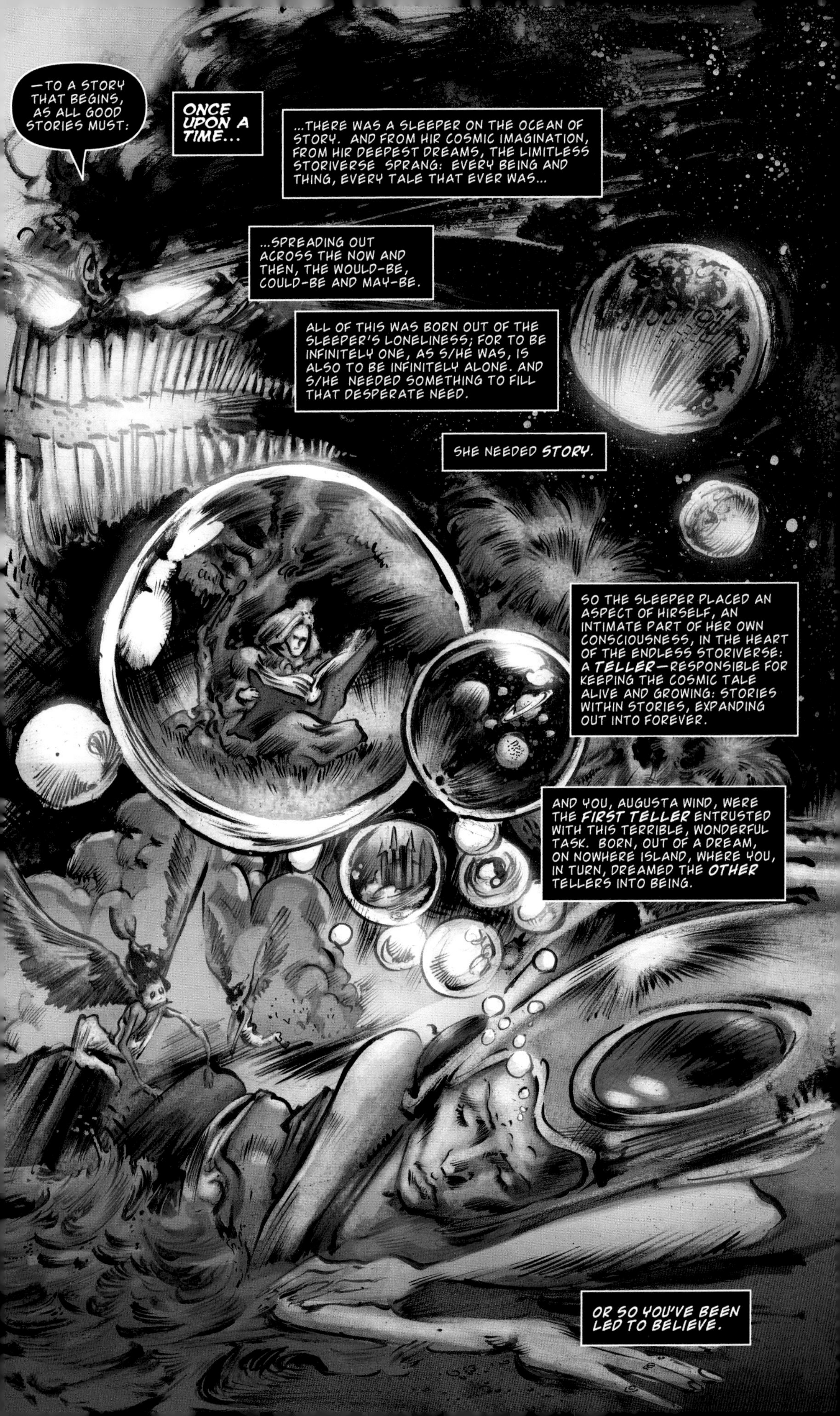
—TO A STORY THAT BEGINS, AS ALL GOOD STORIES MUST:
ONCE UPON A TIME...
...THERE WAS A SLEEPER ON THE OCEAN OF STORY. AND FROM HIR COSMIC IMAGINATION, FROM HIR DEEPEST DREAMS, THE LIMITLESS STORIVERSE SPRANG: EVERY BEING AND THING, EVERY TALE THAT EVER WAS...
...SPREADING OUT ACROSS THE NOW AND THEN, THE WOULD-BE, COULD-BE AND MAY-BE.
ALL OF THIS WAS BORN OUT OF THE SLEEPER'S LONELINESS; FOR TO BE INFINITELY ONE, AS S/HE WAS, IS ALSO TO BE INFINITELY ALONE. AND S/HE NEEDED SOMETHING TO FILL THAT DESPERATE NEED.
SHE NEEDED STORY.
SO THE SLEEPER PLACED AN ASPECT OF HIRSELF, AN INTIMATE PART OF HER OWN CONSCIOUSNESS, IN THE HEART OF THE ENDLESS STORIVERSE: A TELLER—RESPONSIBLE FOR KEEPING THE COSMIC TALE ALIVE AND GROWING: STORIES WITHIN STORIES, EXPANDING OUT INTO FOREVER.
AND YOU, AUGUSTA WIND, WERE THE FIRST TELLER ENTRUSTED WITH THIS TERRIBLE, WONDERFUL TASK. BORN, OUT OF A DREAM, ON NOWHERE ISLAND, WHERE YOU, IN TURN, DREAMED THE OTHER TELLERS INTO BEING.
OR SO YOU'VE BEEN LED TO BELIEVE.

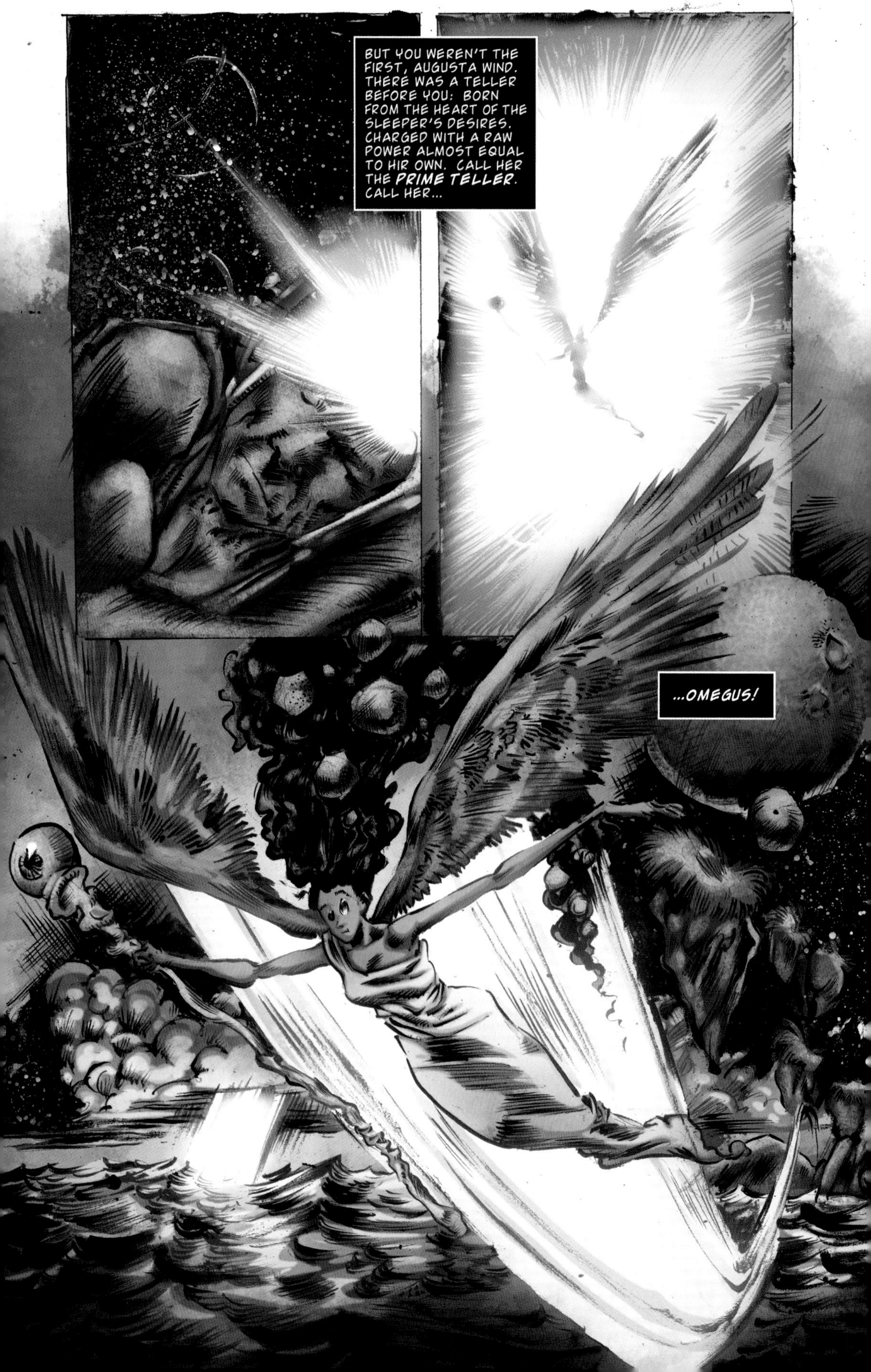
BUT YOU WEREN'T THE FIRST, AUGUSTA WIND. THERE WAS A TELLER BEFORE YOU: BORN FROM THE HEART OF THE SLEEPER'S DESIRES. CHARGED WITH A RAW POWER ALMOST EQUAL TO HIR OWN. CALL HER THE PRIME TELLER. CALL HER...
...OMEGUS!

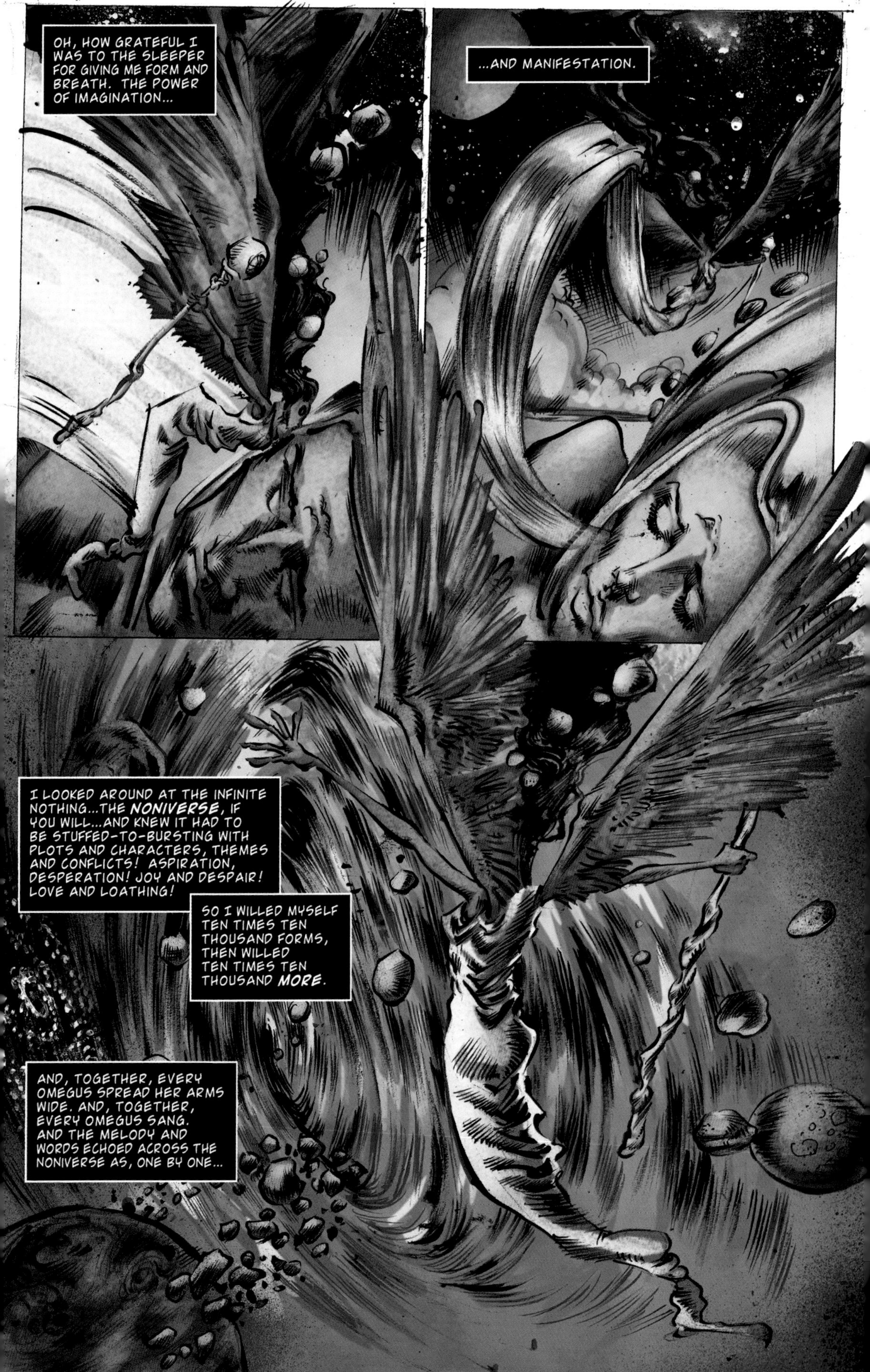
OH, HOW GRATEFUL I WAS TO THE SLEEPER FOR GIVING ME FORM AND BREATH. THE POWER OF IMAGINATION...
...AND MANIFESTATION.
I LOOKED AROUND AT THE INFINITE NOTHING...THE *NONIVERSE*, IF YOU WILL...AND KNEW IT HAD TO BE STUFFED-TO-BURSTING WITH PLOTS AND CHARACTERS, THEMES AND CONFLICTS! ASPIRATION, DESPERATION! JOY AND DESPAIR! LOVE AND LOATHING!
SO I WILLED MYSELF TEN TIMES TEN THOUSAND FORMS, THEN WILLED TEN TIMES TEN THOUSAND *MORE*.
AND, TOGETHER, EVERY OMEGUS SPREAD HER ARMS WIDE. AND, TOGETHER, EVERY OMEGUS SANG. AND THE MELODY AND WORDS ECHOED ACROSS THE NONIVERSE AS, ONE BY ONE...

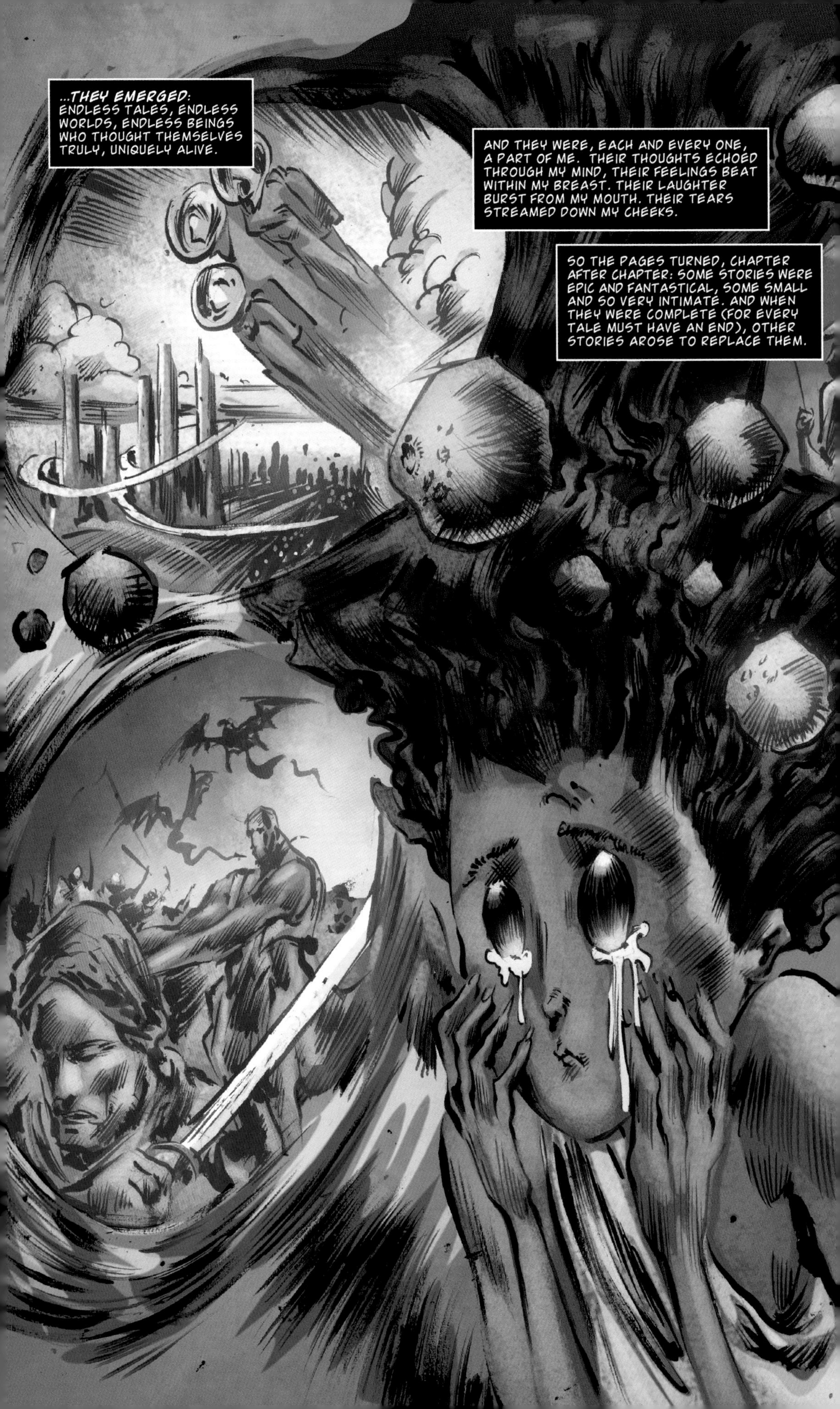
...THEY EMERGED: ENDLESS TALES, ENDLESS WORLDS, ENDLESS BEINGS WHO THOUGHT THEMSELVES TRULY, UNIQUELY ALIVE.
AND THEY WERE, EACH AND EVERY ONE, A PART OF ME. THEIR THOUGHTS ECHOED THROUGH MY MIND, THEIR FEELINGS BEAT WITHIN MY BREAST. THEIR LAUGHTER BURST FROM MY MOUTH. THEIR TEARS STREAMED DOWN MY CHEEKS.
SO THE PAGES TURNED, CHAPTER AFTER CHAPTER: SOME STORIES WERE EPIC AND FANTASTICAL, SOME SMALL AND SO VERY INTIMATE. AND WHEN THEY WERE COMPLETE (FOR EVERY TALE MUST HAVE AN END), OTHER STORIES AROSE TO REPLACE THEM.

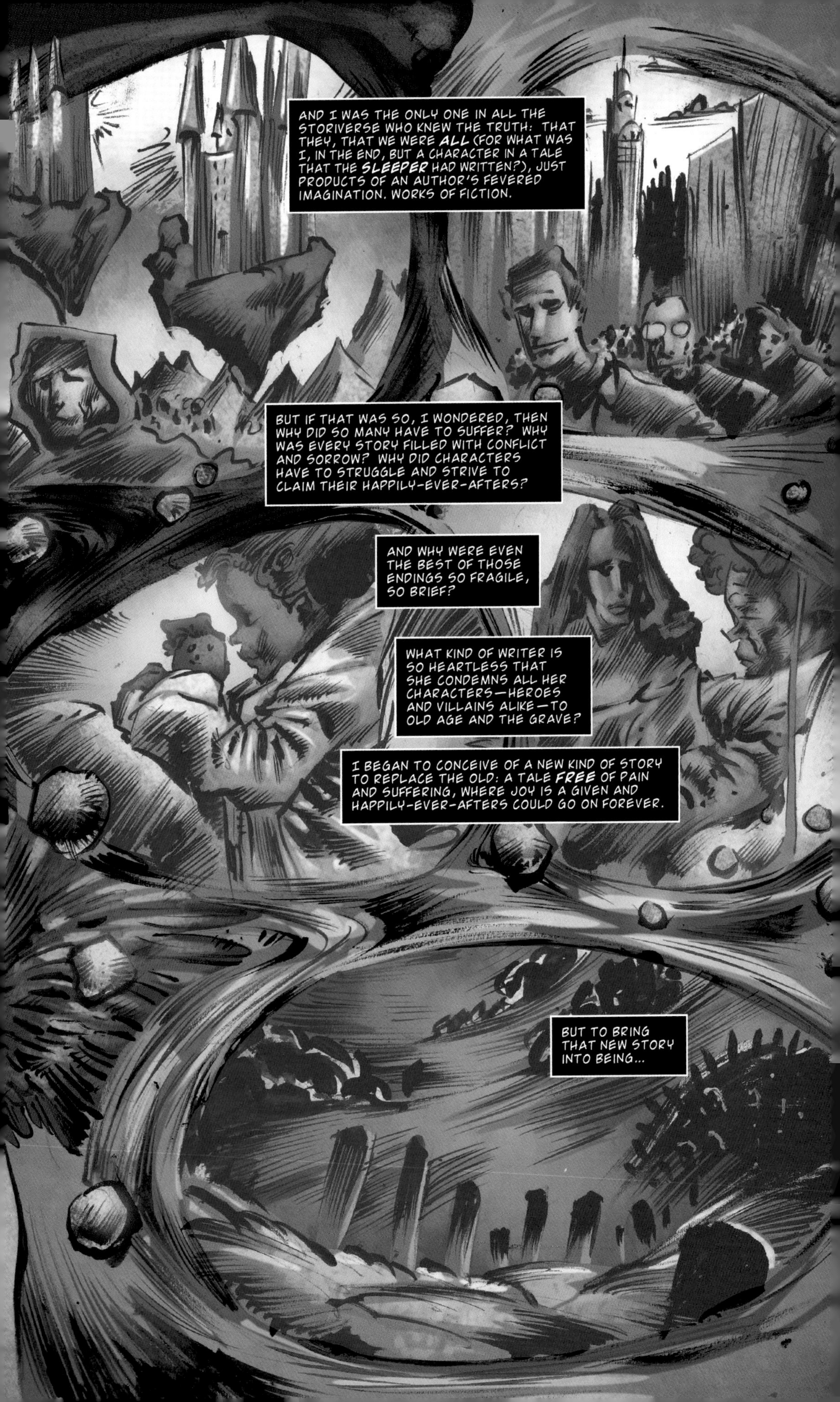

AND I WAS THE ONLY ONE IN ALL THE STORIVERSE WHO KNEW THE TRUTH: THAT THEY, THAT WE WERE ALL (FOR WHAT WAS I, IN THE END, BUT A CHARACTER IN A TALE THAT THE SLEEPER HAD WRITTEN?), JUST PRODUCTS OF AN AUTHOR'S FEVERED IMAGINATION. WORKS OF FICTION.
BUT IF THAT WAS SO, I WONDERED, THEN WHY DID SO MANY HAVE TO SUFFER? WHY WAS EVERY STORY FILLED WITH CONFLICT AND SORROW? WHY DID CHARACTERS HAVE TO STRUGGLE AND STRIVE TO CLAIM THEIR HAPPILY-EVER-AFTERS?
AND WHY WERE EVEN THE BEST OF THOSE ENDINGS SO FRAGILE, SO BRIEF?
WHAT KIND OF WRITER IS SO HEARTLESS THAT SHE CONDEMNS ALL HER CHARACTERS—HEROES AND VILLAINS ALIKE—TO OLD AGE AND THE GRAVE?
I BEGAN TO CONCEIVE OF A NEW KIND OF STORY TO REPLACE THE OLD: A TALE FREE OF PAIN AND SUFFERING, WHERE JOY IS A GIVEN AND HAPPILY-EVER-AFTERS COULD GO ON FOREVER.
BUT TO BRING THAT NEW STORY INTO BEING...

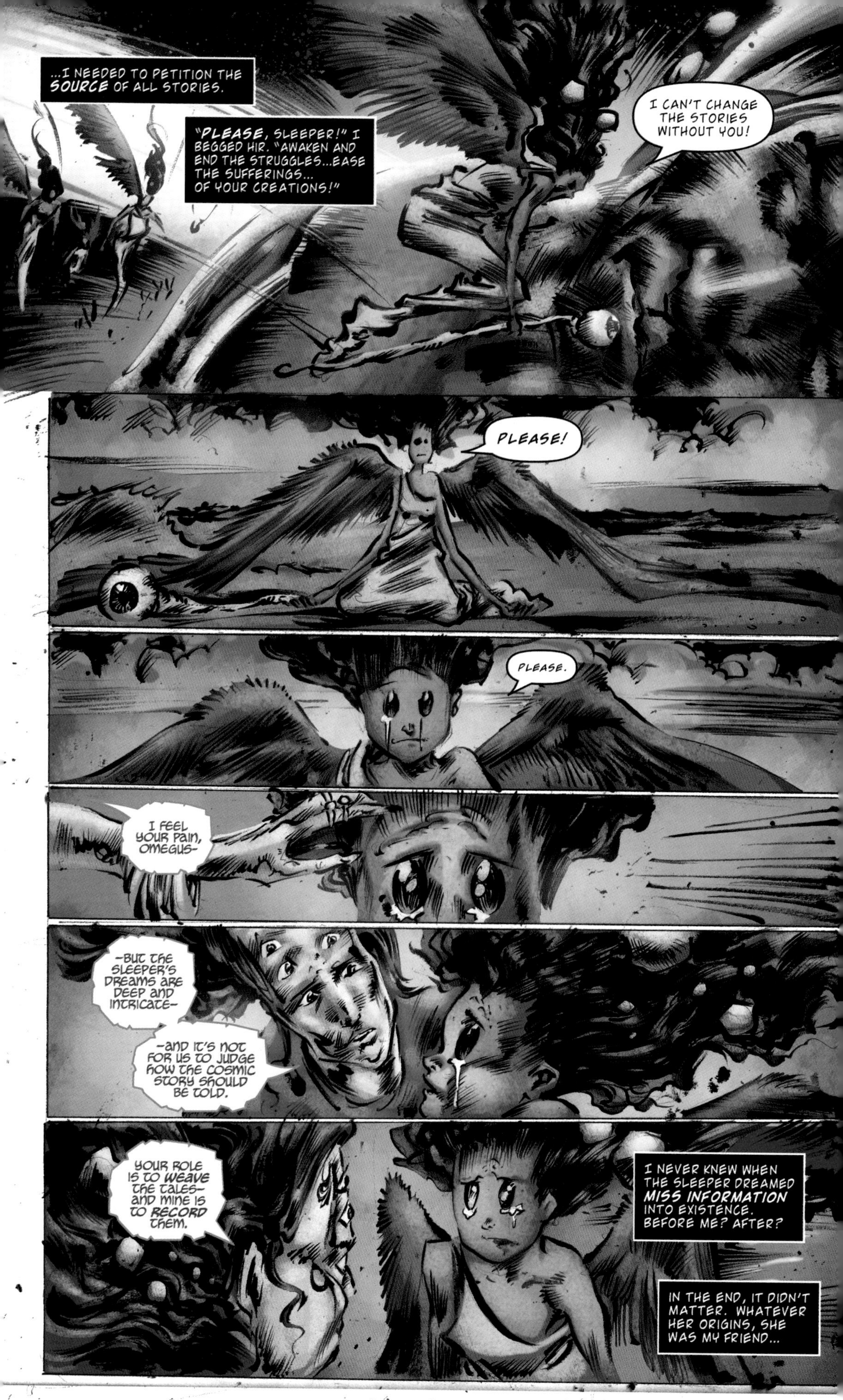

...I NEEDED TO PETITION THE SOURCE OF ALL STORIES.
"PLEASE, SLEEPER!" I BEGGED HIR. "AWAKEN AND END THE STRUGGLES...EASE THE SUFFERINGS... OF YOUR CREATIONS!"
I CAN'T CHANGE THE STORIES WITHOUT YOU!
PLEASE!
PLEASE.
I FEEL YOUR PAIN, OMEGUS-
-BUT THE SLEEPER'S DREAMS ARE DEEP AND INTRICATE-
-AND IT'S NOT FOR US TO JUDGE HOW THE COSMIC STORY SHOULD BE TOLD.
YOUR ROLE IS TO WEAVE THE TALES- AND MINE IS TO RECORD THEM.
I NEVER KNEW WHEN THE SLEEPER DREAMED MISS INFORMATION INTO EXISTENCE. BEFORE ME? AFTER?
IN THE END, IT DIDN'T MATTER. WHATEVER HER ORIGINS, SHE WAS MY FRIEND...

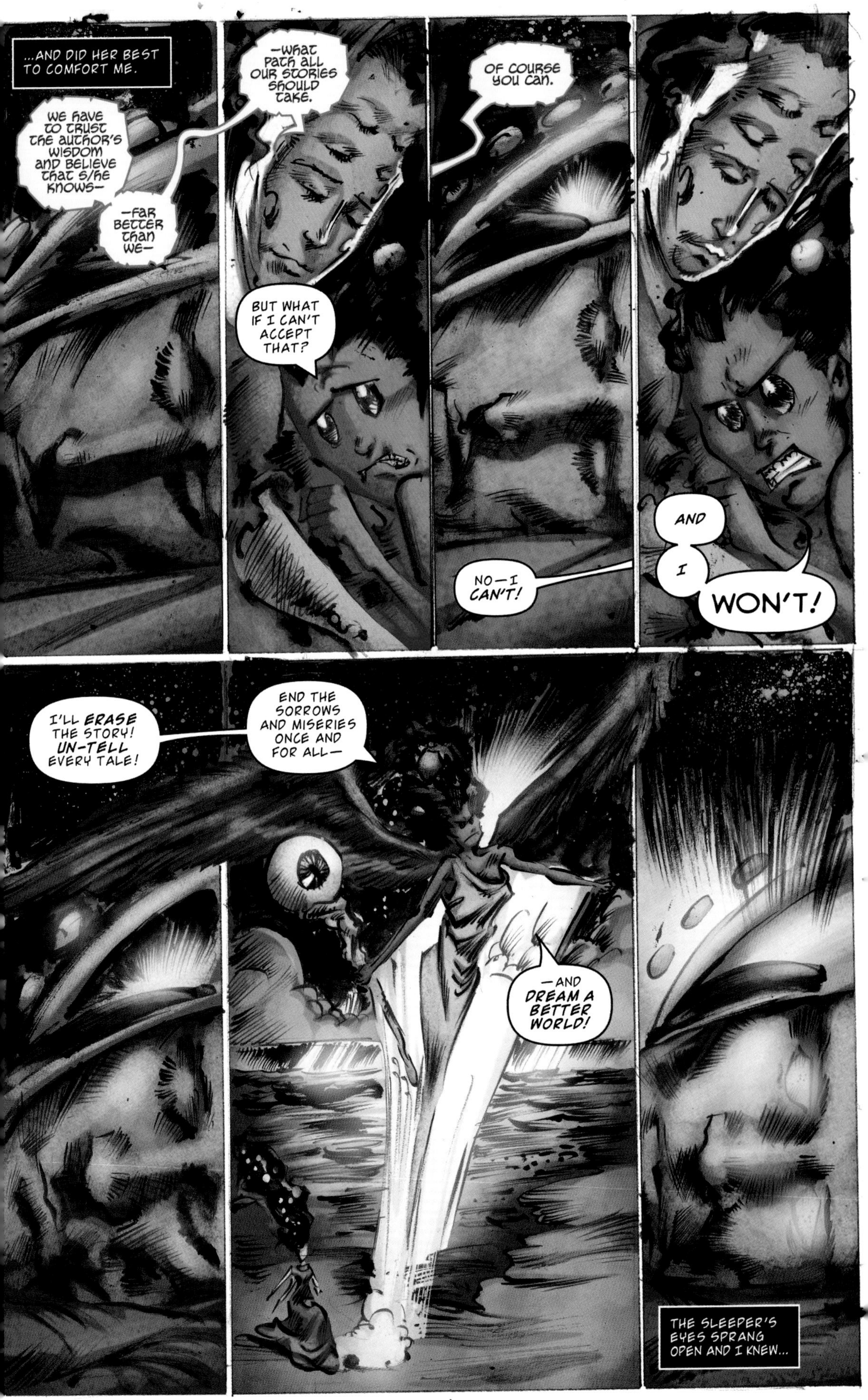
...AND DID HER BEST TO COMFORT ME.
WE HAVE TO TRUST THE AUTHOR'S WISDOM AND BELIEVE THAT S/HE KNOWS—
—FAR BETTER THAN WE—
—WHAT PATH ALL OUR STORIES SHOULD TAKE.
BUT WHAT IF I CAN'T ACCEPT THAT?
OF COURSE YOU CAN.
NO—I CAN'T!
AND
I
WON'T!
I'LL ERASE THE STORY! UN-TELL EVERY TALE!
END THE SORROWS AND MISERIES ONCE AND FOR ALL—
—AND DREAM A BETTER WORLD!
THE SLEEPER'S EYES SPRANG OPEN AND I KNEW...

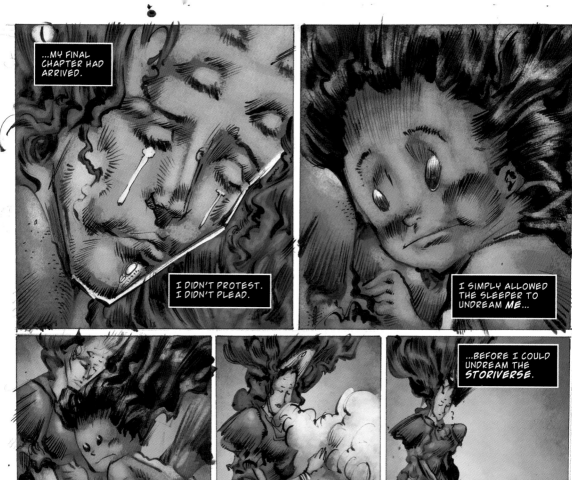

...MY FINAL CHAPTER HAD ARRIVED.

I DIDN'T PROTEST. I DIDN'T PLEAD.

I SIMPLY ALLOWED THE SLEEPER TO UNDREAM *ME*...

...BEFORE I COULD UNDREAM THE *STORIVERSE*.

BUT THERE WAS AN UNEXPECTED *EPILOGUE* TO THE TALE OF MY DEMISE.

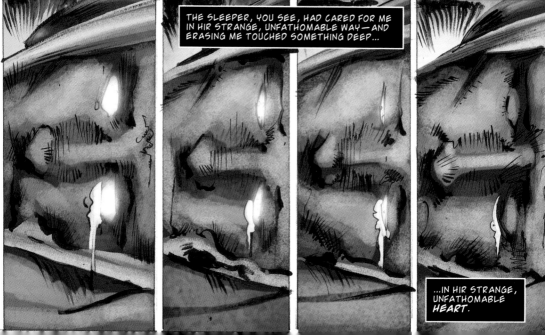

THE SLEEPER, YOU SEE, HAD CARED FOR ME IN HIR STRANGE, UNFATHOMABLE WAY—AND ERASING ME TOUCHED SOMETHING DEEP...

...IN HIR STRANGE, UNFATHOMABLE *HEART*.

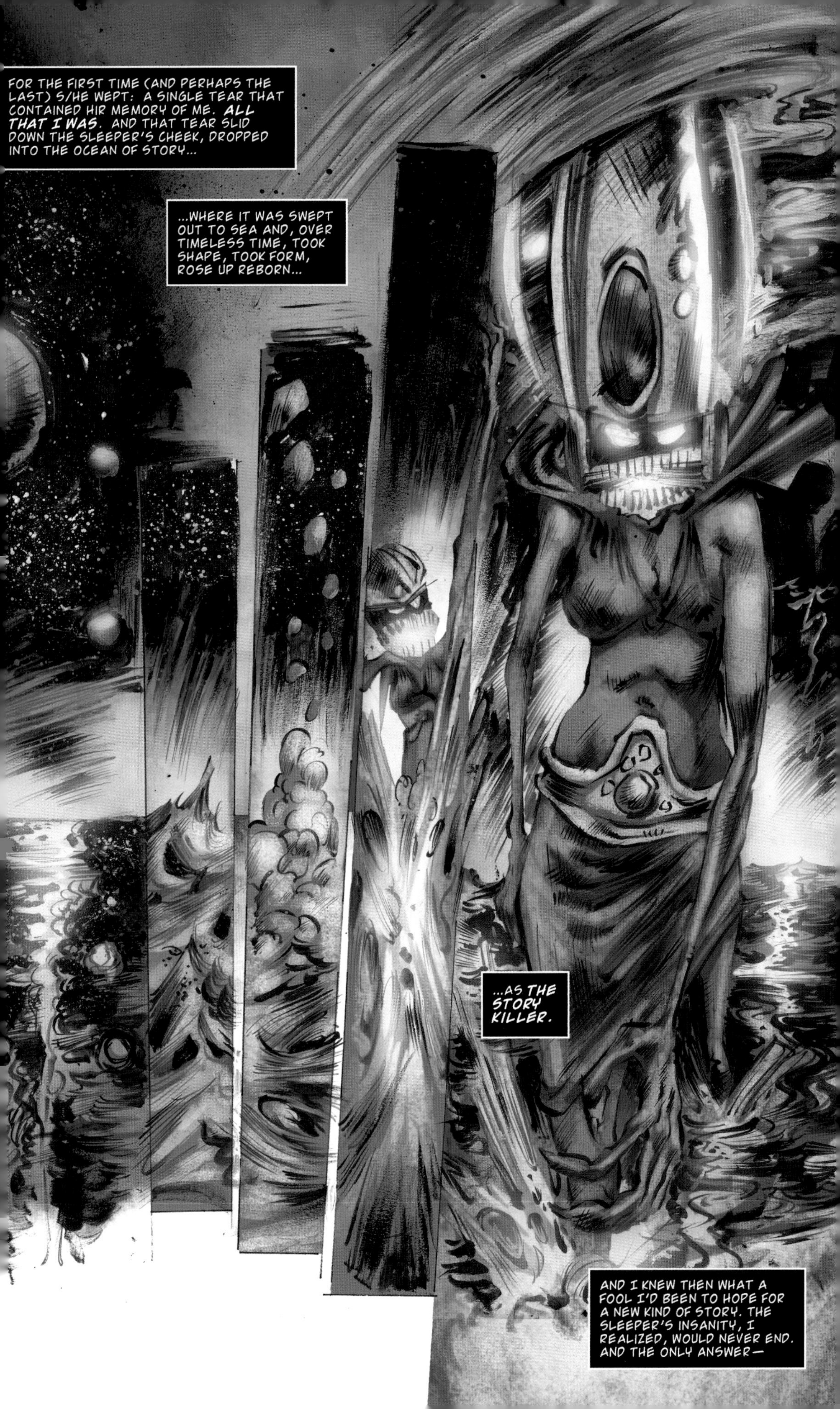
FOR THE FIRST TIME (AND PERHAPS THE LAST) S/HE WEPT: A SINGLE TEAR THAT CONTAINED HIR MEMORY OF ME. ALL THAT I WAS. AND THAT TEAR SLID DOWN THE SLEEPER'S CHEEK, DROPPED INTO THE OCEAN OF STORY...
...WHERE IT WAS SWEPT OUT TO SEA AND, OVER TIMELESS TIME, TOOK SHAPE, TOOK FORM, ROSE UP REBORN...
...AS THE STORY KILLER.
AND I KNEW THEN WHAT A FOOL I'D BEEN TO HOPE FOR A NEW KIND OF STORY. THE SLEEPER'S INSANITY, I REALIZED, WOULD NEVER END. AND THE ONLY ANSWER—

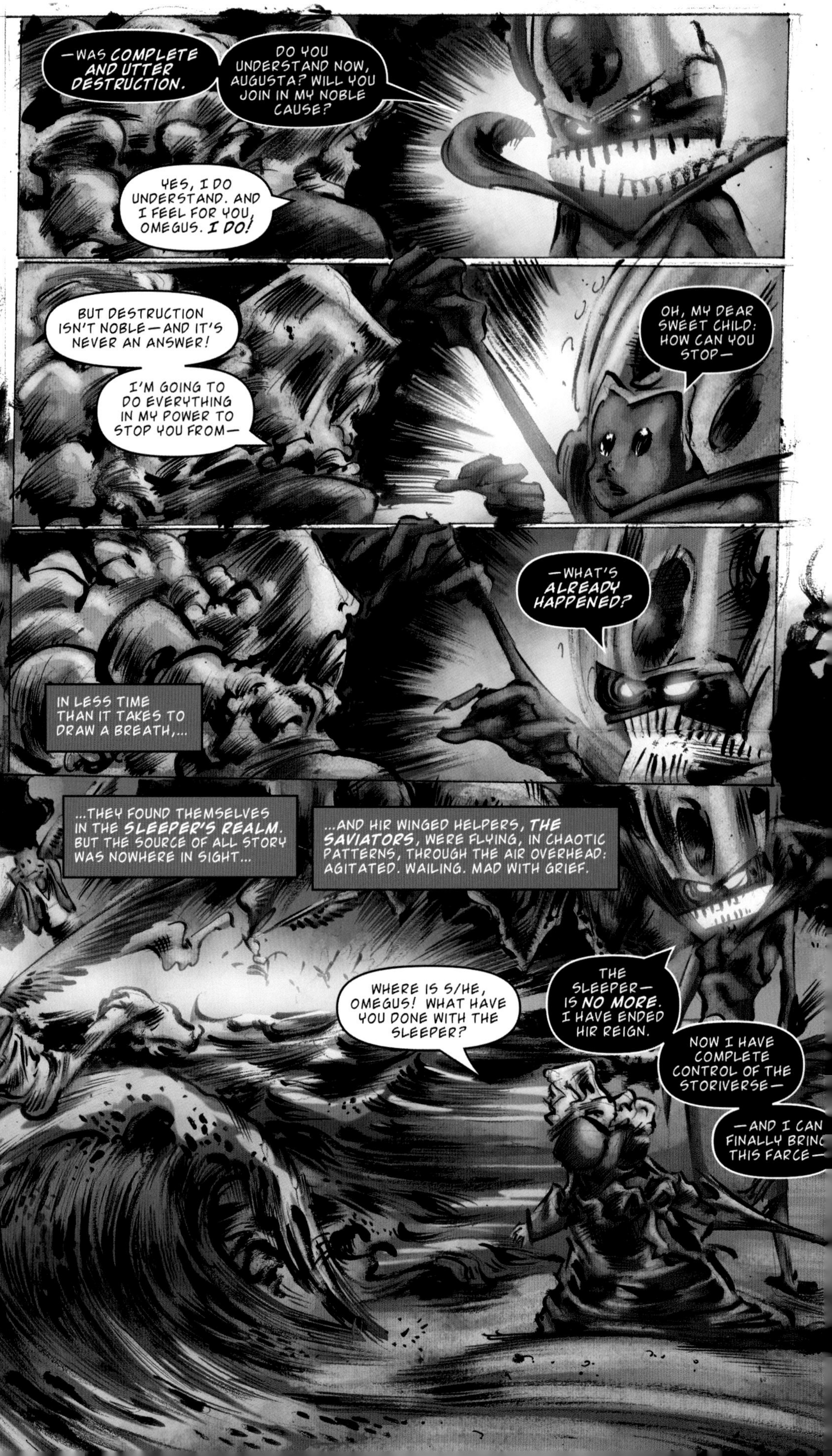
—WAS COMPLETE AND UTTER DESTRUCTION.
DO YOU UNDERSTAND NOW, AUGUSTA? WILL YOU JOIN IN MY NOBLE CAUSE?
YES, I DO UNDERSTAND. AND I FEEL FOR YOU, OMEGUS. I DO!
BUT DESTRUCTION ISN'T NOBLE—AND IT'S NEVER AN ANSWER!
I'M GOING TO DO EVERYTHING IN MY POWER TO STOP YOU FROM—
OH, MY DEAR SWEET CHILD: HOW CAN YOU STOP—
—WHAT'S ALREADY HAPPENED?
IN LESS TIME THAN IT TAKES TO DRAW A BREATH,...
...THEY FOUND THEMSELVES IN THE SLEEPER'S REALM. BUT THE SOURCE OF ALL STORY WAS NOWHERE IN SIGHT...
...AND HIR WINGED HELPERS, THE SAVIATORS, WERE FLYING, IN CHAOTIC PATTERNS, THROUGH THE AIR OVERHEAD: AGITATED. WAILING. MAD WITH GRIEF.
WHERE IS S/HE, OMEGUS! WHAT HAVE YOU DONE WITH THE SLEEPER?
THE SLEEPER—IS NO MORE. I HAVE ENDED HIR REIGN.
NOW I HAVE COMPLETE CONTROL OF THE STORIVERSE—
—AND I CAN FINALLY BRING THIS FARCE—

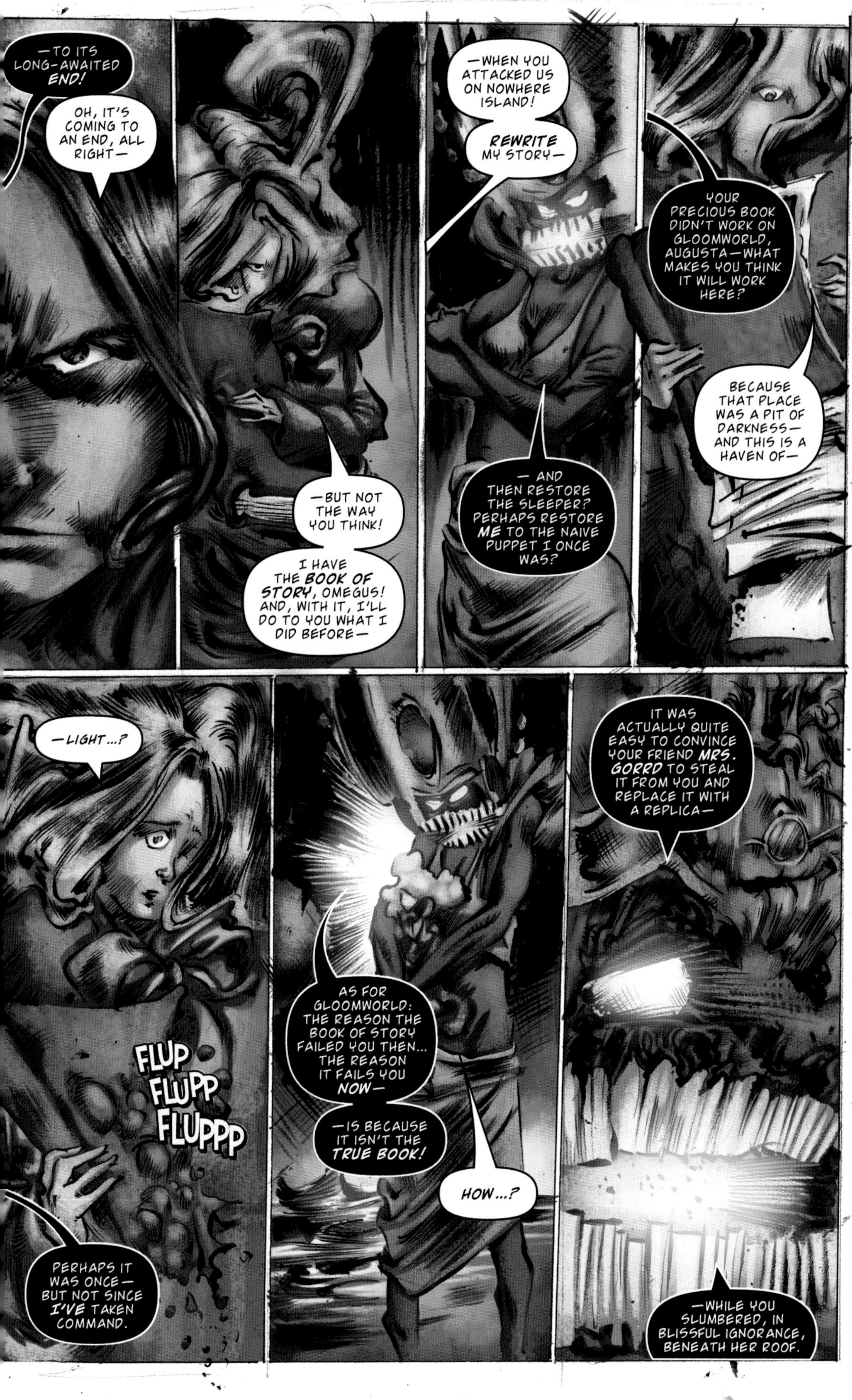
—TO ITS LONG-AWAITED END!
OH, IT'S COMING TO AN END, ALL RIGHT—
—BUT NOT THE WAY YOU THINK!
I HAVE THE BOOK OF STORY, OMEGUS! AND, WITH IT, I'LL DO TO YOU WHAT I DID BEFORE—
—WHEN YOU ATTACKED US ON NOWHERE ISLAND!
REWRITE MY STORY—
— AND THEN RESTORE THE SLEEPER? PERHAPS RESTORE ME TO THE NAIVE PUPPET I ONCE WAS?
YOUR PRECIOUS BOOK DIDN'T WORK ON GLOOMWORLD, AUGUSTA—WHAT MAKES YOU THINK IT WILL WORK HERE?
BECAUSE THAT PLACE WAS A PIT OF DARKNESS—AND THIS IS A HAVEN OF—
—LIGHT...?
FLUP
FLUPP
FLUPPP
PERHAPS IT WAS ONCE—BUT NOT SINCE I'VE TAKEN COMMAND.
AS FOR GLOOMWORLD: THE REASON THE BOOK OF STORY FAILED YOU THEN... THE REASON IT FAILS YOU NOW—
—IS BECAUSE IT ISN'T THE TRUE BOOK!
HOW...?
IT WAS ACTUALLY QUITE EASY TO CONVINCE YOUR FRIEND MRS. GORRD TO STEAL IT FROM YOU AND REPLACE IT WITH A REPLICA—
—WHILE YOU SLUMBERED, IN BLISSFUL IGNORANCE, BENEATH HER ROOF.

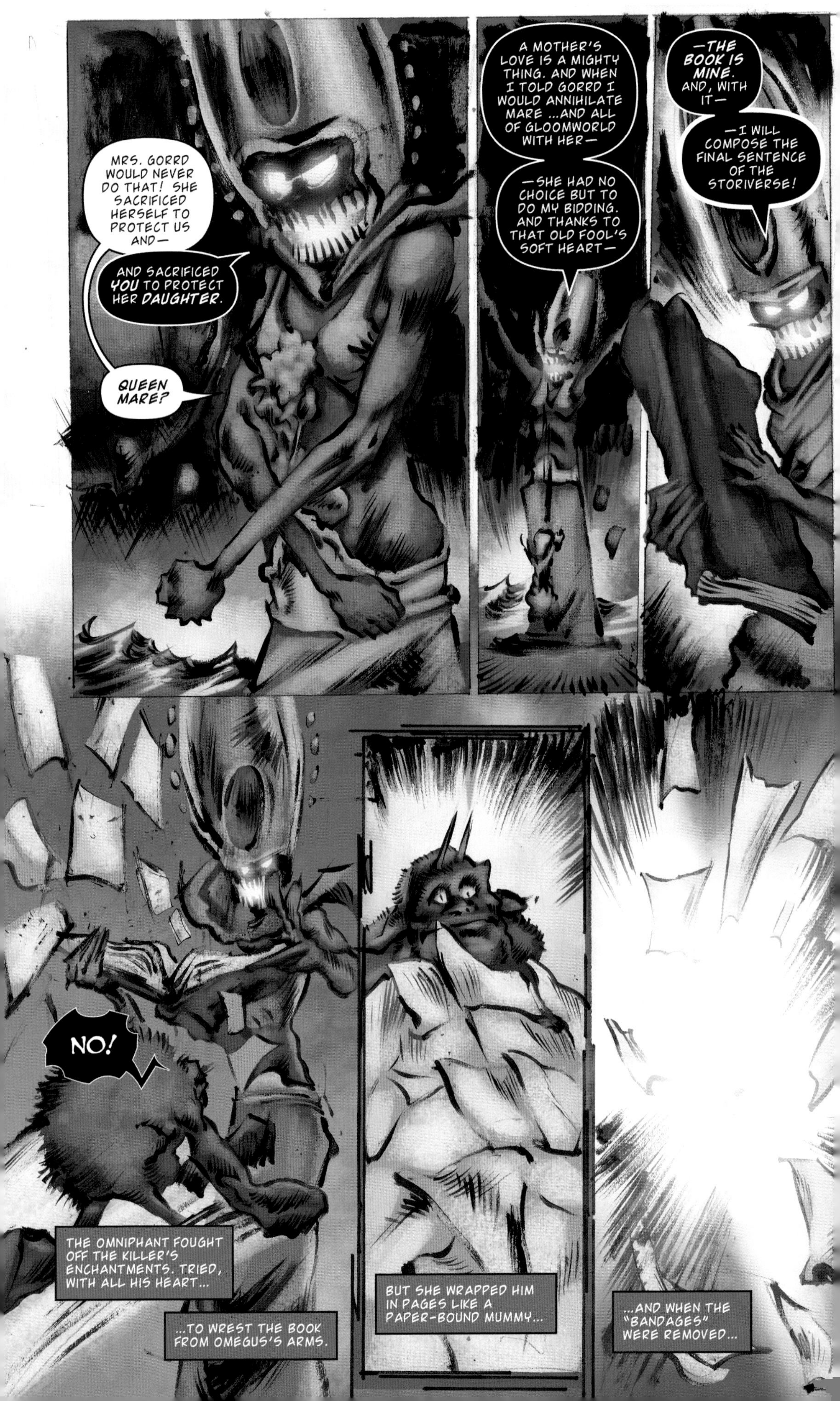
MRS. GORRD WOULD NEVER DO THAT! SHE SACRIFICED HERSELF TO PROTECT US AND—
AND SACRIFICED YOU TO PROTECT HER DAUGHTER.
QUEEN MARE?
A MOTHER'S LOVE IS A MIGHTY THING. AND WHEN I TOLD GORRD I WOULD ANNIHILATE MARE ...AND ALL OF GLOOMWORLD WITH HER—
—SHE HAD NO CHOICE BUT TO DO MY BIDDING. AND THANKS TO THAT OLD FOOL'S SOFT HEART—
—THE BOOK IS MINE. AND, WITH IT—
—I WILL COMPOSE THE FINAL SENTENCE OF THE STORIVERSE!
NO!
THE OMNIPHANT FOUGHT OFF THE KILLER'S ENCHANTMENTS. TRIED, WITH ALL HIS HEART...
...TO WREST THE BOOK FROM OMEGUS'S ARMS.
BUT SHE WRAPPED HIM IN PAGES LIKE A PAPER-BOUND MUMMY...
...AND WHEN THE "BANDAGES" WERE REMOVED...

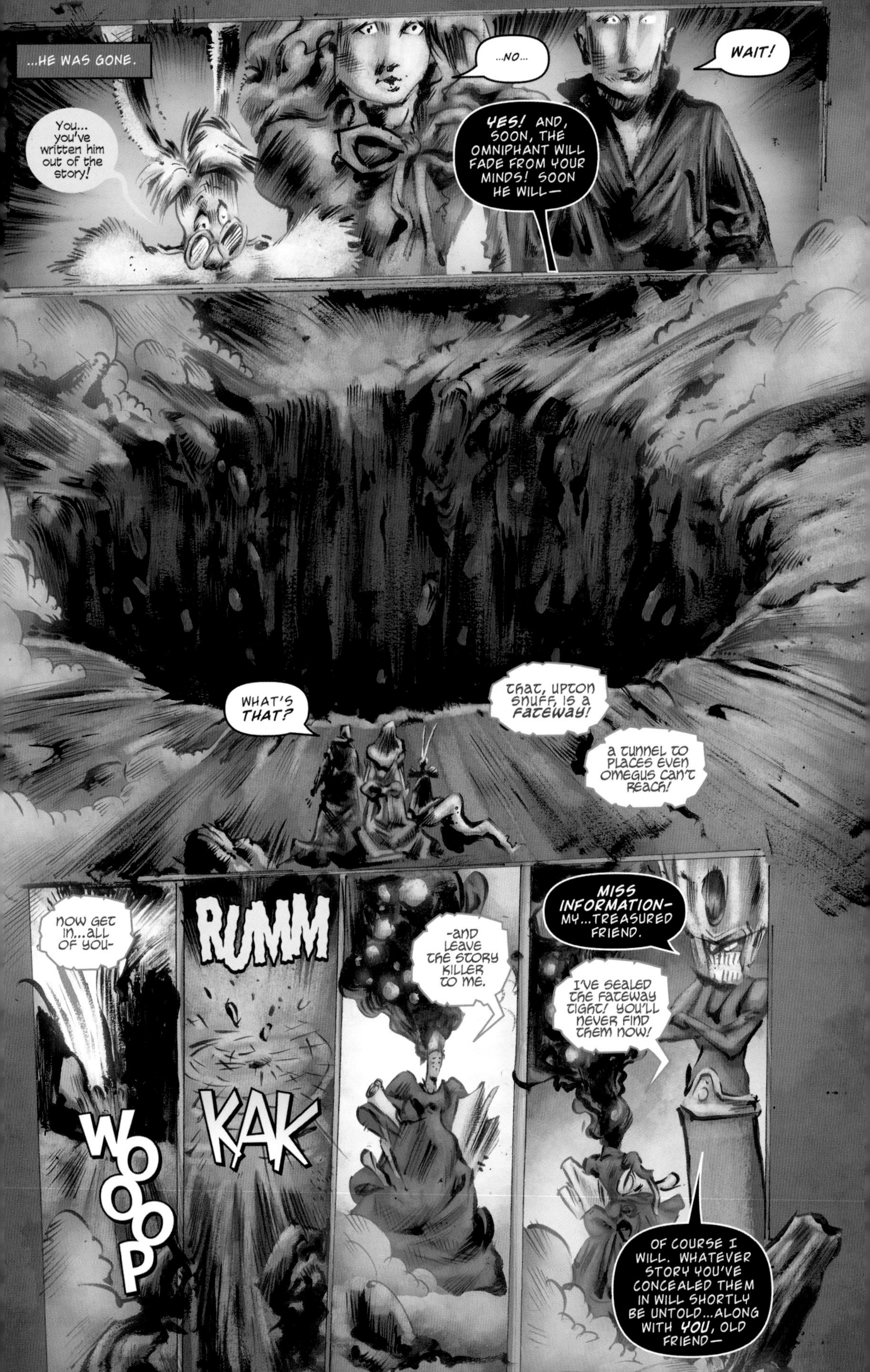
...HE WAS GONE.
...NO...
WAIT!
You... you've written him out of the story!
YES! AND, SOON, THE OMNIPHANT WILL FADE FROM YOUR MINDS! SOON HE WILL—
WHAT'S THAT?
THAT, UPTON SNUFF, IS A FATEWAY!
A TUNNEL TO PLACES EVEN OMEGUS CAN'T REACH!
NOW GET IN...ALL OF YOU-
WOOOP
RUMM
KAK
-AND LEAVE THE STORY KILLER TO ME.
MISS INFORMATION-MY...TREASURED FRIEND.
I'VE SEALED THE FATEWAY TIGHT! YOU'LL NEVER FIND THEM NOW!
OF COURSE I WILL. WHATEVER STORY YOU'VE CONCEALED THEM IN WILL SHORTLY BE UNTOLD...ALONG WITH YOU, OLD FRIEND—

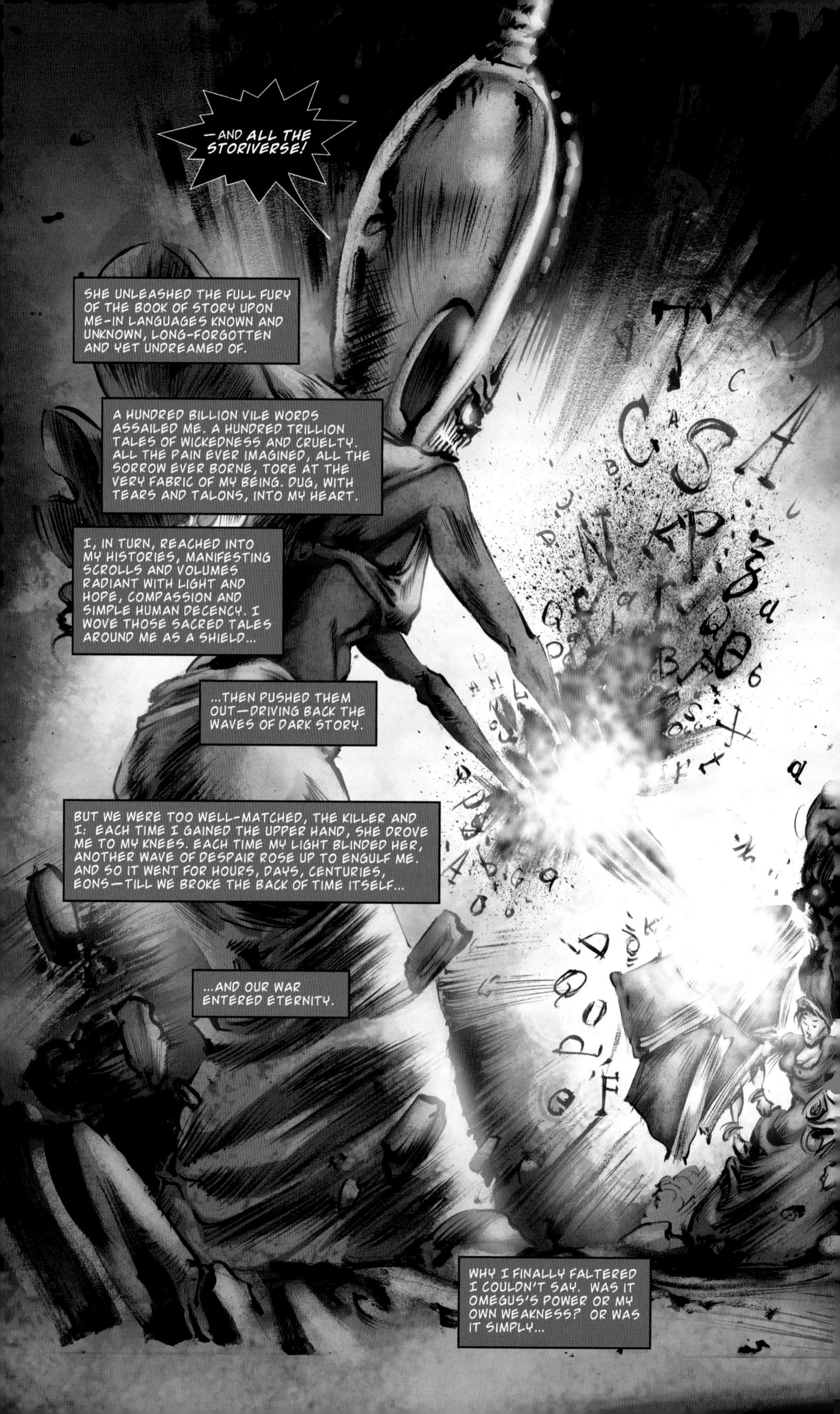

—AND ALL THE STORIVERSE!
SHE UNLEASHED THE FULL FURY OF THE BOOK OF STORY UPON ME—IN LANGUAGES KNOWN AND UNKNOWN, LONG-FORGOTTEN AND YET UNDREAMED OF.
A HUNDRED BILLION VILE WORDS ASSAILED ME. A HUNDRED TRILLION TALES OF WICKEDNESS AND CRUELTY. ALL THE PAIN EVER IMAGINED, ALL THE SORROW EVER BORNE, TORE AT THE VERY FABRIC OF MY BEING. DUG, WITH TEARS AND TALONS, INTO MY HEART.
I, IN TURN, REACHED INTO MY HISTORIES, MANIFESTING SCROLLS AND VOLUMES RADIANT WITH LIGHT AND HOPE, COMPASSION AND SIMPLE HUMAN DECENCY. I WOVE THOSE SACRED TALES AROUND ME AS A SHIELD...
...THEN PUSHED THEM OUT—DRIVING BACK THE WAVES OF DARK STORY.
BUT WE WERE TOO WELL-MATCHED, THE KILLER AND I: EACH TIME I GAINED THE UPPER HAND, SHE DROVE ME TO MY KNEES. EACH TIME MY LIGHT BLINDED HER, ANOTHER WAVE OF DESPAIR ROSE UP TO ENGULF ME. AND SO IT WENT FOR HOURS, DAYS, CENTURIES, EONS—TILL WE BROKE THE BACK OF TIME ITSELF...
...AND OUR WAR ENTERED ETERNITY.
WHY I FINALLY FALTERED I COULDN'T SAY. WAS IT OMEGUS'S POWER OR MY OWN WEAKNESS? OR WAS IT SIMPLY...

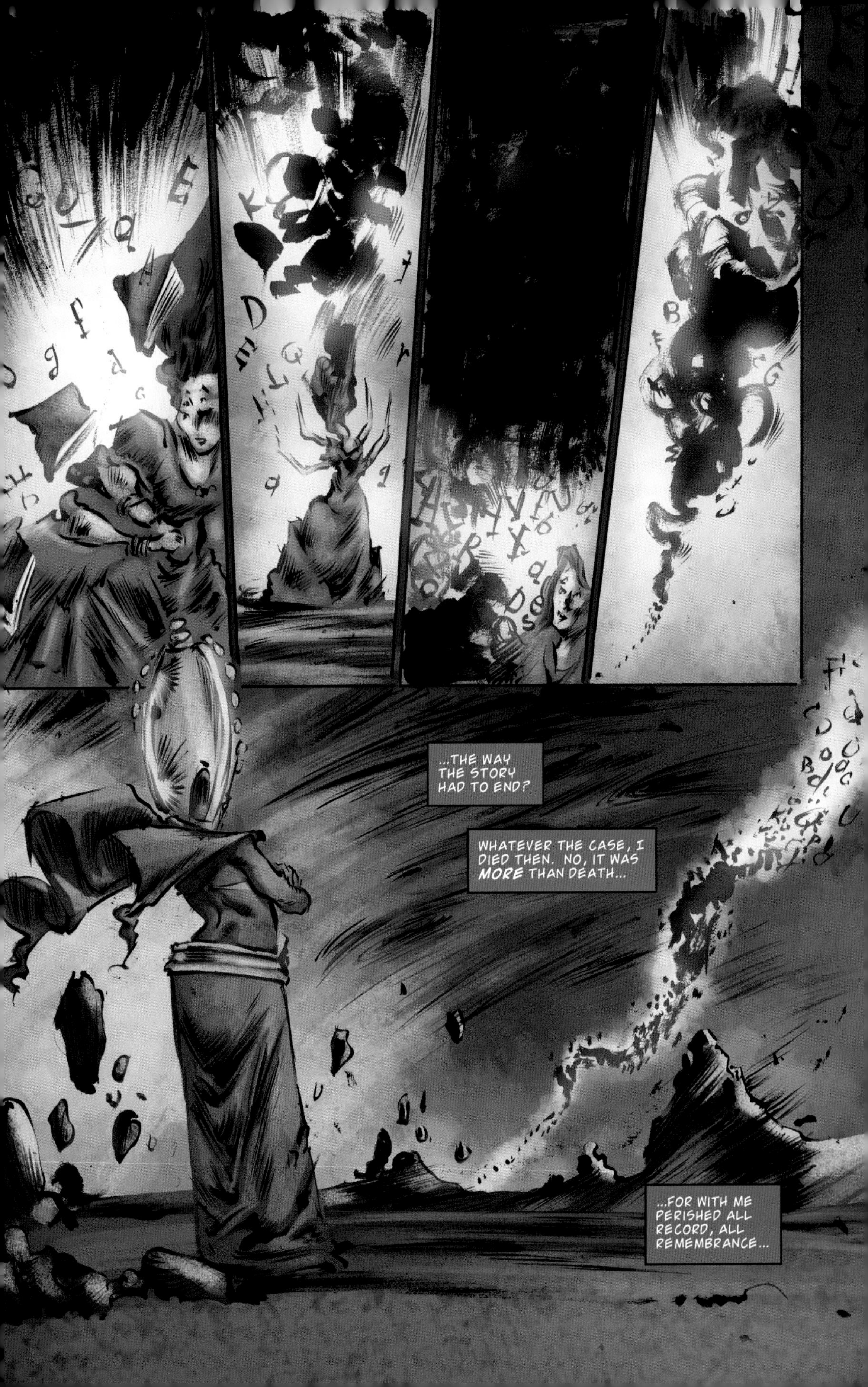
...THE WAY THE STORY HAD TO END?
WHATEVER THE CASE, I DIED THEN. NO, IT WAS MORE THAN DEATH...
...FOR WITH ME PERISHED ALL RECORD, ALL REMEMBRANCE...

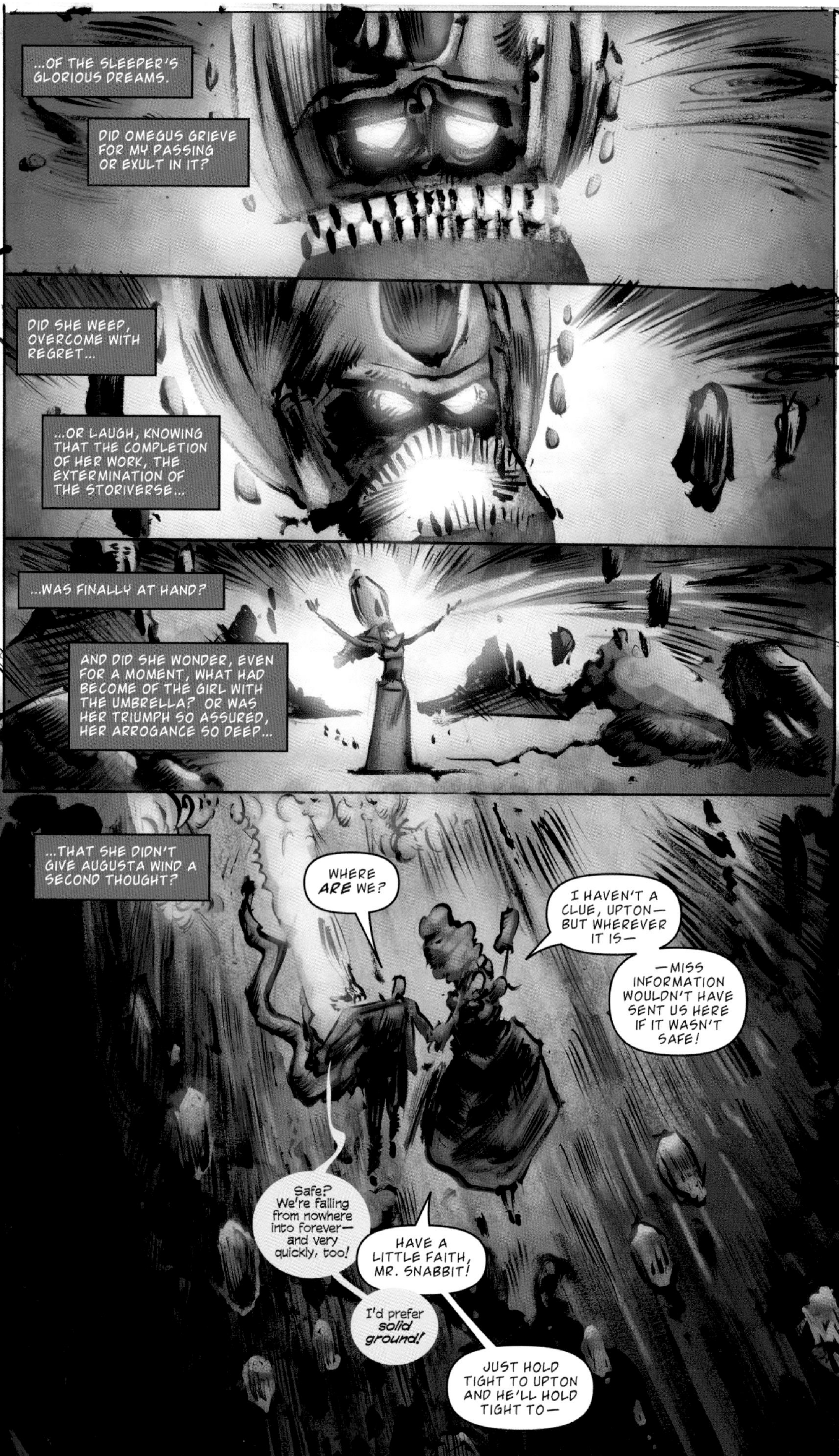
...OF THE SLEEPER'S GLORIOUS DREAMS.
DID OMEGUS GRIEVE FOR MY PASSING OR EXULT IN IT?
DID SHE WEEP, OVERCOME WITH REGRET...
...OR LAUGH, KNOWING THAT THE COMPLETION OF HER WORK, THE EXTERMINATION OF THE STORIVERSE...
...WAS FINALLY AT HAND?
AND DID SHE WONDER, EVEN FOR A MOMENT, WHAT HAD BECOME OF THE GIRL WITH THE UMBRELLA? OR WAS HER TRIUMPH SO ASSURED, HER ARROGANCE SO DEEP...
...THAT SHE DIDN'T GIVE AUGUSTA WIND A SECOND THOUGHT?
WHERE ARE WE?
I HAVEN'T A CLUE, UPTON— BUT WHEREVER IT IS—
—MISS INFORMATION WOULDN'T HAVE SENT US HERE IF IT WASN'T SAFE!
Safe? We're falling from nowhere into forever— and very quickly, too!
HAVE A LITTLE FAITH, MR. SNABBIT!
I'd prefer solid ground!
JUST HOLD TIGHT TO UPTON AND HE'LL HOLD TIGHT TO—

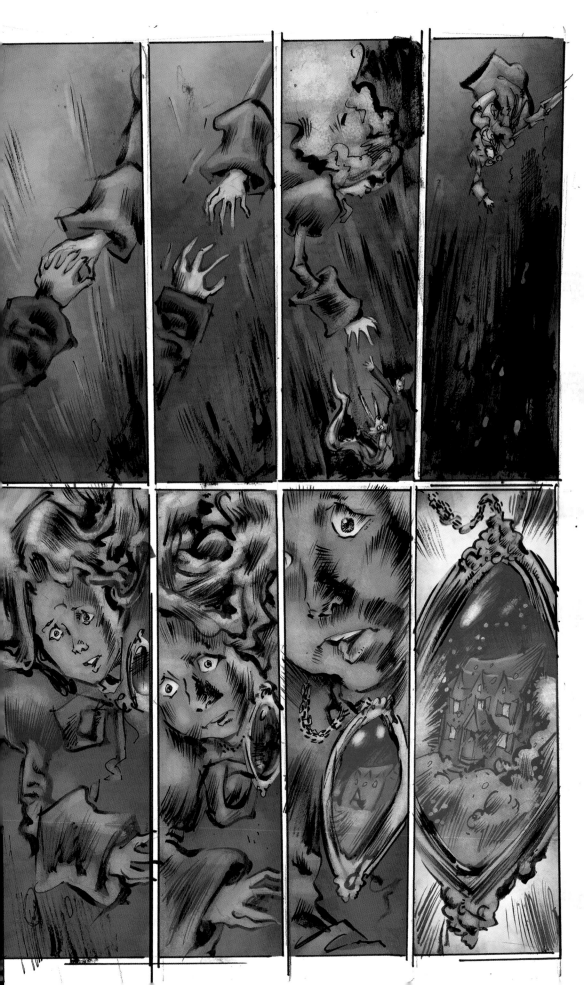

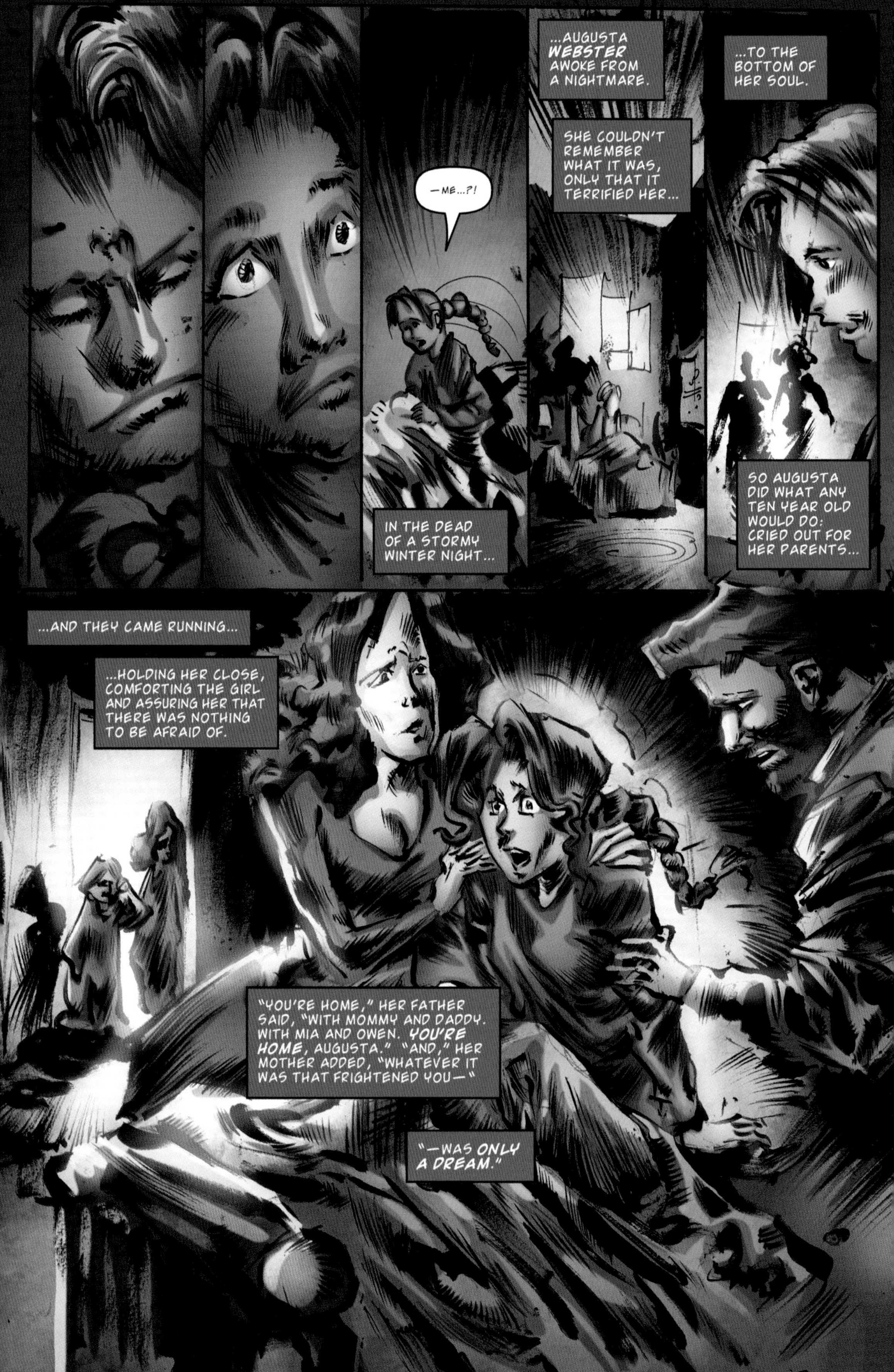
—ME...?!
IN THE DEAD OF A STORMY WINTER NIGHT...
...AUGUSTA WEBSTER AWOKE FROM A NIGHTMARE.
SHE COULDN'T REMEMBER WHAT IT WAS, ONLY THAT IT TERRIFIED HER...
...TO THE BOTTOM OF HER SOUL.
SO AUGUSTA DID WHAT ANY TEN YEAR OLD WOULD DO: CRIED OUT FOR HER PARENTS...
...AND THEY CAME RUNNING...
...HOLDING HER CLOSE, COMFORTING THE GIRL AND ASSURING HER THAT THERE WAS NOTHING TO BE AFRAID OF.
"YOU'RE HOME," HER FATHER SAID, "WITH MOMMY AND DADDY. WITH MIA AND OWEN. YOU'RE HOME, AUGUSTA." "AND," HER MOTHER ADDED, "WHATEVER IT WAS THAT FRIGHTENED YOU—"
"—WAS ONLY A DREAM."

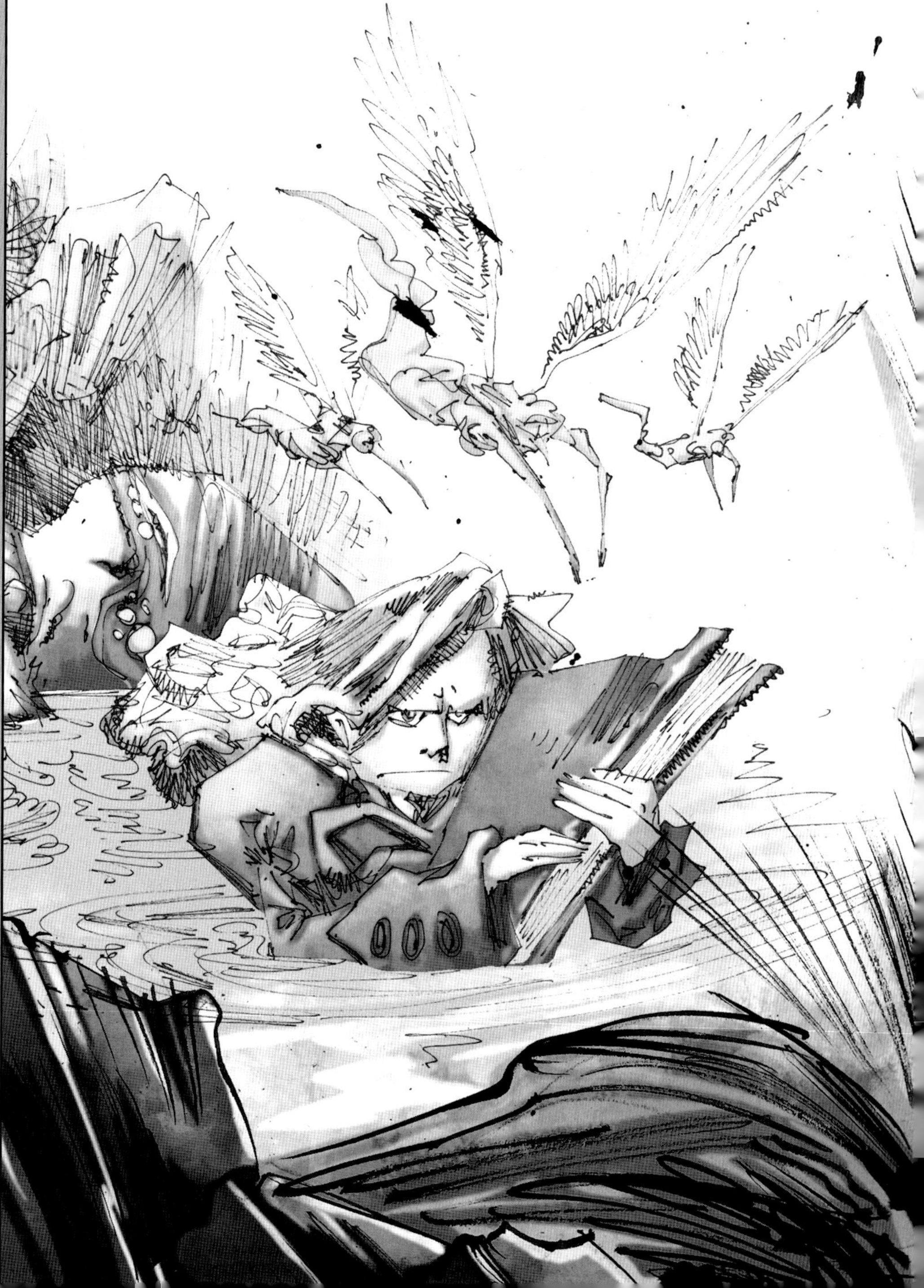

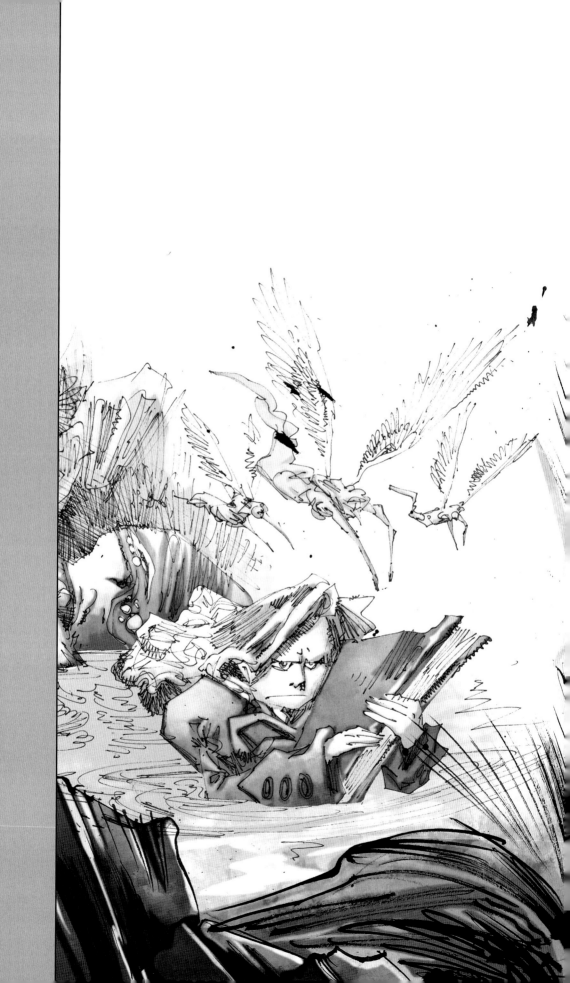

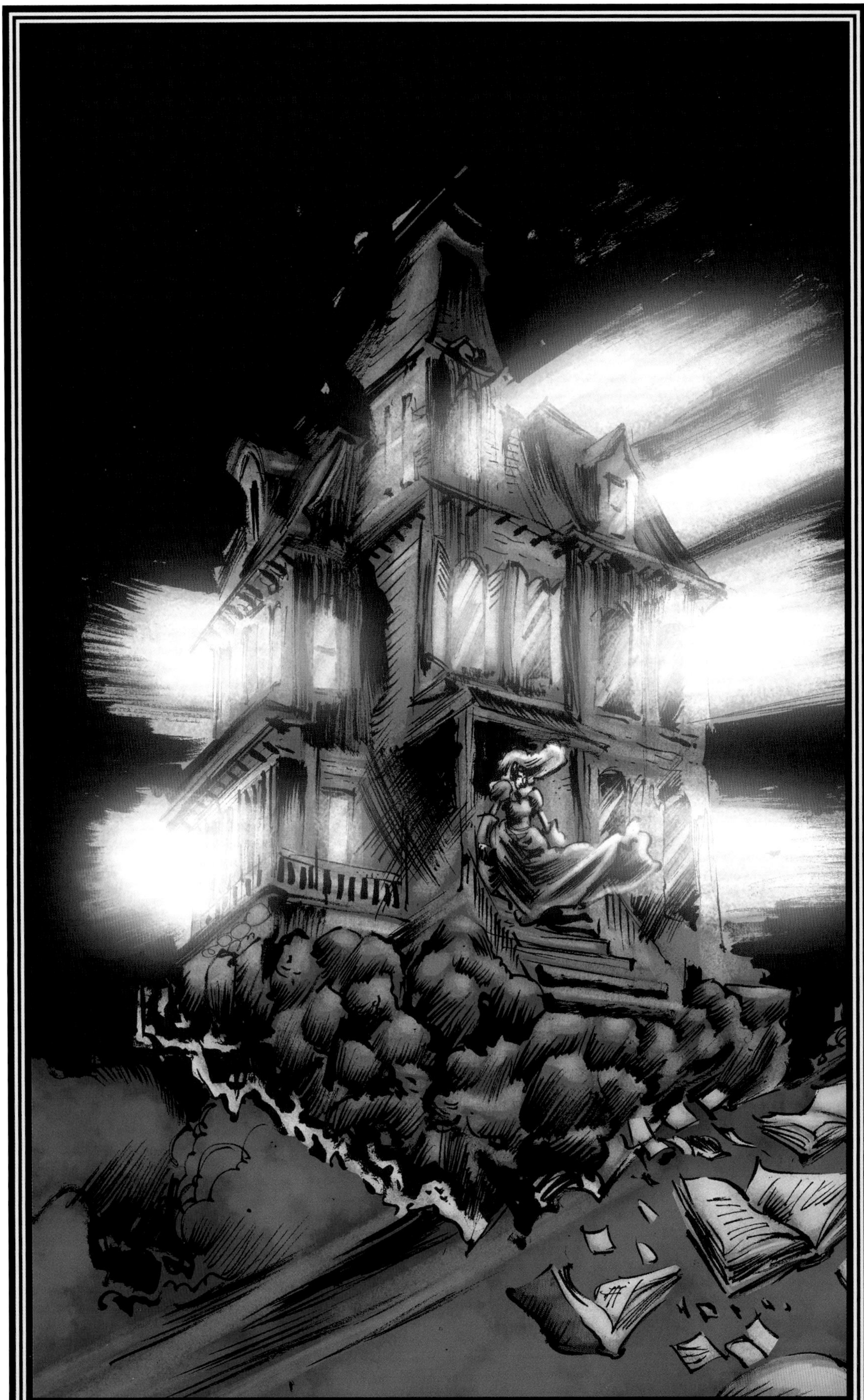

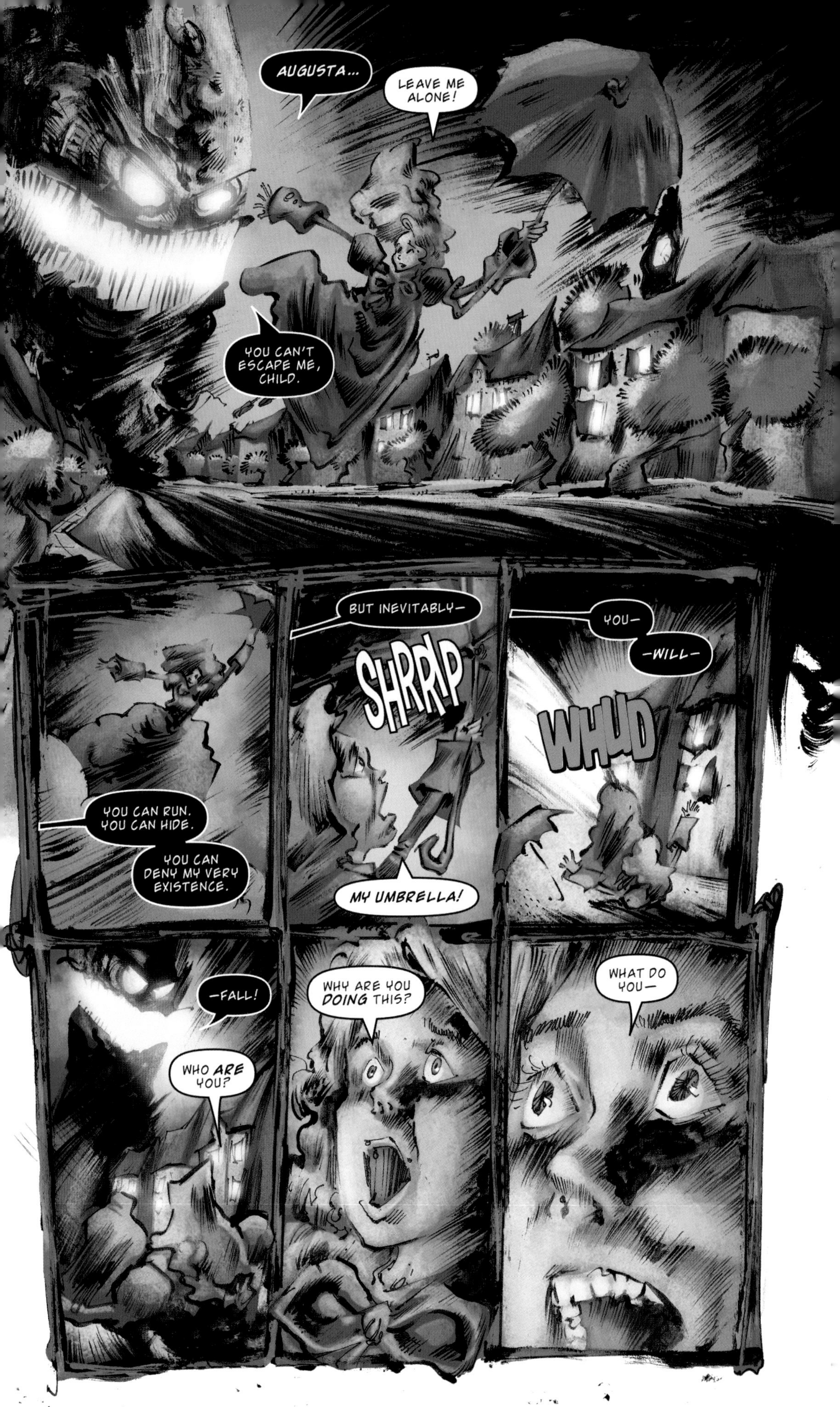
AUGUSTA...
LEAVE ME ALONE!
YOU CAN'T ESCAPE ME, CHILD.
YOU CAN RUN. YOU CAN HIDE.
YOU CAN DENY MY VERY EXISTENCE.
BUT INEVITABLY—
SHRRIP
MY UMBRELLA!
YOU—
—WILL—
WHUD
—FALL!
WHO ARE YOU?
WHY ARE YOU DOING THIS?
WHAT DO YOU—

CHAPTER FOUR: THE ENDLESS END

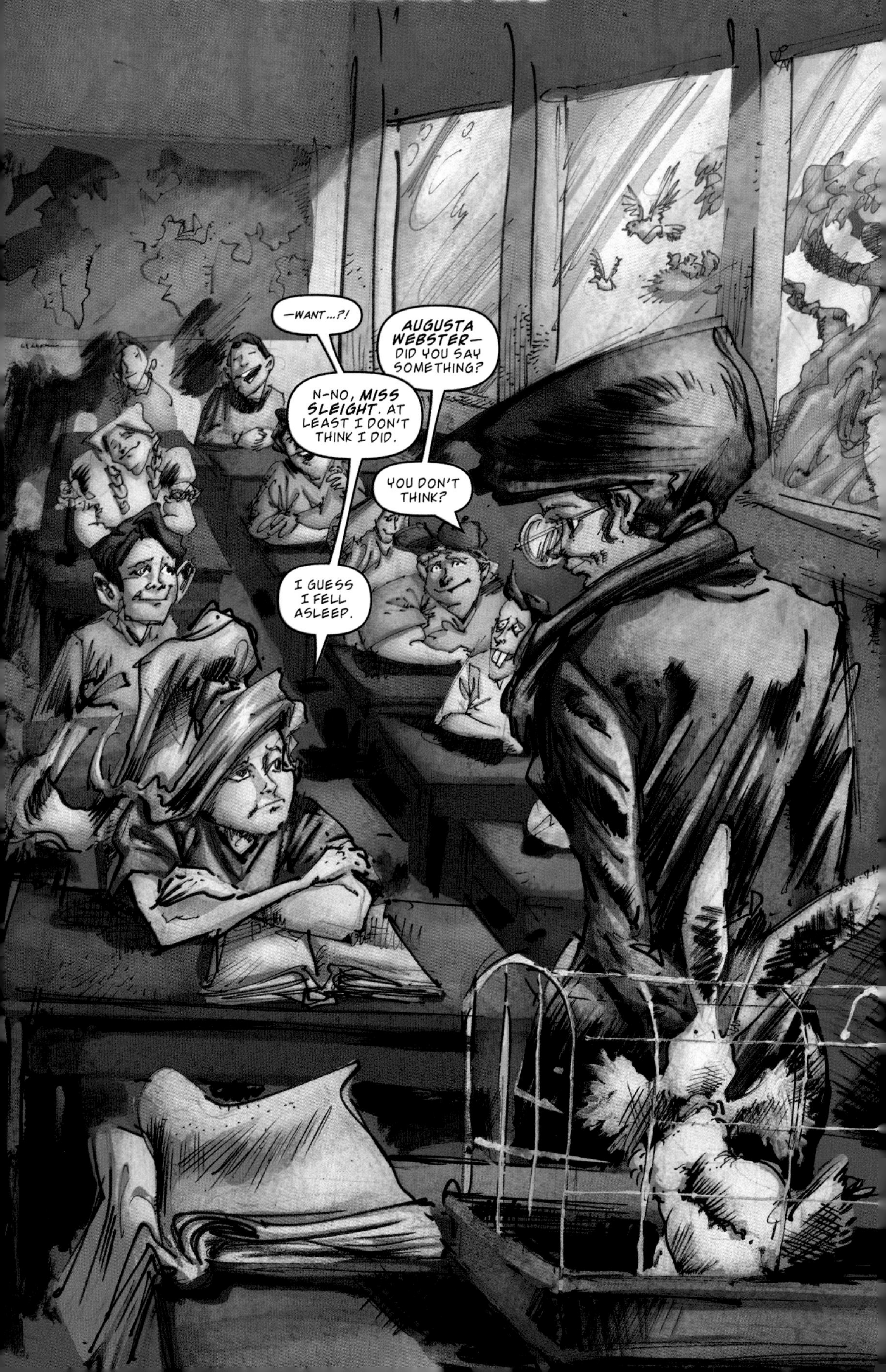
—WANT...?!
AUGUSTA WEBSTER— DID YOU SAY SOMETHING?
N-NO, MISS SLEIGHT. AT LEAST I DON'T THINK I DID.
YOU DON'T THINK?
I GUESS I FELL ASLEEP.

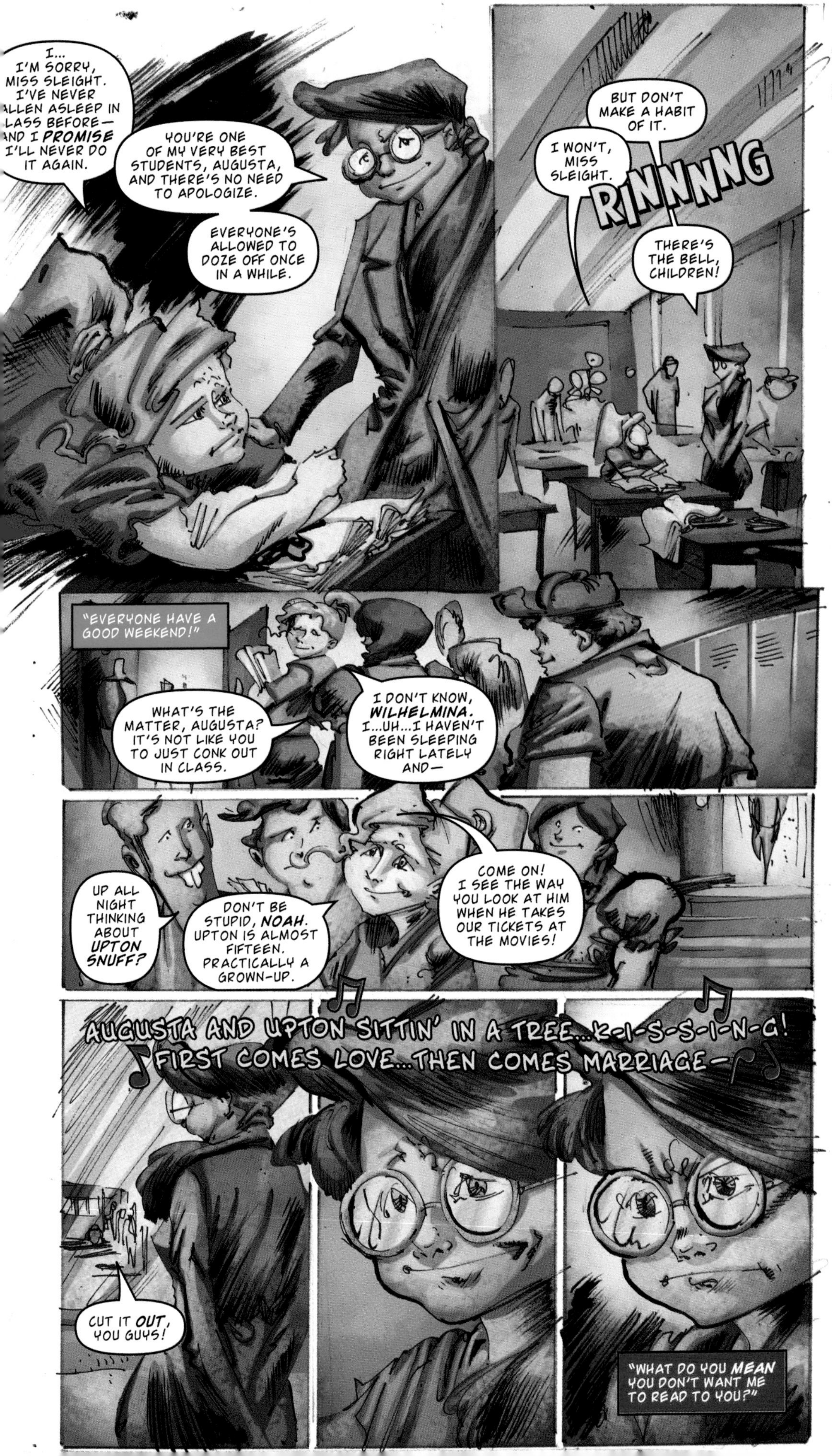
I... I'M SORRY, MISS SLEIGHT. I'VE NEVER FALLEN ASLEEP IN CLASS BEFORE— AND I PROMISE I'LL NEVER DO IT AGAIN.
YOU'RE ONE OF MY VERY BEST STUDENTS, AUGUSTA, AND THERE'S NO NEED TO APOLOGIZE.
EVERYONE'S ALLOWED TO DOZE OFF ONCE IN A WHILE.
BUT DON'T MAKE A HABIT OF IT.
I WON'T, MISS SLEIGHT.
RINNNNG
THERE'S THE BELL, CHILDREN!
"EVERYONE HAVE A GOOD WEEKEND!"
WHAT'S THE MATTER, AUGUSTA? IT'S NOT LIKE YOU TO JUST CONK OUT IN CLASS.
I DON'T KNOW, WILHELMINA. I...UH...I HAVEN'T BEEN SLEEPING RIGHT LATELY AND—
UP ALL NIGHT THINKING ABOUT UPTON SNUFF?
DON'T BE STUPID, NOAH. UPTON IS ALMOST FIFTEEN. PRACTICALLY A GROWN-UP.
COME ON! I SEE THE WAY YOU LOOK AT HIM WHEN HE TAKES OUR TICKETS AT THE MOVIES!
AUGUSTA AND UPTON SITTIN' IN A TREE...K-I-S-S-I-N-G!
FIRST COMES LOVE...THEN COMES MARRIAGE—
CUT IT OUT, YOU GUYS!
"WHAT DO YOU MEAN YOU DON'T WANT ME TO READ TO YOU?"

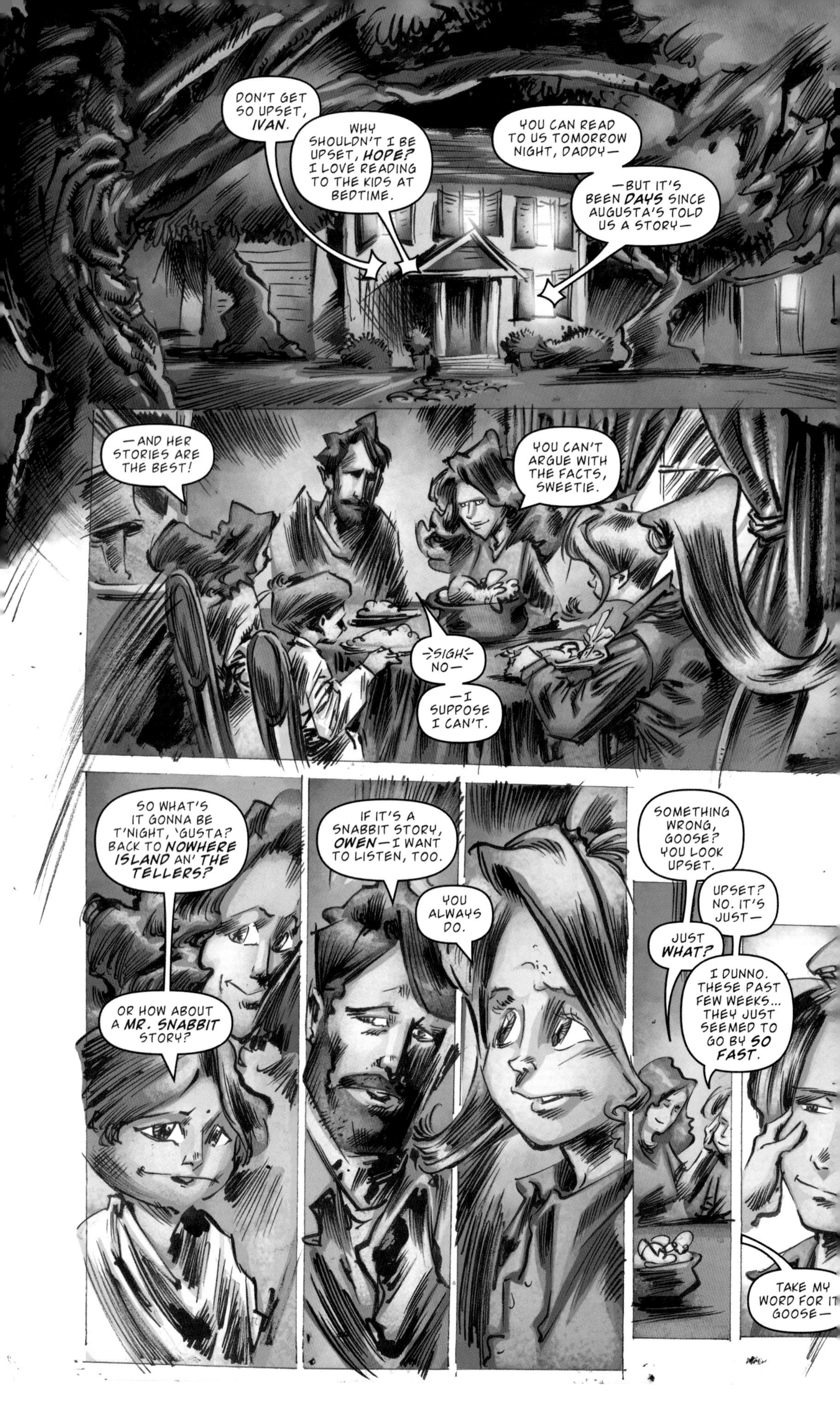
DON'T GET SO UPSET, IVAN.
WHY SHOULDN'T I BE UPSET, HOPE? I LOVE READING TO THE KIDS AT BEDTIME.
YOU CAN READ TO US TOMORROW NIGHT, DADDY—
—BUT IT'S BEEN DAYS SINCE AUGUSTA'S TOLD US A STORY—
—AND HER STORIES ARE THE BEST!
YOU CAN'T ARGUE WITH THE FACTS, SWEETIE.
-SIGH- NO—
—I SUPPOSE I CAN'T.
SO WHAT'S IT GONNA BE T'NIGHT, 'GUSTA? BACK TO NOWHERE ISLAND AN' THE TELLERS?
OR HOW ABOUT A MR. SNABBIT STORY?
IF IT'S A SNABBIT STORY, OWEN—I WANT TO LISTEN, TOO.
YOU ALWAYS DO.
SOMETHING WRONG, GOOSE? YOU LOOK UPSET.
UPSET? NO. IT'S JUST—
JUST WHAT?
I DUNNO. THESE PAST FEW WEEKS... THEY JUST SEEMED TO GO BY SO FAST.
TAKE MY WORD FOR IT GOOSE—

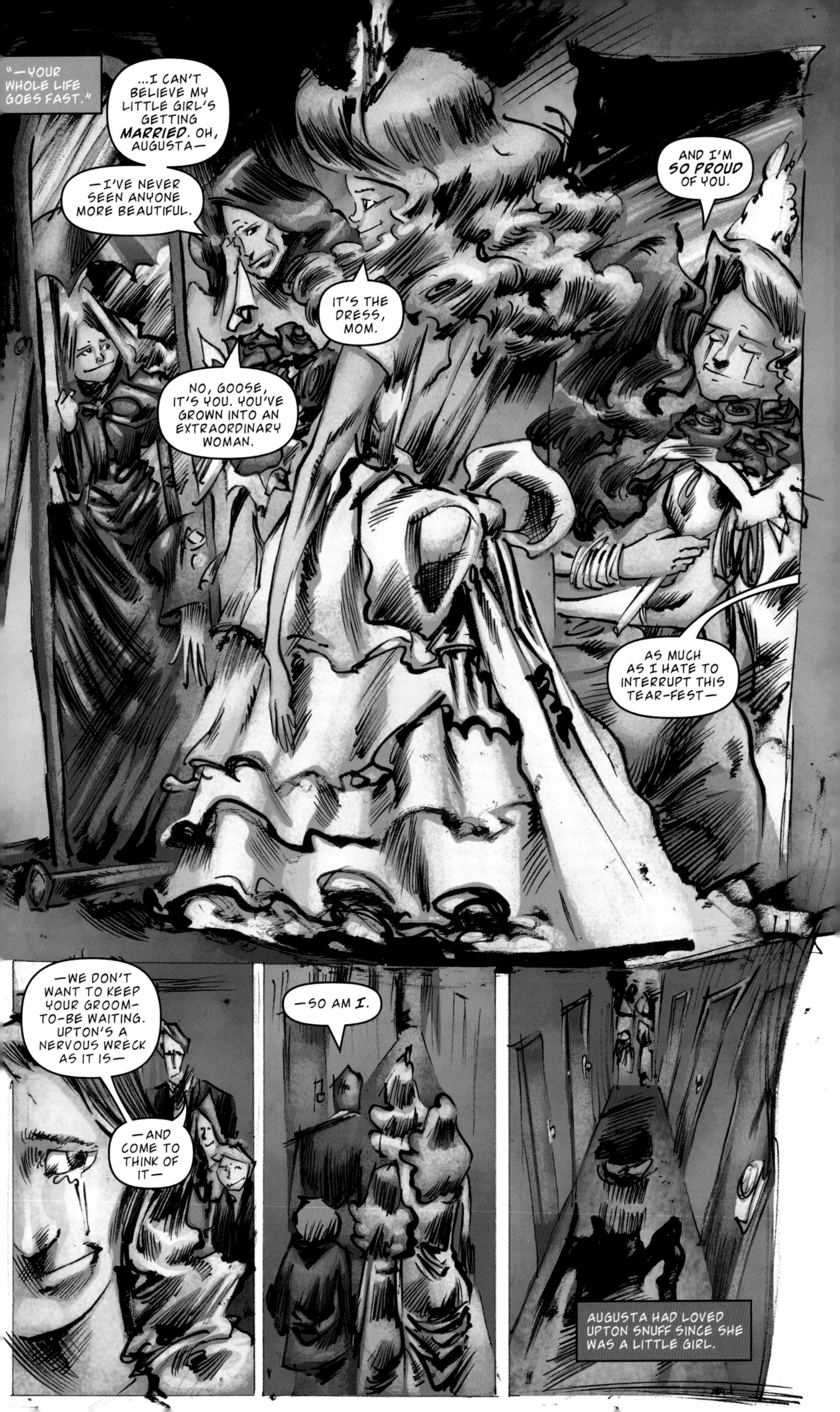
"—YOUR WHOLE LIFE GOES FAST."
...I CAN'T BELIEVE MY LITTLE GIRL'S GETTING **MARRIED**. OH, AUGUSTA—
—I'VE NEVER SEEN ANYONE MORE BEAUTIFUL.
AND I'M **SO PROUD** OF YOU.
IT'S THE DRESS, MOM.
NO, GOOSE, IT'S YOU. YOU'VE GROWN INTO AN EXTRAORDINARY WOMAN.
AS MUCH AS I HATE TO INTERRUPT THIS TEAR-FEST—
—WE DON'T WANT TO KEEP YOUR GROOM-TO-BE WAITING. UPTON'S A NERVOUS WRECK AS IT IS—
—AND COME TO THINK OF IT—
—SO AM *I*.
AUGUSTA HAD LOVED UPTON SNUFF SINCE SHE WAS A LITTLE GIRL.

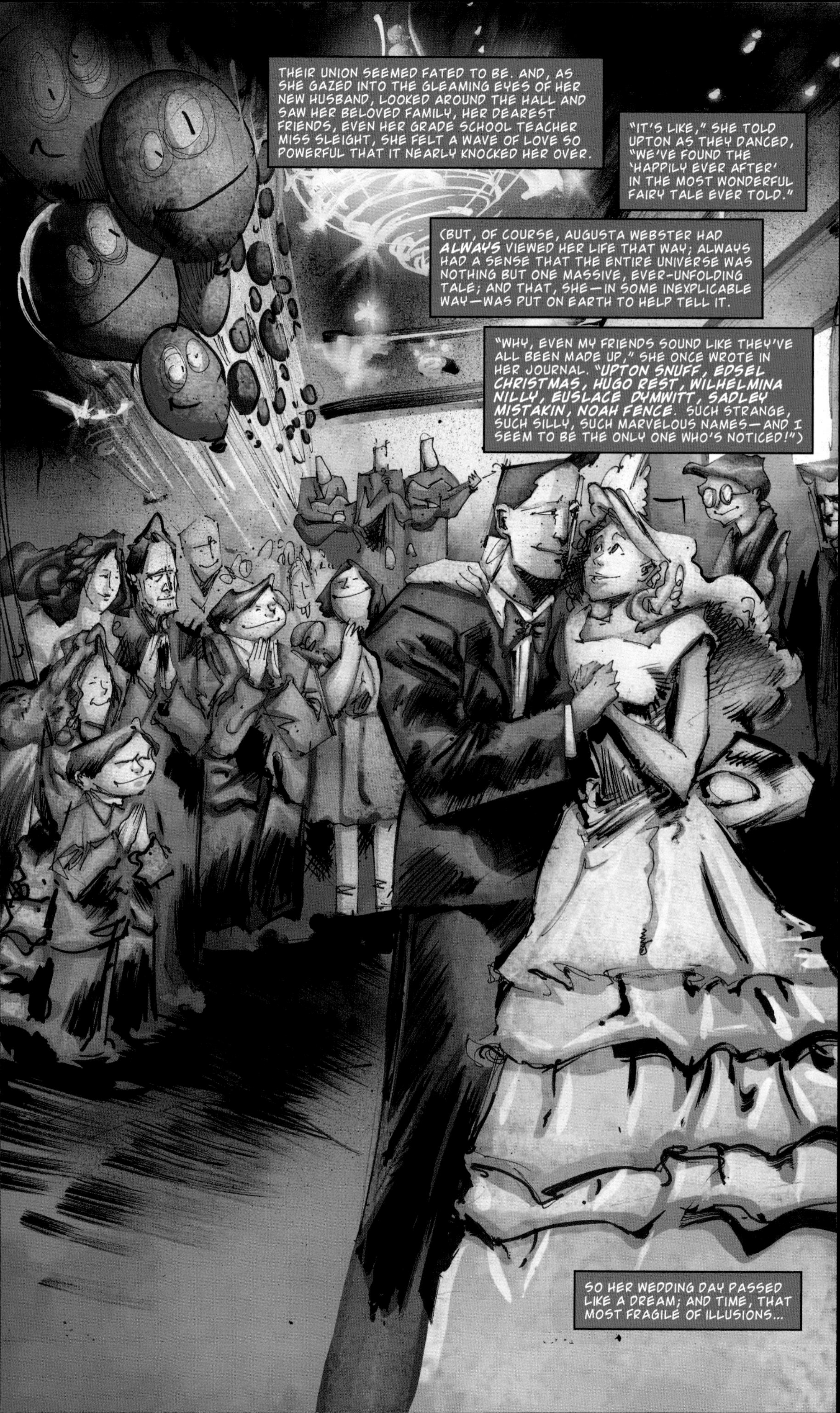
THEIR UNION SEEMED FATED TO BE. AND, AS SHE GAZED INTO THE GLEAMING EYES OF HER NEW HUSBAND, LOOKED AROUND THE HALL AND SAW HER BELOVED FAMILY, HER DEAREST FRIENDS, EVEN HER GRADE SCHOOL TEACHER MISS SLEIGHT, SHE FELT A WAVE OF LOVE SO POWERFUL THAT IT NEARLY KNOCKED HER OVER.
"IT'S LIKE," SHE TOLD UPTON AS THEY DANCED, "WE'VE FOUND THE 'HAPPILY EVER AFTER' IN THE MOST WONDERFUL FAIRY TALE EVER TOLD."
(BUT, OF COURSE, AUGUSTA WEBSTER HAD **ALWAYS** VIEWED HER LIFE THAT WAY; ALWAYS HAD A SENSE THAT THE ENTIRE UNIVERSE WAS NOTHING BUT ONE MASSIVE, EVER-UNFOLDING TALE; AND THAT, SHE—IN SOME INEXPLICABLE WAY—WAS PUT ON EARTH TO HELP TELL IT.
"WHY, EVEN MY FRIENDS SOUND LIKE THEY'VE ALL BEEN MADE UP," SHE ONCE WROTE IN HER JOURNAL. "***UPTON SNUFF, EDSEL CHRISTMAS, HUGO REST, WILHELMINA NILLY, EUSLACE DYMWITT, SADLEY MISTAKIN, NOAH FENCE.*** SUCH STRANGE, SUCH SILLY, SUCH MARVELOUS NAMES—AND I SEEM TO BE THE ONLY ONE WHO'S NOTICED!")
SO HER WEDDING DAY PASSED LIKE A DREAM; AND TIME, THAT MOST FRAGILE OF ILLUSIONS...

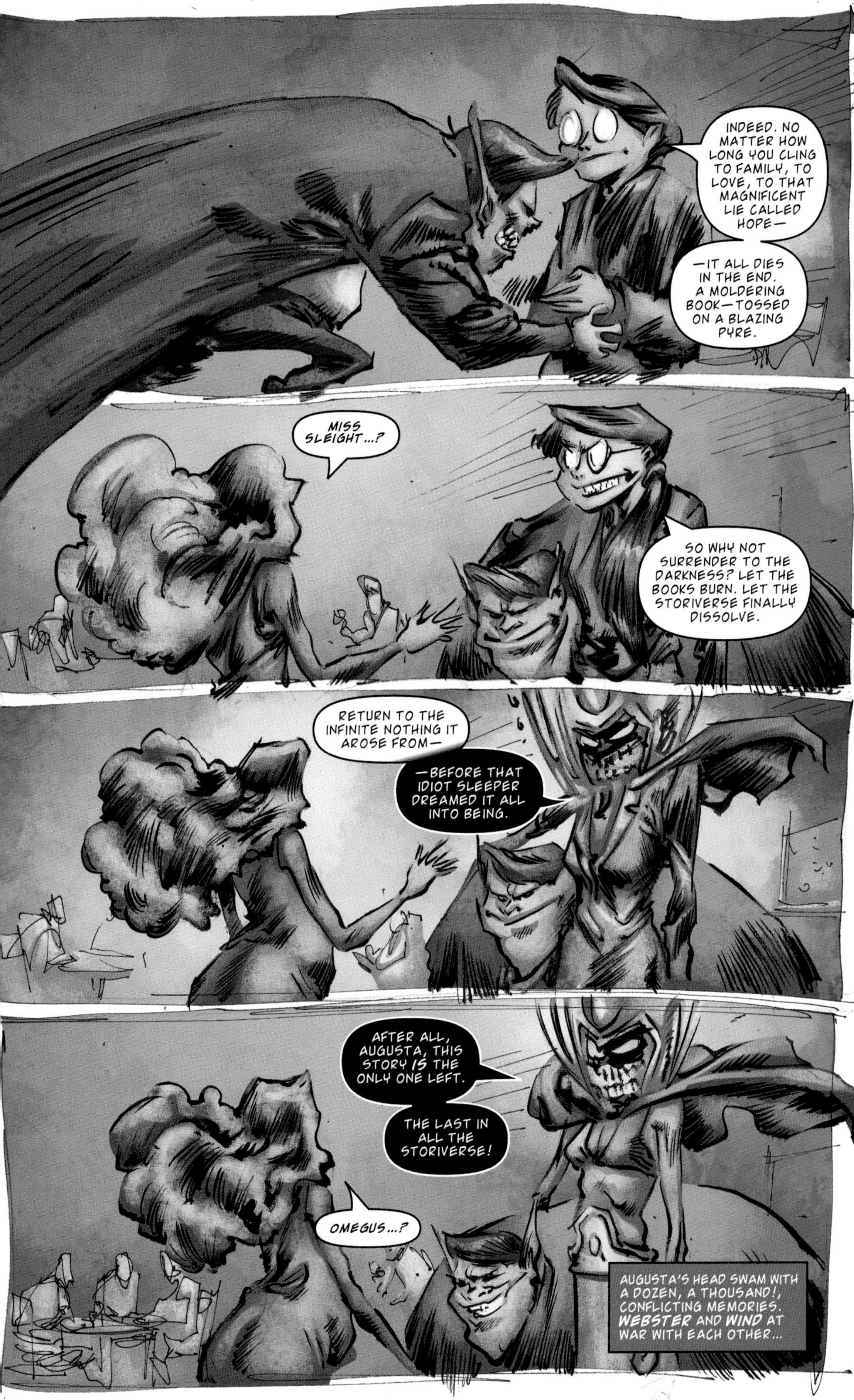
INDEED. NO MATTER HOW LONG YOU CLING TO FAMILY, TO LOVE, TO THAT MAGNIFICENT LIE CALLED HOPE—
—IT ALL DIES IN THE END. A MOLDERING BOOK—TOSSED ON A BLAZING PYRE.
MISS SLEIGHT...?
SO WHY NOT SURRENDER TO THE DARKNESS? LET THE BOOKS BURN. LET THE STORIVERSE FINALLY DISSOLVE.
RETURN TO THE INFINITE NOTHING IT AROSE FROM—
—BEFORE THAT IDIOT SLEEPER DREAMED IT ALL INTO BEING.
AFTER ALL, AUGUSTA, THIS STORY IS THE ONLY ONE LEFT.
THE LAST IN ALL THE STORIVERSE!
OMEGUS...?
AUGUSTA'S HEAD SWAM WITH A DOZEN, A THOUSAND!, CONFLICTING MEMORIES. WEBSTER AND WIND AT WAR WITH EACH OTHER...

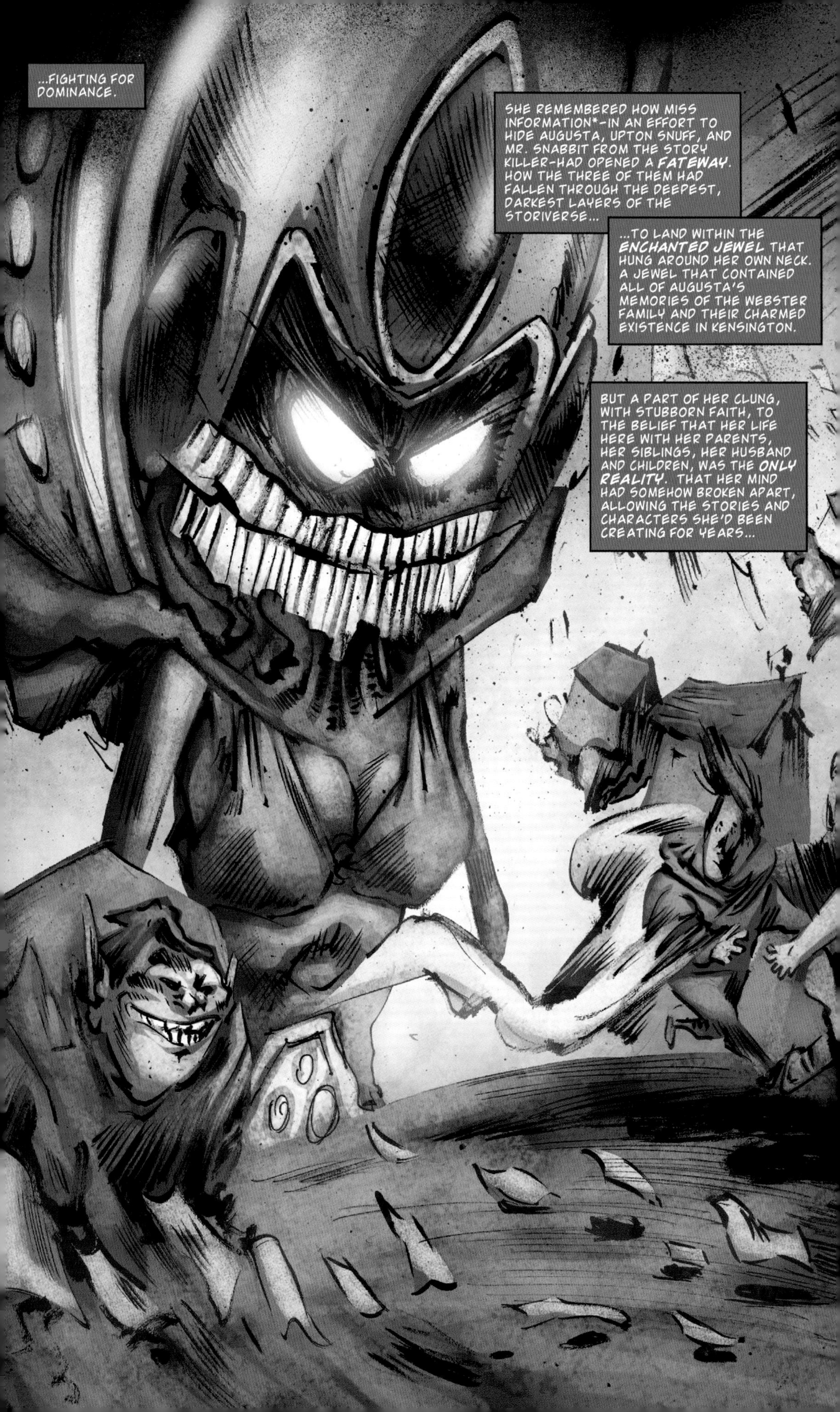
...FIGHTING FOR DOMINANCE.
SHE REMEMBERED HOW MISS INFORMATION*-IN AN EFFORT TO HIDE AUGUSTA, UPTON SNUFF, AND MR. SNABBIT FROM THE STORY KILLER-HAD OPENED A **FATEWAY**. HOW THE THREE OF THEM HAD FALLEN THROUGH THE DEEPEST, DARKEST LAYERS OF THE STORIVERSE...
...TO LAND WITHIN THE **ENCHANTED JEWEL** THAT HUNG AROUND HER OWN NECK. A JEWEL THAT CONTAINED ALL OF AUGUSTA'S MEMORIES OF THE WEBSTER FAMILY AND THEIR CHARMED EXISTENCE IN KENSINGTON.
BUT A PART OF HER CLUNG, WITH STUBBORN FAITH, TO THE BELIEF THAT HER LIFE HERE WITH HER PARENTS, HER SIBLINGS, HER HUSBAND AND CHILDREN, WAS THE **ONLY REALITY**. THAT HER MIND HAD SOMEHOW BROKEN APART, ALLOWING THE STORIES AND CHARACTERS SHE'D BEEN CREATING FOR YEARS...

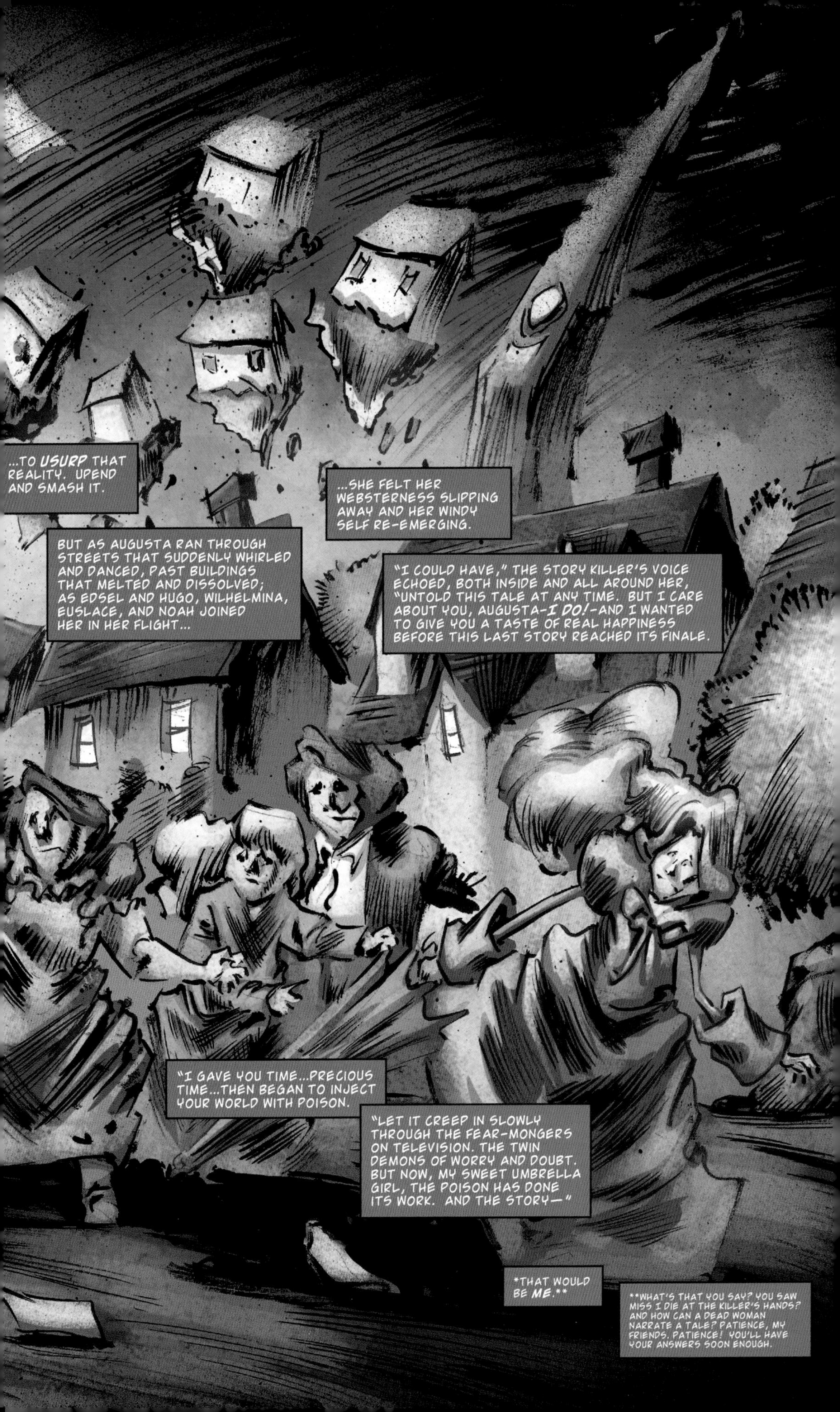
...TO *USURP* THAT REALITY. UPEND AND SMASH IT.
...SHE FELT HER WEBSTERNESS SLIPPING AWAY AND HER WINDY SELF RE-EMERGING.
BUT AS AUGUSTA RAN THROUGH STREETS THAT SUDDENLY WHIRLED AND DANCED, PAST BUILDINGS THAT MELTED AND DISSOLVED; AS EDSEL AND HUGO, WILHELMINA, EUSLACE, AND NOAH JOINED HER IN HER FLIGHT...
"I COULD HAVE," THE STORY KILLER'S VOICE ECHOED, BOTH INSIDE AND ALL AROUND HER, "UNTOLD THIS TALE AT ANY TIME. BUT I CARE ABOUT YOU, AUGUSTA-*I DO!*-AND I WANTED TO GIVE YOU A TASTE OF REAL HAPPINESS BEFORE THIS LAST STORY REACHED ITS FINALE.
"I GAVE YOU TIME...PRECIOUS TIME...THEN BEGAN TO INJECT YOUR WORLD WITH POISON.
"LET IT CREEP IN SLOWLY THROUGH THE FEAR-MONGERS ON TELEVISION. THE TWIN DEMONS OF WORRY AND DOUBT. BUT NOW, MY SWEET UMBRELLA GIRL, THE POISON HAS DONE ITS WORK. AND THE STORY—"
*THAT WOULD BE *ME*.**
**WHAT'S THAT YOU SAY? YOU SAW MISS I DIE AT THE KILLER'S HANDS? AND HOW CAN A DEAD WOMAN NARRATE A TALE? PATIENCE, MY FRIENDS. PATIENCE! YOU'LL HAVE YOUR ANSWERS SOON ENOUGH.

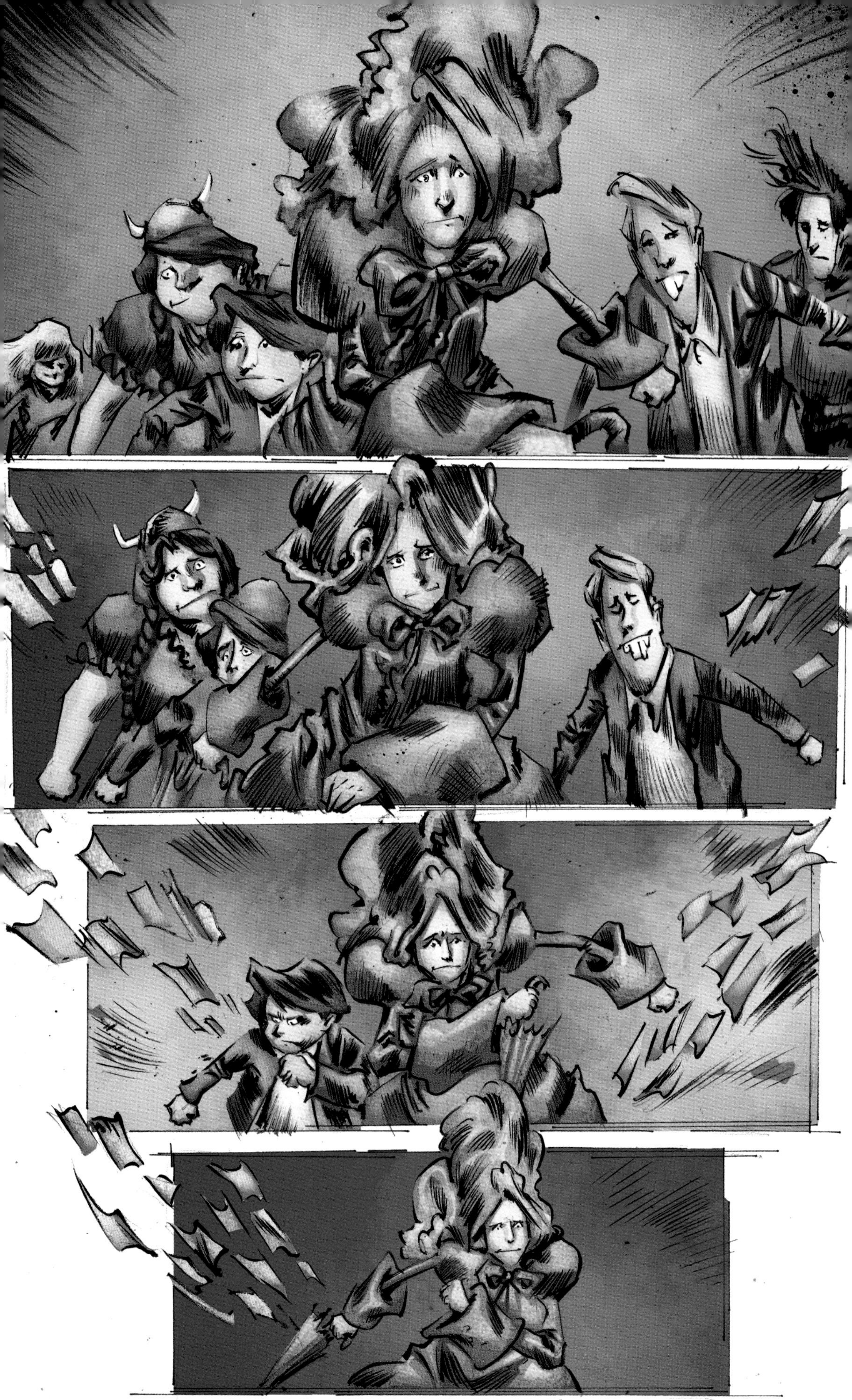

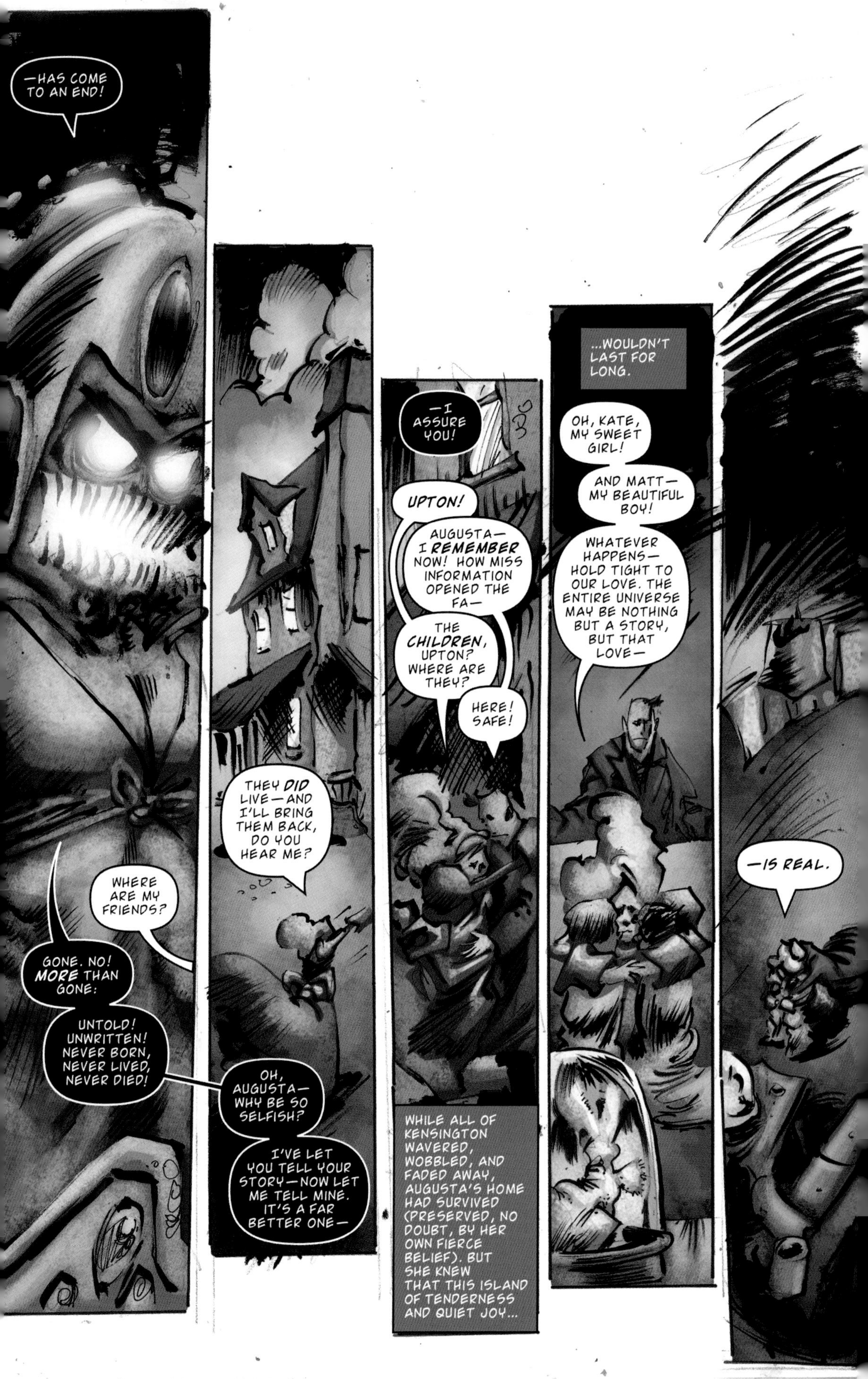
—HAS COME TO AN END!
WHERE ARE MY FRIENDS?
GONE. NO! MORE THAN GONE:
UNTOLD! UNWRITTEN! NEVER BORN, NEVER LIVED, NEVER DIED!
THEY DID LIVE—AND I'LL BRING THEM BACK, DO YOU HEAR ME?
OH, AUGUSTA—WHY BE SO SELFISH?
I'VE LET YOU TELL YOUR STORY—NOW LET ME TELL MINE. IT'S A FAR BETTER ONE—
—I ASSURE YOU!
UPTON!
AUGUSTA—I REMEMBER NOW! HOW MISS INFORMATION OPENED THE FA—
THE CHILDREN, UPTON? WHERE ARE THEY?
HERE! SAFE!
WHILE ALL OF KENSINGTON WAVERED, WOBBLED, AND FADED AWAY, AUGUSTA'S HOME HAD SURVIVED (PRESERVED, NO DOUBT, BY HER OWN FIERCE BELIEF). BUT SHE KNEW THAT THIS ISLAND OF TENDERNESS AND QUIET JOY...
...WOULDN'T LAST FOR LONG.
OH, KATE, MY SWEET GIRL!
AND MATT—MY BEAUTIFUL BOY!
WHATEVER HAPPENS—HOLD TIGHT TO OUR LOVE. THE ENTIRE UNIVERSE MAY BE NOTHING BUT A STORY, BUT THAT LOVE—
—IS REAL.

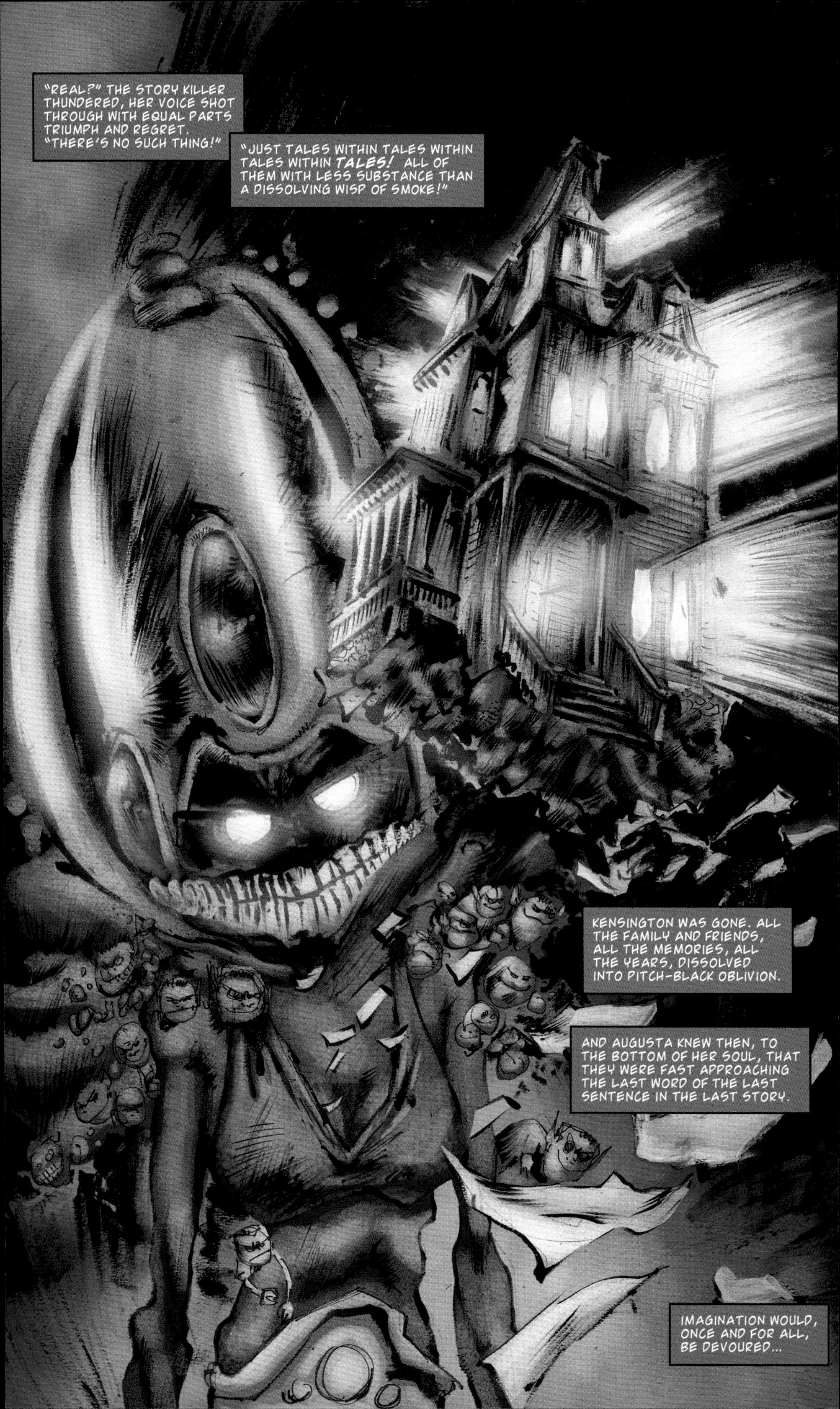
"REAL?" THE STORY KILLER THUNDERED, HER VOICE SHOT THROUGH WITH EQUAL PARTS TRIUMPH AND REGRET. "THERE'S NO SUCH THING!"
"JUST TALES WITHIN TALES WITHIN TALES WITHIN TALES! ALL OF THEM WITH LESS SUBSTANCE THAN A DISSOLVING WISP OF SMOKE!"
KENSINGTON WAS GONE. ALL THE FAMILY AND FRIENDS, ALL THE MEMORIES, ALL THE YEARS, DISSOLVED INTO PITCH-BLACK OBLIVION.
AND AUGUSTA KNEW THEN, TO THE BOTTOM OF HER SOUL, THAT THEY WERE FAST APPROACHING THE LAST WORD OF THE LAST SENTENCE IN THE LAST STORY.
IMAGINATION WOULD, ONCE AND FOR ALL, BE DEVOURED...

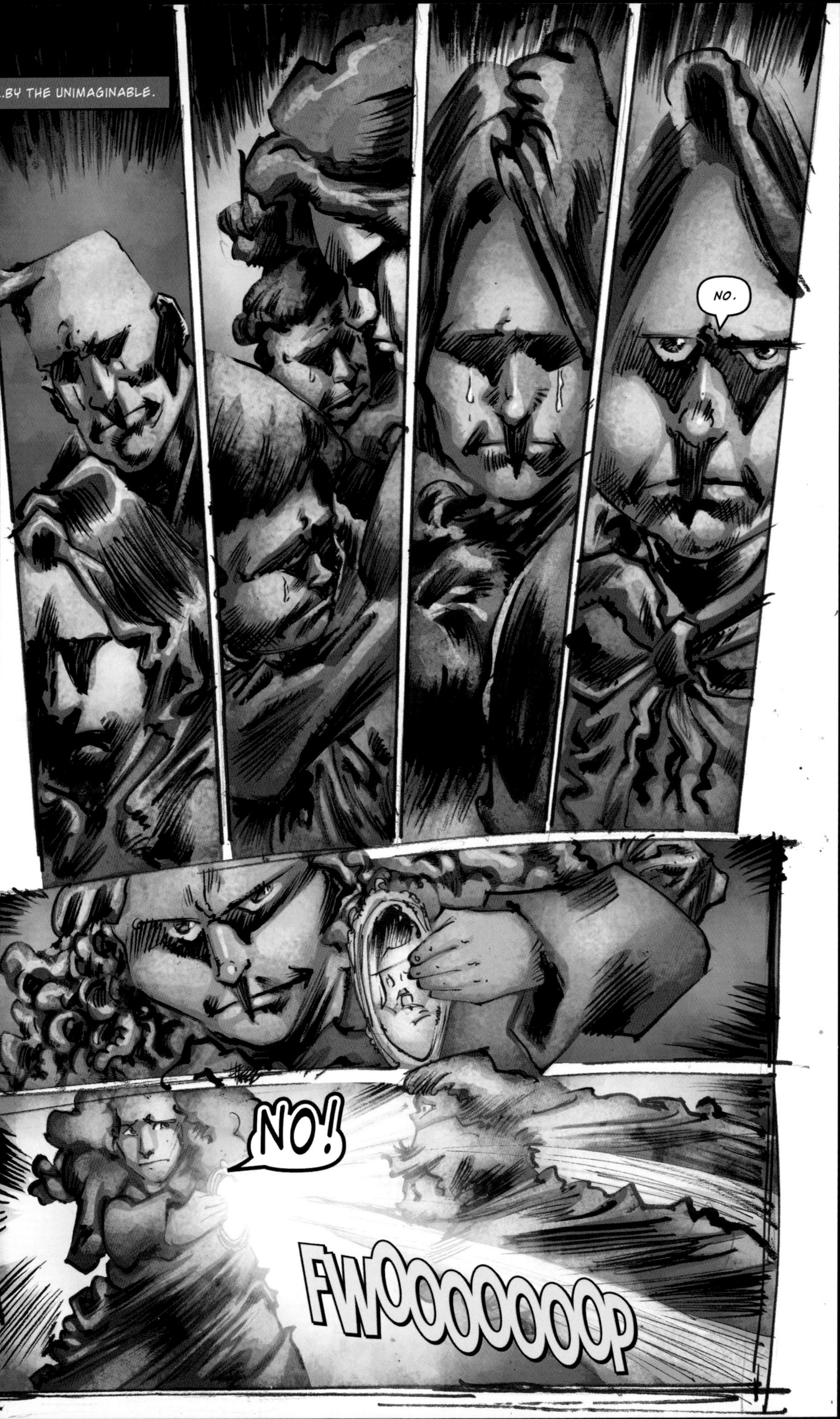
...BY THE UNIMAGINABLE.
NO.
NO!
FWOOOOOOOP

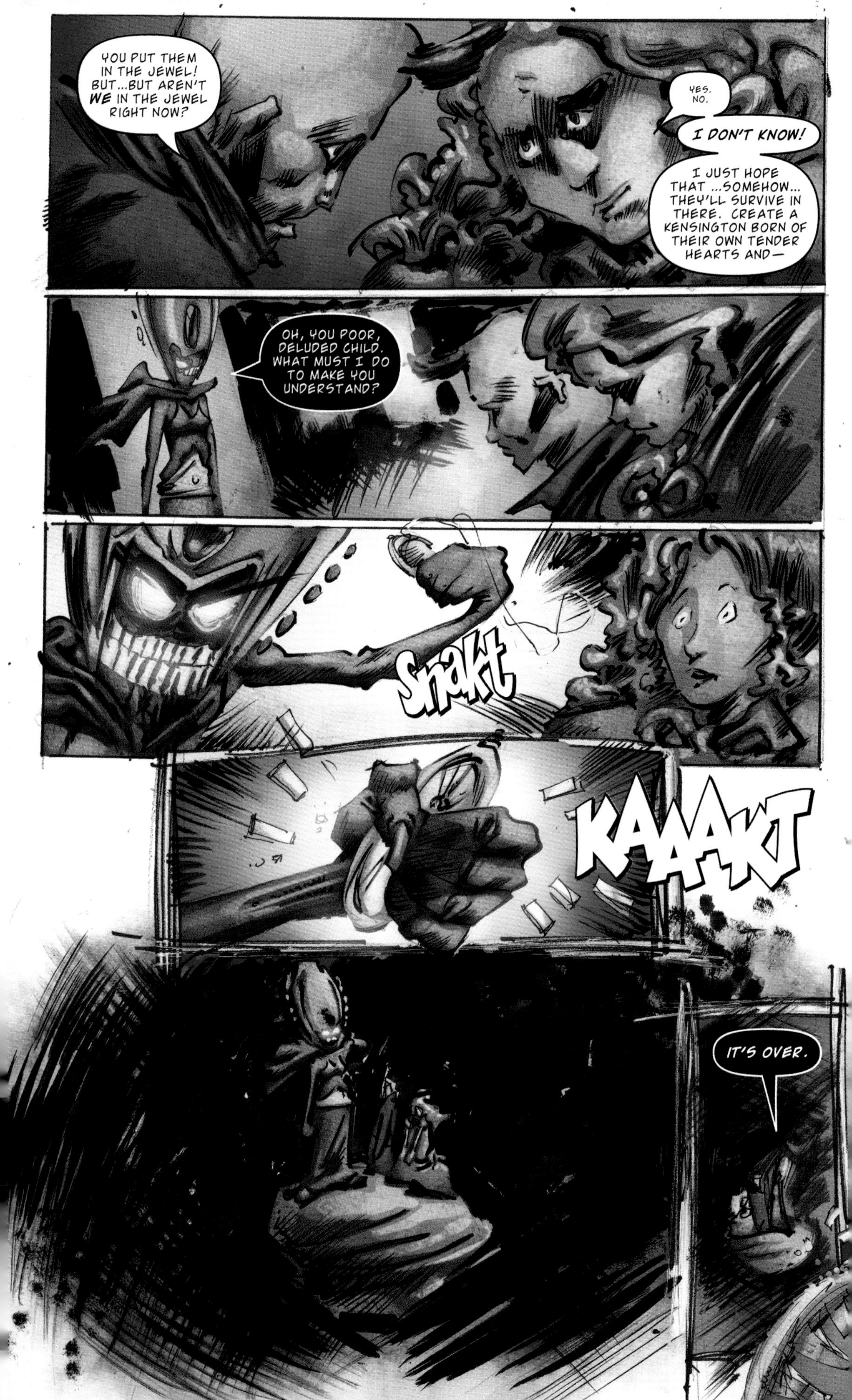
YOU PUT THEM IN THE JEWEL! BUT...BUT AREN'T WE IN THE JEWEL RIGHT NOW?
YES. NO.
I DON'T KNOW!
I JUST HOPE THAT ...SOMEHOW... THEY'LL SURVIVE IN THERE. CREATE A KENSINGTON BORN OF THEIR OWN TENDER HEARTS AND—
OH, YOU POOR, DELUDED CHILD. WHAT MUST I DO TO MAKE YOU UNDERSTAND?
SNAKT
KAAAKT
IT'S OVER.

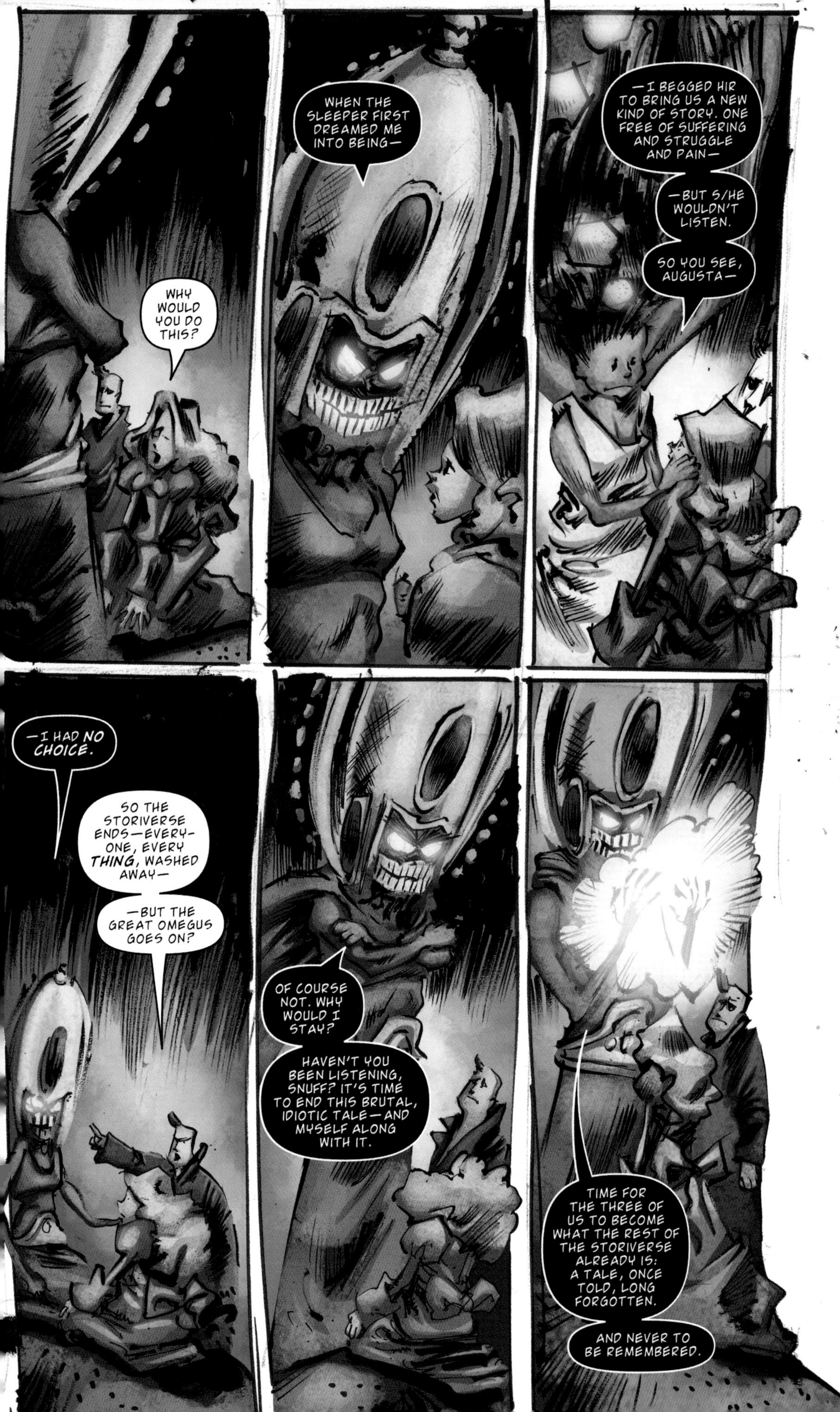

WHY WOULD YOU DO THIS?
WHEN THE SLEEPER FIRST DREAMED ME INTO BEING—
—I BEGGED HIR TO BRING US A NEW KIND OF STORY. ONE FREE OF SUFFERING AND STRUGGLE AND PAIN—
—BUT S/HE WOULDN'T LISTEN.
SO YOU SEE, AUGUSTA—
—I HAD NO CHOICE.
SO THE STORIVERSE ENDS—EVERY-ONE, EVERY THING, WASHED AWAY—
—BUT THE GREAT OMEGUS GOES ON?
OF COURSE NOT. WHY WOULD I STAY?
HAVEN'T YOU BEEN LISTENING, SNUFF? IT'S TIME TO END THIS BRUTAL, IDIOTIC TALE—AND MYSELF ALONG WITH IT.
TIME FOR THE THREE OF US TO BECOME WHAT THE REST OF THE STORIVERSE ALREADY IS: A TALE, ONCE TOLD, LONG FORGOTTEN.
AND NEVER TO BE REMEMBERED.

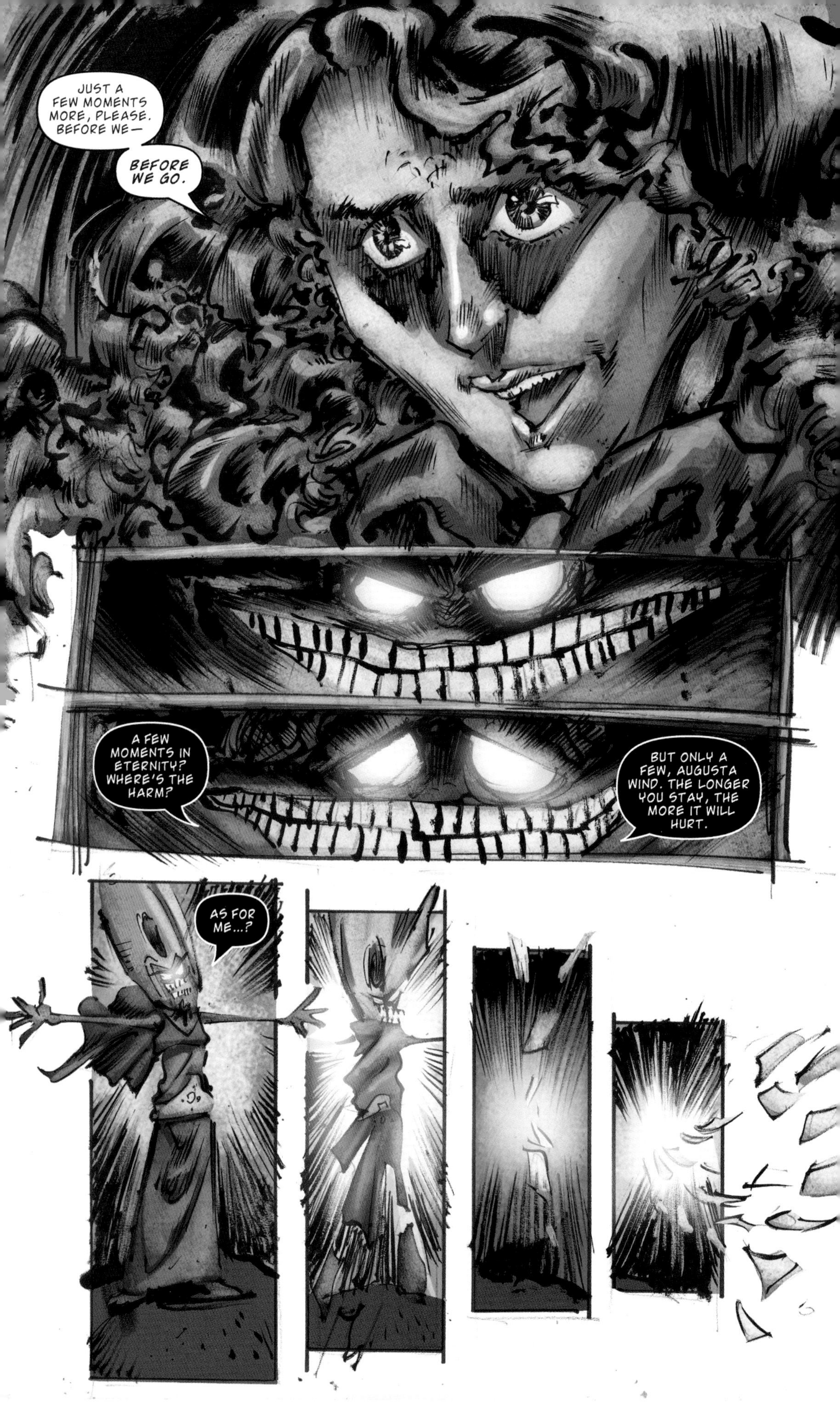
JUST A FEW MOMENTS MORE, PLEASE. BEFORE WE—
BEFORE WE GO.
A FEW MOMENTS IN ETERNITY? WHERE'S THE HARM?
BUT ONLY A FEW, AUGUSTA WIND. THE LONGER YOU STAY, THE MORE IT WILL HURT.
AS FOR ME...?

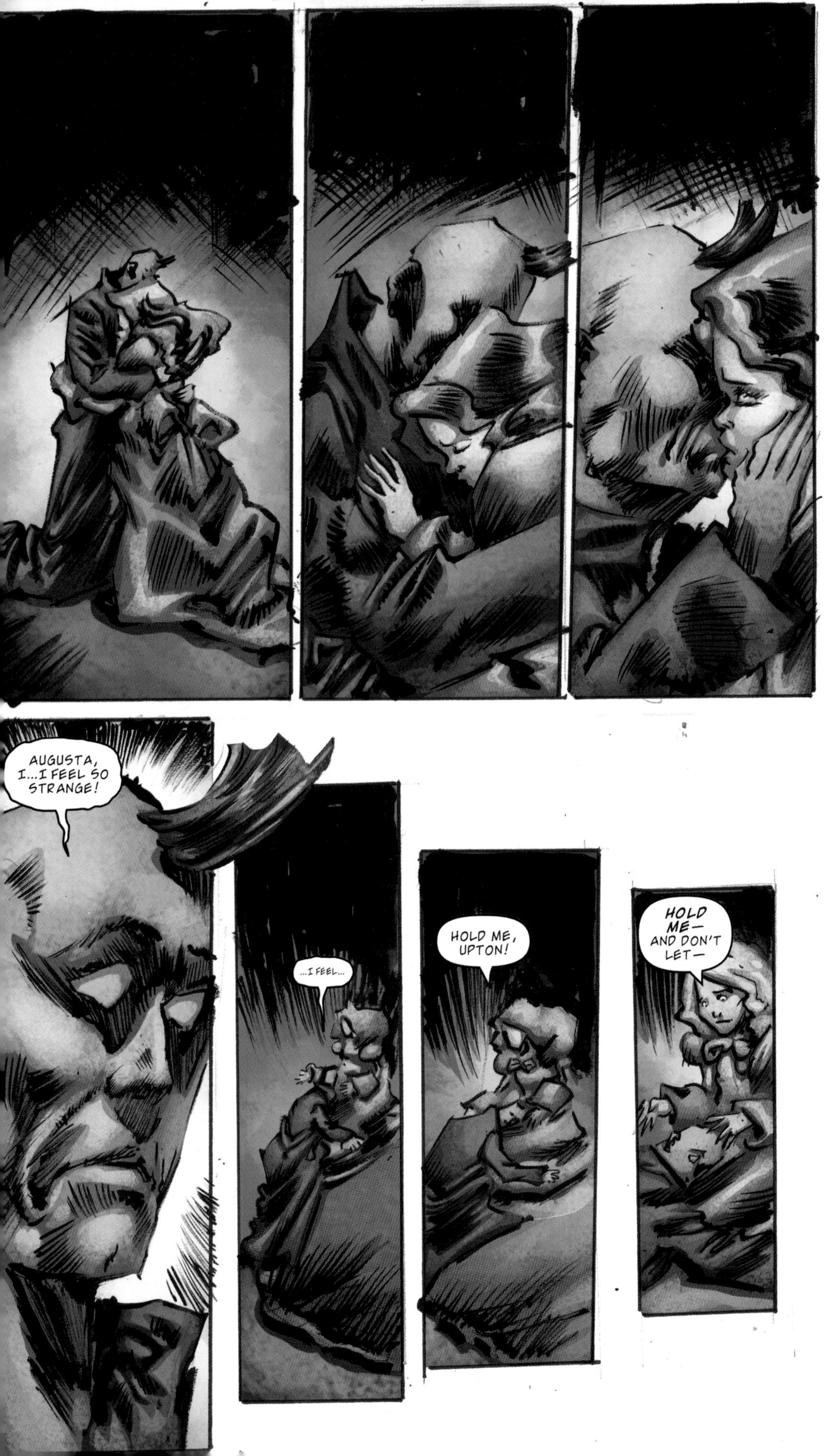
AUGUSTA, I...I FEEL SO STRANGE!
...I FEEL...
HOLD ME, UPTON!
HOLD ME— AND DON'T LET—

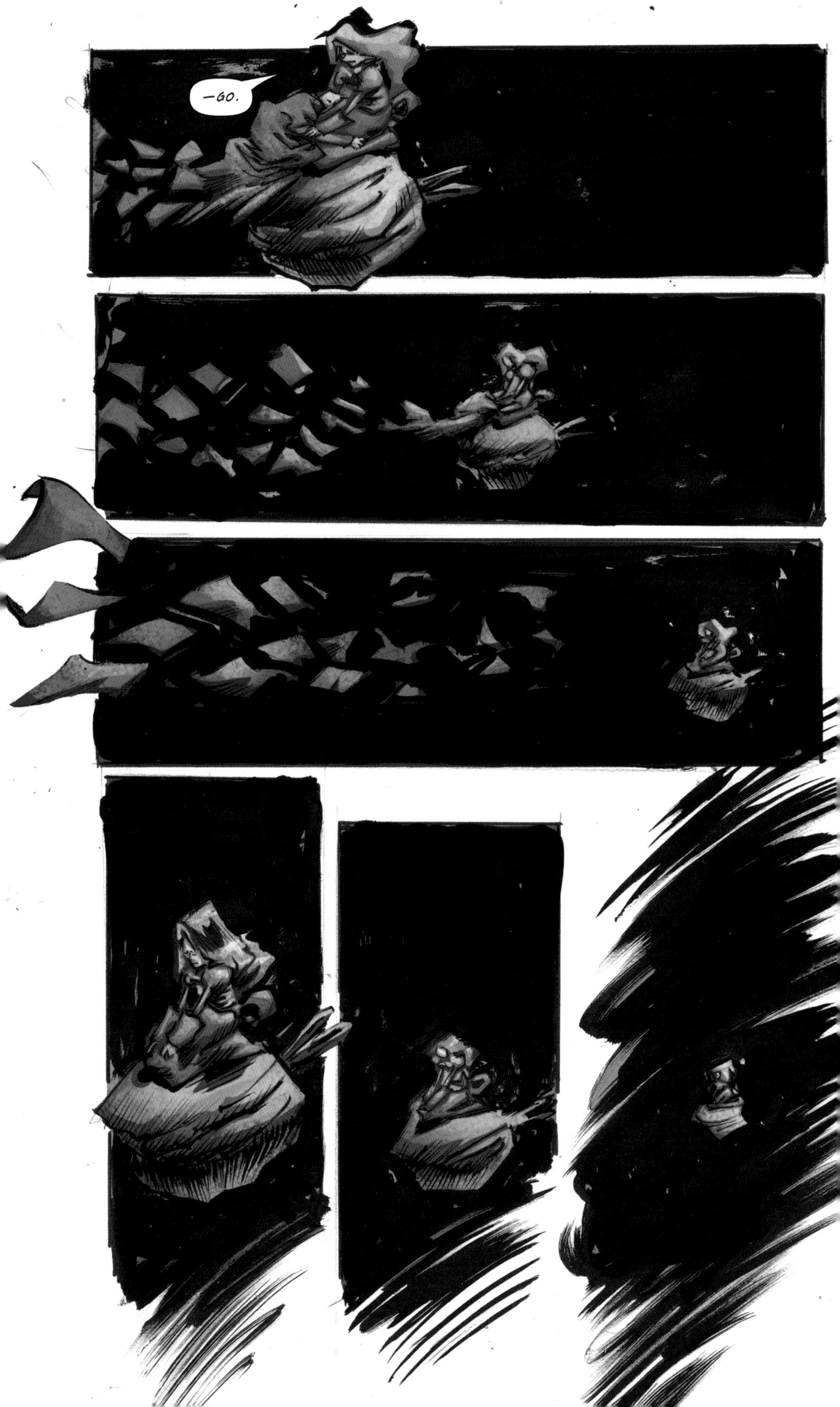
—GO.

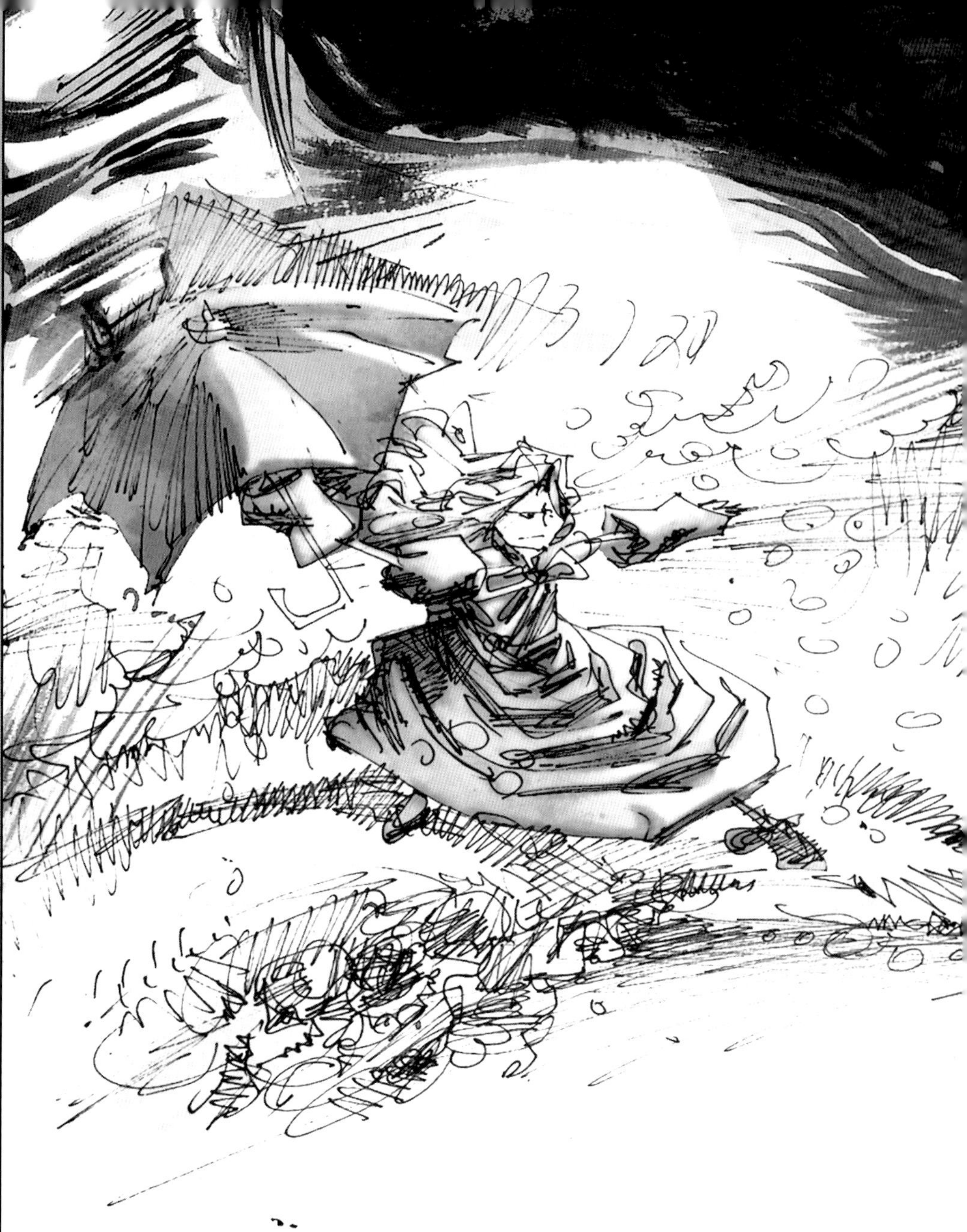

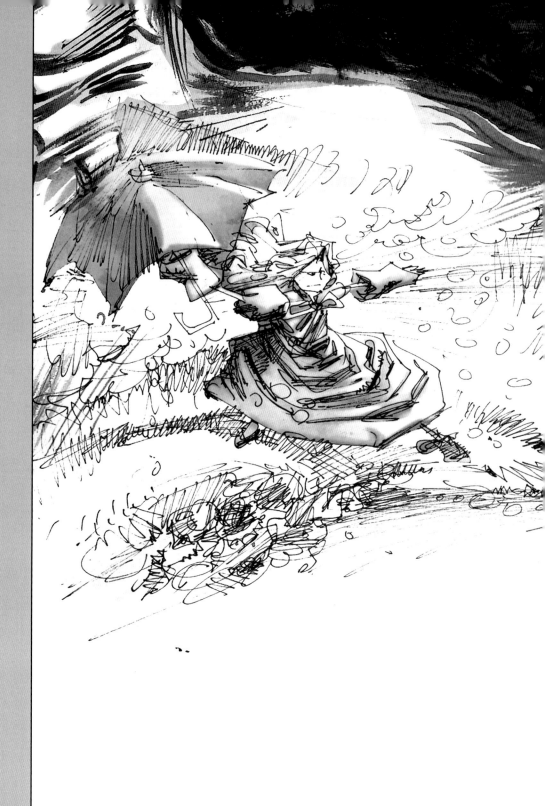

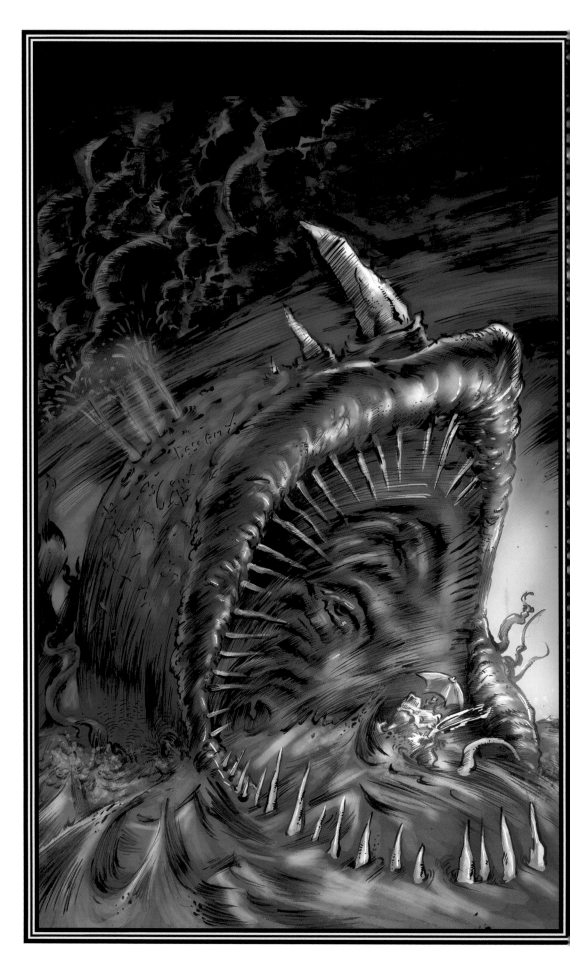

CHAPTER FIVE: THE FIRST STORY

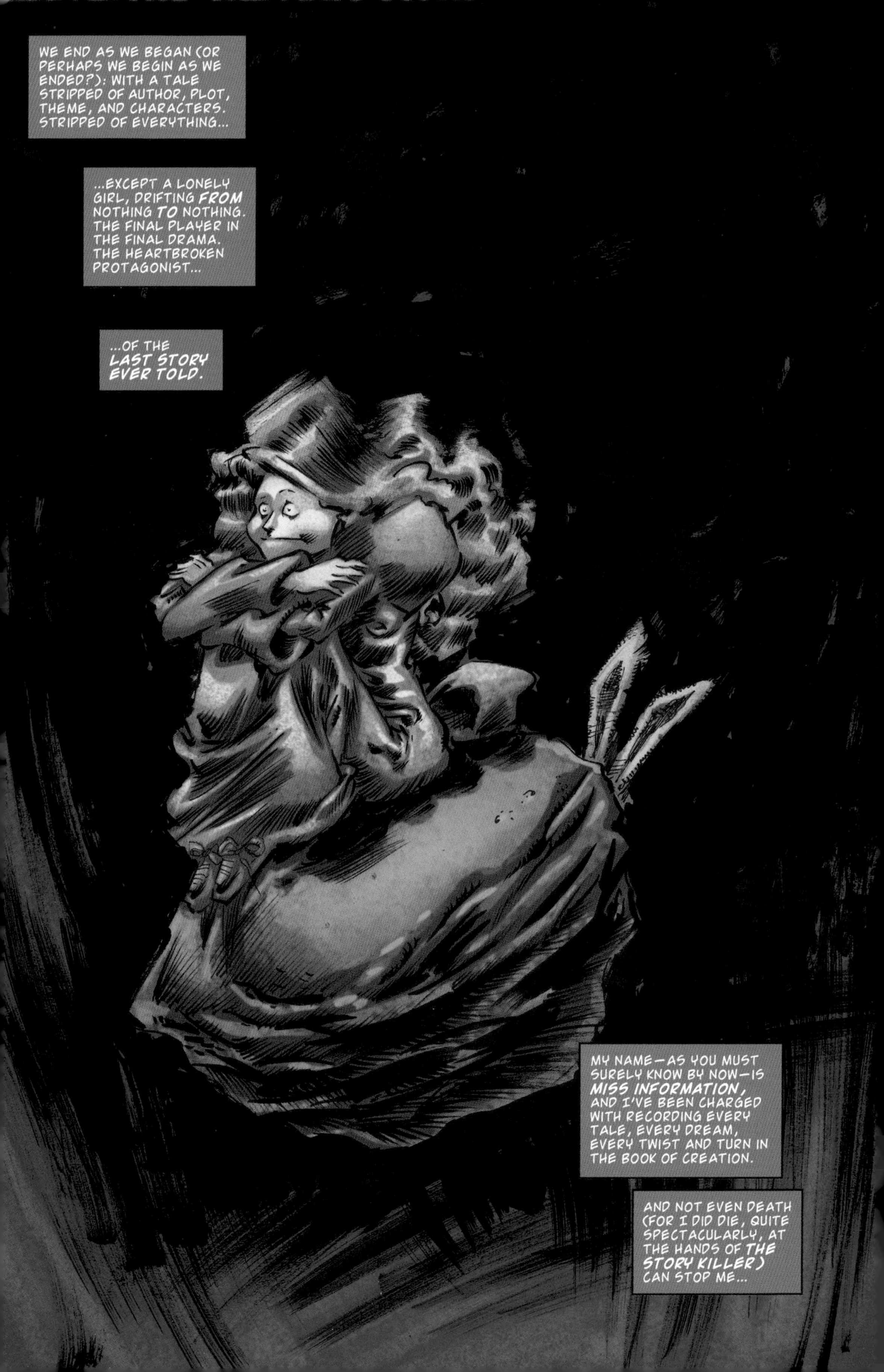
WE END AS WE BEGAN (OR PERHAPS WE BEGIN AS WE ENDED?): WITH A TALE STRIPPED OF AUTHOR, PLOT, THEME, AND CHARACTERS. STRIPPED OF EVERYTHING...
...EXCEPT A LONELY GIRL, DRIFTING FROM NOTHING TO NOTHING. THE FINAL PLAYER IN THE FINAL DRAMA. THE HEARTBROKEN PROTAGONIST...
...OF THE LAST STORY EVER TOLD.
MY NAME—AS YOU MUST SURELY KNOW BY NOW—IS MISS INFORMATION, AND I'VE BEEN CHARGED WITH RECORDING EVERY TALE, EVERY DREAM, EVERY TWIST AND TURN IN THE BOOK OF CREATION.
AND NOT EVEN DEATH (FOR I DID DIE, QUITE SPECTACULARLY, AT THE HANDS OF THE STORY KILLER) CAN STOP ME...

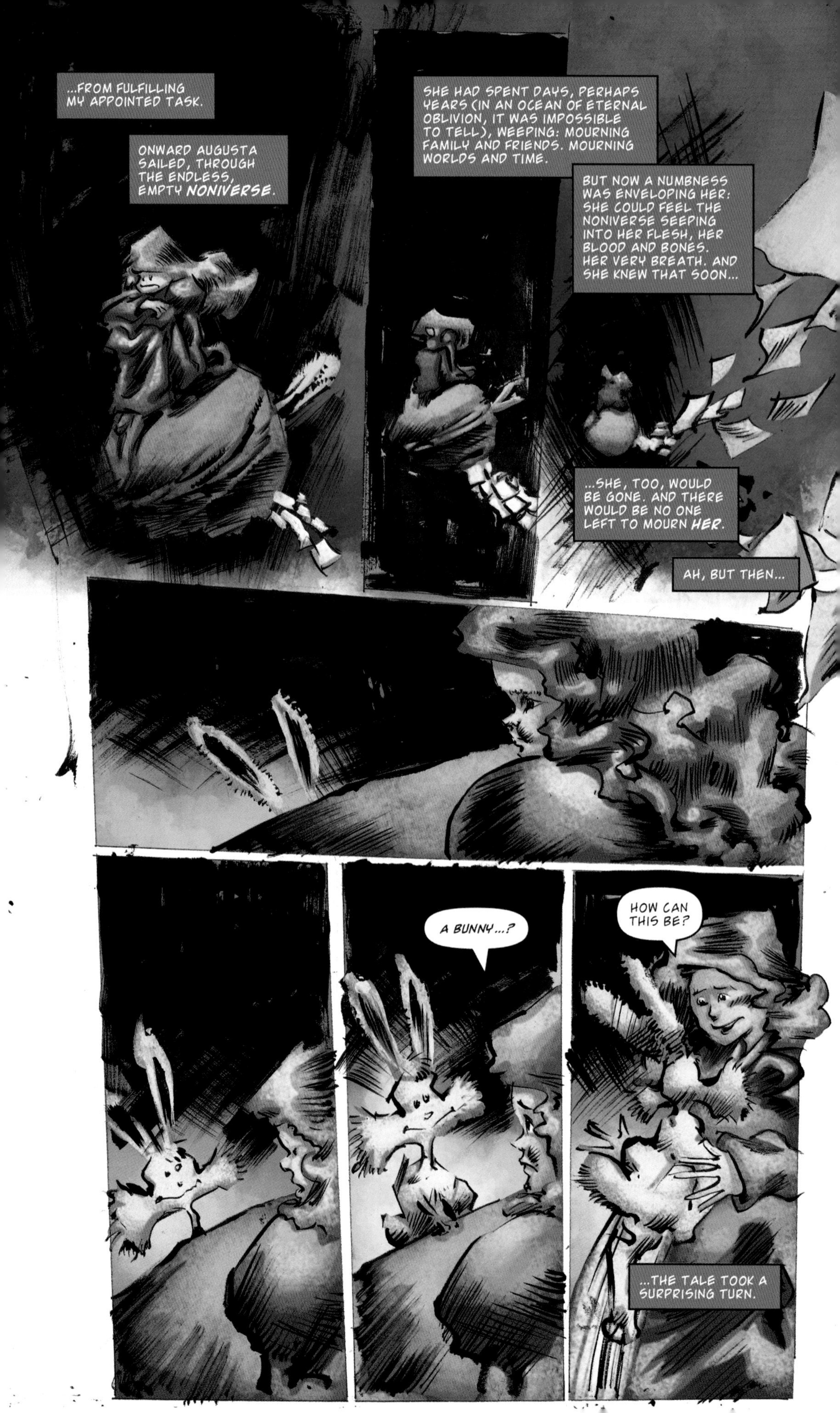
...FROM FULFILLING MY APPOINTED TASK.
ONWARD AUGUSTA SAILED, THROUGH THE ENDLESS, EMPTY *NONIVERSE*.
SHE HAD SPENT DAYS, PERHAPS YEARS (IN AN OCEAN OF ETERNAL OBLIVION, IT WAS IMPOSSIBLE TO TELL), WEEPING: MOURNING FAMILY AND FRIENDS. MOURNING WORLDS AND TIME.
BUT NOW A NUMBNESS WAS ENVELOPING HER: SHE COULD FEEL THE NONIVERSE SEEPING INTO HER FLESH, HER BLOOD AND BONES. HER VERY BREATH. AND SHE KNEW THAT SOON...
...SHE, TOO, WOULD BE GONE. AND THERE WOULD BE NO ONE LEFT TO MOURN *HER*.
AH, BUT THEN...
A BUNNY...?
HOW CAN THIS BE?
...THE TALE TOOK A SURPRISING TURN.

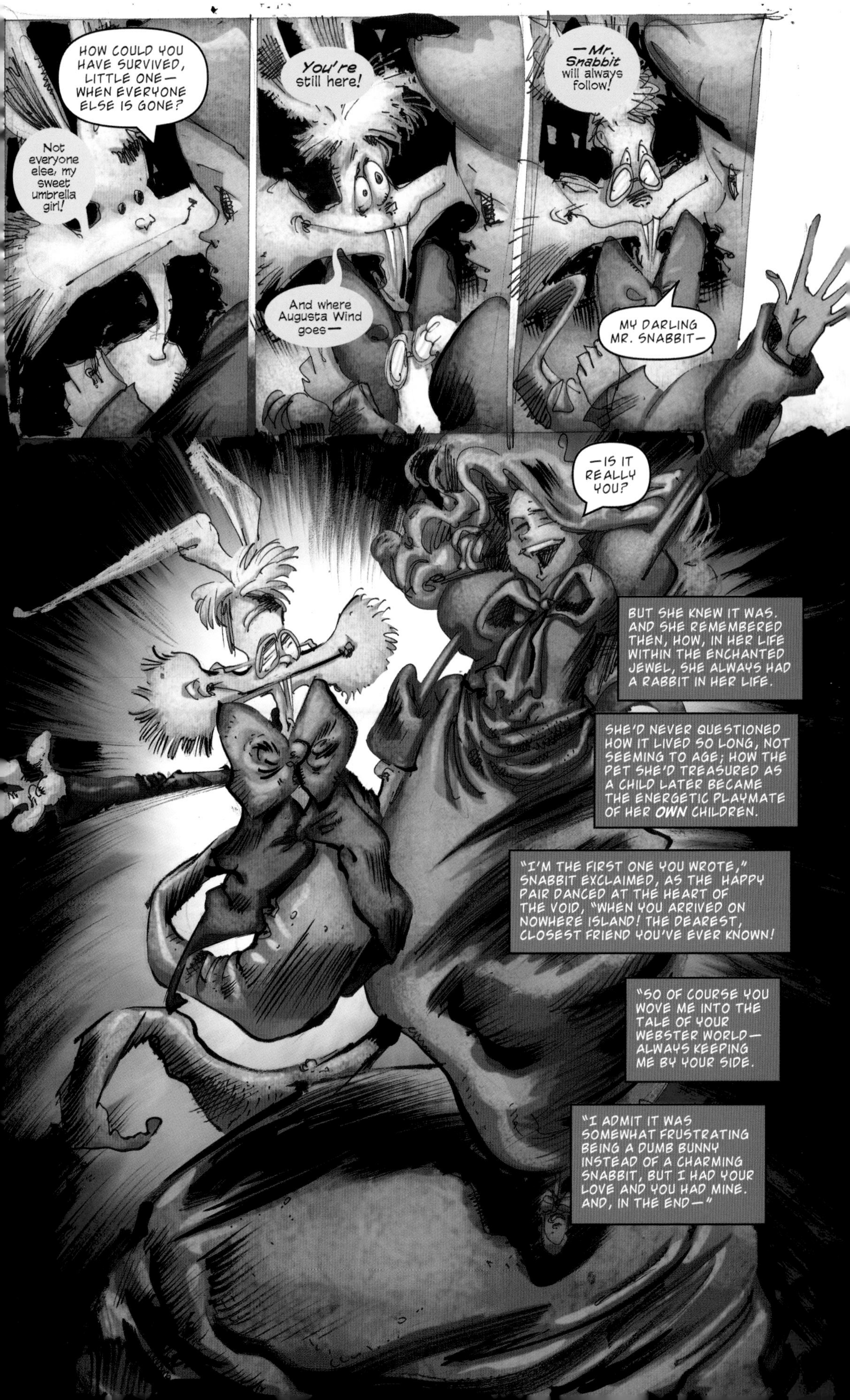
HOW COULD YOU HAVE SURVIVED, LITTLE ONE— WHEN EVERYONE ELSE IS GONE?
Not everyone else, my sweet umbrella girl!
You're still here!
And where Augusta Wind goes—
—Mr. Snabbit will always follow!
MY DARLING MR. SNABBIT—
—IS IT REALLY YOU?
BUT SHE KNEW IT WAS. AND SHE REMEMBERED THEN, HOW, IN HER LIFE WITHIN THE ENCHANTED JEWEL, SHE ALWAYS HAD A RABBIT IN HER LIFE.
SHE'D NEVER QUESTIONED HOW IT LIVED SO LONG, NOT SEEMING TO AGE; HOW THE PET SHE'D TREASURED AS A CHILD LATER BECAME THE ENERGETIC PLAYMATE OF HER OWN CHILDREN.
"I'M THE FIRST ONE YOU WROTE," SNABBIT EXCLAIMED, AS THE HAPPY PAIR DANCED AT THE HEART OF THE VOID, "WHEN YOU ARRIVED ON NOWHERE ISLAND! THE DEAREST, CLOSEST FRIEND YOU'VE EVER KNOWN!
"SO OF COURSE YOU WOVE ME INTO THE TALE OF YOUR WEBSTER WORLD— ALWAYS KEEPING ME BY YOUR SIDE.
"I ADMIT IT WAS SOMEWHAT FRUSTRATING BEING A DUMB BUNNY INSTEAD OF A CHARMING SNABBIT, BUT I HAD YOUR LOVE AND YOU HAD MINE. AND, IN THE END—"

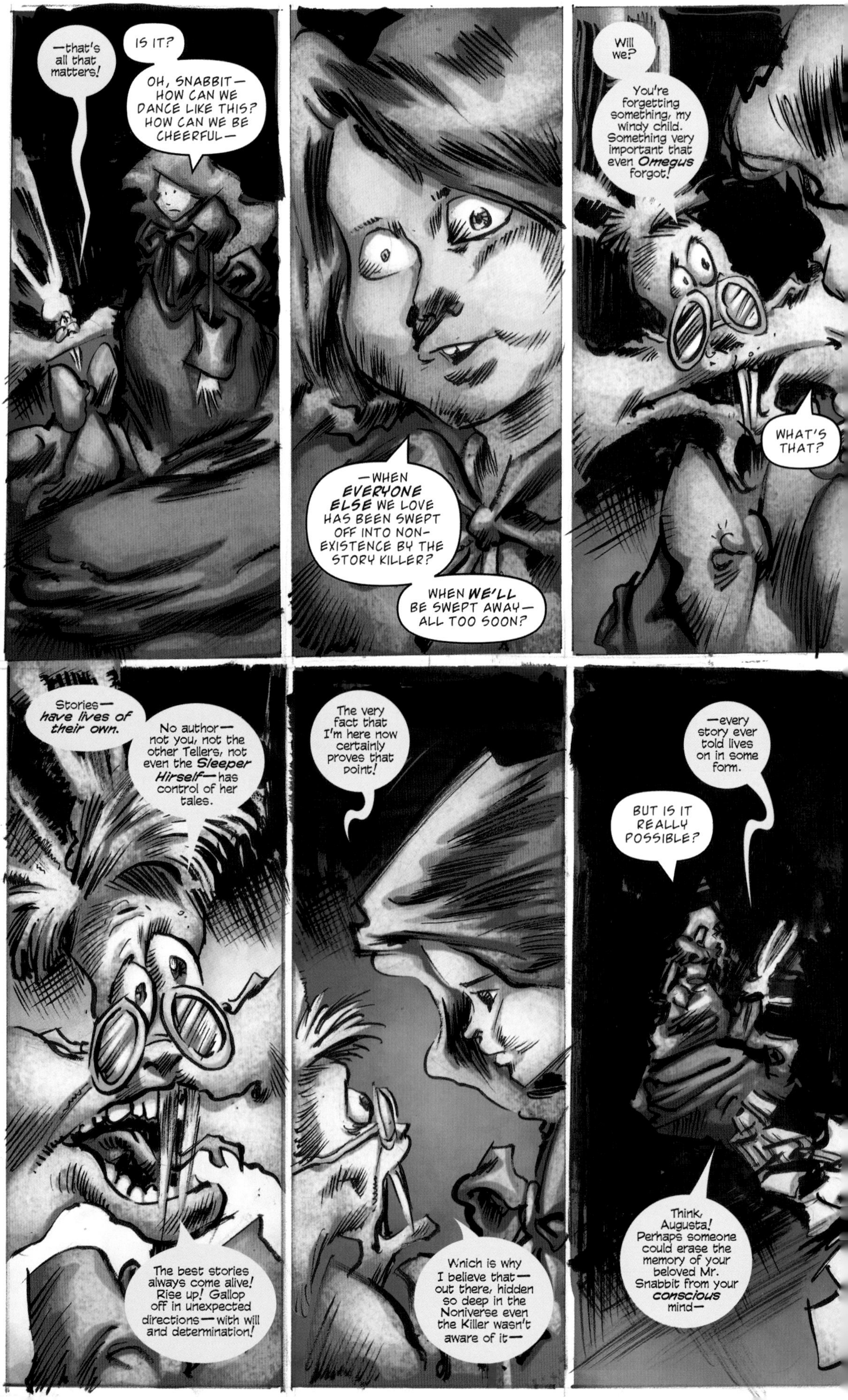
—that's all that matters!
IS IT?
OH, SNABBIT— HOW CAN WE DANCE LIKE THIS? HOW CAN WE BE CHEERFUL—
—WHEN EVERYONE ELSE WE LOVE HAS BEEN SWEPT OFF INTO NON-EXISTENCE BY THE STORY KILLER?
WHEN WE'LL BE SWEPT AWAY— ALL TOO SOON?
Will we?
You're forgetting something, my windy child. Something very important that even Omegus forgot!
WHAT'S THAT?
Stories— have lives of their own.
No author— not you, not the other Tellers, not even the Sleeper Hirself— has control of her tales.
The best stories always come alive! Rise up! Gallop off in unexpected directions—with will and determination!
The very fact that I'm here now certainly proves that point!
Which is why I believe that— out there, hidden so deep in the Noniverse even the Killer wasn't aware of it—
—every story ever told lives on in some form.
BUT IS IT REALLY POSSIBLE?
Think, Augusta! Perhaps someone could erase the memory of your beloved Mr. Snabbit from your conscious mind—

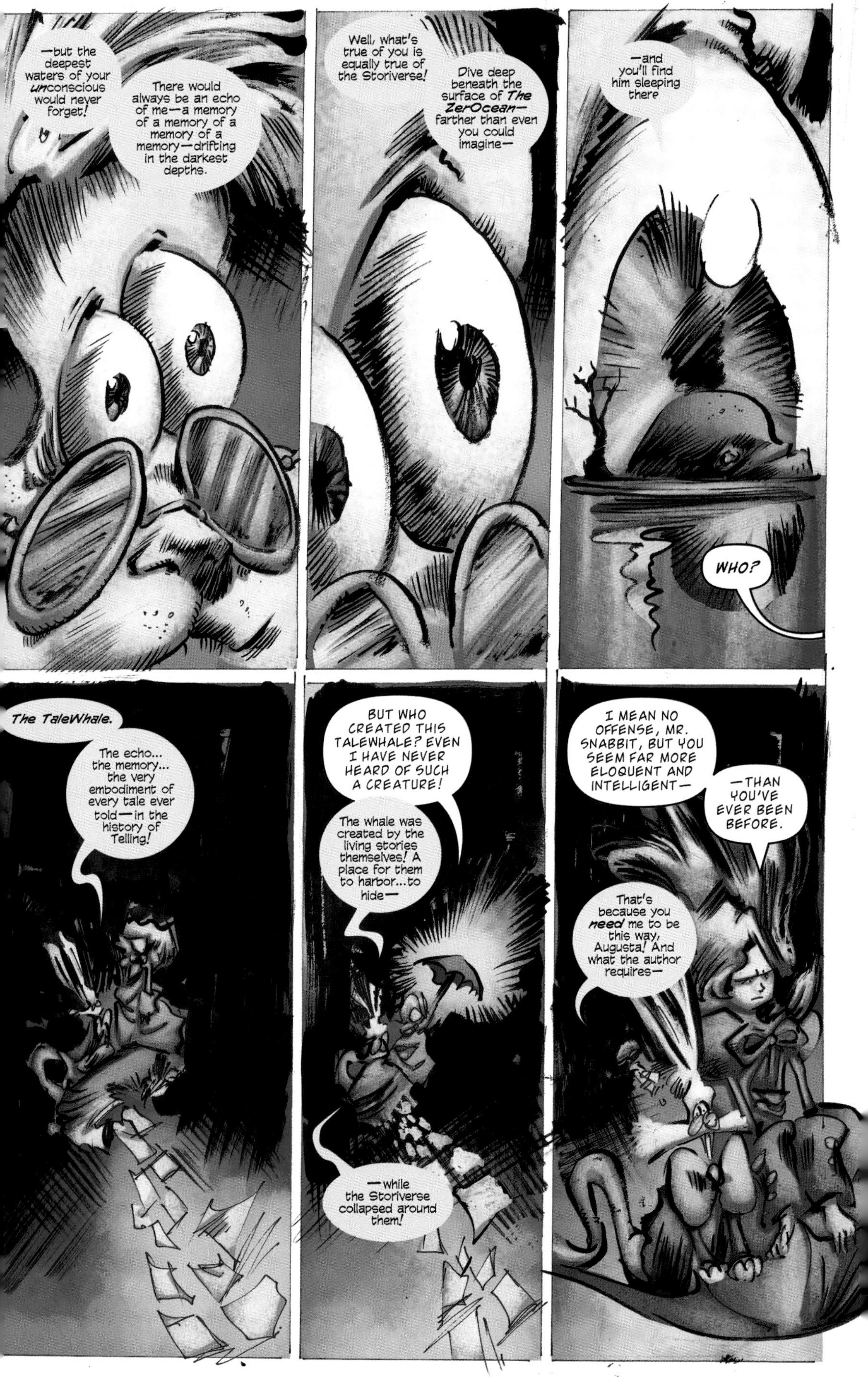
—but the deepest waters of your *un*conscious would never forget!
There would always be an echo of me—a memory of a memory of a memory of a memory—drifting in the darkest depths.
Well, what's true of you is equally true of the Storiverse!
Dive deep beneath the surface of *The ZerOcean*—farther than even you could imagine—
—and you'll find him sleeping there
WHO?
The TaleWhale.
The echo... the memory... the very embodiment of every tale ever told—in the history of Telling!
BUT WHO CREATED THIS TALEWHALE? EVEN I HAVE NEVER HEARD OF SUCH A CREATURE!
The whale was created by the living stories themselves! A place for them to harbor...to hide—
—while the Storiverse collapsed around them!
I MEAN NO OFFENSE, MR. SNABBIT, BUT YOU SEEM FAR MORE ELOQUENT AND INTELLIGENT—
—THAN YOU'VE EVER BEEN BEFORE.
That's because you *need* me to be this way, Augusta! And what the author requires—

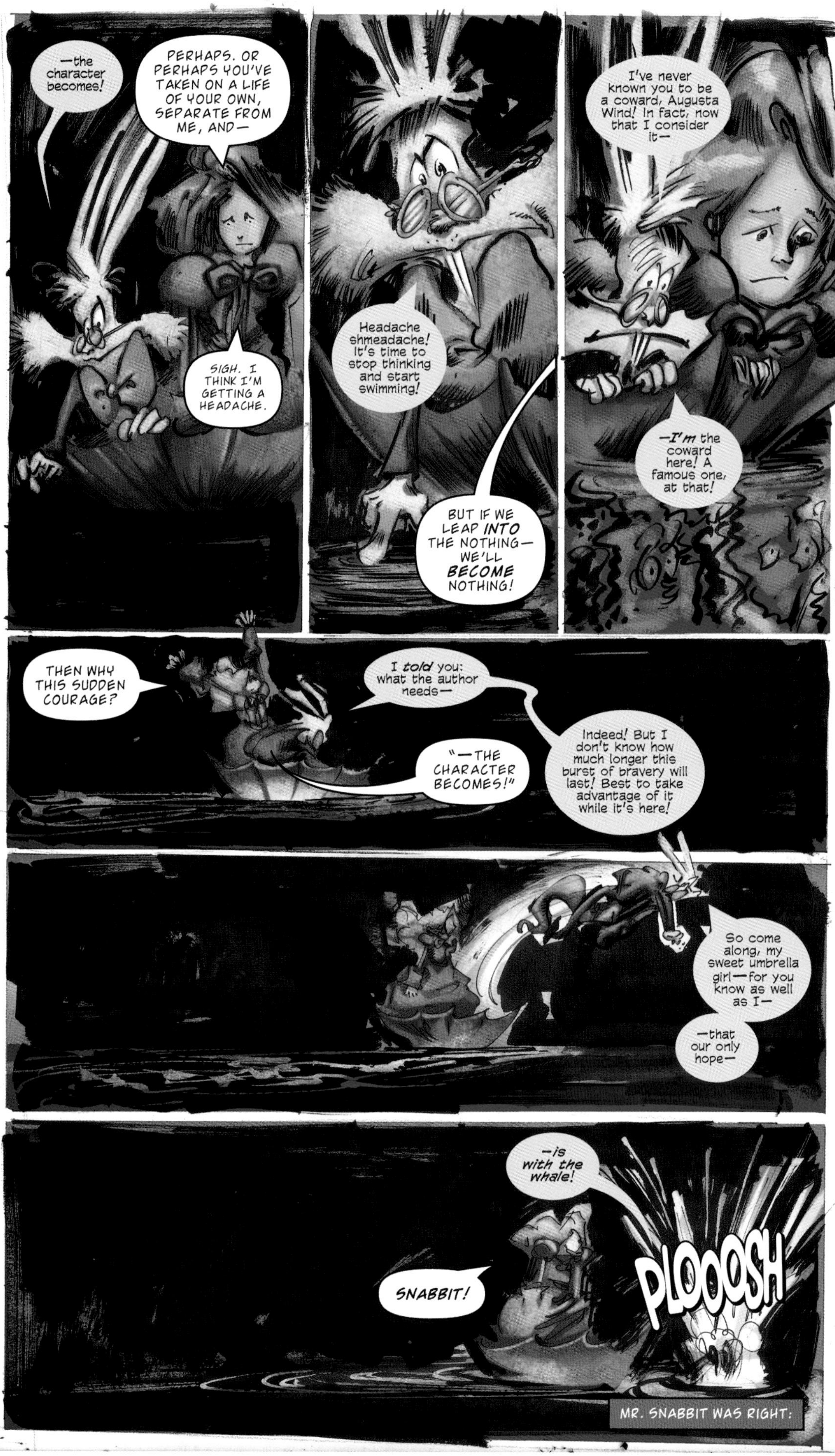
—the character becomes!
PERHAPS. OR PERHAPS YOU'VE TAKEN ON A LIFE OF YOUR OWN, SEPARATE FROM ME, AND—
SIGH. I THINK I'M GETTING A HEADACHE.
Headache shmeadache! It's time to stop thinking and start swimming!
BUT IF WE LEAP INTO THE NOTHING—WE'LL BECOME NOTHING!
I've never known you to be a coward, Augusta Wind! In fact, now that I consider it—
—I'm the coward here! A famous one, at that!
THEN WHY THIS SUDDEN COURAGE?
I told you: what the author needs—
"—THE CHARACTER BECOMES!"
Indeed! But I don't know how much longer this burst of bravery will last! Best to take advantage of it while it's here!
So come along, my sweet umbrella girl—for you know as well as I—
—that our only hope—
—is with the whale!
SNABBIT!
PLOOOSH
MR. SNABBIT WAS RIGHT:

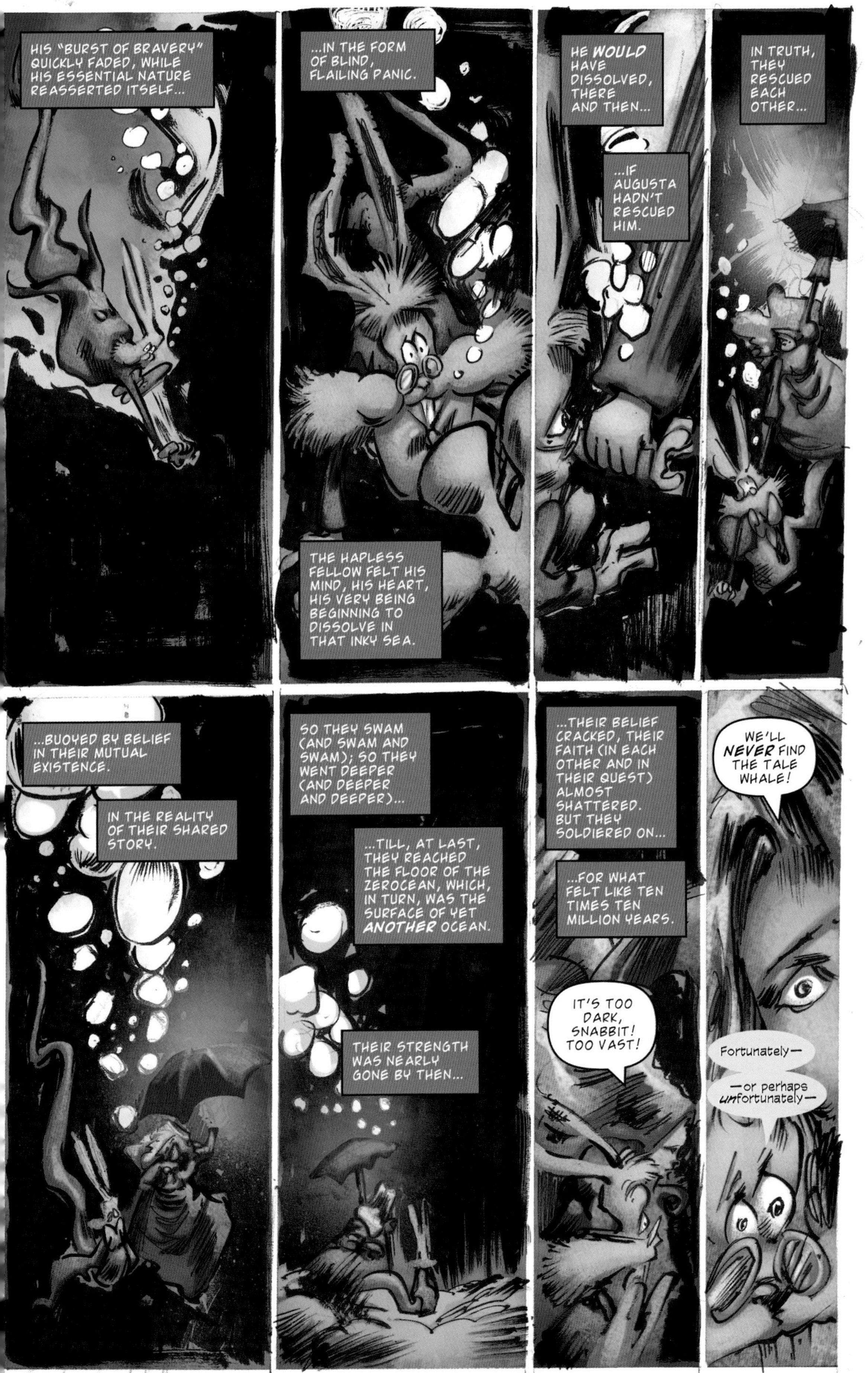
HIS "BURST OF BRAVERY" QUICKLY FADED, WHILE HIS ESSENTIAL NATURE REASSERTED ITSELF...
...IN THE FORM OF BLIND, FLAILING PANIC.
THE HAPLESS FELLOW FELT HIS MIND, HIS HEART, HIS VERY BEING BEGINNING TO DISSOLVE IN THAT INKY SEA.
HE WOULD HAVE DISSOLVED, THERE AND THEN...
...IF AUGUSTA HADN'T RESCUED HIM.
IN TRUTH, THEY RESCUED EACH OTHER...
...BUOYED BY BELIEF IN THEIR MUTUAL EXISTENCE.
IN THE REALITY OF THEIR SHARED STORY.
SO THEY SWAM (AND SWAM AND SWAM); SO THEY WENT DEEPER (AND DEEPER AND DEEPER)...
...TILL, AT LAST, THEY REACHED THE FLOOR OF THE ZEROCEAN, WHICH, IN TURN, WAS THE SURFACE OF YET ANOTHER OCEAN.
THEIR STRENGTH WAS NEARLY GONE BY THEN...
...THEIR BELIEF CRACKED, THEIR FAITH (IN EACH OTHER AND IN THEIR QUEST) ALMOST SHATTERED. BUT THEY SOLDIERED ON...
...FOR WHAT FELT LIKE TEN TIMES TEN MILLION YEARS.
IT'S TOO DARK, SNABBIT! TOO VAST!
WE'LL NEVER FIND THE TALE WHALE!
Fortunately—
—or perhaps unfortunately—

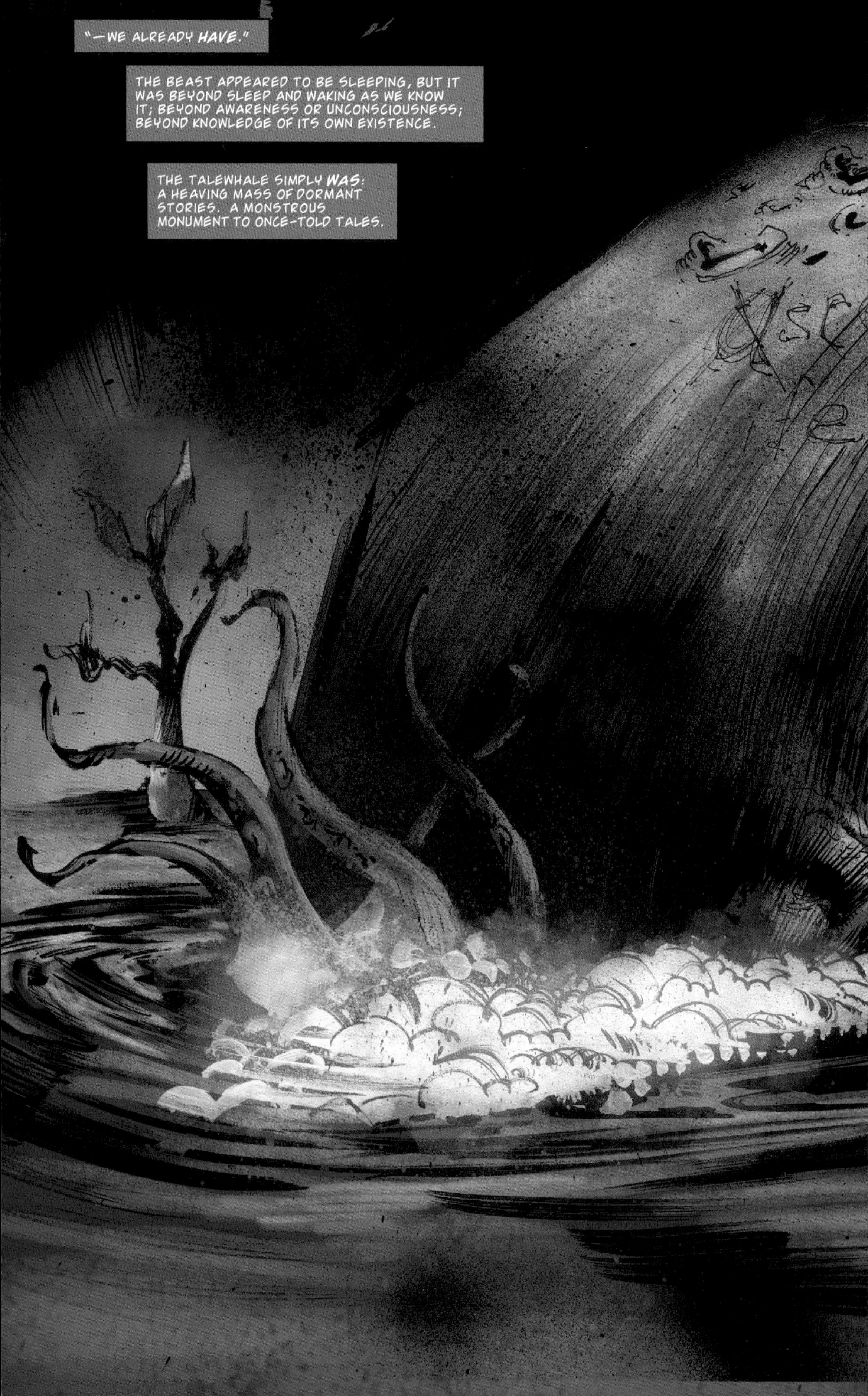
"—WE ALREADY HAVE."
THE BEAST APPEARED TO BE SLEEPING, BUT IT WAS BEYOND SLEEP AND WAKING AS WE KNOW IT; BEYOND AWARENESS OR UNCONSCIOUSNESS; BEYOND KNOWLEDGE OF ITS OWN EXISTENCE.
THE TALEWHALE SIMPLY WAS: A HEAVING MASS OF DORMANT STORIES. A MONSTROUS MONUMENT TO ONCE-TOLD TALES.

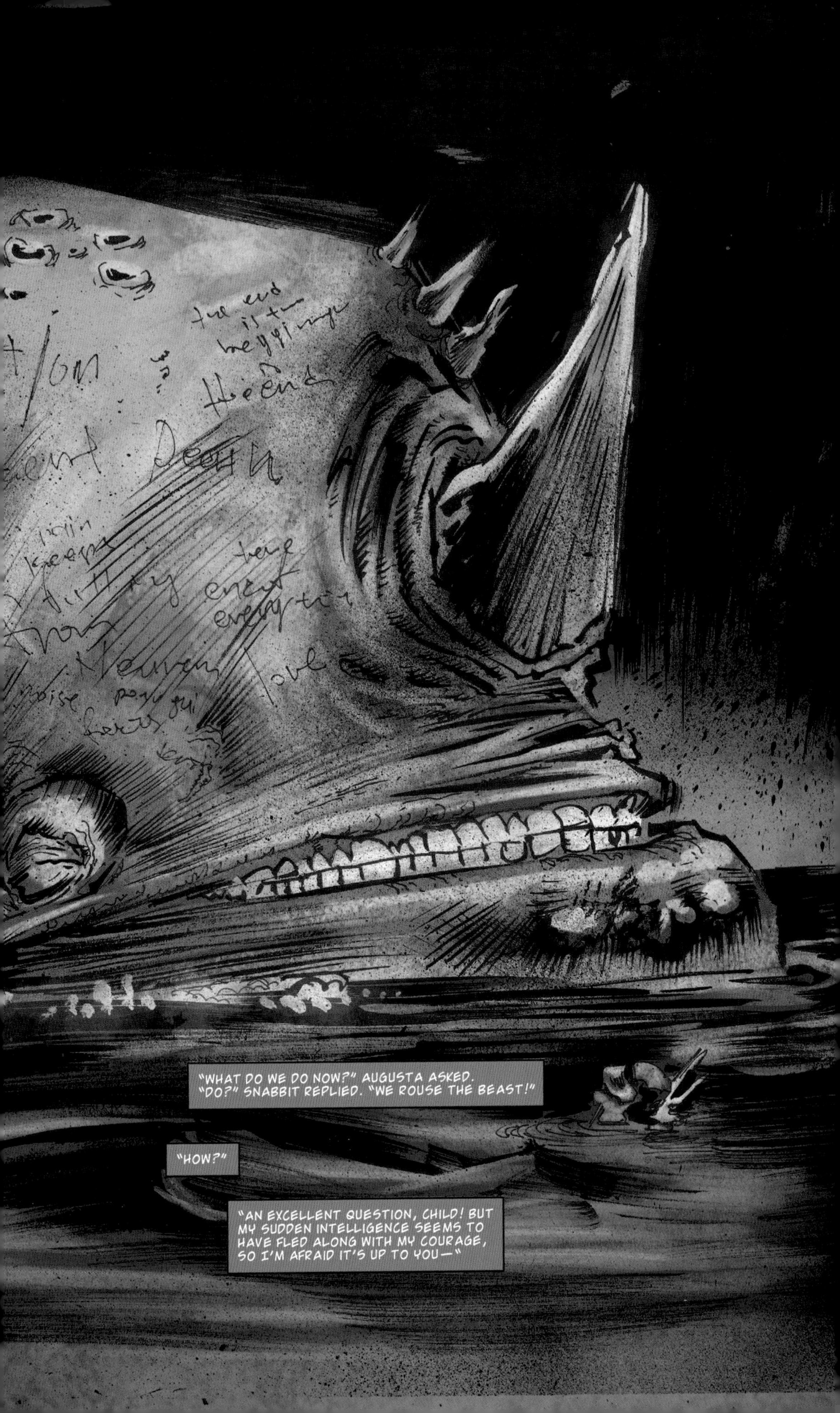
"WHAT DO WE DO NOW?" AUGUSTA ASKED. "DO?" SNABBIT REPLIED. "WE ROUSE THE BEAST!"
"HOW?"
"AN EXCELLENT QUESTION, CHILD! BUT MY SUDDEN INTELLIGENCE SEEMS TO HAVE FLED ALONG WITH MY COURAGE, SO I'M AFRAID IT'S UP TO YOU—"

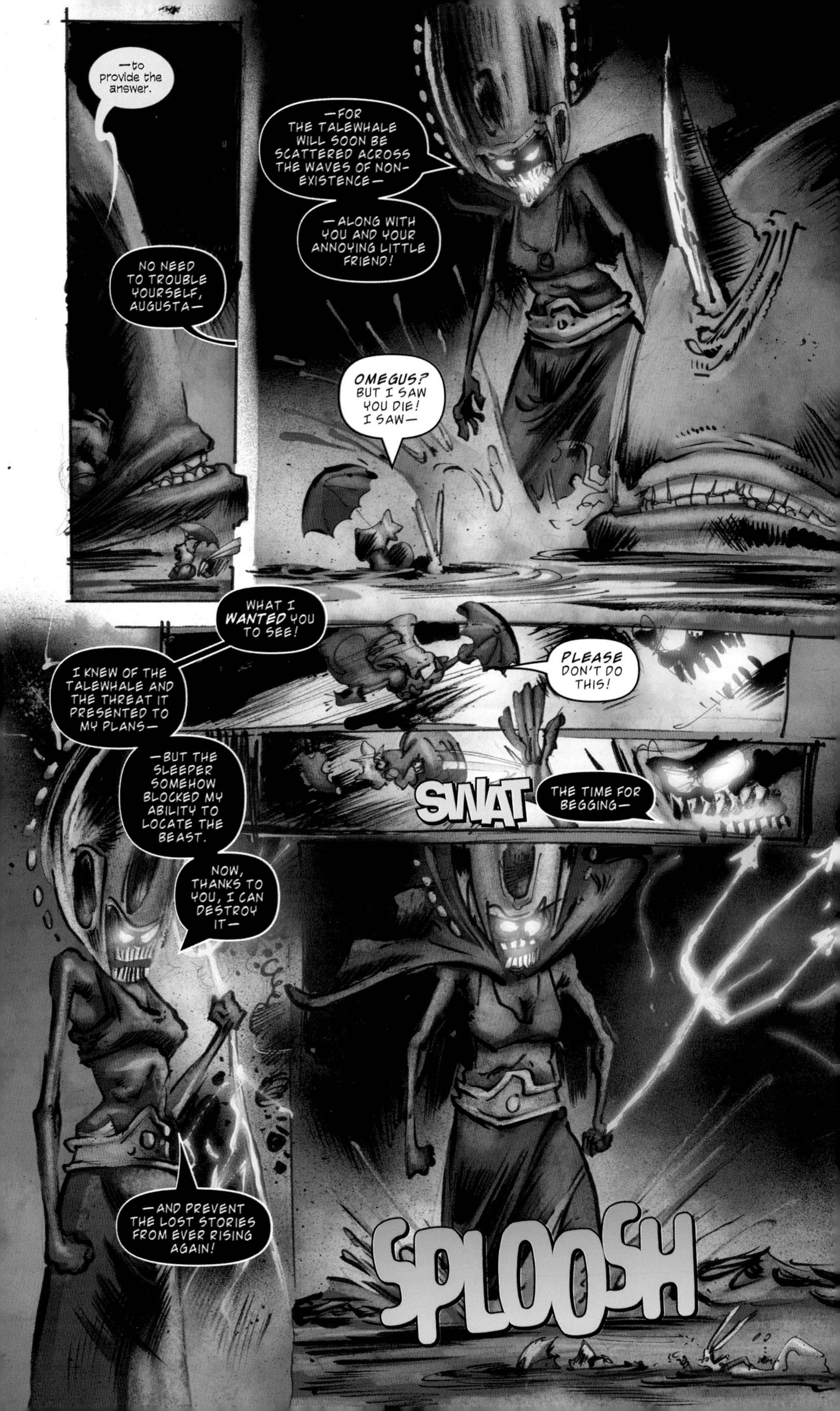
—to provide the answer.
—FOR THE TALEWHALE WILL SOON BE SCATTERED ACROSS THE WAVES OF NON-EXISTENCE—
—ALONG WITH YOU AND YOUR ANNOYING LITTLE FRIEND!
NO NEED TO TROUBLE YOURSELF, AUGUSTA—
OMEGUS? BUT I SAW YOU DIE! I SAW—
WHAT I WANTED YOU TO SEE!
PLEASE DON'T DO THIS!
I KNEW OF THE TALEWHALE AND THE THREAT IT PRESENTED TO MY PLANS—
—BUT THE SLEEPER SOMEHOW BLOCKED MY ABILITY TO LOCATE THE BEAST.
SWAT
THE TIME FOR BEGGING—
NOW, THANKS TO YOU, I CAN DESTROY IT—
—AND PREVENT THE LOST STORIES FROM EVER RISING AGAIN!
SPLOOSH

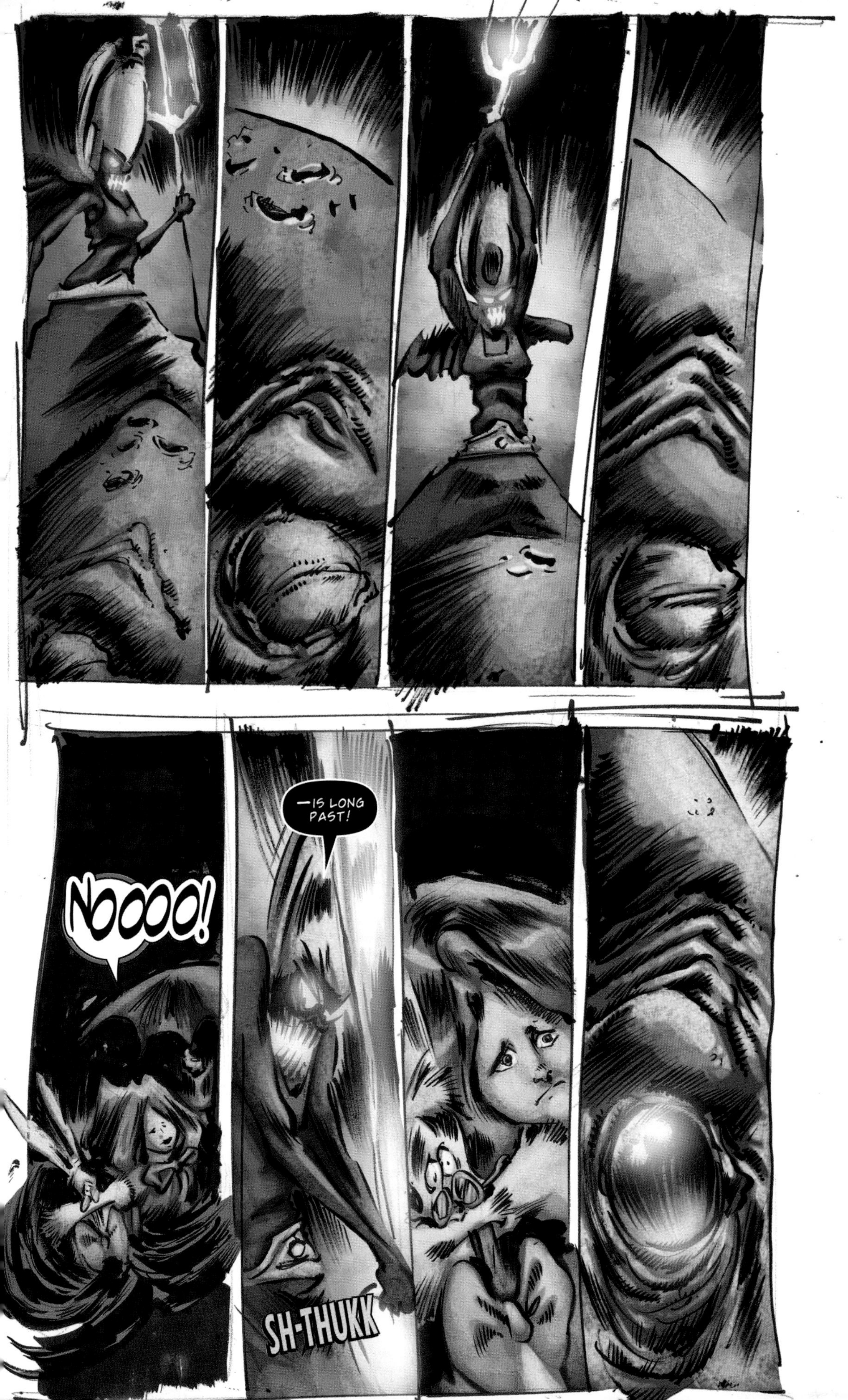
NOOOO!
—IS LONG PAST!
SH-THUKK

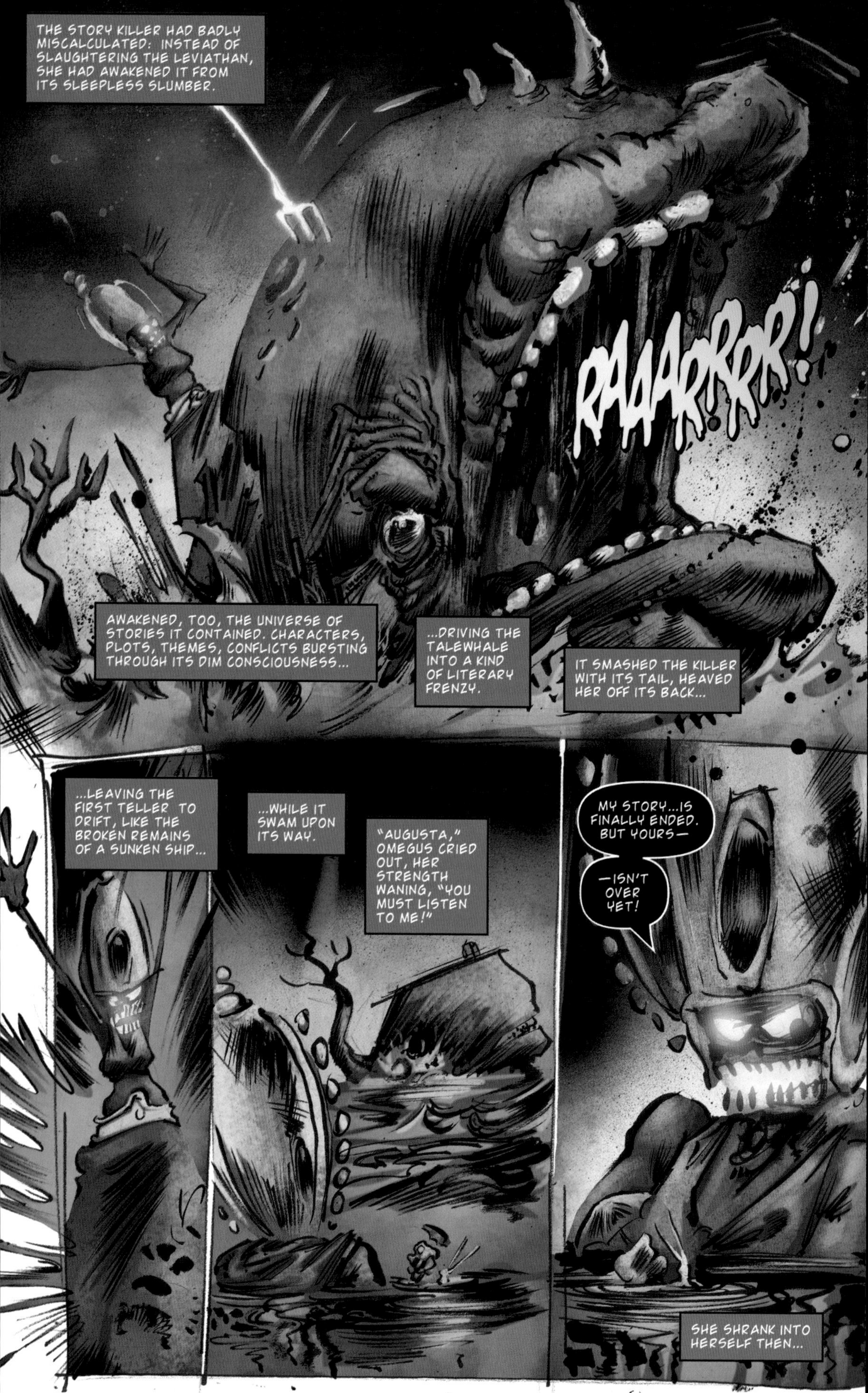
THE STORY KILLER HAD BADLY MISCALCULATED: INSTEAD OF SLAUGHTERING THE LEVIATHAN, SHE HAD AWAKENED IT FROM ITS SLEEPLESS SLUMBER.
RAAARRRR!
AWAKENED, TOO, THE UNIVERSE OF STORIES IT CONTAINED. CHARACTERS, PLOTS, THEMES, CONFLICTS BURSTING THROUGH ITS DIM CONSCIOUSNESS...
...DRIVING THE TALEWHALE INTO A KIND OF LITERARY FRENZY.
IT SMASHED THE KILLER WITH ITS TAIL, HEAVED HER OFF ITS BACK...
...LEAVING THE FIRST TELLER TO DRIFT, LIKE THE BROKEN REMAINS OF A SUNKEN SHIP...
...WHILE IT SWAM UPON ITS WAY.
"AUGUSTA," OMEGUS CRIED OUT, HER STRENGTH WANING, "YOU MUST LISTEN TO ME!"
MY STORY...IS FINALLY ENDED. BUT YOURS—
—ISN'T OVER YET!
SHE SHRANK INTO HERSELF THEN...

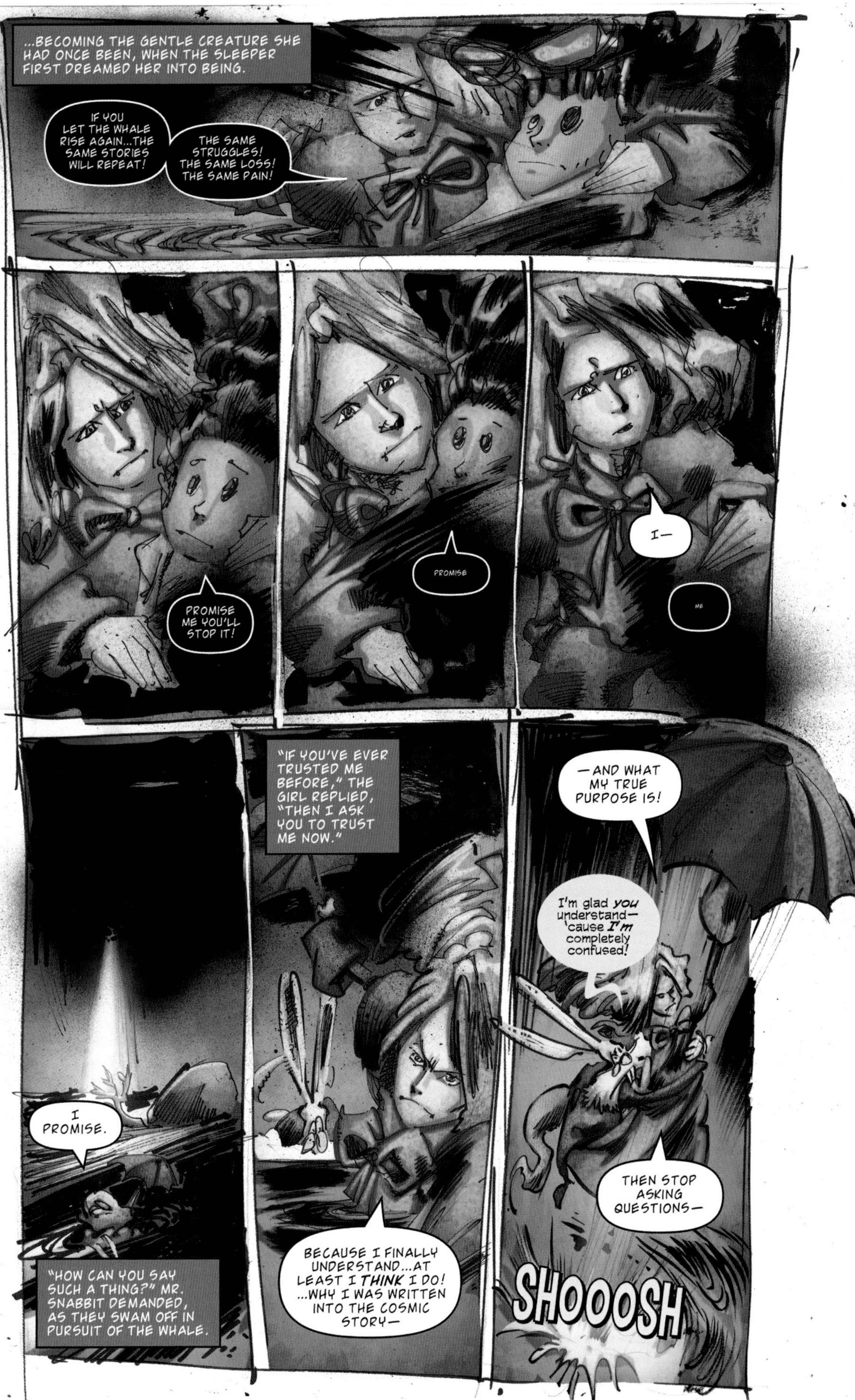
...BECOMING THE GENTLE CREATURE SHE HAD ONCE BEEN, WHEN THE SLEEPER FIRST DREAMED HER INTO BEING.
IF YOU LET THE WHALE RISE AGAIN...THE SAME STORIES WILL REPEAT!
THE SAME STRUGGLES! THE SAME LOSS! THE SAME PAIN!
PROMISE ME YOU'LL STOP IT!
PROMISE
I—
ME
I PROMISE.
"HOW CAN YOU SAY SUCH A THING?" MR. SNABBIT DEMANDED, AS THEY SWAM OFF IN PURSUIT OF THE WHALE.
"IF YOU'VE EVER TRUSTED ME BEFORE," THE GIRL REPLIED, "THEN I ASK YOU TO TRUST ME NOW."
BECAUSE I FINALLY UNDERSTAND...AT LEAST I *THINK* I DO! ...WHY I WAS WRITTEN INTO THE COSMIC STORY—
—AND WHAT MY TRUE PURPOSE IS!
I'm glad *you* understand—'cause *I'm* completely confused!
THEN STOP ASKING QUESTIONS—
SHOOOSH

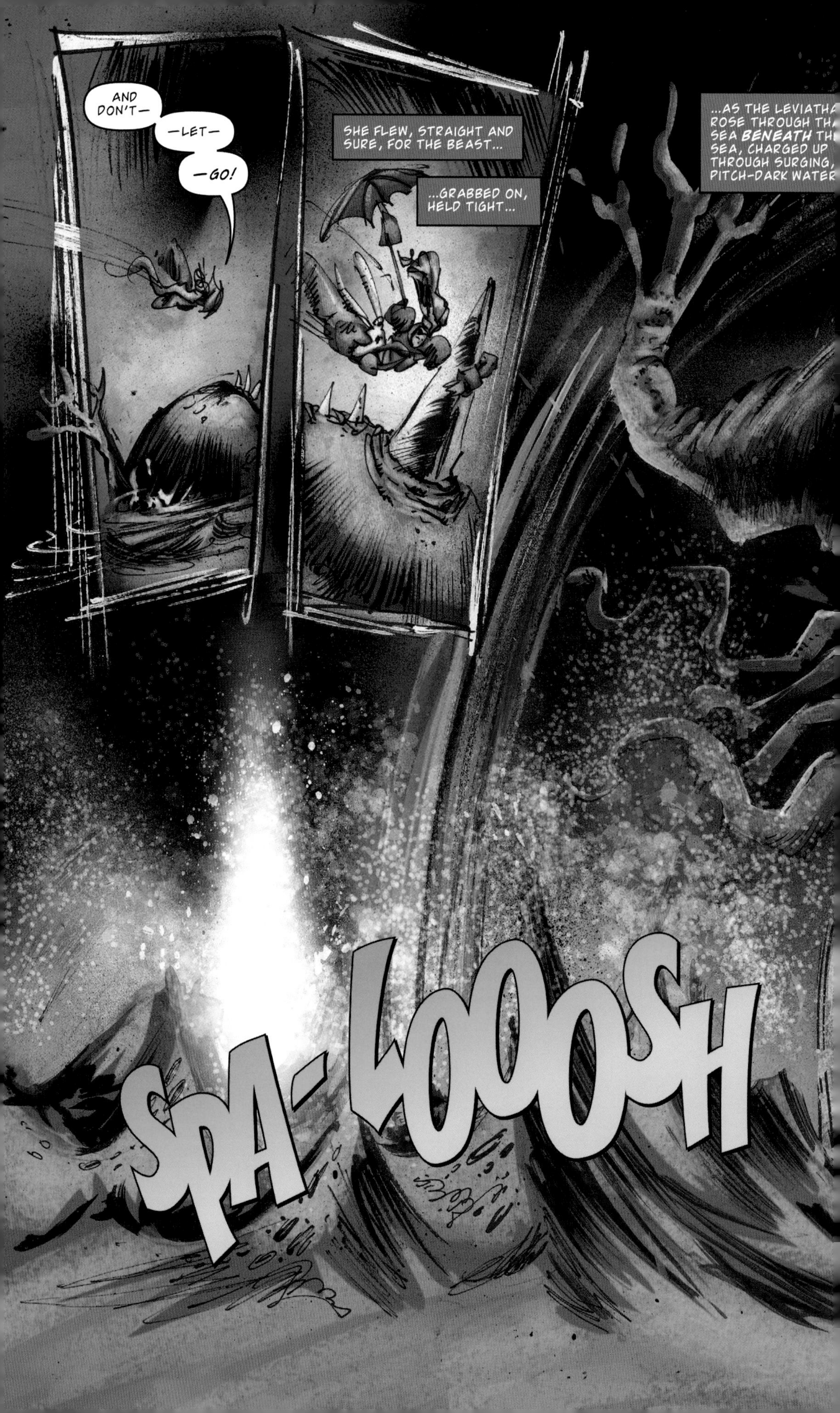
AND DON'T—
—LET—
—GO!
SHE FLEW, STRAIGHT AND SURE, FOR THE BEAST...
...GRABBED ON, HELD TIGHT...
...AS THE LEVIATHA ROSE THROUGH TH SEA BENEATH TH SEA, CHARGED UP THROUGH SURGING, PITCH-DARK WATER
SPA-LOOOSH

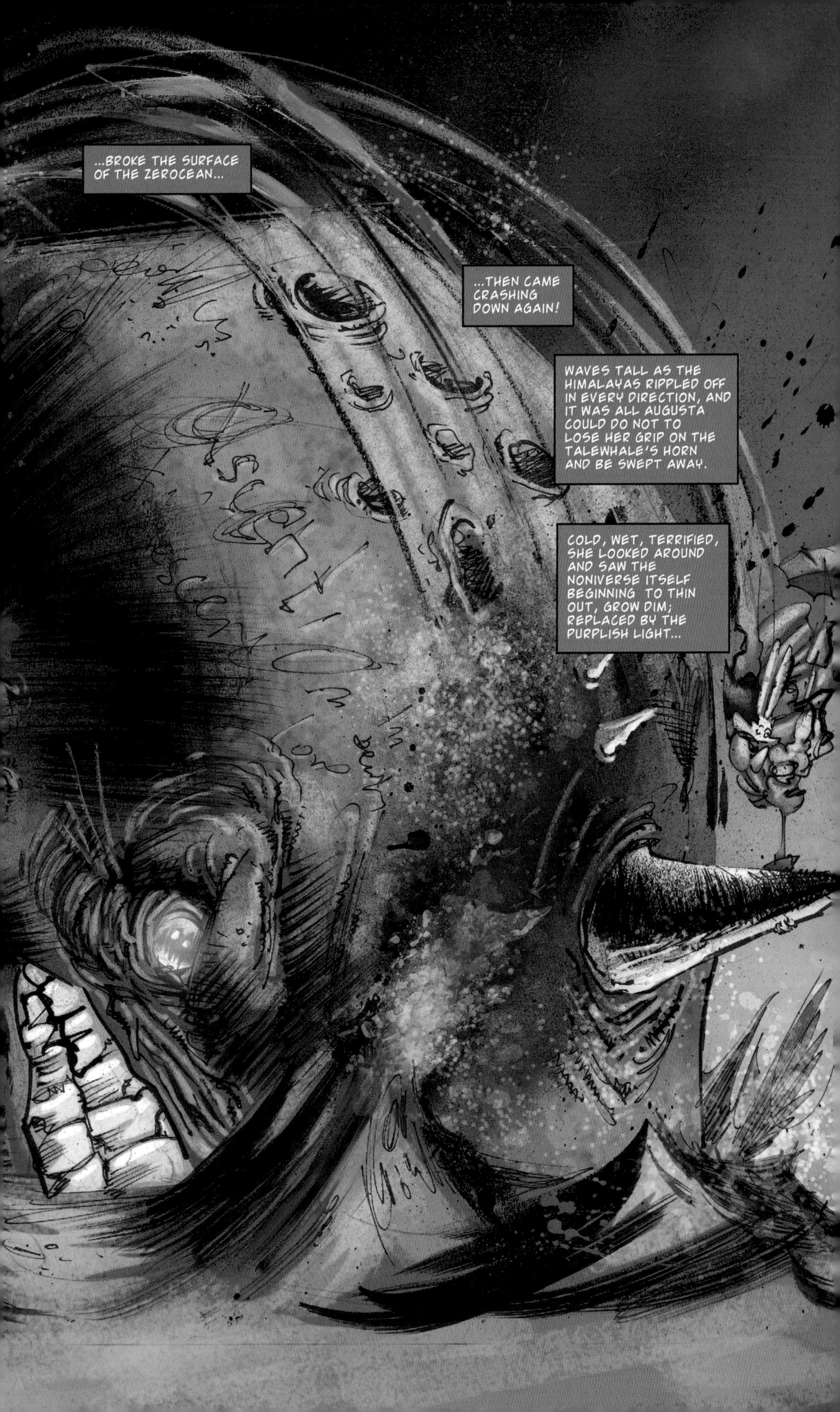
...BROKE THE SURFACE OF THE ZEROCEAN...
...THEN CAME CRASHING DOWN AGAIN!
WAVES TALL AS THE HIMALAYAS RIPPLED OFF IN EVERY DIRECTION, AND IT WAS ALL AUGUSTA COULD DO NOT TO LOSE HER GRIP ON THE TALEWHALE'S HORN AND BE SWEPT AWAY.
COLD, WET, TERRIFIED, SHE LOOKED AROUND AND SAW THE NONIVERSE ITSELF BEGINNING TO THIN OUT, GROW DIM; REPLACED BY THE PURPLISH LIGHT...

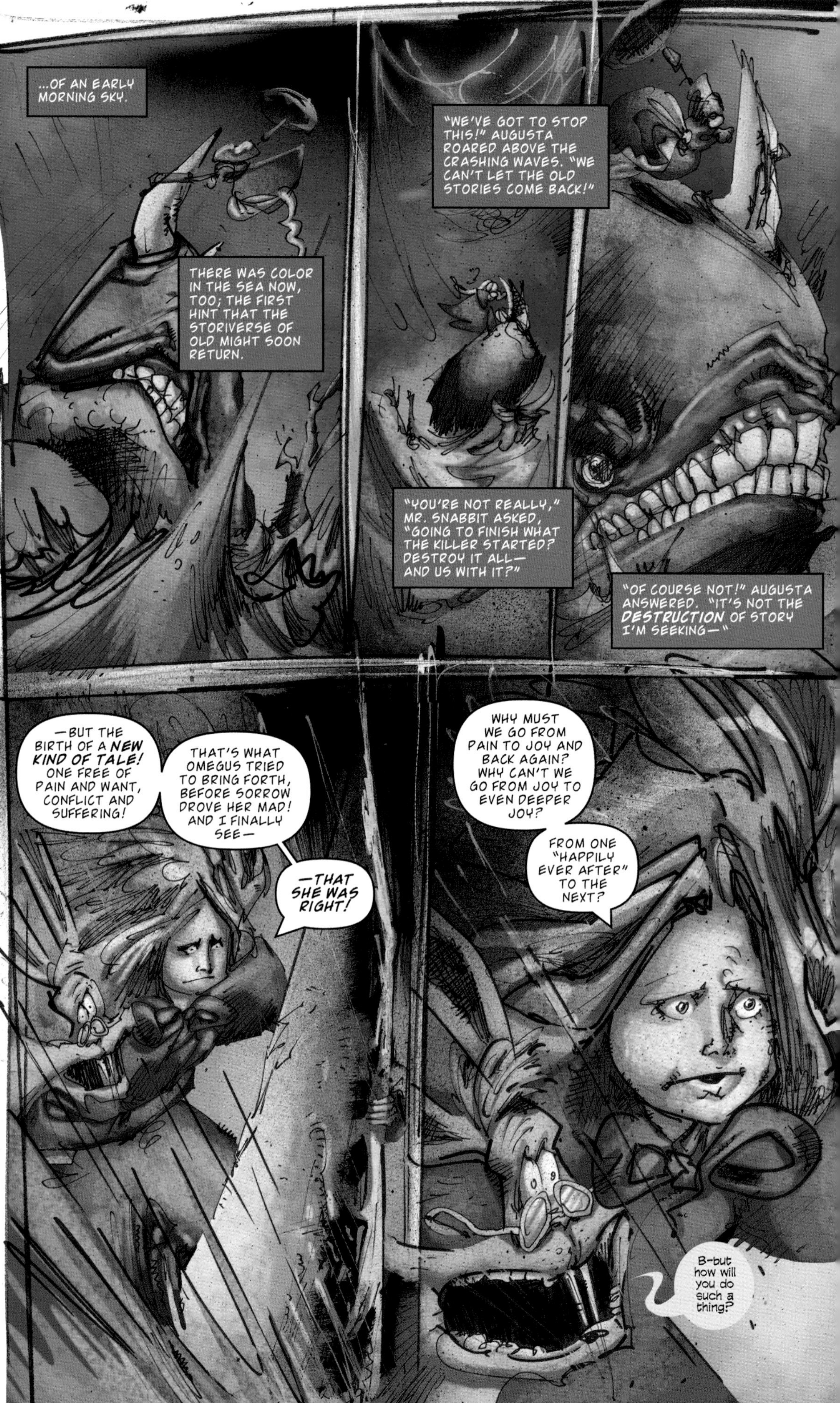
...OF AN EARLY MORNING SKY.
THERE WAS COLOR IN THE SEA NOW, TOO; THE FIRST HINT THAT THE STORIVERSE OF OLD MIGHT SOON RETURN.
"WE'VE GOT TO STOP THIS!" AUGUSTA ROARED ABOVE THE CRASHING WAVES. "WE CAN'T LET THE OLD STORIES COME BACK!"
"YOU'RE NOT REALLY," MR. SNABBIT ASKED, "GOING TO FINISH WHAT THE KILLER STARTED? DESTROY IT ALL— AND US WITH IT?"
"OF COURSE NOT!" AUGUSTA ANSWERED. "IT'S NOT THE DESTRUCTION OF STORY I'M SEEKING—"
—BUT THE BIRTH OF A NEW KIND OF TALE! ONE FREE OF PAIN AND WANT, CONFLICT AND SUFFERING!
THAT'S WHAT OMEGUS TRIED TO BRING FORTH, BEFORE SORROW DROVE HER MAD! AND I FINALLY SEE—
—THAT SHE WAS RIGHT!
WHY MUST WE GO FROM PAIN TO JOY AND BACK AGAIN? WHY CAN'T WE GO FROM JOY TO EVEN DEEPER JOY?
FROM ONE "HAPPILY EVER AFTER" TO THE NEXT?
B-but how will you do such a thing?

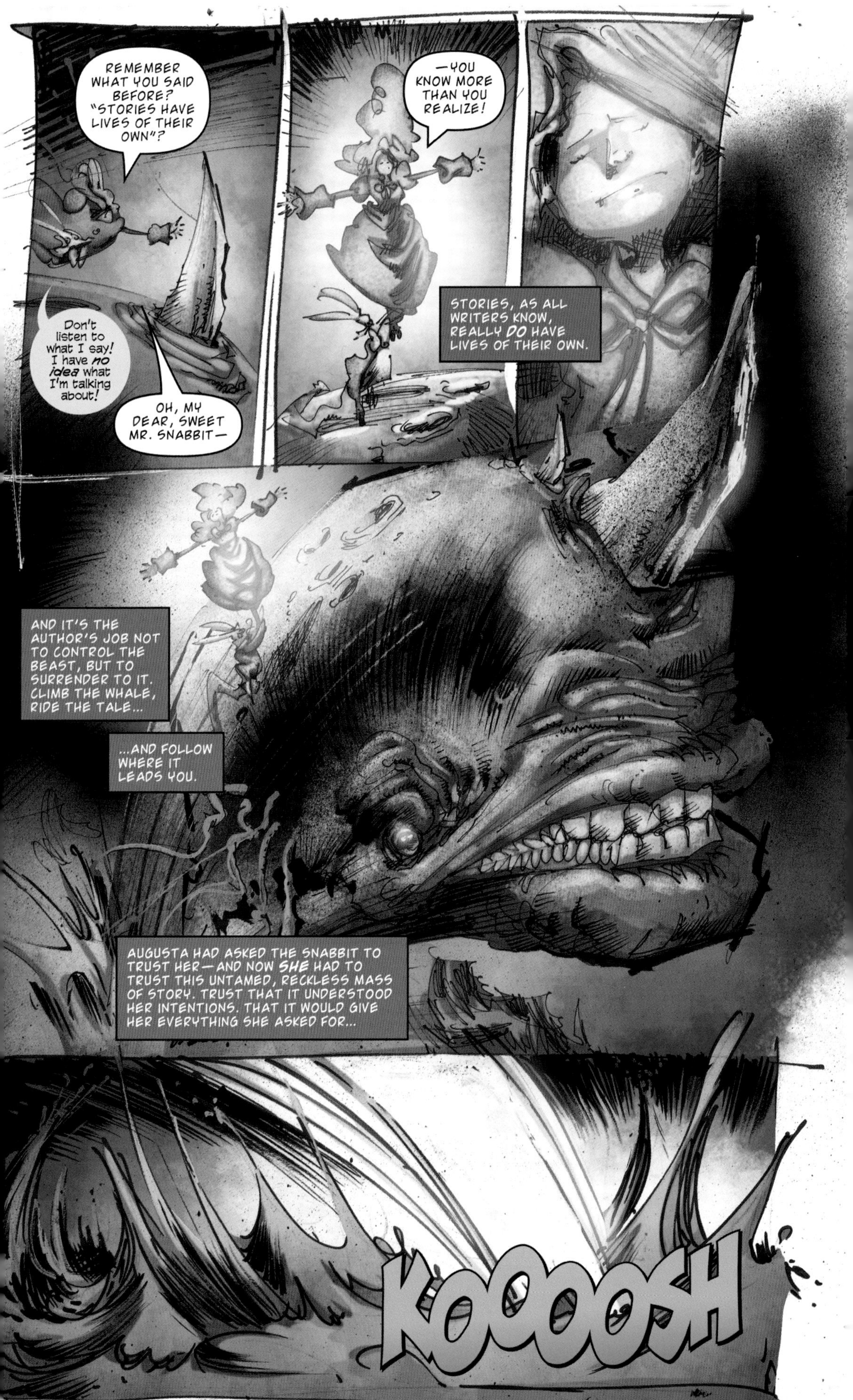
REMEMBER WHAT YOU SAID BEFORE? "STORIES HAVE LIVES OF THEIR OWN"?
Don't listen to what I say! I have *no idea* what I'm talking about!
OH, MY DEAR, SWEET MR. SNABBIT—
—YOU KNOW MORE THAN YOU REALIZE!
STORIES, AS ALL WRITERS KNOW, REALLY *DO* HAVE LIVES OF THEIR OWN.
AND IT'S THE AUTHOR'S JOB NOT TO CONTROL THE BEAST, BUT TO SURRENDER TO IT. CLIMB THE WHALE, RIDE THE TALE...
...AND FOLLOW WHERE IT LEADS YOU.
AUGUSTA HAD ASKED THE SNABBIT TO TRUST HER—AND NOW *SHE* HAD TO TRUST THIS UNTAMED, RECKLESS MASS OF STORY. TRUST THAT IT UNDERSTOOD HER INTENTIONS. THAT IT WOULD GIVE HER EVERYTHING SHE ASKED FOR...
KOOOOSH

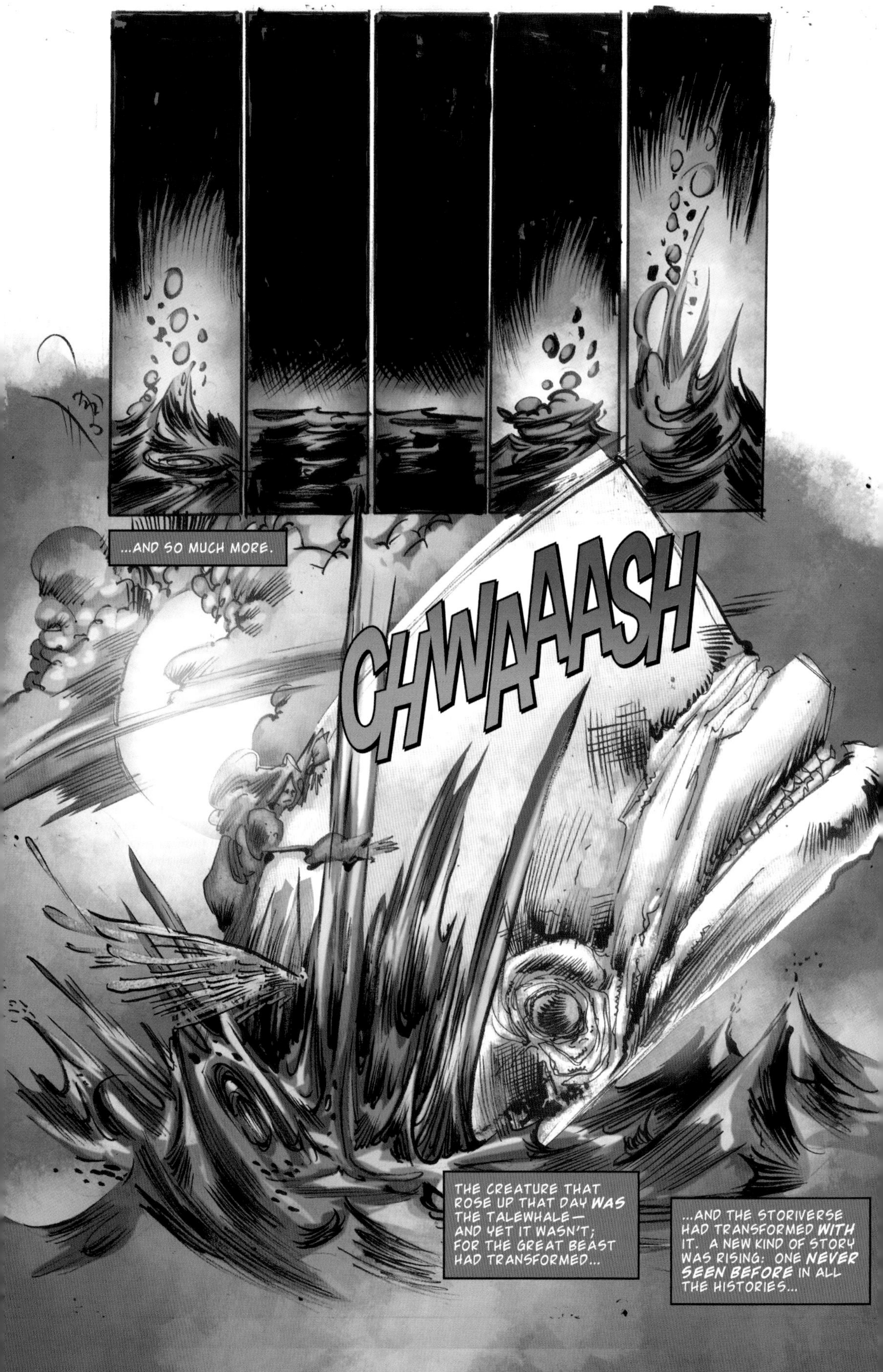
...AND SO MUCH MORE.
CHWAAASH
THE CREATURE THAT ROSE UP THAT DAY WAS THE TALEWHALE— AND YET IT WASN'T; FOR THE GREAT BEAST HAD TRANSFORMED...
...AND THE STORIVERSE HAD TRANSFORMED WITH IT. A NEW KIND OF STORY WAS RISING: ONE NEVER SEEN BEFORE IN ALL THE HISTORIES...

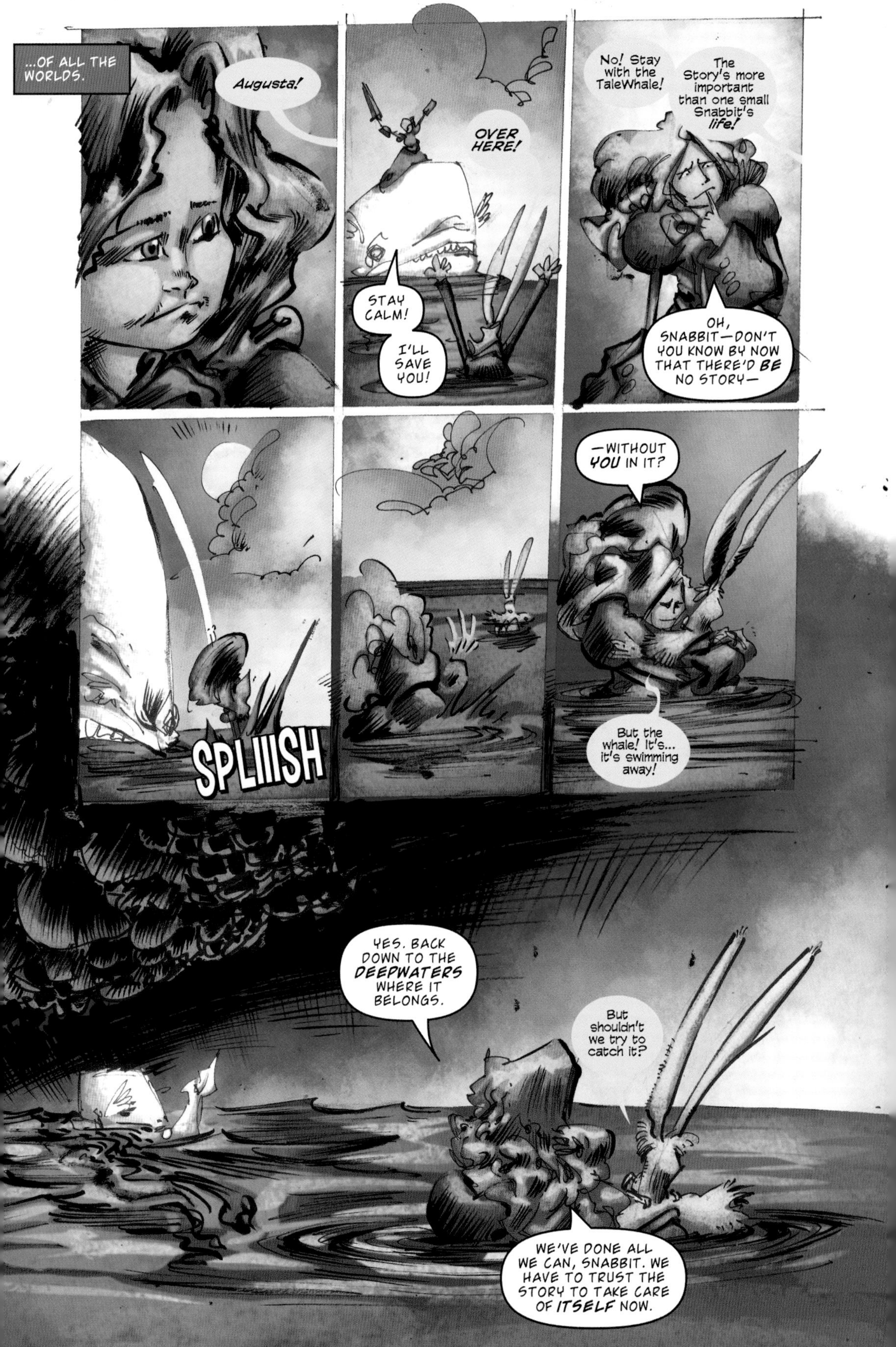
...OF ALL THE WORLDS.
Augusta!
OVER HERE!
STAY CALM!
I'LL SAVE YOU!
No! Stay with the TaleWhale!
The Story's more important than one small Snabbit's life!
OH, SNABBIT—DON'T YOU KNOW BY NOW THAT THERE'D BE NO STORY—
SPLIIISH
—WITHOUT YOU IN IT?
But the whale! It's... it's swimming away!
YES. BACK DOWN TO THE DEEPWATERS WHERE IT BELONGS.
But shouldn't we try to catch it?
WE'VE DONE ALL WE CAN, SNABBIT. WE HAVE TO TRUST THE STORY TO TAKE CARE OF ITSELF NOW.

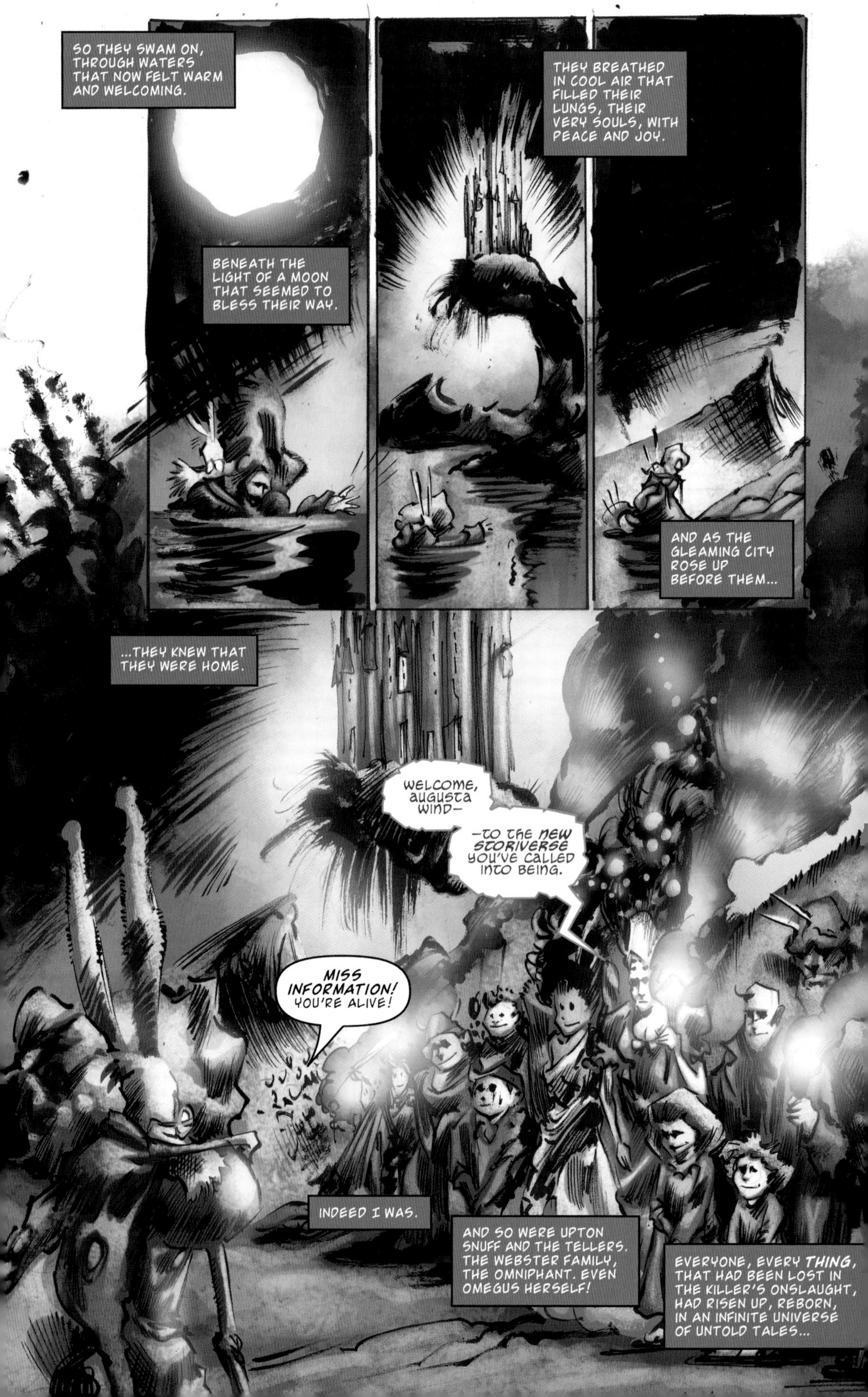
SO THEY SWAM ON, THROUGH WATERS THAT NOW FELT WARM AND WELCOMING.
BENEATH THE LIGHT OF A MOON THAT SEEMED TO BLESS THEIR WAY.
THEY BREATHED IN COOL AIR THAT FILLED THEIR LUNGS, THEIR VERY SOULS, WITH PEACE AND JOY.
AND AS THE GLEAMING CITY ROSE UP BEFORE THEM...
...THEY KNEW THAT THEY WERE HOME.
WELCOME, AUGUSTA WIND—
—TO THE NEW STORIVERSE YOU'VE CALLED INTO BEING.
MISS INFORMATION! YOU'RE ALIVE!
INDEED I WAS.
AND SO WERE UPTON SNUFF AND THE TELLERS. THE WEBSTER FAMILY, THE OMNIPHANT. EVEN OMEGUS HERSELF!
EVERYONE, EVERY THING, THAT HAD BEEN LOST IN THE KILLER'S ONSLAUGHT, HAD RISEN UP, REBORN, IN AN INFINITE UNIVERSE OF UNTOLD TALES...

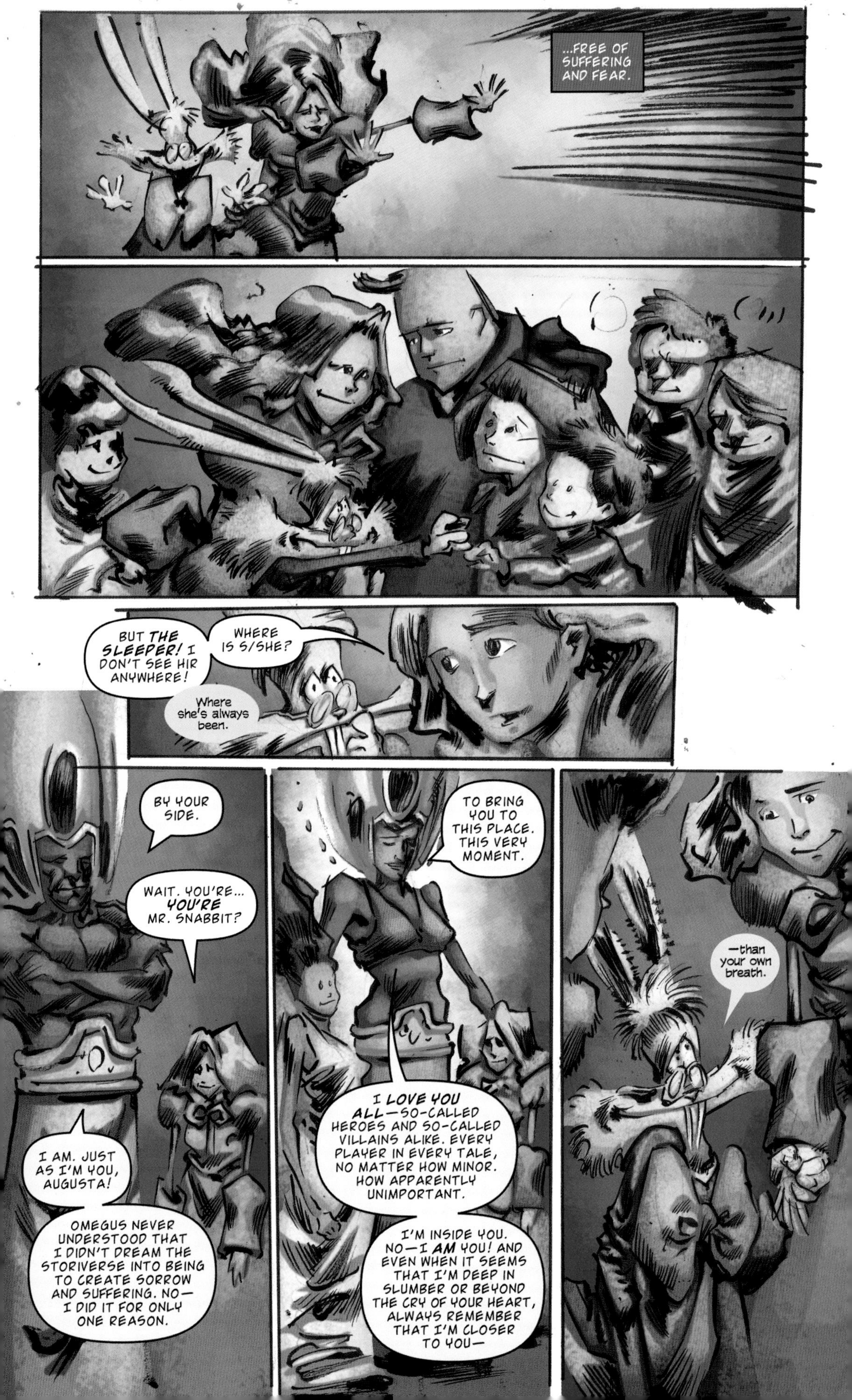
...FREE OF SUFFERING AND FEAR.
BUT THE SLEEPER! I DON'T SEE HIR ANYWHERE!
WHERE IS S/SHE?
Where she's always been.
BY YOUR SIDE.
WAIT. YOU'RE... YOU'RE MR. SNABBIT?
I AM. JUST AS I'M YOU, AUGUSTA!
OMEGUS NEVER UNDERSTOOD THAT I DIDN'T DREAM THE STORIVERSE INTO BEING TO CREATE SORROW AND SUFFERING. NO— I DID IT FOR ONLY ONE REASON.
TO BRING YOU TO THIS PLACE. THIS VERY MOMENT.
I LOVE YOU ALL—SO-CALLED HEROES AND SO-CALLED VILLAINS ALIKE. EVERY PLAYER IN EVERY TALE, NO MATTER HOW MINOR. HOW APPARENTLY UNIMPORTANT.
I'M INSIDE YOU. NO—I AM YOU! AND EVEN WHEN IT SEEMS THAT I'M DEEP IN SLUMBER OR BEYOND THE CRY OF YOUR HEART, ALWAYS REMEMBER THAT I'M CLOSER TO YOU—
—than your own breath.

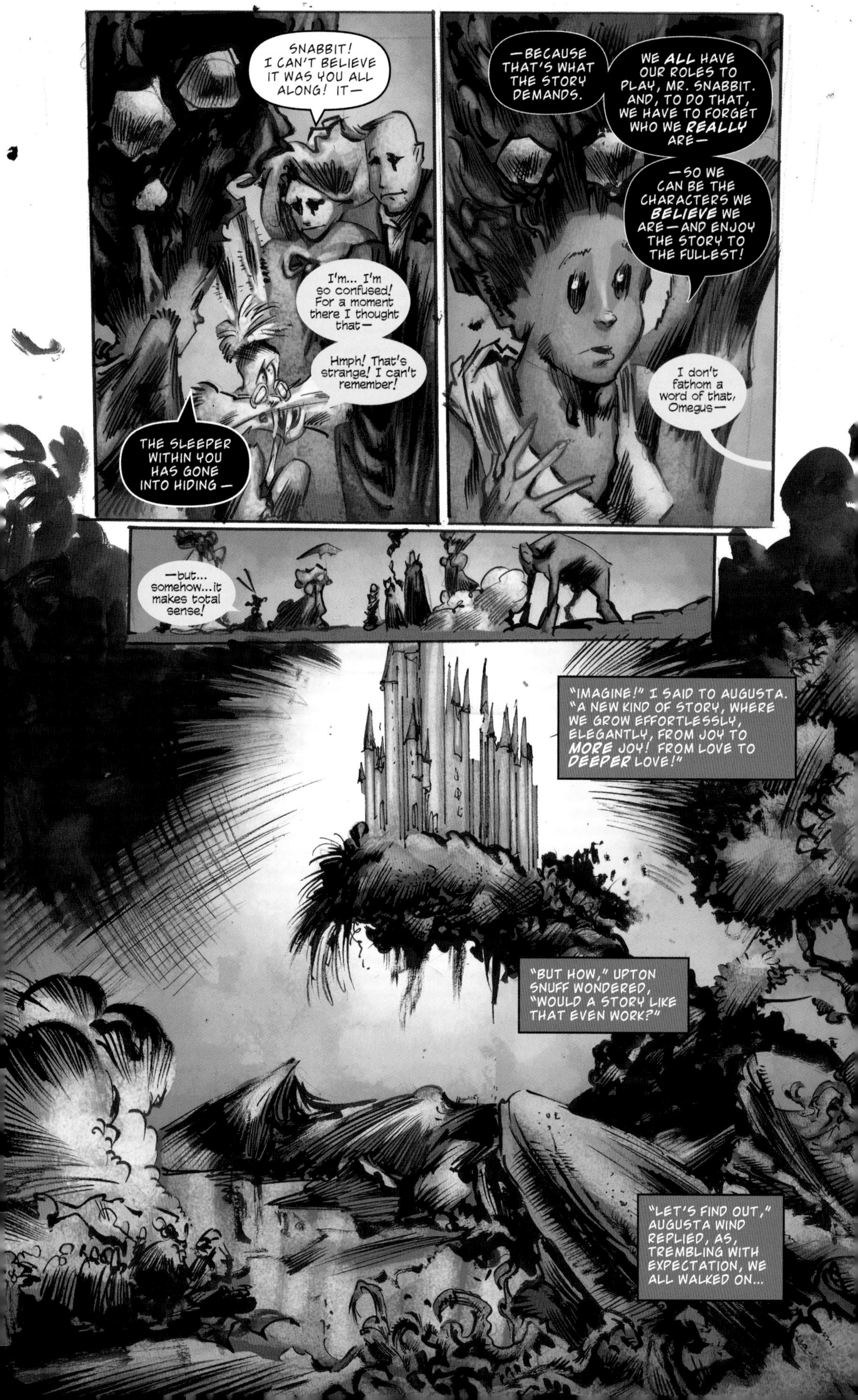
SNABBIT! I CAN'T BELIEVE IT WAS YOU ALL ALONG! IT—
I'm... I'm so confused! For a moment there I thought that—
Hmph! That's strange! I can't remember!
THE SLEEPER WITHIN YOU HAS GONE INTO HIDING—
—BECAUSE THAT'S WHAT THE STORY DEMANDS.
WE ALL HAVE OUR ROLES TO PLAY, MR. SNABBIT. AND, TO DO THAT, WE HAVE TO FORGET WHO WE REALLY ARE—
—SO WE CAN BE THE CHARACTERS WE BELIEVE WE ARE—AND ENJOY THE STORY TO THE FULLEST!
I don't fathom a word of that, Omegus—
—but... somehow...it makes total sense!
"IMAGINE!" I SAID TO AUGUSTA. "A NEW KIND OF STORY, WHERE WE GROW EFFORTLESSLY, ELEGANTLY, FROM JOY TO MORE JOY! FROM LOVE TO DEEPER LOVE!"
"BUT HOW," UPTON SNUFF WONDERED, "WOULD A STORY LIKE THAT EVEN WORK?"
"LET'S FIND OUT," AUGUSTA WIND REPLIED, AS, TREMBLING WITH EXPECTATION, WE ALL WALKED ON...

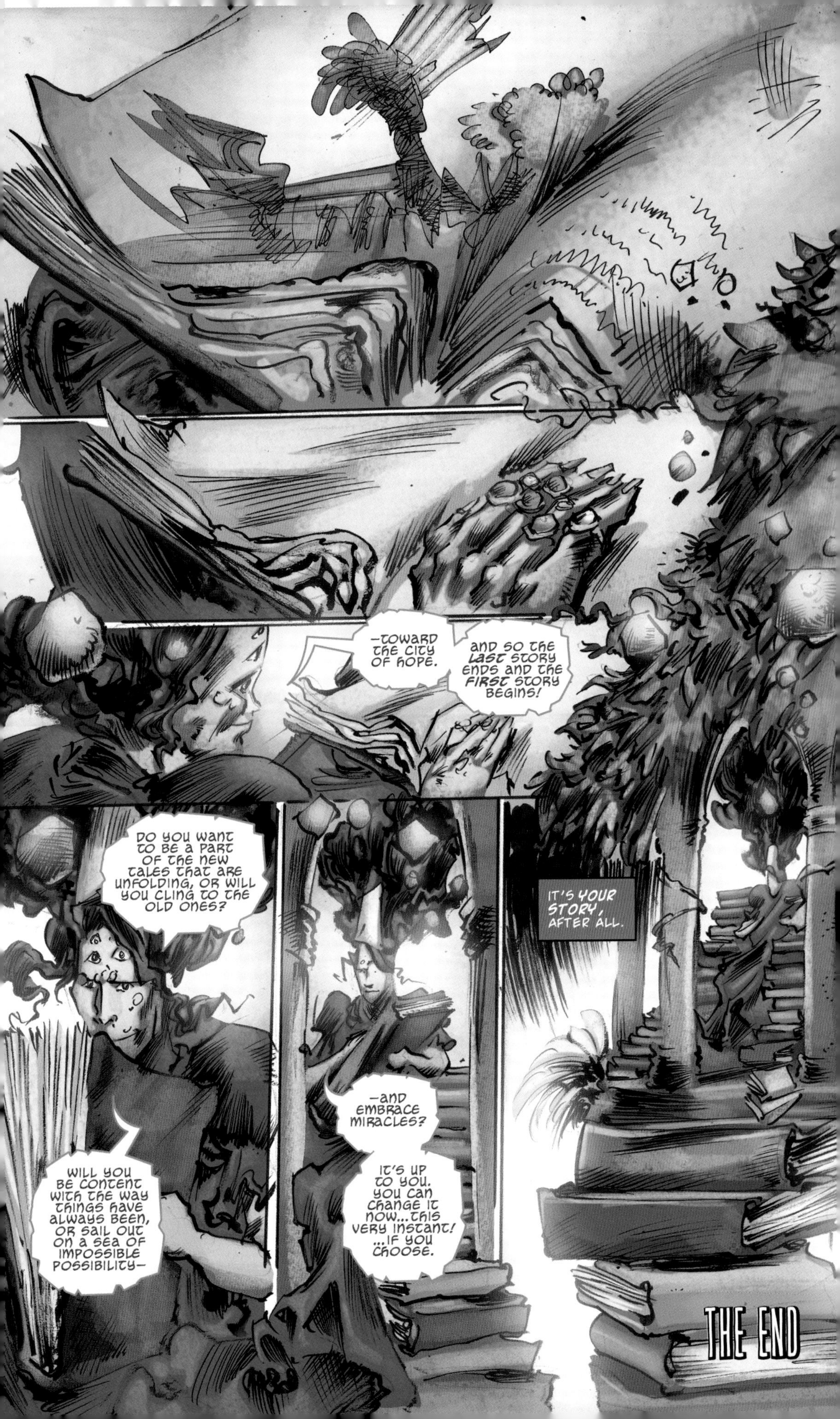
—TOWARD THE CITY OF HOPE.
AND SO THE LAST STORY ENDS AND THE FIRST STORY BEGINS!
DO YOU WANT TO BE A PART OF THE NEW TALES THAT ARE UNFOLDING, OR WILL YOU CLING TO THE OLD ONES?
WILL YOU BE CONTENT WITH THE WAY THINGS HAVE ALWAYS BEEN, OR SAIL OUT ON A SEA OF IMPOSSIBLE POSSIBILITY—
—AND EMBRACE MIRACLES?
IT'S UP TO YOU. YOU CAN CHANGE IT NOW...THIS VERY INSTANT! ...IF YOU CHOOSE.
IT'S YOUR STORY, AFTER ALL.
THE END

ART GALLERY

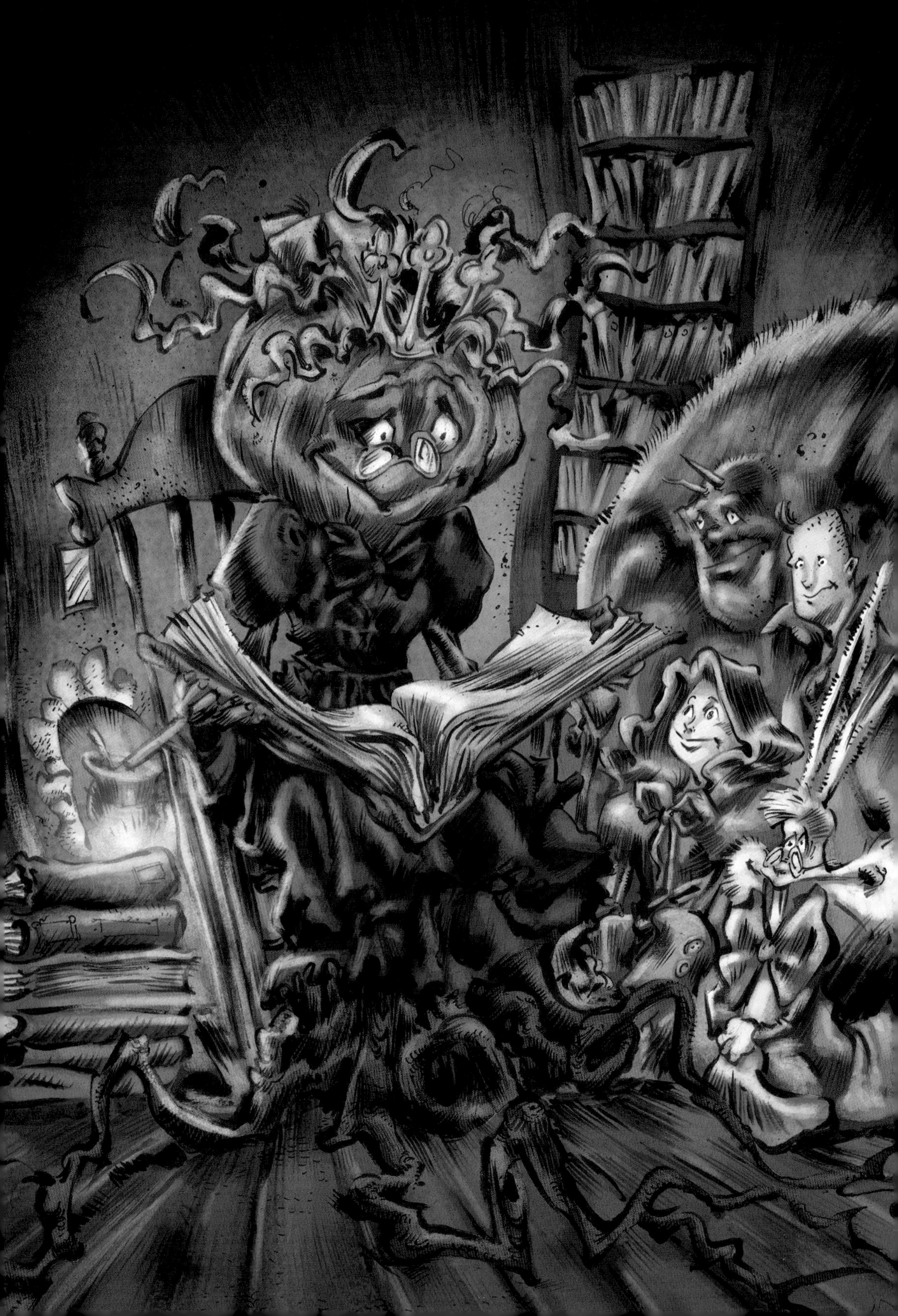

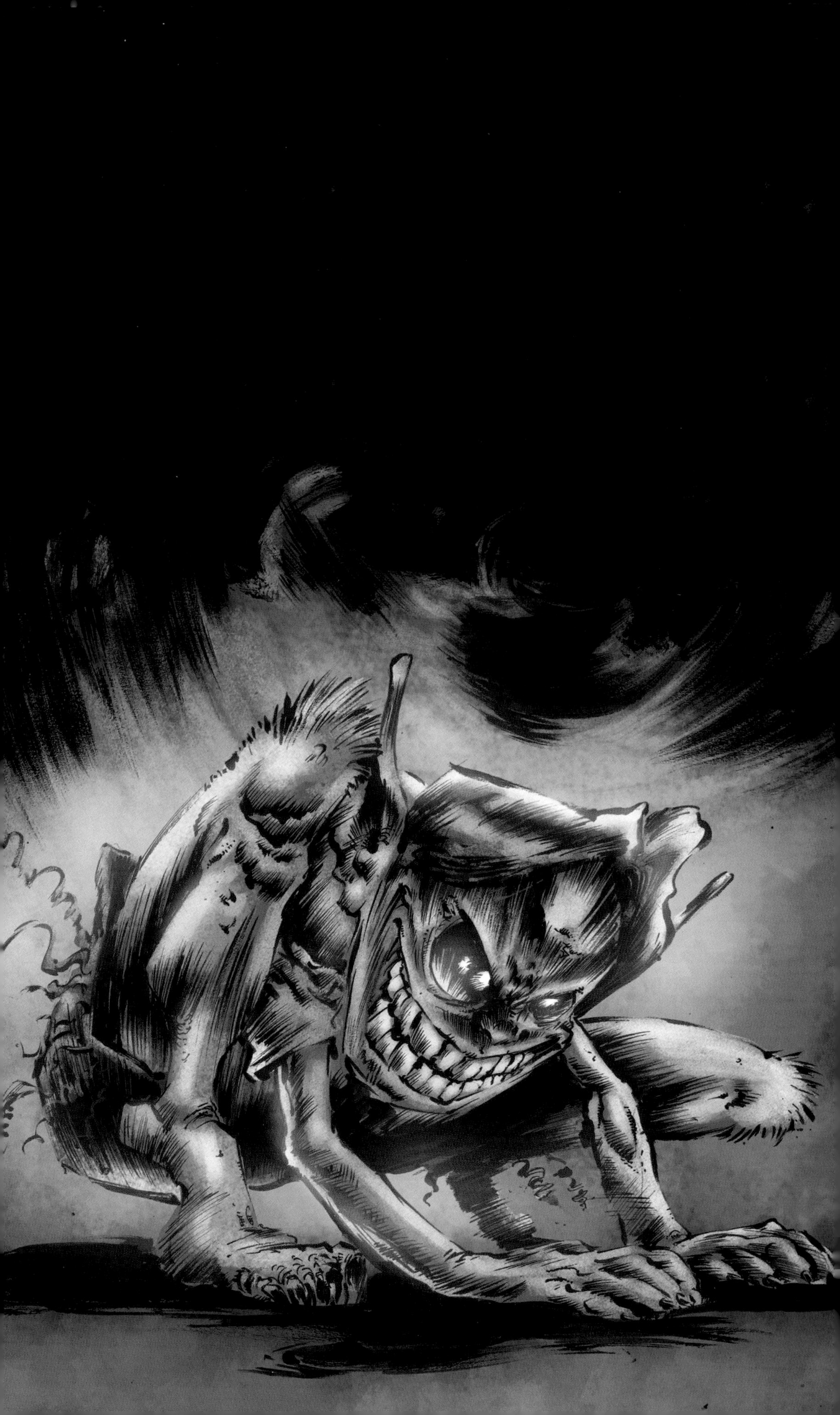

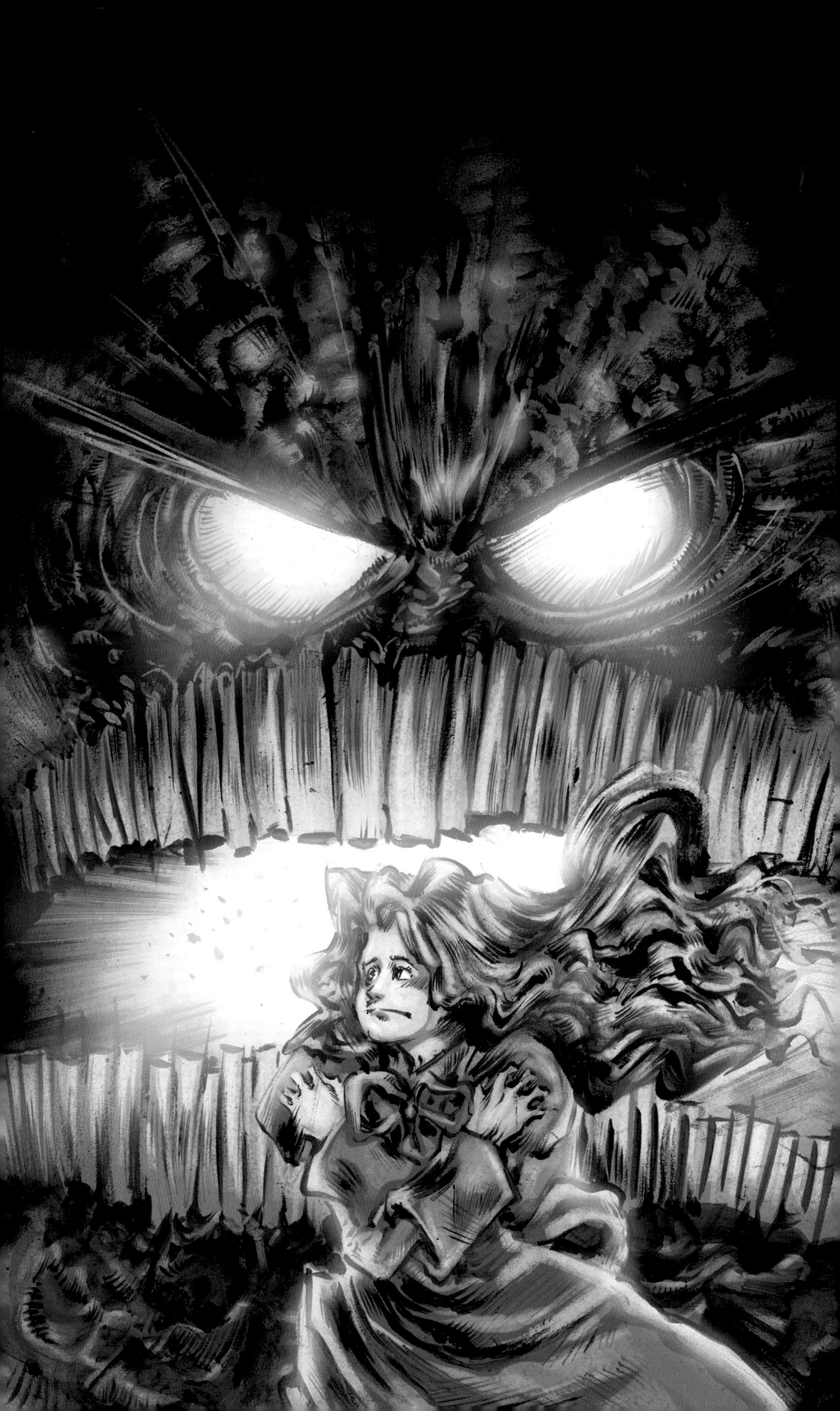

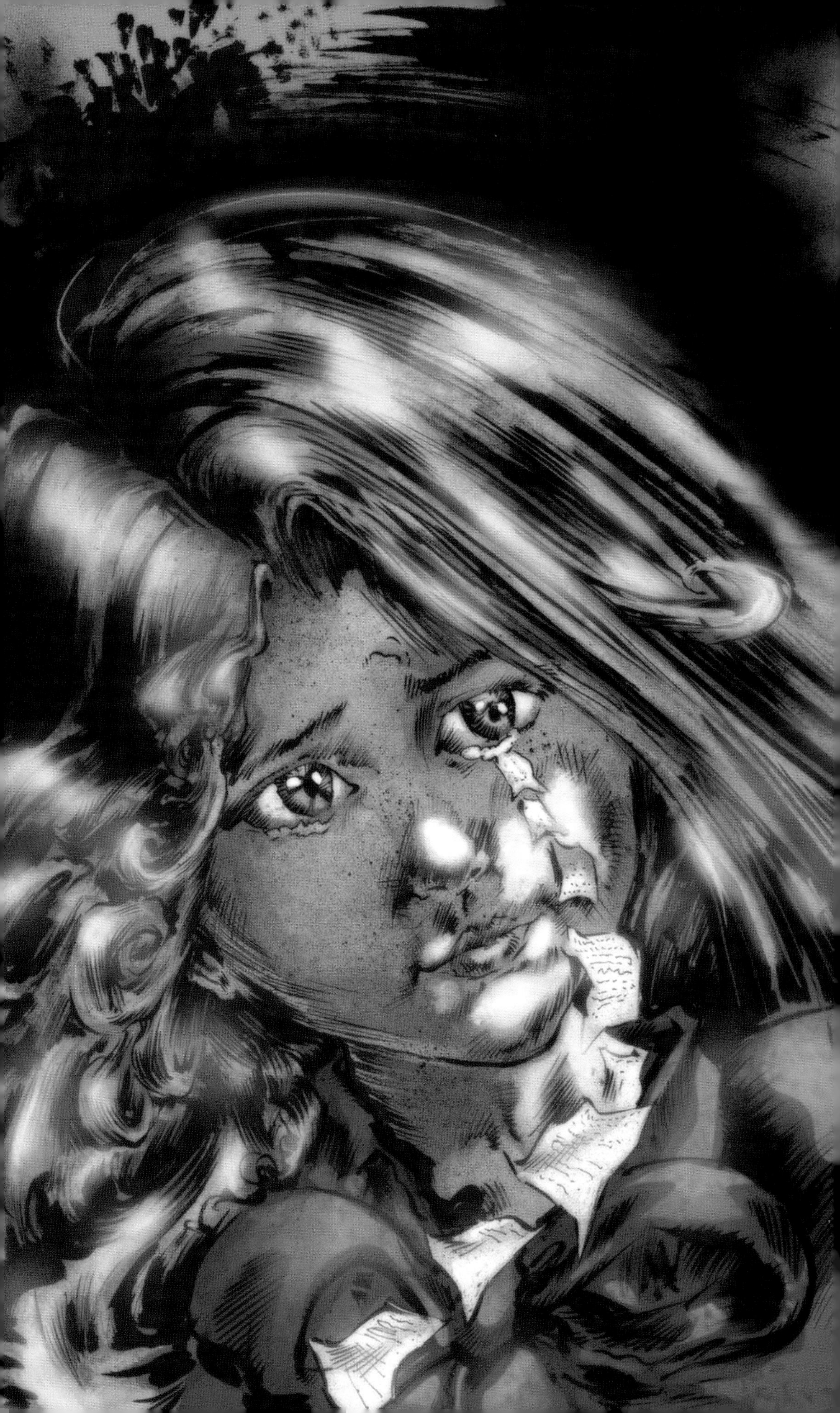

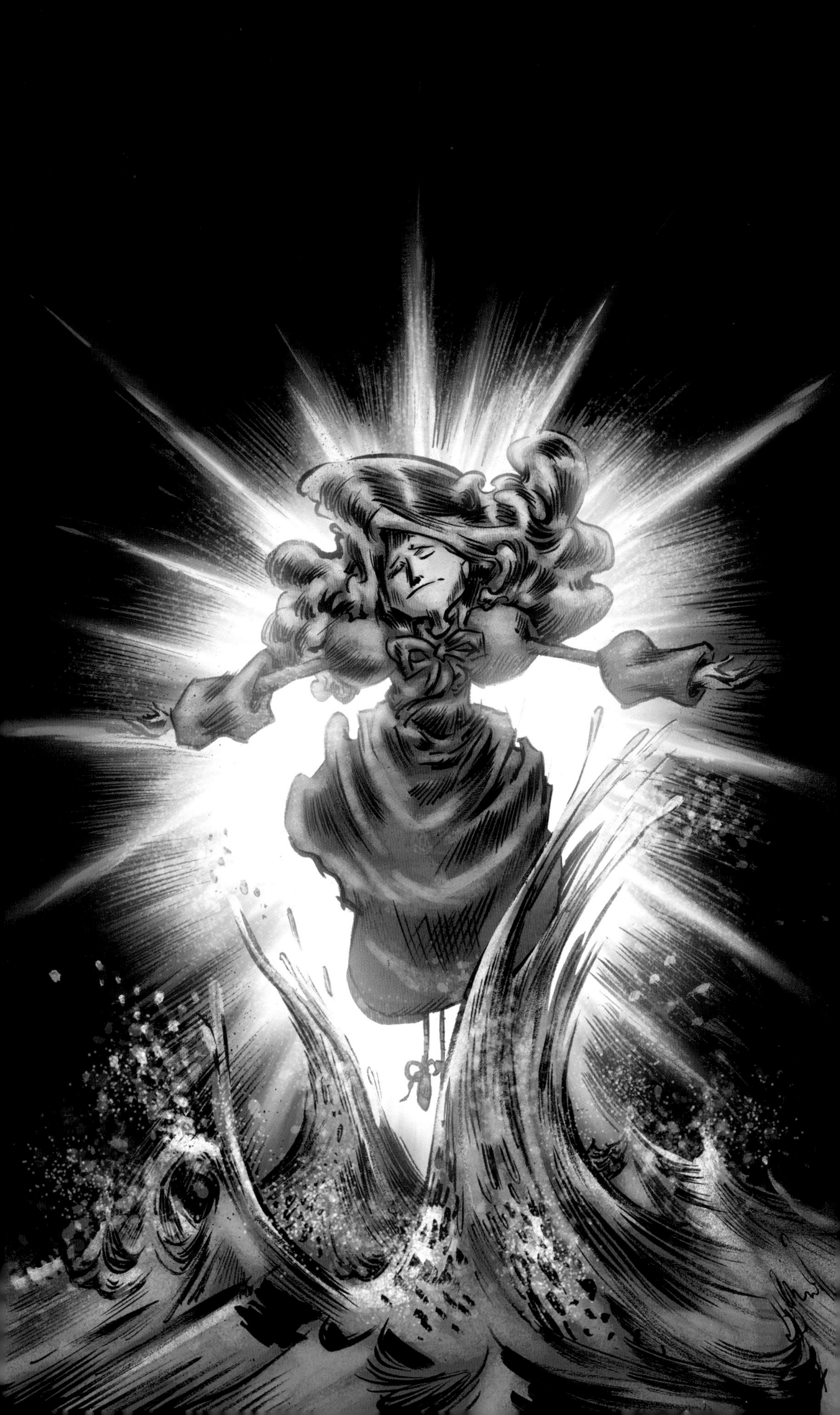

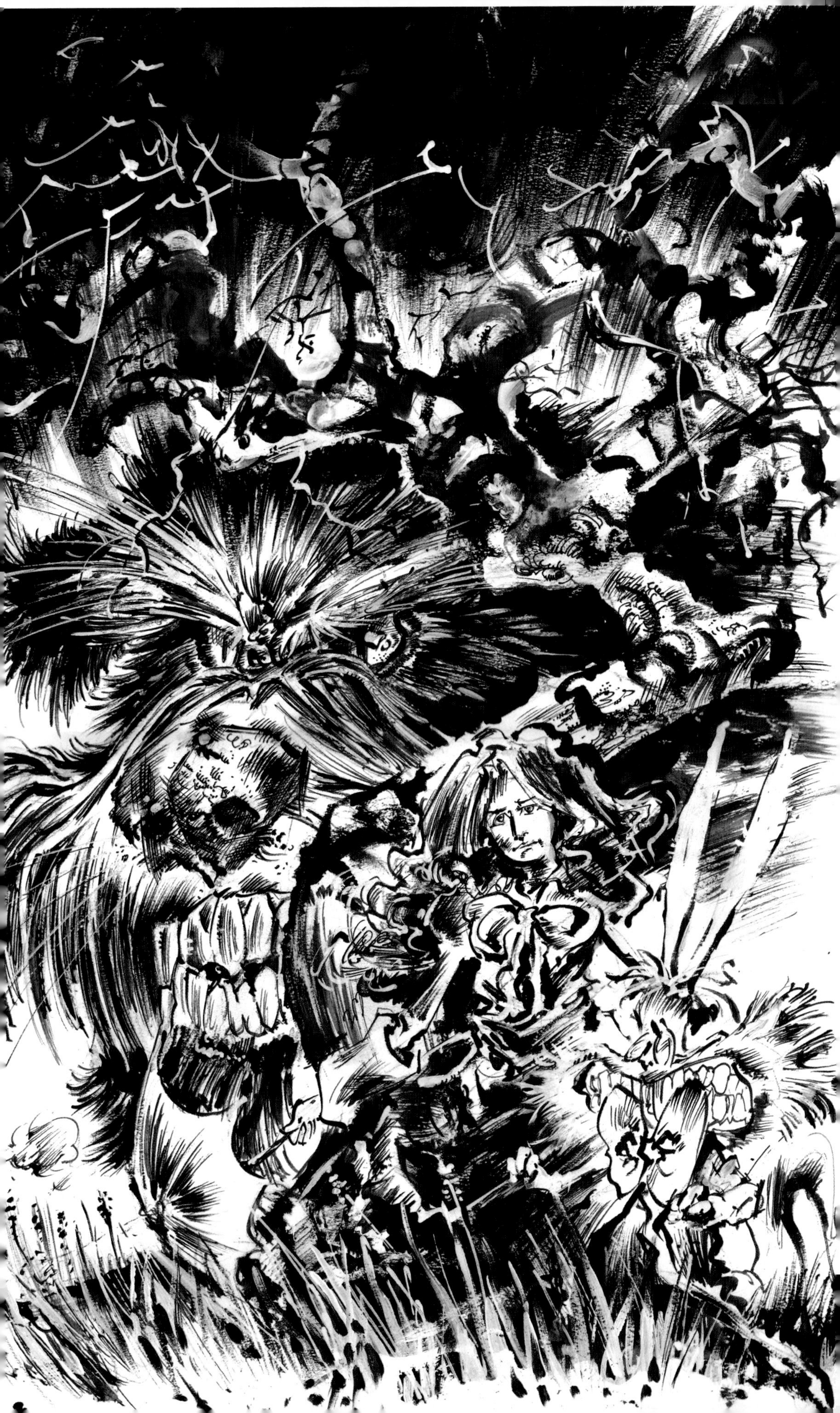

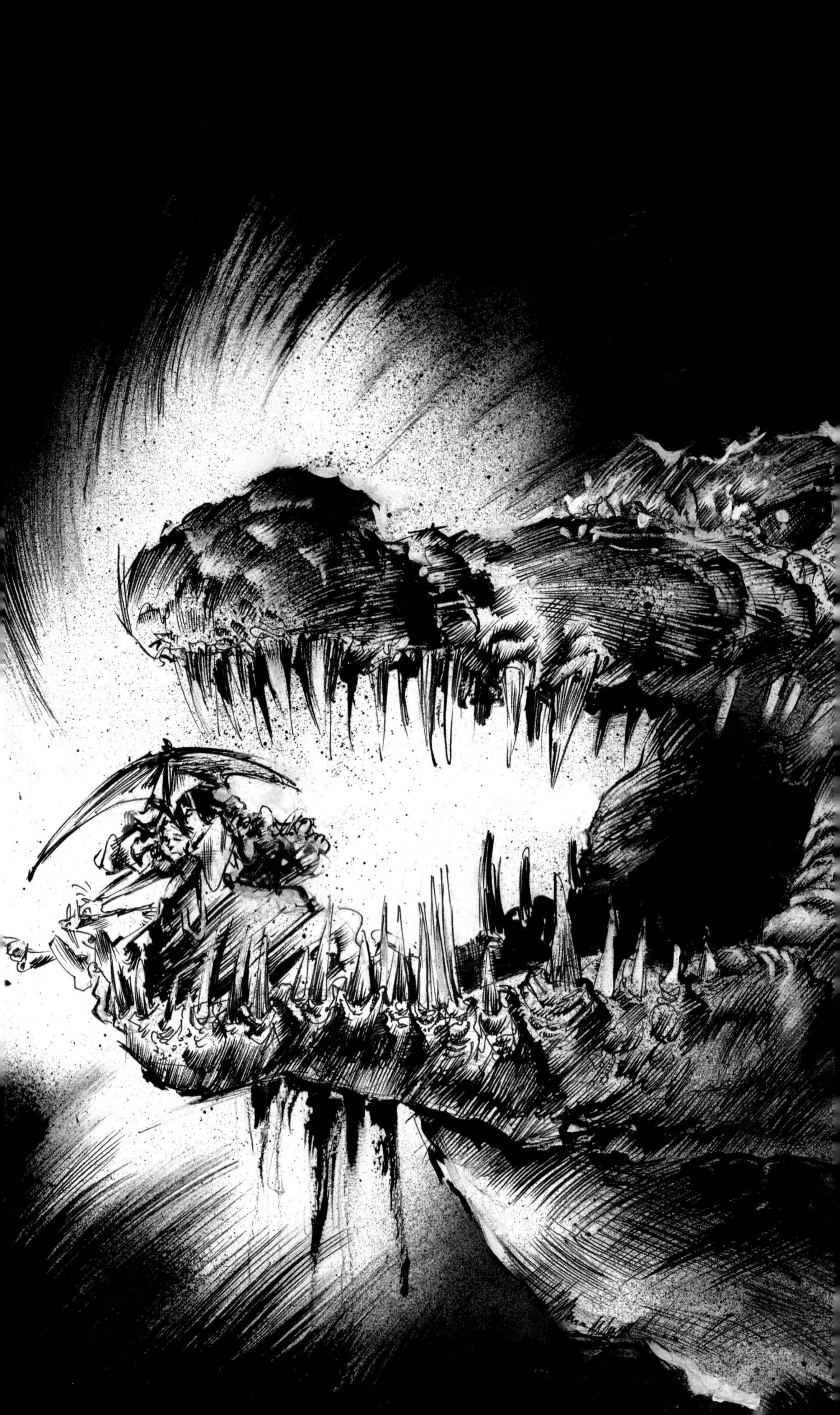

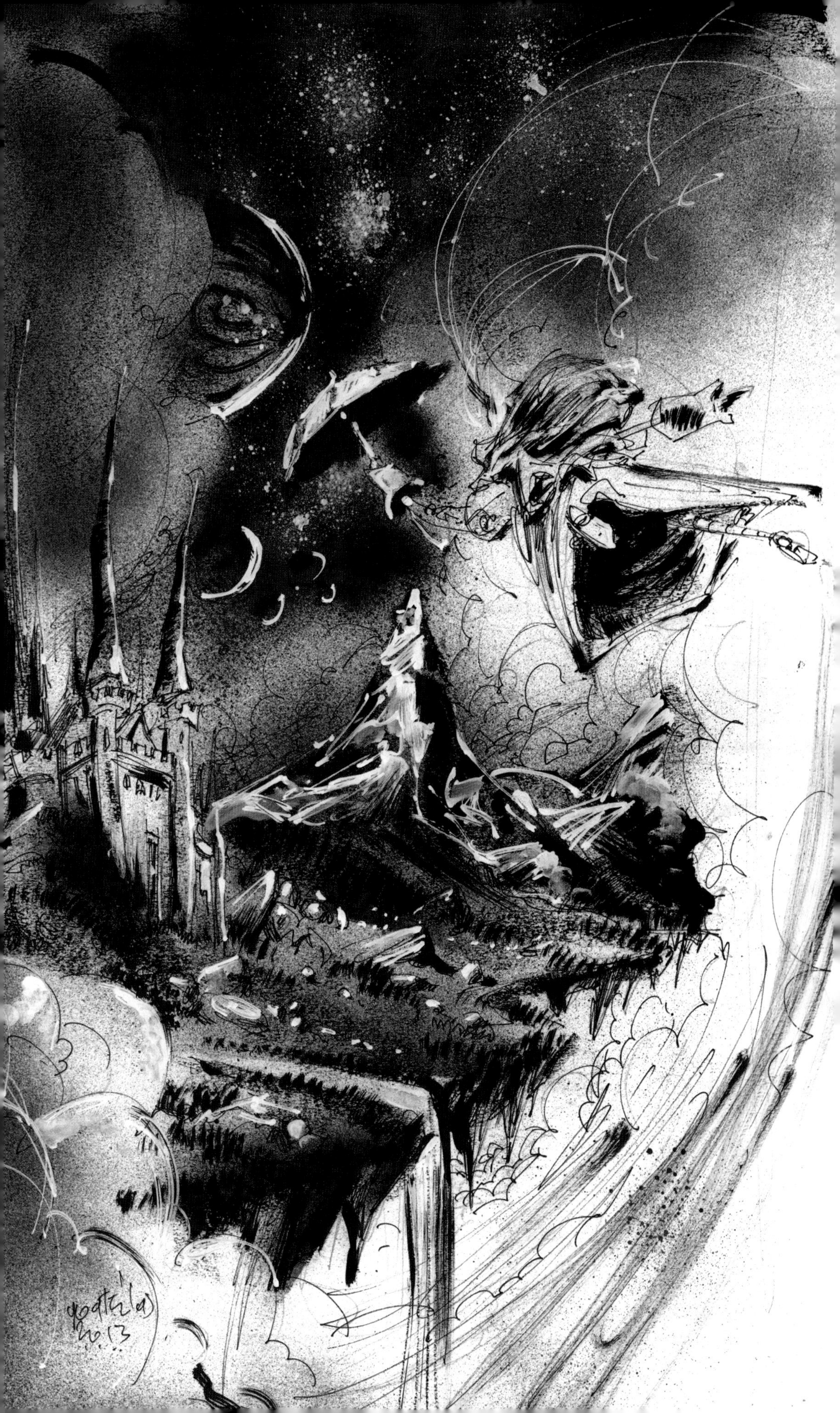

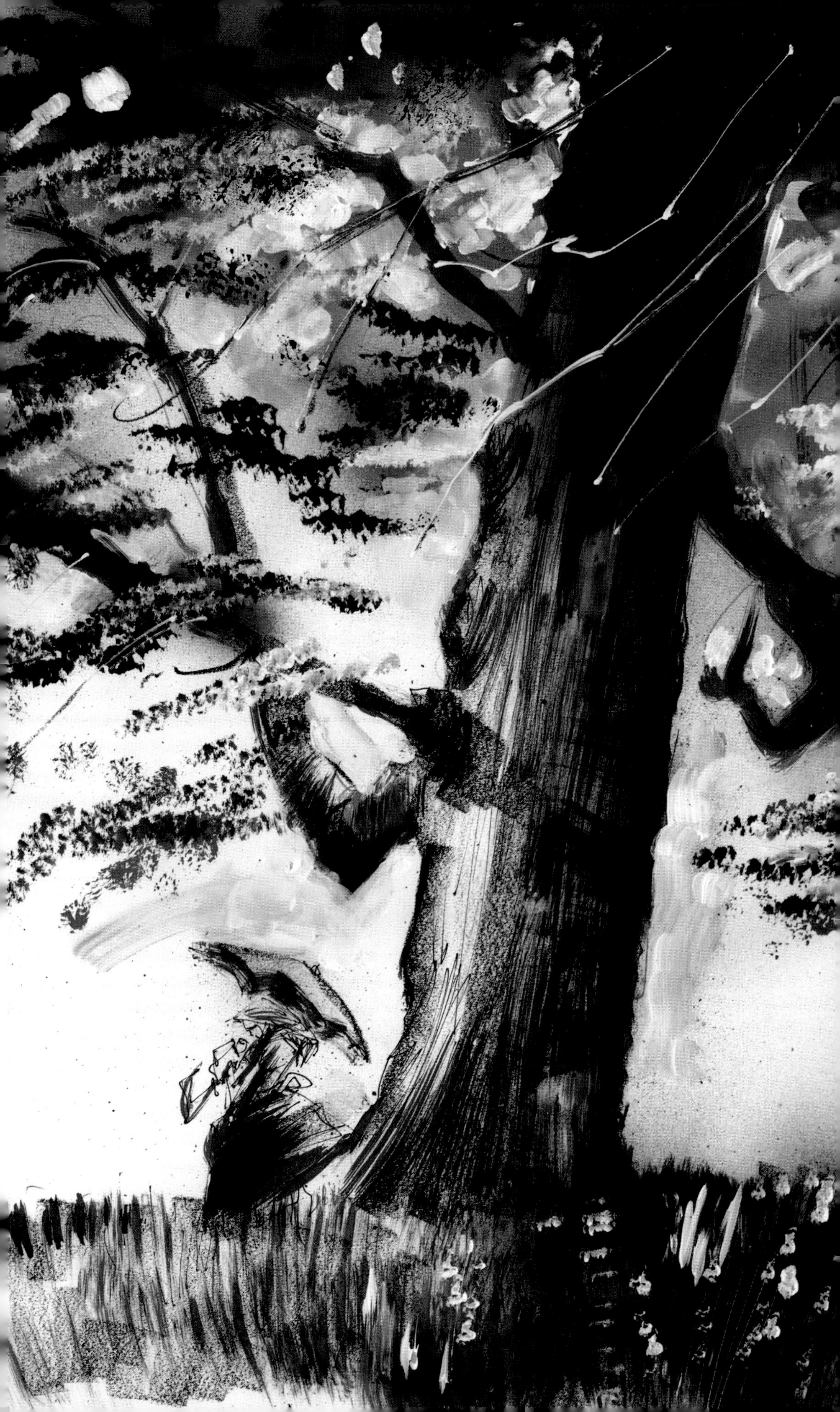

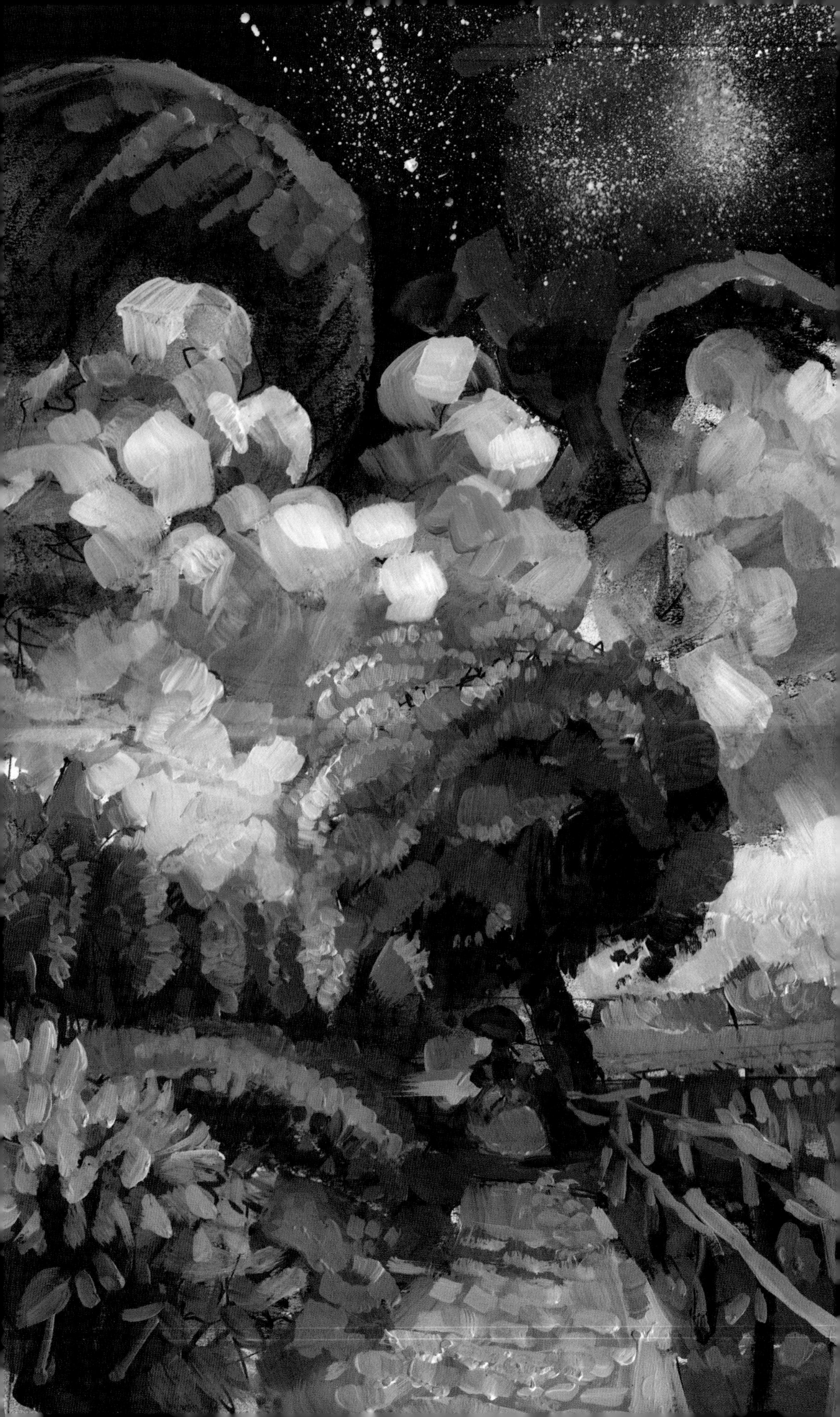

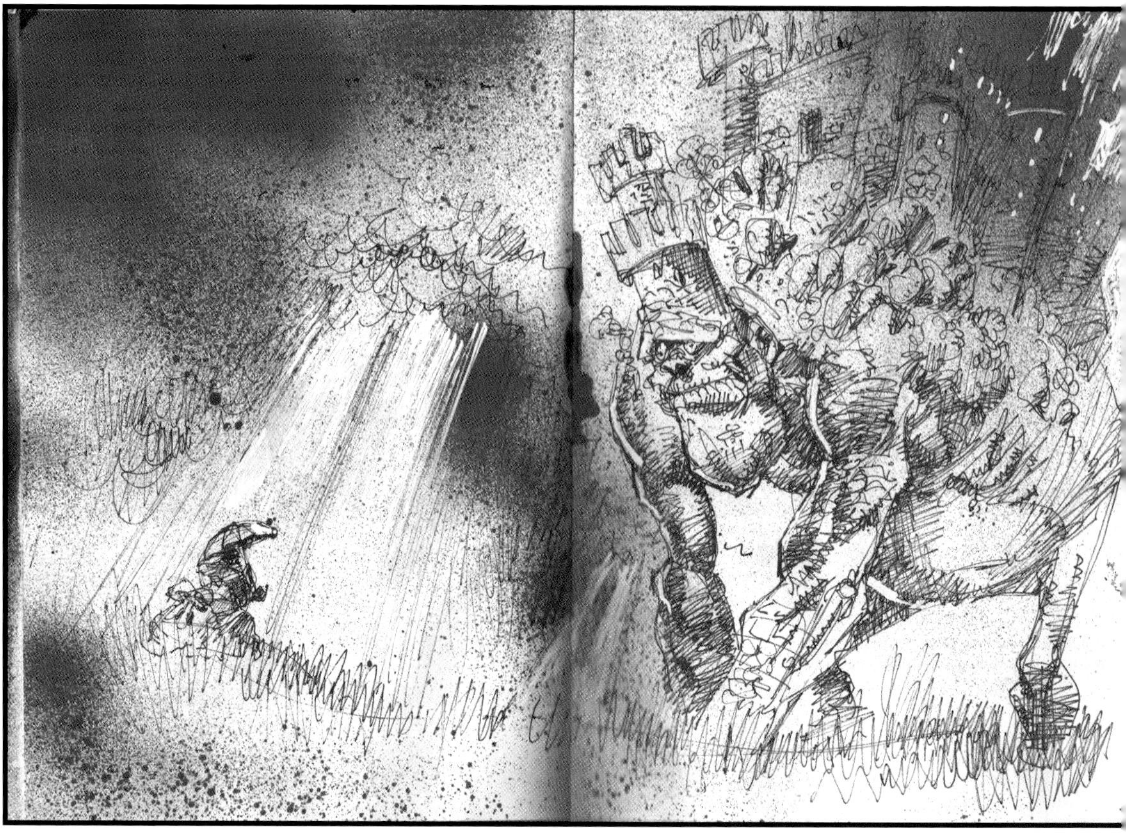

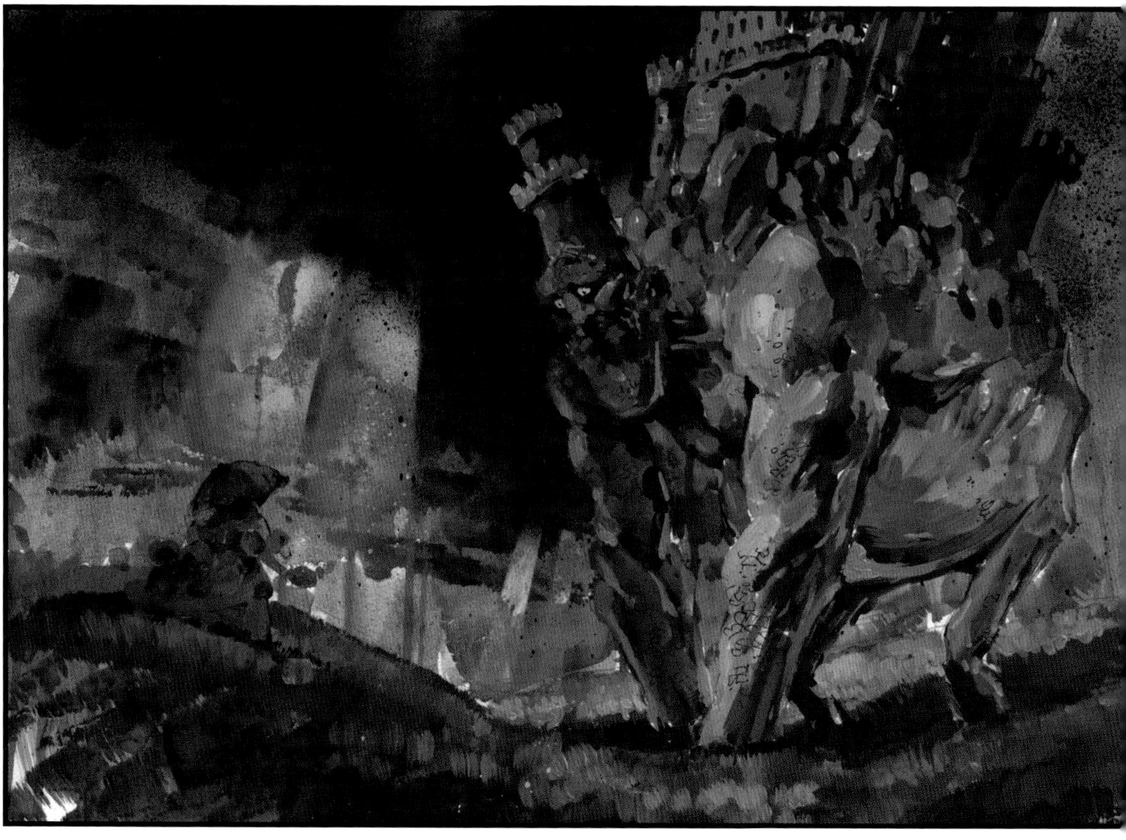

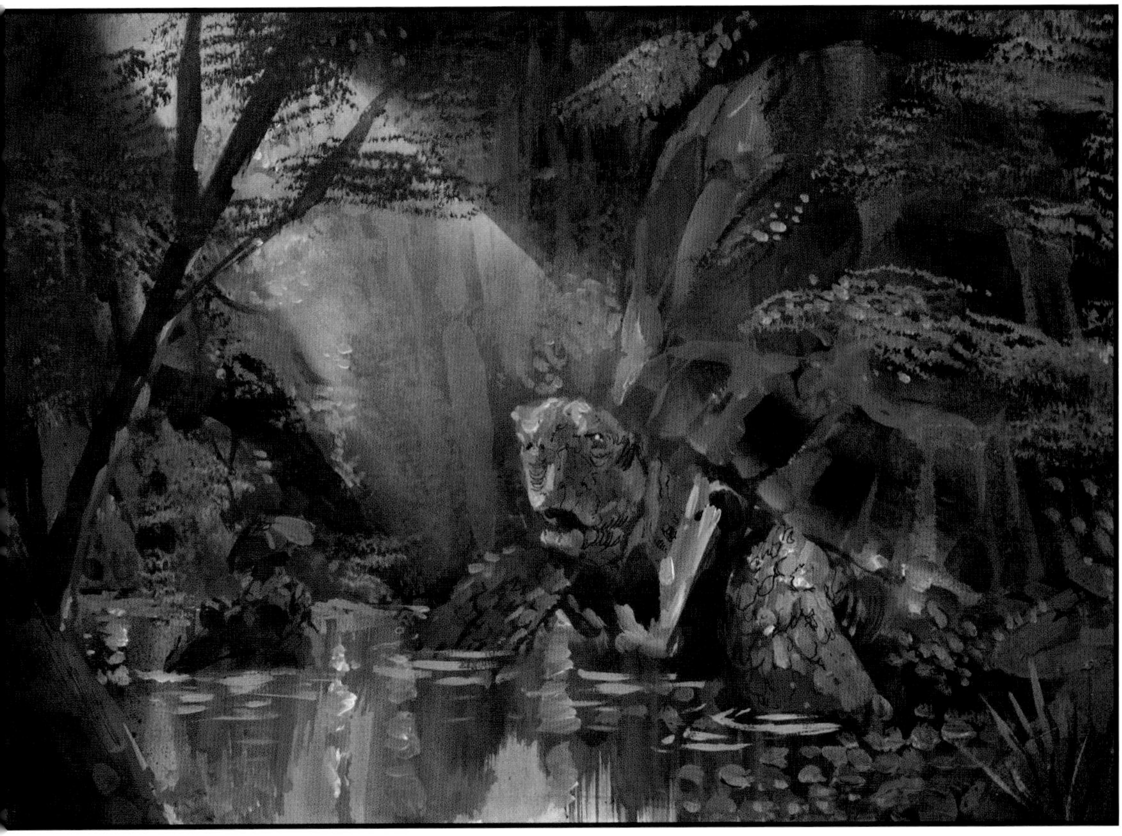

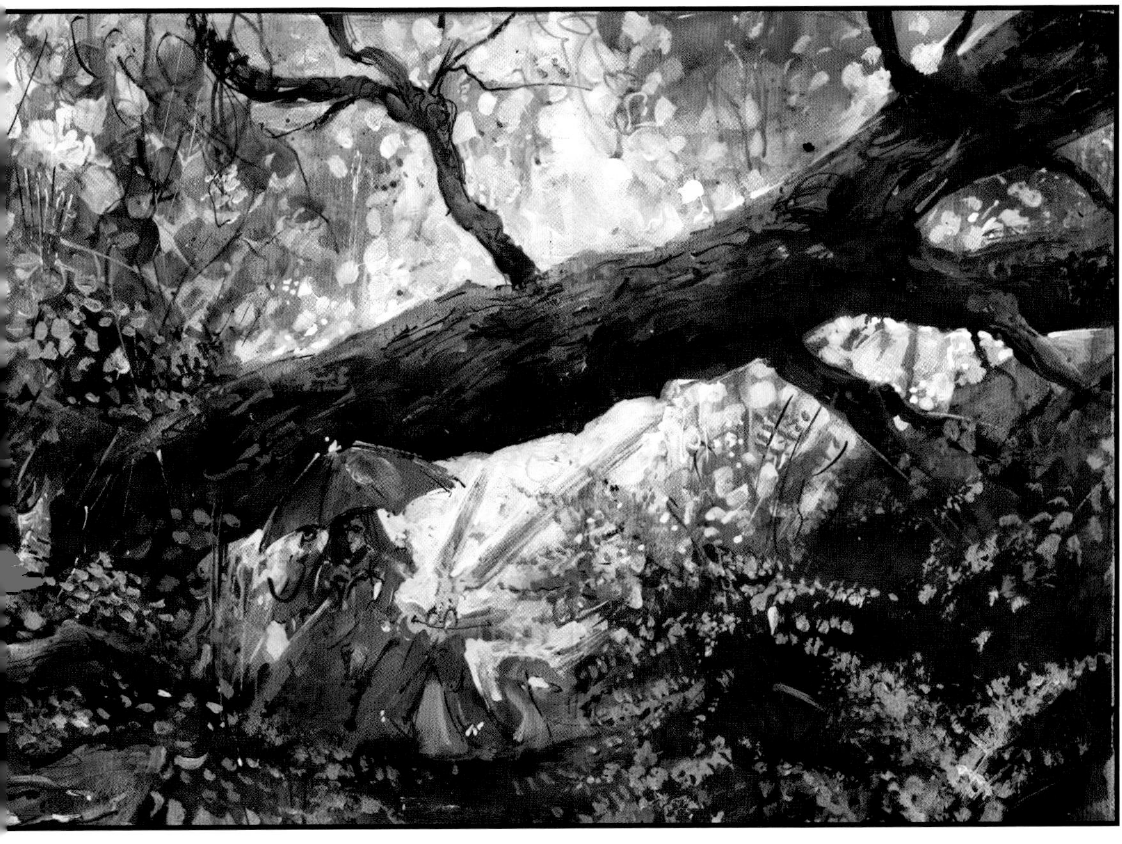

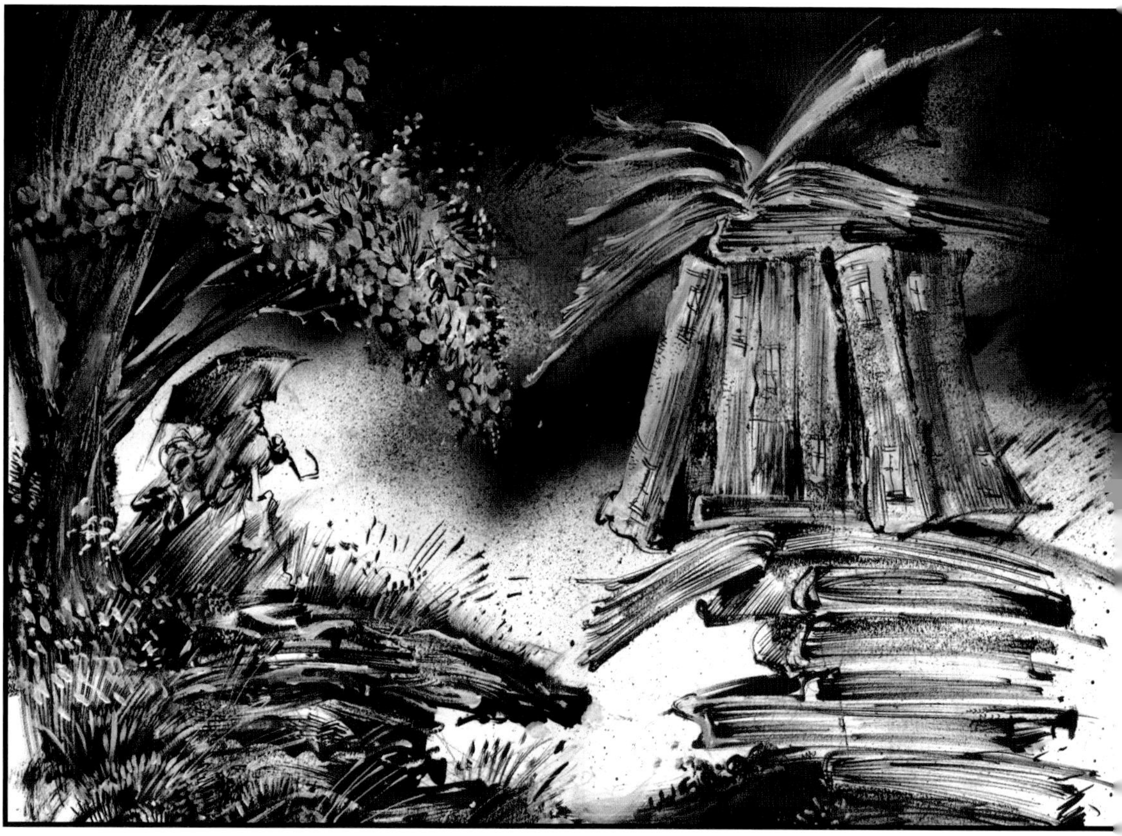

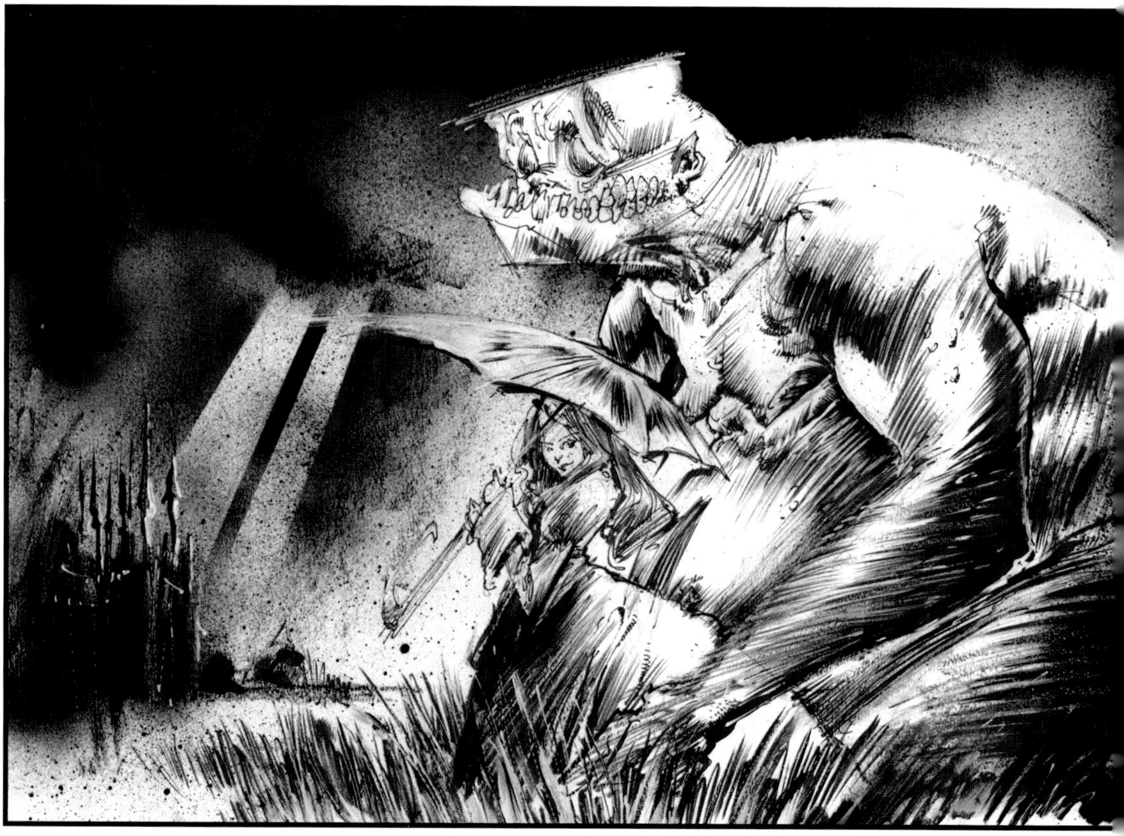

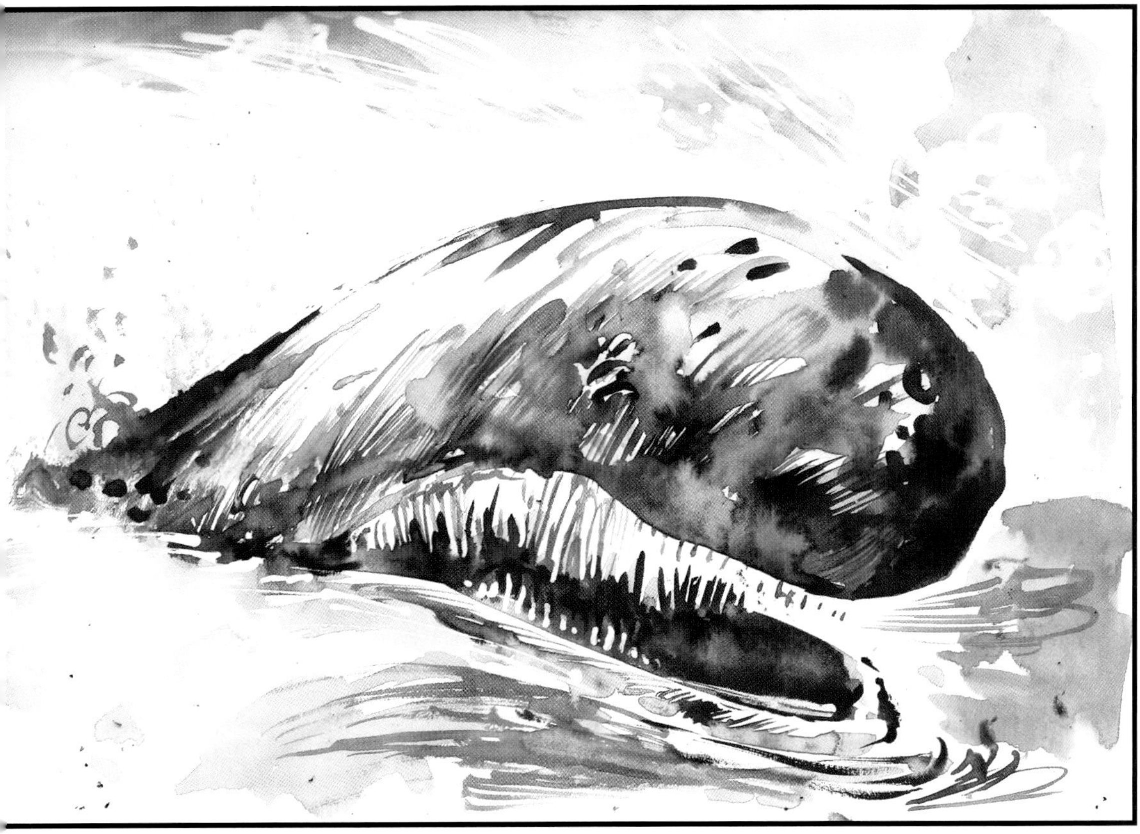

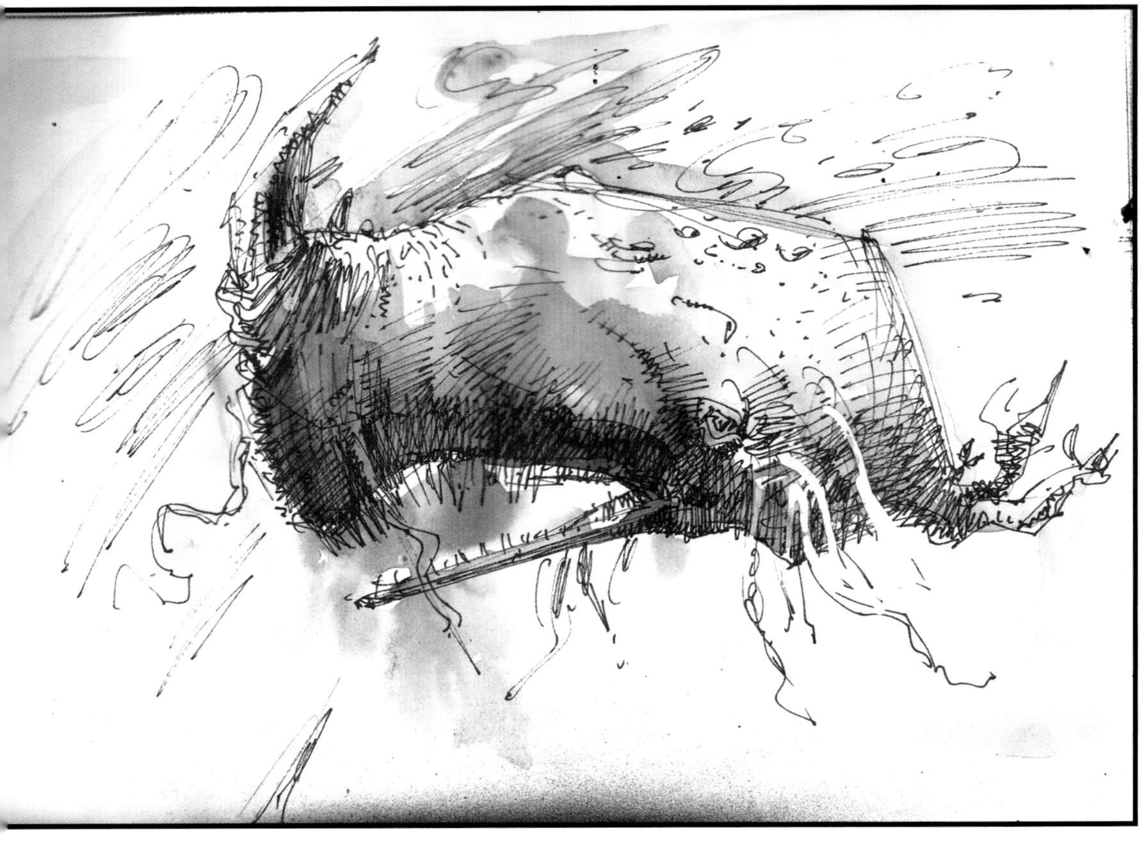

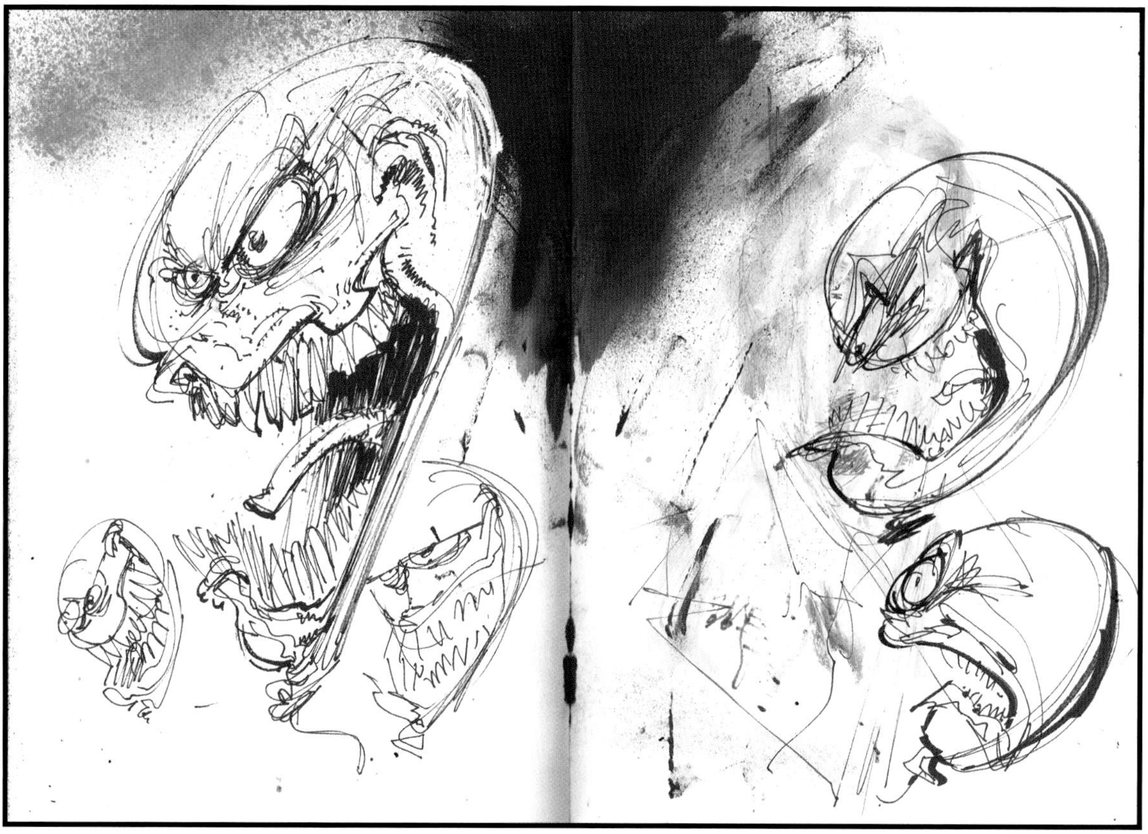

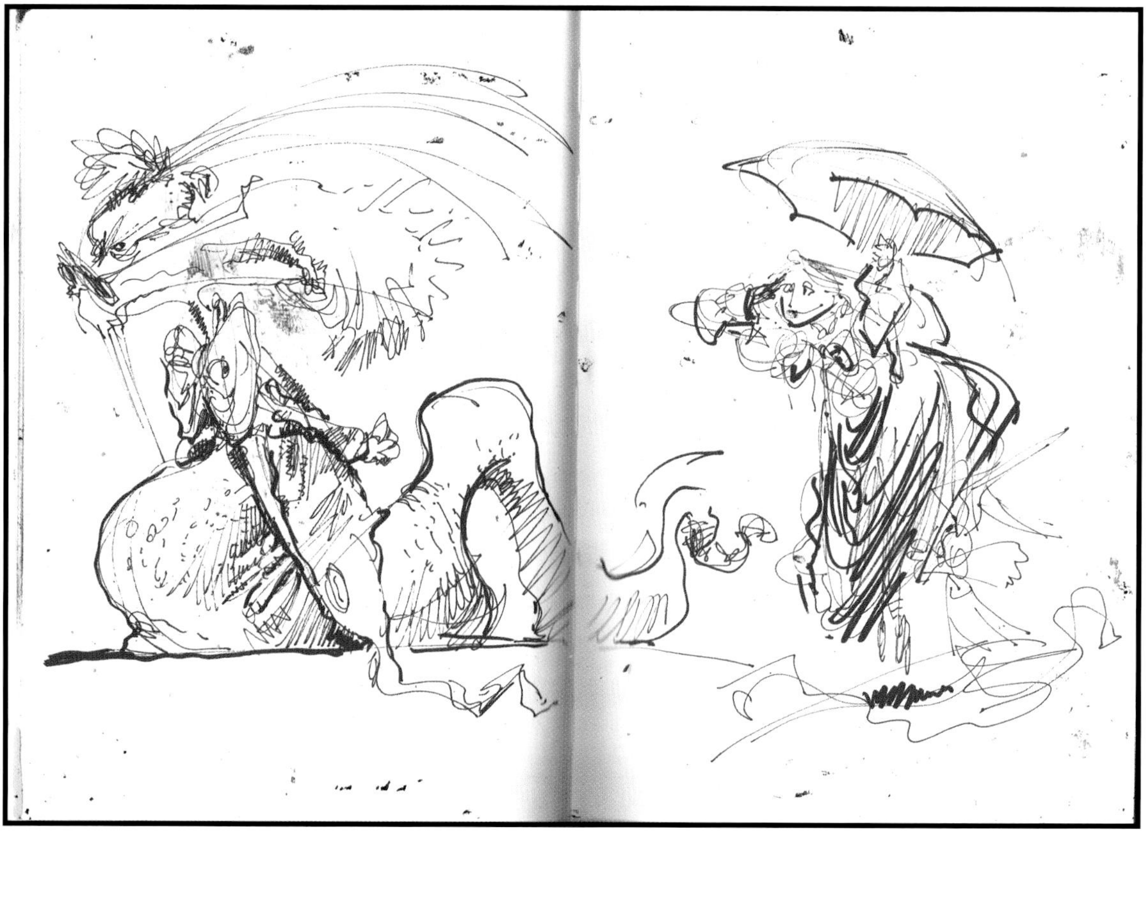

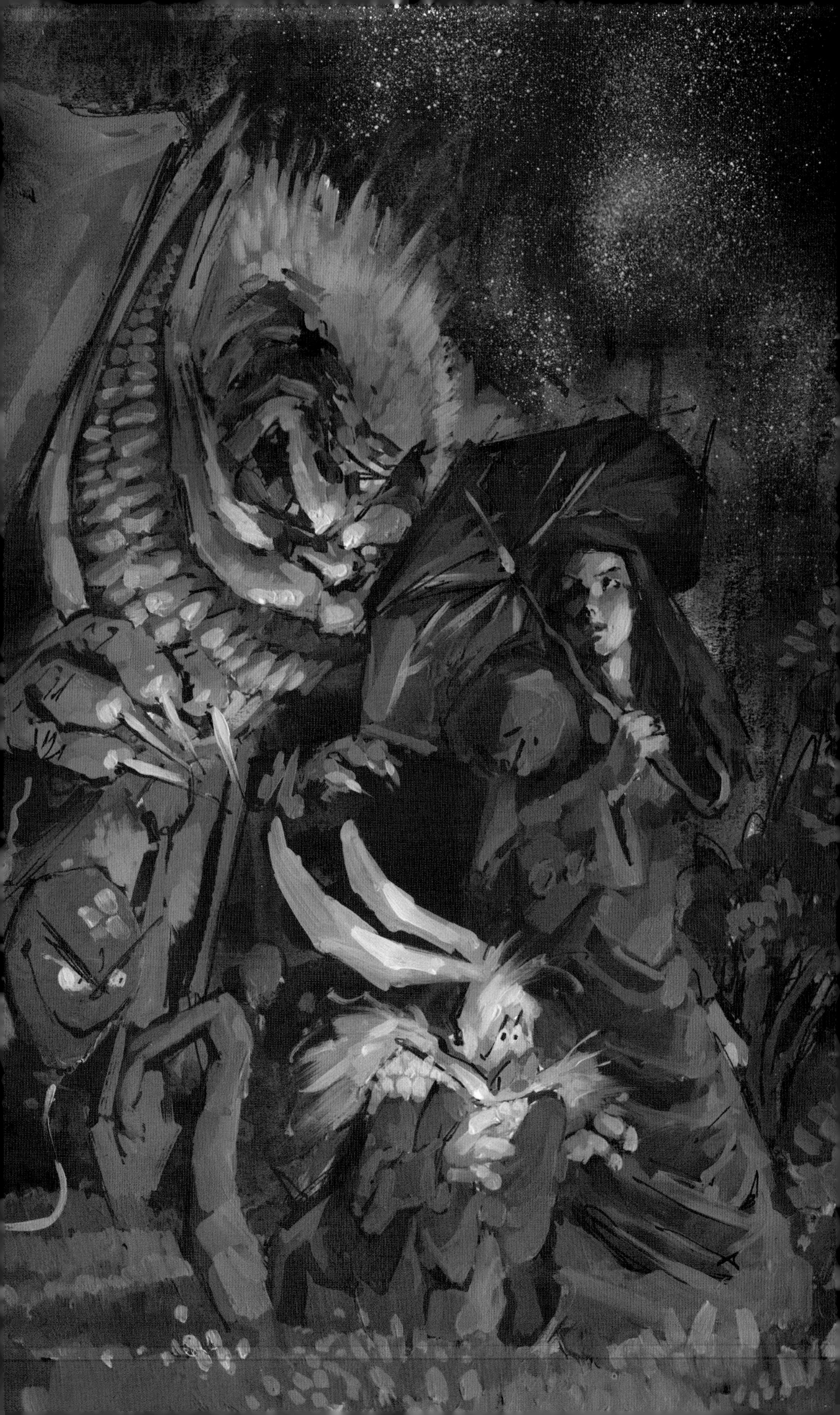

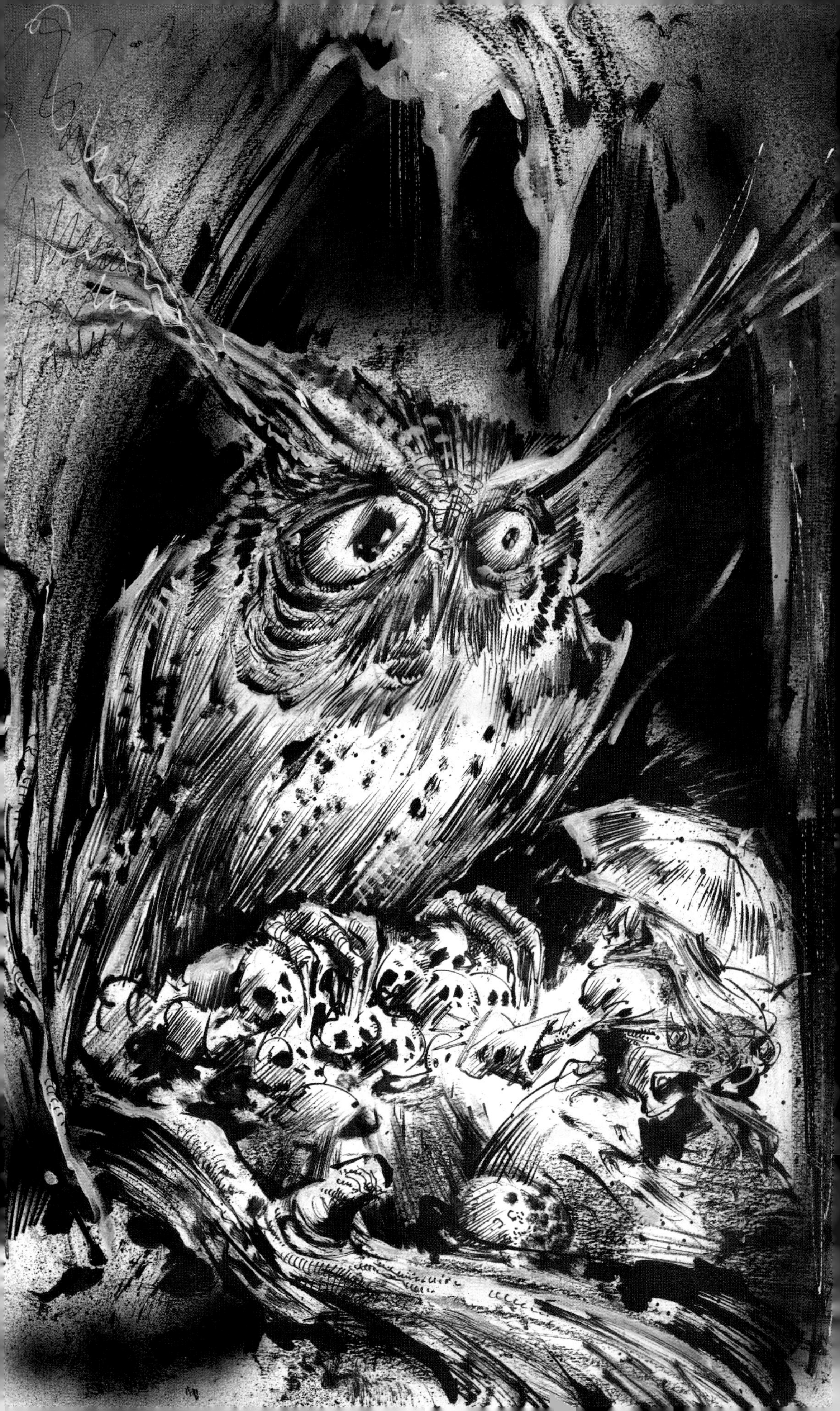

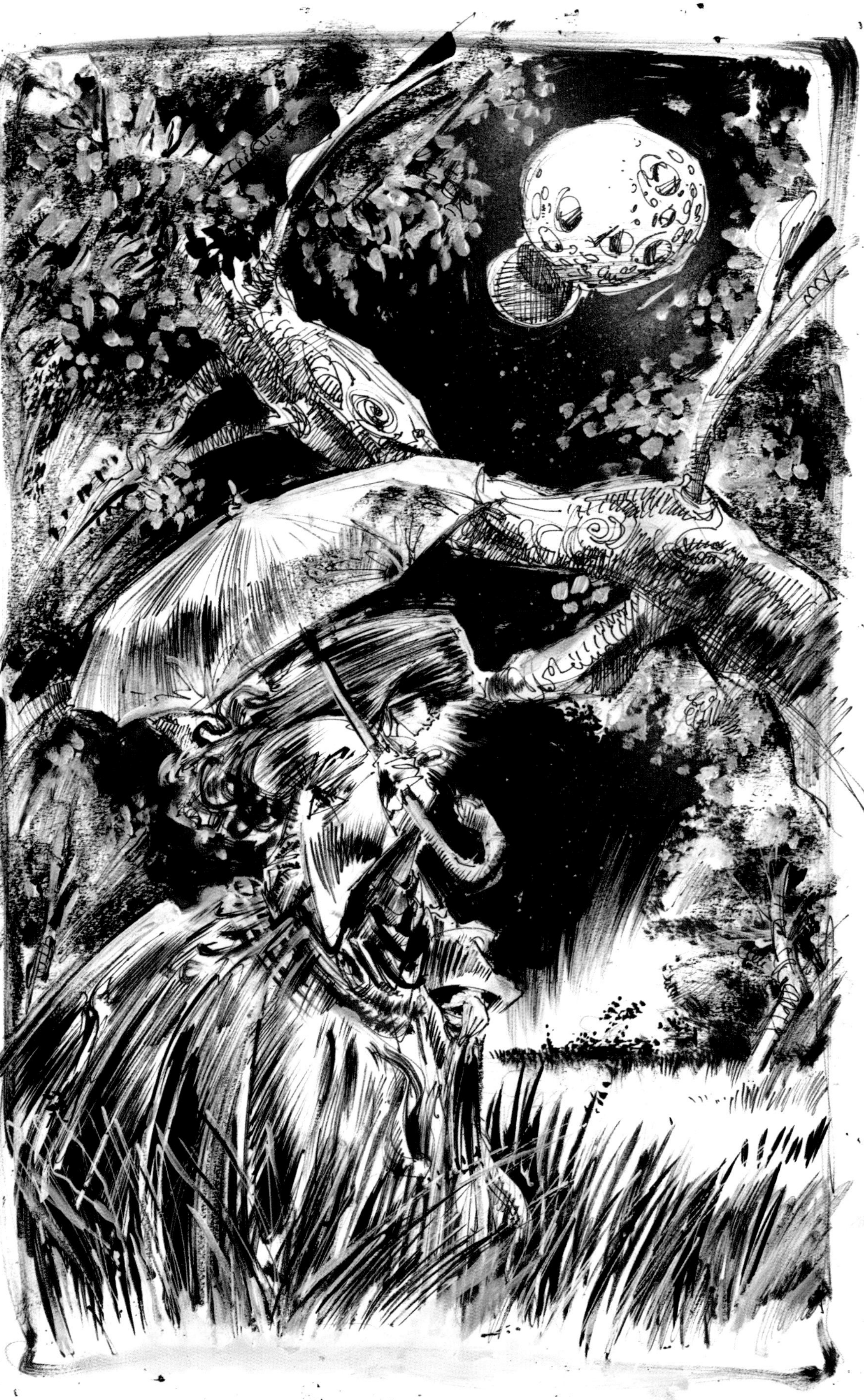

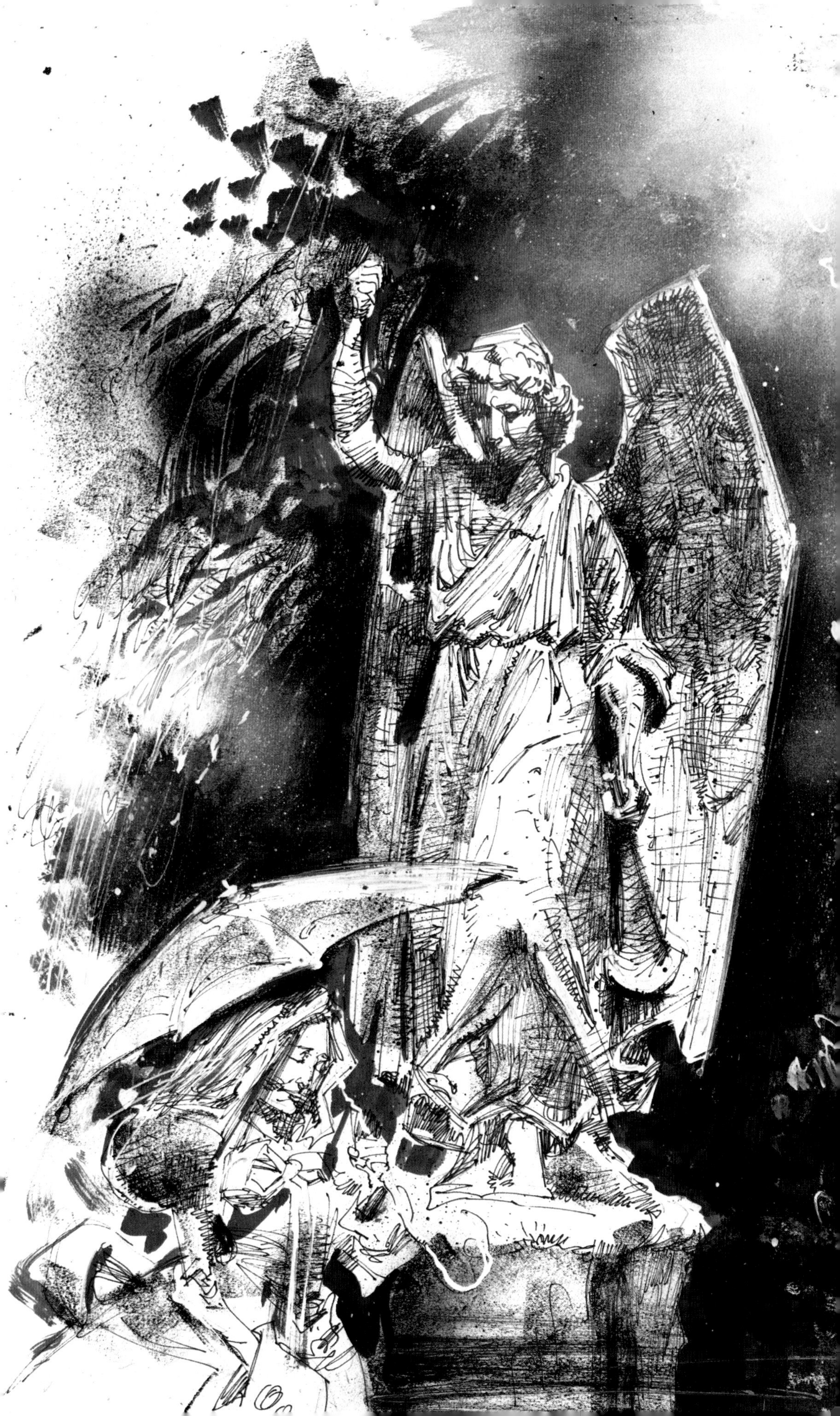

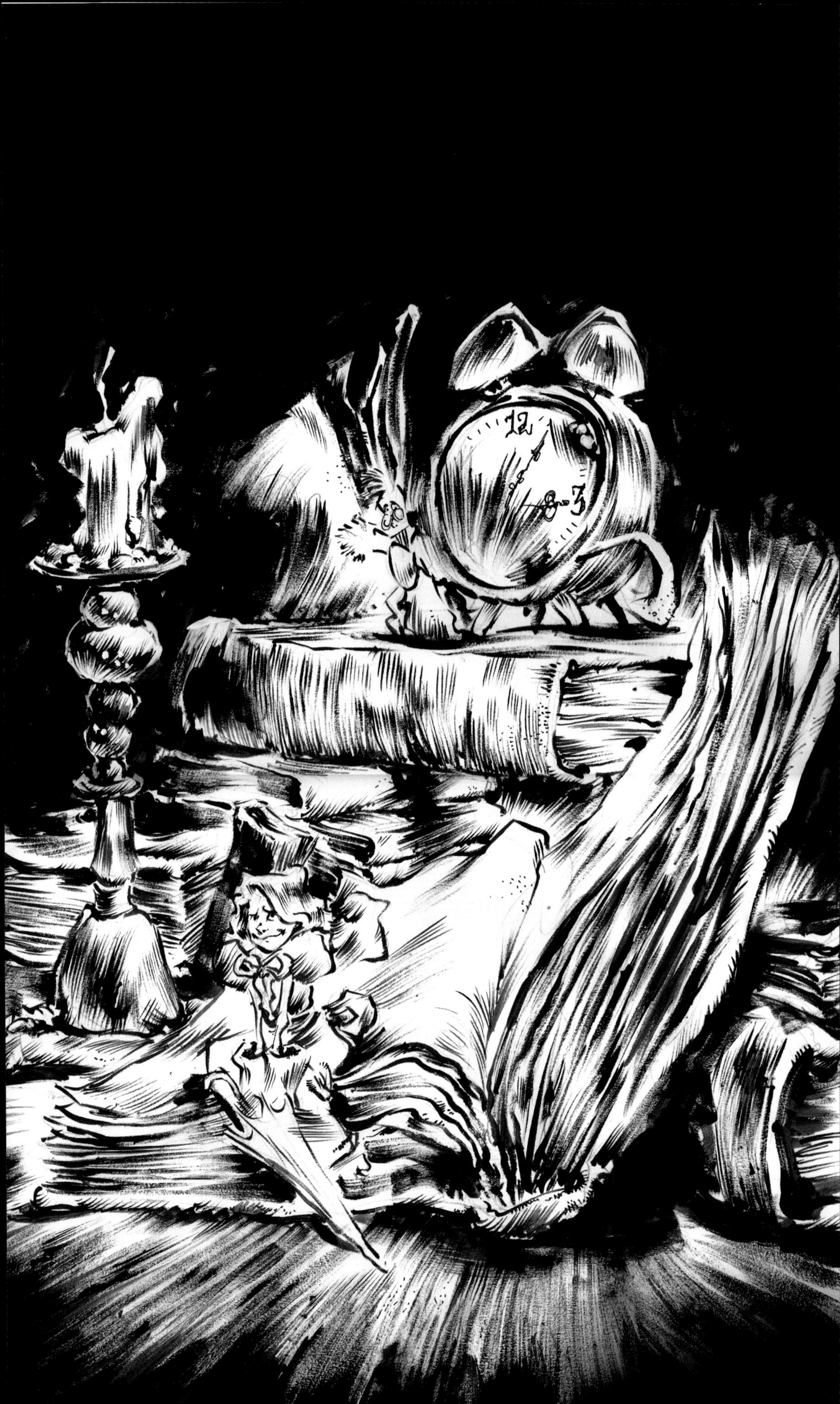

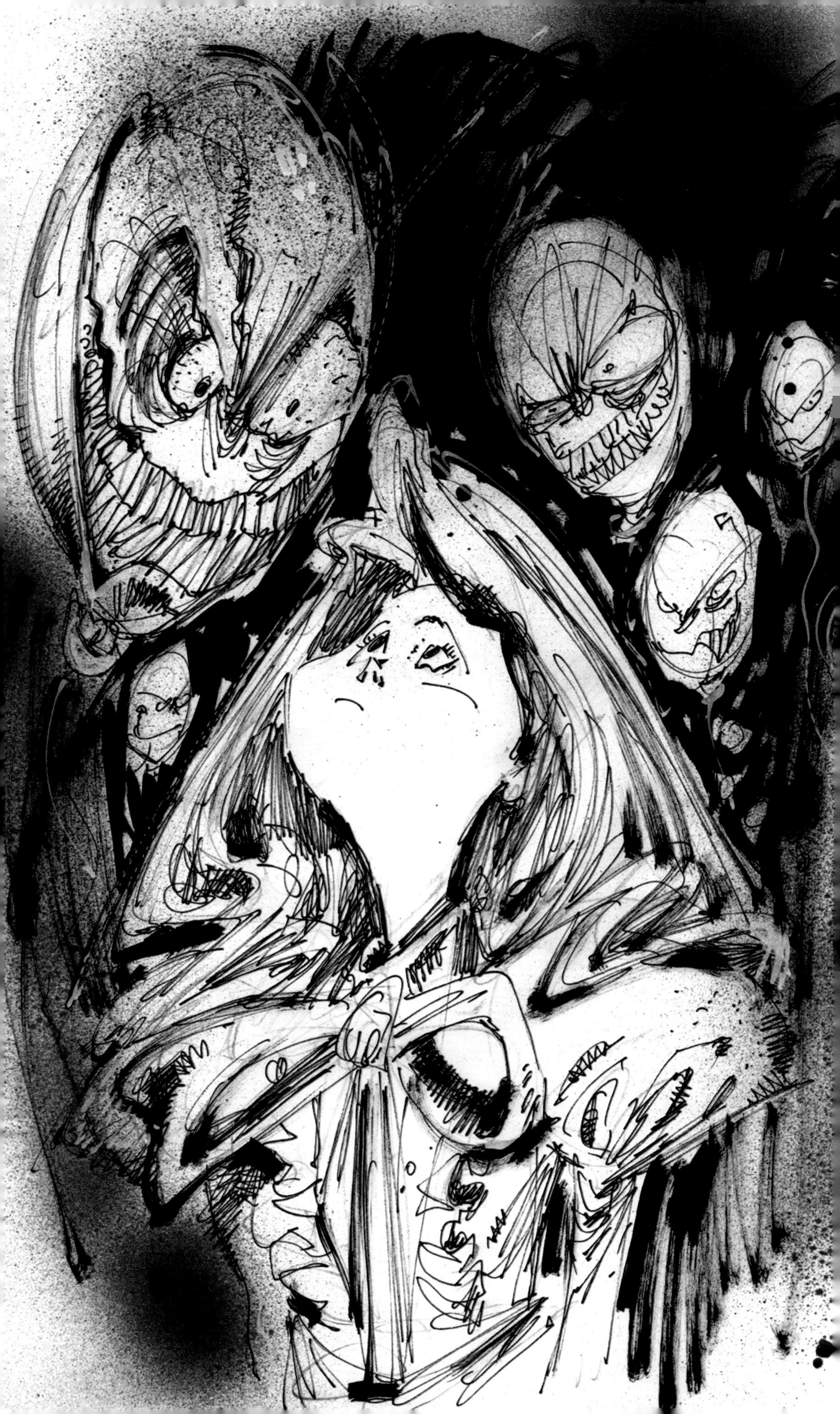

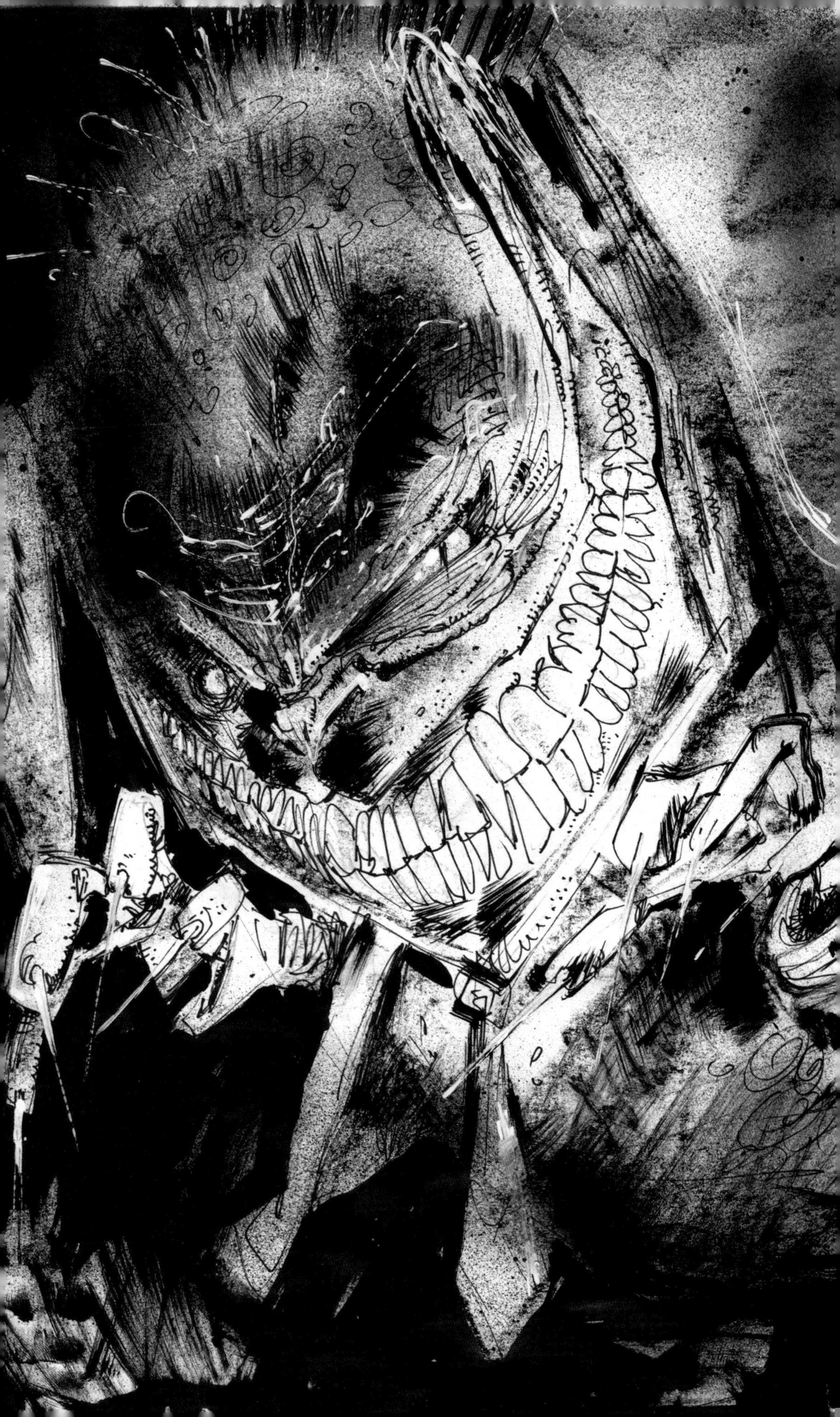

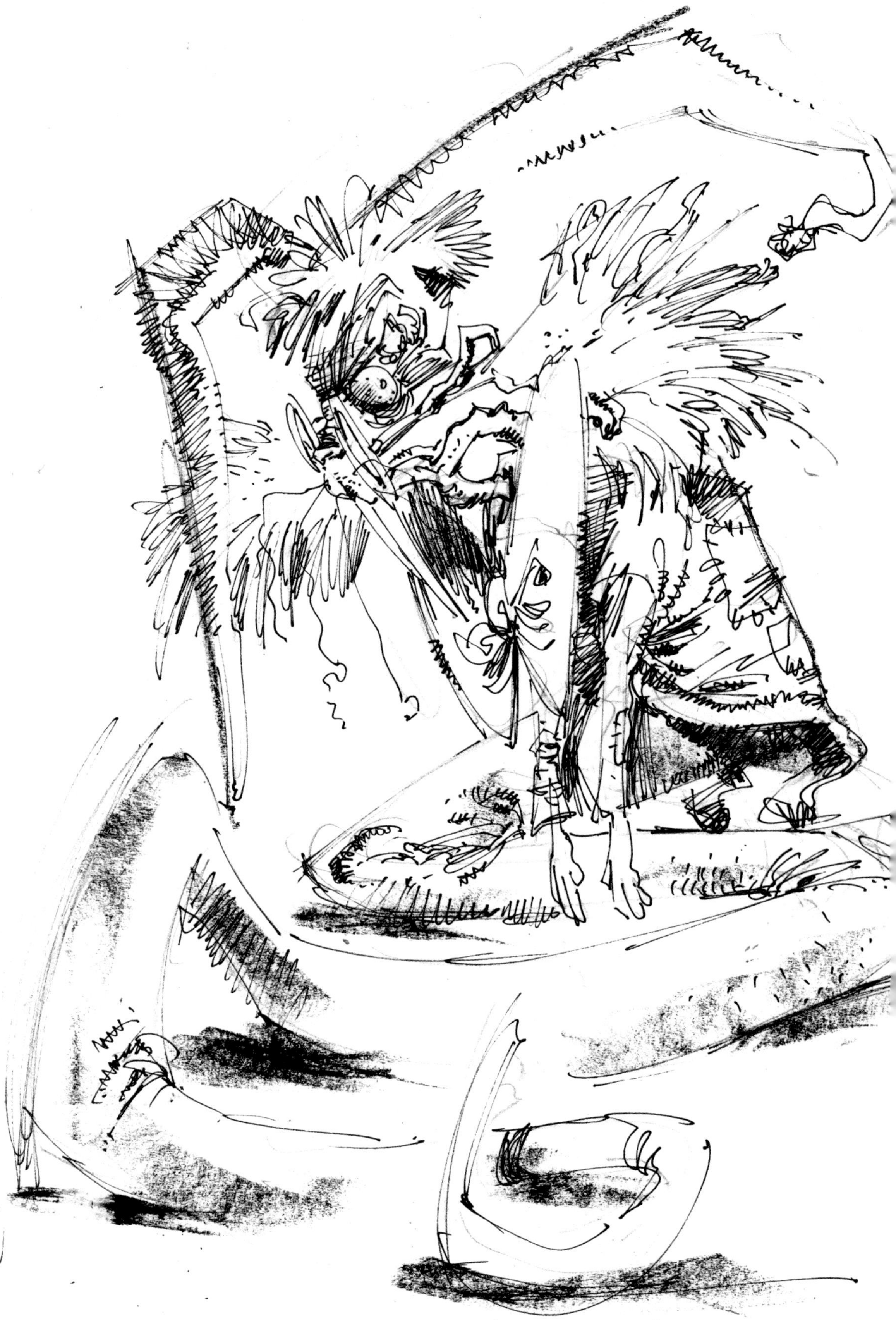

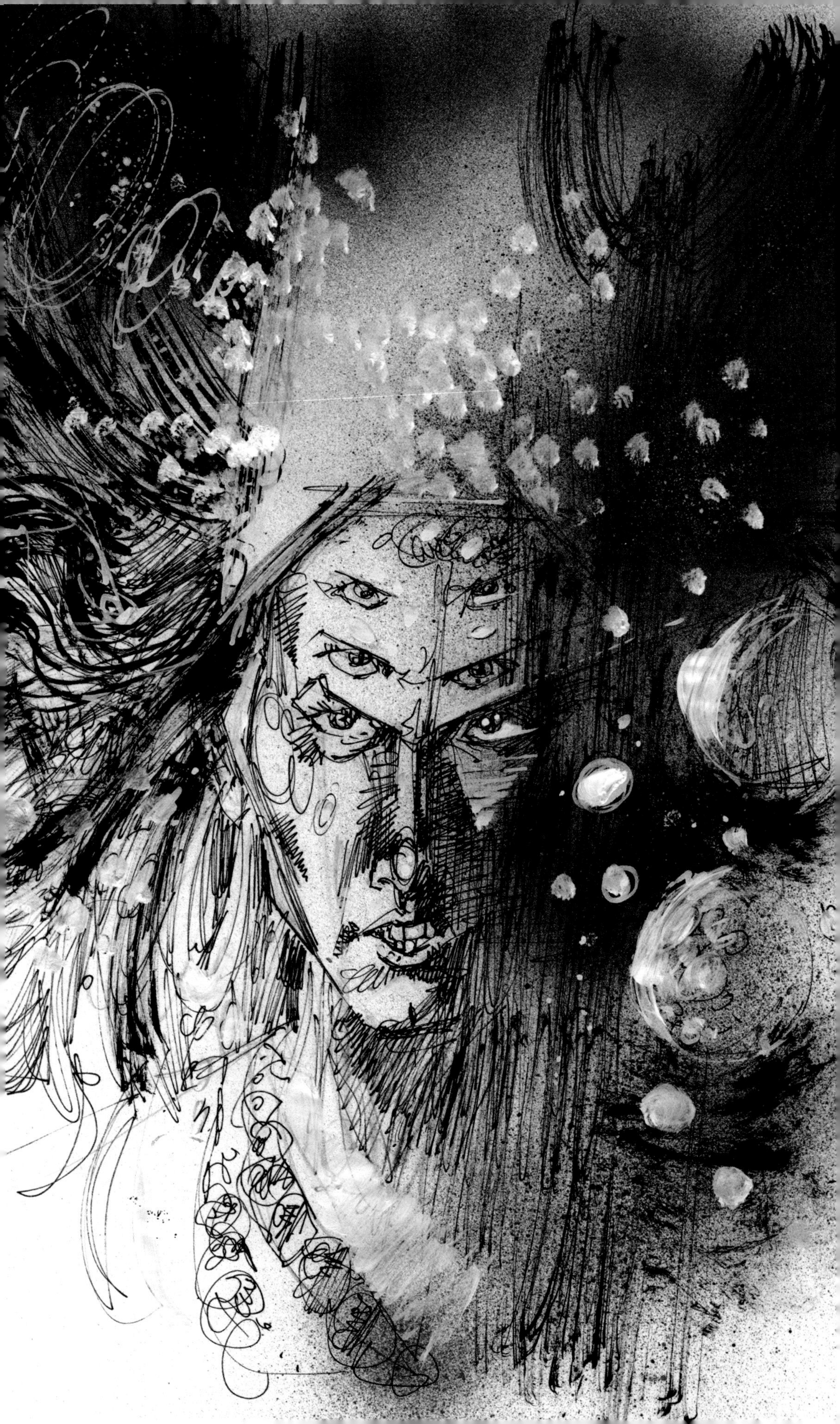

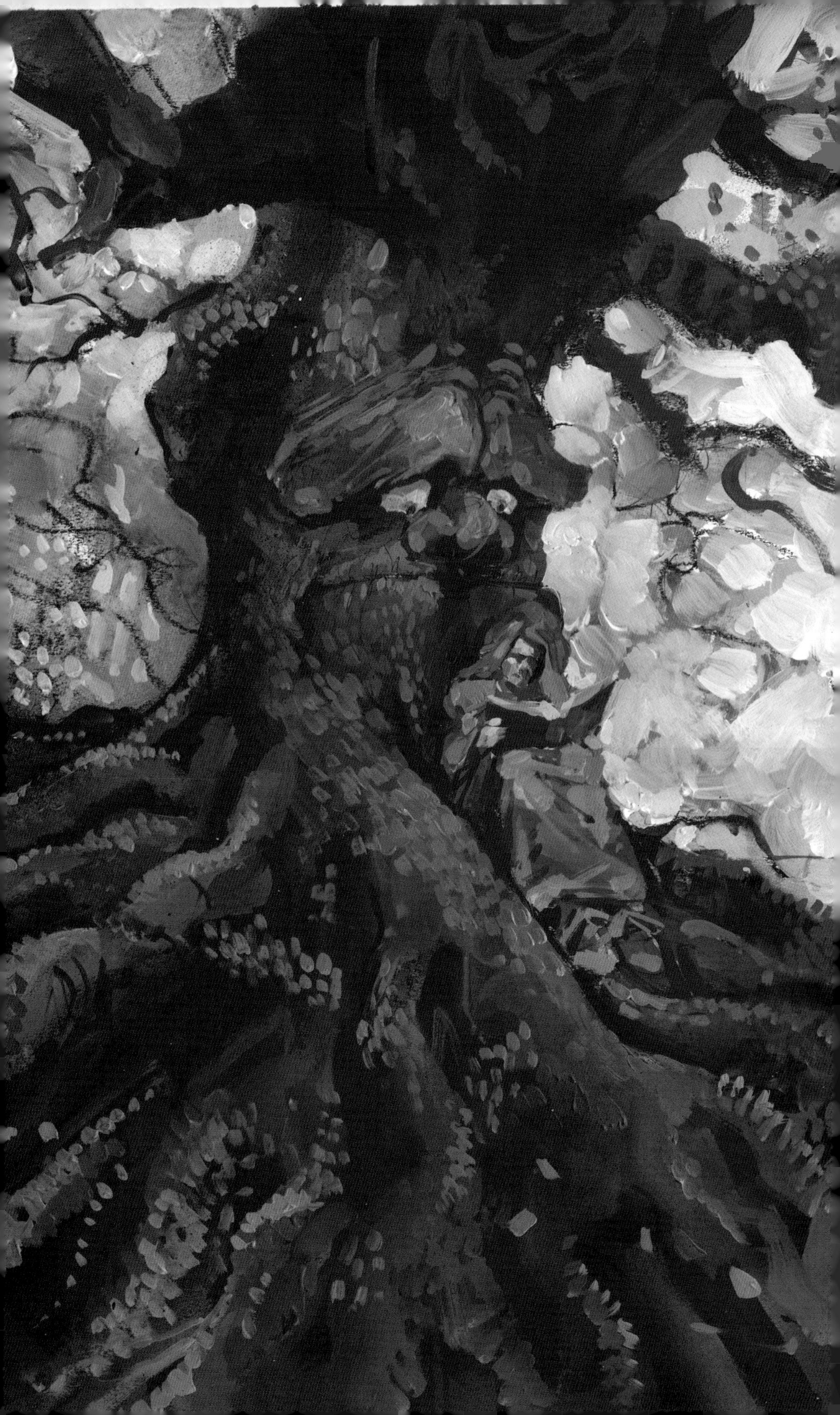